Croatian

lonely planet

phrasebooks
and
Gordana & Ivan Ivetac

Croatian phrasebook
2nd edition – October 2010

Published by
Lonely Planet Publications Pty Ltd ABN 36 005 607 983
90 Maribyrnong St, Footscray, Victoria 3011, Australia

Lonely Planet Offices
Australia Locked Bag 1, Footscray, Victoria 3011
USA 150 Linden St, Oakland CA 94607
UK 2nd fl, 186 City Rd, London, EC1V 2NT

Cover illustration Yukiyoshi Kamimura

ISBN 978 1 74104 566 6

10 9 8 7 6 5 4 3 2

Printed by Toppan Security Printing Pte. Ltd.
Printed in Singapore

Mixed Sources
Product group from well-managed forests and other controlled sources
www.fsc.org Cert no. SGS-COC-005002
© 1996 Forest Stewardship Council

acknowledgments

Editor Francesca Coles would like to acknowledge the following for their contributions to this phrasebook:

Gordana and Ivan Ivetac for their polished translations and linguistic and cultural expertise. Both Gordana and Ivan are NAATI accredited Croatian to English translators and interpreters with extensive experience in the field. Gordana also teaches a course on the cultural and ethical aspects of interpreting at RMIT. Ivan (a native of the town of Pula in coastal Croatia) has a BA in Italian and Philosophy and is completing a PhD in Molecular Biology at Monash University.

Editors Quentin Frayne, Piers Kelly and Annelies Mertens for advice, feedback and companionship along the way.

In-house Croatian speakers Zeljko Basic and Jack Gavran for help with the transliteration system and queries generally.

Freelance editor Adrienne Costanzo for her eagle-eyed proofing.

Wendy Wright for the inside illustrations and Daniel New for the cover.

Paul Piaia for assistance with the map.

Lonely Planet Language Products

Publishing Manager: Karin Vidstrup Monk
Commissioning Editors: Karina Coates/Ben Handicott
Editors: Francesca Coles, Meladel Mistica and Jodie Martire
Layout Designer: David Kemp
Project Manager: Fabrice Rocher
Managing Editors: Karin Vidstrup Monk/Annelies Mertens
Layout Manager: Adriana Mammarella
Series Designers: Yukiyoshi Kamimura/Brendan Dempsey
Cartographer: Wayne Murphy

make the most of this phrasebook ...

Anyone can speak another language! It's all about confidence. Don't worry if you can't remember your school language lessons or if you've never learnt a language before. Even if you learn the very basics (on the inside covers of this book), your travel experience will be the better for it. You have nothing to lose and everything to gain when the locals hear you making an effort.

finding things in this book

For easy navigation, this book is in sections. The Tools chapters are the ones you'll thumb through time and again. The Practical section covers basic travel situations like catching transport and finding a bed. The Social section gives you conversational phrases, pick-up lines, the ability to express opinions – so you can get to know people. Food has a section all of its own: gourmets and vegetarians are covered and local dishes feature. Safe Travel equips you with health and police phrases, just in case. Remember the colours of each section and you'll find everything easily; or use the comprehensive Index. Otherwise, check the two-way traveller's Dictionary for the word you need.

being understood

Throughout this book you'll see coloured phrases on each page. They're phonetic guides to help you pronounce the language. You don't even need to look at the language itself, but you'll get used to the way we've represented particular sounds. The pronunciation chapter in Tools will explain more, but you can feel confident that if you read the coloured phrase slowly, you'll be understood.

communication tips

Body language, ways of doing things, sense of humour – all have a role to play in every culture. 'Local talk' boxes show you common ways of saying things, or everyday language to drop into conversation. 'Listen for ...' boxes supply the phrases you may hear. They start with the phonetic guide (because you'll hear it before you know what's being said) and then lead in to the language and the English translation.

CONTENTS

croatian

official language
widely understood
generally understood

For more details, see the **introduction.**

Croatian is the language of one of the world's newest countries. Like the country itself, Croatian has an intriguing, cosmopolitan, and at times fraught, history.

Croatian's linguistic ancestor was brought to the region in the sixth and seventh centuries AD by the South Slavs who may have crossed the Danube from the region now known as Poland. This ancestral language split off into two branches: East South Slavic, which later evolved into Bulgarian and Macedonian, and West South Slavic, of which Slovene, Serbian and Croatian are all descendants.

Croatia may be a peaceful country today but the Balkan region to which it belongs has a long history of invasion and conflict. These upheavals have enriched and politicised the language. The invasion by Charlemagne's armies and forced conversion to the Roman Church in AD 803 left its mark on Croatian in the form of words borrowed from Latin and the adoption of the Latin alphabet rather than the Cyrillic alphabet (with which Serbian is written). Subsequent invasions by the Hapsburg, Ottoman and Venetian empires added vibrancy to the language through the influx of German, Turkish and Venetian dialect loan words. Many words from the standard Italian of Croatia's neighbour Italy have also added colour.

Croatian is not really a separate language from Serbian or Bosnian. Linguists

---

at a glance ...

language name:
Croatian

name in language:
hrvatski jezik
hr·vat·skee *je·*zeek

language family: Slavic

approximate number of speakers: 5 million

close relatives:
Bosnian, Macedonian, Serbian and Slovenian

donations to English:
cravat, dalmatian

---

introduction

commonly refer to the language spoken in Croatia, Serbia and Bosnia-Hercegovina under the umbrella term Serbo-Croatian while acknowledging dialectical difference. Croats, Serbs and Bosnians themselves generally maintain that they speak different languages, however. This polarisation of language identities reflects the desire to retain separate ethnic identities.

The good news is that, if you venture into Serbia or Montenegro, you'll be able to enrich your travel experience there by using this phrasebook. Croatian is also a handy lingua franca in any of the other states that made up part of the former Yugoslavia, as it's an official language in Bosnia-Hercegovina. People in Macedonia and Slovenia, who speak closely related languages, generally understand Croatian.

Croatian has plenty of appeal. As well as its rich vocabulary, it has a lovely repertoire of soft lisping sounds such as *sh*, *zh* and *ch* and a lilting musical rhythm due to its use of high and low pitches. It also has an intriguing grammar, quite different from English. It is, however, readily understandable.

Take this phrasebook with you to help make your trip hassle free. It's packed with all the practical language information you'll need and it will also open up a world of possibilities for social interaction and cultural exchange with the locals. Need more encouragement? Remember, the contact you make through using Croatian will make your travel experience unique. Local knowledge, new relationships and a sense of satisfaction are on the tip of your tongue, so don't just stand there – say something!

abbreviations used in this book

m	masculine	pol	polite
f	feminine	inf	informal
n	neuter	imp	imperfective
sg	singular	perf	perfective
pl	plural	lit	literally

Croatian pronunciation is quite straightforward for English speakers as many of the sounds are similar to English sounds. Some claim, in fact, that for English speakers, Croatian pronunciation is the easiest to master among the European languages.

vowel sounds

There are seven vowel sounds in Croatian. In the written language, vowels that appear next to each other don't run together to form diphthongs (vowel sound combinations) as in English. When you see two or more vowels written next to each other in a Croatian word, pronounce each vowel separately.

symbol	english equivalent	croatian example	transliteration
a	father	*zdravo*	zdra·vaw
ai	aisle	*ajvar*	ai·var
aw	raw	*brod*	brawd
e	let	*pet*	pet
ee	bee	*sidro*	see·draw
oo	book	*skupo*	skoo·paw
oy	boy	*tvoj*	tvoy

consonant sounds

Croatian consonant sounds all have equivalents, or close equivalents, in English. The rolled r sound can be pronounced in combination with another consonant (or more than one consonant) as a separate syllable, as in the word *Hrvat* hr·vat 'Croatian'. If these syllables without vowels look a bit intimidating, try inserting a slight 'uh' sound before the r to help them run off your tongue more easily. The sound s can appear as a syllable on its own.

symbol	english equivalent	croatian example	transliteration
b	**b**ig	*glazba*	glaz·ba
ch	**ch**illi	*četiri, ćuk*	che·tee·ree, chuk
d	**d**in	*doručak*	daw·roo·chak
f	**f**un	*fotograf*	faw·taw·graf
g	**g**o	*jagoda*	ya·gaw·da
h	**h**it	*hodnik*	hawd·neek
j	**j**am	*džep, đak*	jep, jak
k	**k**ick	*krov*	krawv
l	**l**oud	*lutka*	loot·ka
l'	mi**lli**on	*kašalj*	kash·al'
m	**m**an	*mozak*	maw·zak
n	**n**o	*nafta*	naf·ta
n'	ca**ny**on	*siječanj*	see·ye·chan'
r	**r**ag (but 'rolled')	*radnik*	rad·neek
s	**s**alt	*sastanak*	sas·ta·nak
sh	**sh**ow	*košta*	kawsh·ta
t	**t**in	*sat*	sat
ts	hi**ts**	*prosinac*	pro·see·nats
v	**v**ery	*viza*	vee·za
y	**y**es	*svjetlost*	svyet·lawst
z	**z**oo	*zec*	zets
zh	plea**s**ure	*koža*	kaw·zha

When y comes after another consonant and before a vowel (as in the word *djeca* dye·tsa) it runs together with the preceding consonant and vowel. The preceding consonant is then pronounced with the tongue rising up towards the roof of the mouth. Something similar happens in English when you say 'and you' quickly. You don't need to be too conscious of this feature as it should happen more or less automatically as you follow the pronunciation guides.

stress & pitch accent

Certain syllables in Croatian have stress, which means you emphasise one syllable over another. As a general rule, in two-syllable words stress usually falls on the first syllable. In words of three or more syllables, stress may fall on any syllable except the last. In our pronunciation guides, the stressed syllable is italicised.

Croatian also has what's known as pitch accent. A stressed vowel may have either a rising or a falling pitch and be long or short. The combination of stress, pitch and vowel length in a given syllable can affect the meaning of a word. The word *sam* pronounced with a short vowel and falling pitch means 'alone' and sounds like 'sum'. When it's pronounced with a long vowel with falling pitch however, it means 'I am' and sounds like 'sarm'.

You don't need to worry about reproducing this feature of Croatian and we haven't indicated it in this book, as it only distinguishes meaning in a very few cases. In such cases it should be clear from the context what is meant. You may notice though that the speech of native speakers has an appealing musical lilt to it. You may also notice marks over the vowels in some dictionaries and grammar books to indicate vowel length and pitch.

reading & writing

Croatian is so closely related to Serbian that many people describe them as two dialects of the same language. However, religion and historical circumstances dictated that Croatian be written in the Latin alphabet, like English, rather than the Cyrillic alphabet, like Serbian. The Croatian alphabet has 30 letters, of which three are digraphs (single sounds made up of a combination of two letters). The accents above letters change the pronunciation of letters. The letter *c* for example is pronounced like the 'ts' in 'cats', while the letter č is pronounced like the 'ch' in 'cheese'.

Croatian spelling is absolutely phonetic – there's a fixed regular correspondence between letters and the way they're pronounced even when they're combined into words. What you see is what you say!

letter for letter

The table below shows the correspondences between the Croatian alphabet and the Serbian Cyrillic alphabet. This could come in handy if you venture beyond the confines of Croatia and want to try to read and understand written Serbian.

croatian		serbian		croatian		serbian	
A a	a	А а	a	*L l*	el	Л л	el
B b	be	Б б	be	*Lj lj*	l'	Љ љ	l'
C c	tse	Ц ц	tse	*M m*	em	М м	em
Č č	tch	Ч ч	tch	*N n*	en	Н н	en
Ć ć	ch	Ћ ћ	ch	*Nj nj*	n'	Њ њ	n'
D d	de	Д д	de	*O o*	aw	О о	aw
Dž dž	dzh	Џ џ	dzh	*P p*	pe	П п	pe
Đ đ	j	ђ ђ	j	*R r*	er	Р р	er
E e	e	Е е	e	*S s*	es	С с	es
F f	ef	Ф ф	ef	*Š š*	sh	Ш ш	sh
G g	ge	Г г	ge	*T t*	te	Т т	te
H h	ha	Х х	ha	*U u*	oo	У у	oo
I i	ee	И и	ee	*V v*	ve	В в	ve
J j	y	Ј ј	y	*Z z*	zed	З з	zed
K k	ka	К к	ka	*Ž ž*	zh	Ж ж	zh

This chapter is arranged alphabetically for ease of navigation and is designed to help you go beyond the phrases in this book to create your own sentences. Don't worry too much about the rules of grammar. A couple of well-chosen words and gestures and a desire to communicate will generally help you get your message across.

All illustrations of points shown in the tables (other than examples of verbs) are given in the nominative case unless otherwise stated (for an explanation of case see **me, myself & I**). We haven't given you all the different case forms and endings, but if you want to delve into them there are many good basic textbook grammars of Croatian available, a useful one being *Colloquial Croatian and Serbian* by Celia Hawkesworth (Routledge, 1998).

a/an & the

There are no equivalents of the English articles 'a/an' and 'the'. In Croatian the context indicates whether something is meant to be indefinite (corresponding to 'a/an') or definite (corresponding to 'the').

adjectives see **describing things**

articles see **a/an & the**

be

Below are the present tense forms of the verb *biti* 'be'. The pronouns are in brackets because they're mostly not used in Croatian as the verb endings tell you who's doing the action of the verb, ie who's the subject.

I am	*(ja) sam*	(ya) sam
you are sg inf	*(ti) si*	(tee) see
you are sg pol	*(vi) ste*	(vee) ste
he/she/it is	*(on/ona/ono) je* m/f/n	(awn/*aw*·na/*aw*·naw) ye
we are	*(mi) smo*	(mee) smaw
you are pl	*(vi) ste*	(vee) ste
they are m/f/n	*(oni/one/ona) su*	(*aw*·nee/*aw*·ne/*aw*·na) soo

I'm Australian.

Ja sam Australac/   ya sam a·oo·*stra*·lats/
Australka. m/f   a·oo·*stral*·ka
(lit: I am Australian)

If you want to form a negative sentence with 'be' to express 'I'm/You're not' etc, just add the prefix *ni-* to the forms of *biti* above, eg *nisam, nisi*, etc.

I'm not Croatian.

Ja nisam Hrvat/Hrvatica. m/f   ya *nee*·sam *hr*·vat/hr·*va*·tee·tsa
(lit: I not-am Croat)

case see **me, myself & I**

describing things

Adjectives take different endings depending on the gender of the noun described, whether it's singular or plural and according to case (see **me, myself & I**).

gender/number	adjective ending
masculine singular	ends in a consonant or -i
masculine plural	ends in -i
feminine singular	ends in -a
feminine plural	ends in -e
neuter singular	ends in -o
neuter plural	ends in -a

He's a good man. (masculine noun and adjective)
On je dobar čovjek.   awn ye *daw*·bar *chaw*·vyek
(lit: he is good man)

She's a good woman. (feminine noun and adjective)
Ona je dobra žena.   *aw*·na ye *daw*·bra *zhe*·na
(lit: she is good woman)

doing things

In Croatian each verb has two forms. This is because Croatian makes the distinction between 'action as process' and 'action as completion' and calls the former the imperfective aspect and the latter the perfective aspect.

The imperfective aspect is used for actions that are thought of as continuing, habitual, ongoing or incomplete, while the perfective aspect is for actions that are thought of as complete or limited. Note that verbs in the perfective aspect can't refer to present events because actions in the present are, by nature, unfinished. Both forms of the verb are provided in the dictionary.

past

Talking about the past in Croatian isn't hard. You just take the present tense of the verb *biti* (see **be**) and follow it with a verb form known as the active past participle. Forming the active past participle of most verbs is quite straightforward. The majority of verbs in Croatian end in -*ti* and to turn these verbs into the active past participle you just remove the -*ti* ending and add the endings shown in the table on the next page. The endings agree in gender and number with the subject of a sentence.

gender/number of subject	active past participle ending
masculine singular	-o
masculine plural	-li
feminine singular	-la
feminine plural	-le
neuter singular	-lo
neuter plural	-la

Here's an example with the verb *imati* 'have':

I had a ticket.

Ja sam imao/imala   ya sam ee·*ma*·aw/ee·*ma*·la
kartu. m/f   *kar*·too
(lit: I am had ticket)

present

There are a few intricacies to forming the present tense of verbs in Croatian, more than is possible to outline here. A rule of thumb though, which works for many verbs, is to remove the *-ti* from the infinitive (dictionary form) of a verb and to add the following endings as shown here for the verb *čitati* 'read':

person		ending	present tense form	
I	ja	-m	čitam	*chee*·tam
you sg inf	ti	-š	čitaš	*chee*·tash
he/she/it	on/ona/ono m/f/n	no ending	čita	*chee*·ta
we	mi	-mo	čitamo	chee·*ta*·maw
you sg pol & pl	vi	-te	čitate	chee·*ta*·te
they m/f/n	oni/one/ona	-ju	čitaju	chee·*ta*·yoo

You'll find the present tense forms of the useful verbs 'be' and 'have' under those headings in this phrasebuilder.

future

To talk about future events you use a form of the verb *htjeti* (lit: 'want' but equivalent to 'will' in English) followed by the infinitive (dictionary) form of a verb.

I will	*(ja) ću*	(ja) choo
you will sg inf	*(ti) ćeš*	(tee) chesh
you will sg pol	*(vi) ćete*	(vee) *che*·te
he/she/it will	*(on/ona/ono) će*	(awn/aw·na/aw·ne) che
we will	*(mi) ćemo*	(mee) *che*·maw
you will pl	*(vi) ćete*	(vee) *che*·te
they will m/f/n	*(oni/one/ona) će*	(aw·nee/aw·ne/aw·na) che

I will read.
Ja ću čitati.   ya choo *chee*·ta·tee
(lit: I will read)

gender

In Croatian, all nouns – words that denote a person, thing or idea – have one of three genders: masculine, feminine or neuter. Gender is assigned to words more or less arbitrarily, though masculine and feminine persons and animals mostly carry masculine and feminine gender, respectively.

The gender of nouns is indicated where relevant in this phrasebook and for all nouns in the dictionary. Here are some handy generalisations to help you identify what gender a noun in the singular might be:

- masculine nouns mostly end in a consonant, eg, *muž* 'husband'
- feminine nouns often end in *-a*, eg *žena* 'woman'
- neuter nouns end in *-o* or *-e*, eg *vino* 'wine' and *dijete* 'child'

Verbs can take different endings according to gender too. They reflect the gender of the subject (the doer of the action). One expression that you'll come across frequently in this phrasebook is 'I'd like …' which translates as *Želio/Željela bih …* m/f. The gender markers indicate that if you're a man you select the first option, while if you're a woman you select the second.

I'd like to withdraw money. (man speaking)
| *Želio bih* | zhe·lee·aw beeh |
| *podignuti novac.* | paw·deeg·noo·tee *naw*·vats |
(lit: I-want-m would change money)

I'd like to withdraw money. (woman speaking)
| *Željela bih* | zhe·lye·la beeh |
| *podignuti novac.* | paw·deeg·noo·tee *naw*·vats |
(lit: I-want-f would change money)

---

gender in this book

Throughout this book we've used the abbreviations m, f and n to indicate gender. The order of presentation is masculine, feminine and then neuter.

If a letter or letters have been added to a masculine form to denote a feminine or neuter form these will appear in parentheses, eg *Židov(ka)* 'Jew' which has the masculine form *Žid* and the feminine form *Židovka*. Where the change involves more than the addition of a letter, different words are given separated by a slash. Sometimes, it's just a case of substituting the final letter of a word to make feminine or neuter forms as in this example: *mladi/a* mla·dee/a 'young' which has the masculine form *mladi* and the feminine form *mlada*.

---

have

To say that you have something you just use a form of the verb *imati* 'have' followed by the noun. As the direct object of the sentence, the nouns possessed should be in the accusative case, but you're sure to be understood if you just use the nominative case (dictionary form) of a noun (see **me, myself & I** for an explanation of the word case).

I have	*(ja) imam*	(ja) *ee*·mam
you have **sg inf**	*(ti) imaš*	(tee) *ee*·mash
you have **sg pol**	*(vi) imate*	(vee) *ee*·*ma*·te
he/she/it has	*(on/ona/ono) ima* **m/f/n**	(awn/*aw*·na/ *aw*·naw) *ee*·ma
we have	*(mi) imamo*	(mee) ee·*ma*·maw
you have **pl**	*(vi) imate*	(vee) *ee*·*ma*·te
they have **m/f/n**	*(oni/one/ona) imaju*	(*aw*·nee/*aw*·ne/ *aw*·na) ee·*ma*·yoo

I have a car.

   Imam auto.　　　　　　*ee*·mam *a*·oo·taw
   (lit: I-have car)

me, myself & I

In Croatian, the endings of nouns, adjectives and pronouns may change depending on their 'case'. The case of a word conveys grammatical information. Case can indicate whether a word is the subject (doer of the action), object (undergoer of the action) or indirect object (recipient of an action) of a sentence. These roles are signified by the nominative, accusative and dative cases respectively. It can also indicate possession, location, motion or the means with which something is done. There are seven cases in Croatian. Most of these have equivalents in English prepositions such as 'with', 'into', 'in', 'of' and so on. Other cases have no equivalents in English because English uses a fixed word order to signify basic grammatical relations. Croatian case endings are too numerous to list here but if you really want to learn the language, try to get hold of a comprehensive grammar guide to get you started.

All the nouns, pronouns and adjectives in the phrases in this book are, of course, in the appropriate case so you don't need to worry about this feature of Croatian. It does explain though, why you may see one word in several different guises. The town *Pula* can become *Pulu* or *Puli* when used with prepositions, for example. It also explains why word order in Croatian might sometimes seem muddled up (see **word order**).

more than one

There are a few tricks to forming the plural of nouns in Croatian. In the case of masculine nouns there's a distinction between animate nouns (those referring to living beings, animals etc) and inanimate nouns (those referring to objects).

animate masculine nouns of one syllable	*-ovi* or *-evi*
animate masculine nouns of more than one syllable	*-i*
inanimate masculine nouns	*-ovi* or *-evi*
feminine nouns ending in –a	*-e*
feminine nouns ending in a consonant	*-i*
neuter nouns	*-a*

my & your

A common way of indicating possession is to use what are known as possessive pronouns ('my, your, his, her' etc in English). These agree in gender (masculine or feminine), number (singular or plural) and case (see **me, myself & I**) with the person or thing possessed.

	masculine singular		feminine singular	
my	*moj*	moy	*moja*	moy·a
your	*tvoj*	tvoy	*tvoja*	tvoy·a
his	*njegov*	nye·gawv	*njegova*	nye·gaw·va
her	*njen*	nyen	*njena*	nye·na
our	*naš*	nash	*naša*	na·sha
your	*vaš*	vash	*vaša*	va·sha
their	*njihov*	nyee·hawv	*njihova*	nyee·haw·va

	neuter singular		plural (all genders)	
my	*moje*	moy·e	*moji*	moy·ee
your	*tvoje*	tvoy·e	*tvoji*	tvoy·ee
his	*njegovo*	nye·gaw·vaw	*njegovi*	nye·gaw·vee
her	*njeno*	nye·naw	*njeni*	nye·nee
our	*naše*	na·she	*naši*	na·shee
your	*vaše*	va·she	*vaši*	va·shee
their	*njihovo*	nye·haw·vaw	*njihovi*	nyee·haw·vee

That's my brother and that's my sister.
To je moj brat a to je   taw ye moy brat a taw ye
moja sestra.   moy·a ses·tra
(lit: that is my brother and that is my sister)

negative

Croatian negatives are easy. Just add the word *ne* 'not' before the verb.

I (don't) speak Croatian.
Ja (ne) govorim hrvatski.   ya (ne) gaw·vaw·reem hr·vat·skee
(lit: I (not) speak Croatian)

Ne is used with all negative forms like *nikada* 'never' and *nitko* 'nobody' etc.

I never drink spirits.
Ja nikada ne pijem   ya nee·ka·da ne pee·yem
žestoka alkoholna pića. zhe·staw·ka al·kaw·hawl·na pee·cha
(lit: I never not drink strong alcoholic drinks)

personal pronouns

Personal pronouns are not usually necessary in the subject position (for the doer, eg 'I'), unless you want to emphasise who the doer is. This is because the doer is indicated with a verb ending. As for the direct object (undergoer of the action) pronouns, they have long and short forms indicated by the brackets. The short forms are neutral while the long forms are for emphasis. The short forms are generally much more common.

subject (nominative case) pronouns					
I	*ja*	ya	we	*mi*	mee
you sg inf	*ti*	tee	you pl	*vi*	vee
you sg pol	*vi*	vee			
he	*on*	awn	they m/f/n	*oni/ one/ ona*	*aw*·nee/ *aw*·ne/ *aw*·na
she	*ona*	*aw*·na			
it	*ono*	*aw*·naw			

direct object (accusative case) pronouns					
me	*me(ne)*	*me*(·ne)	us	*nas*	nas
you sg inf	*te(be)*	*te*(·be)	you pl	*vas*	vas
you sg pol	*vas*	vas			
him	*(nje)ga*	(nye·)ga	them m/f/n	*(nj)ih*	(ny)eeh
her	*nju/je**	nyoo/ye			
it	*(nje)ga*	(nye·)ga			

* long form *nju* and short form *je*.

The polite form of 'you', *vi*, can be used when addressing strangers, older people or people in positions of authority. When talking to family, friends or peers you can use the informal form *ti*.

In this phrasebook we've generally given phrases in the polite form but where you see the abbreviation **inf** you have an informal option to use where appropriate.

plural see more than one

pointing things out

To point things out in Croatian you use the words *evo/eno* 'here/there is' or 'here/there are' before the thing that you're drawing attention to.

There's my sister.
   Eno moje sestre.   *e·*naw *moy·*e se·stre
   (lit: there-is my sister)

If you want to indicate that there's an absence of something, you use the word *nema* 'there is not'.

There's no-one home.
   Nema nikoga doma.   *ne·*ma *nee·*kaw·ga *daw·*ma
   (lit: there-is-not nobody home)

Another way to or point out a person or object is to use one of the following words for 'this/these' or 'that/those' and 'that over there' (ie, referring to a thing further away) before the noun.

this		that		that over there	
ovaj m	*aw·*vai	*taj* m	tai	*onaj* m	*aw·*nai
ova f	*aw·*va	*ta* f	ta	*ona* f	*aw·*na
ovo n	*aw·*vaw	*to* n	taw	*ono* n	*aw·*naw

This island is beautiful.
   Ovaj otok je predivan.   *aw·*vai *aw·*tawk ye *pre·*dee·van
   (lit: this island is beautiful)

polite & informal see personal pronouns

possession see my & your and have

questions

Questions may be introduced by the use of question words as in English. These are the most common ones:

what	što	shtaw
What are you doing?	Što radite?	shtaw ra·dee·te
who	tko	tkaw
Who are you?	Tko ste vi?	tkaw ste vee
where	gdje	gdye
Where do you live?	Gdje živite?	gdye zhee·vee·te
where to	kamo	ka·maw
Where are you going to?	Kamo idete?	ka·maw ee·de·te
why	zašto	za·shtaw
Why are you visiting Croatia?	Zašto posjećujete Hrvatsku?	za·shtaw paw·sye·choo·ye·te hr·vat·skoo
how	kako	ka·kaw
How are you?	Kako ste?	ka·kaw ste
when/ at what time	kada	ka·da
When do you leave?	Kada krećete?	ka·da kre·che·te
how much	koliko	kaw·lee·kaw
How much is a ticket?	Koliko je jedna karta?	kaw·lee·kaw ye yed·na kar·ta

To form a yes-no type question you insert the word *li* (a question particle) immediately after the main verb in the question. The verb must always come first in the question sentence.

Have you been to Croatia before?
   Jesi li bio/bila ikada   ye·see lee bee·aw/bee·la ee·ka·da
   u Hrvatskoj? m/f   oo hr·vat·skoy
   (lit: are-you *li* been ever in Croatia)

The simplest way to form questions is to keep the structure of a statement but raise your intonation (making your voice rise in pitch) towards the end of the sentence.

You can also form questions by adding the expression *zar ne* 'isn't it' to the end of a statement, which usually implies that you'll get a positive response.

Beautiful day, isn't it?
   Predivan dan, zar ne?   pre·dee·van dan zar ne
   (lit: beautiful day isn't it)

You can just use *zar* on its own at the start of a question but this gives a tone of surprise to the question.

You're studying Croatian?
   Zar učiš Hrvatski?   zar oo·cheesh hr·vat·skee
   (lit: really you-are-studying Croatian)

talking about location

You can specify the location of something by using a preposition (like 'in') in front of the place, just as you do in English. In Croatian, prepositions change the case (see **me, myself & I**) of the nouns that they come before. You don't need to worry about this as people will understand you if you just pick nouns referring to a place out of a dictionary. English and Croatian prepositions don't necessarily translate one-for-one so that, for example, you may see 'at' translated as *kod*, *pri*, *na* or *u* in different contexts.

I'd like to get off at Pula.
   Želim izaći u Puli.   zhe·leem ee·za·chee oo poo·lee
   (lit: I-want get-off at Pula)

verbs see doing things

word order

Generally, basic sentences in Croatian follow the same word order as in English (subject first, followed by the verb, followed by the object). However, because Croatian has case (see **me, myself & I**) to indicate who did what to whom, sentences do not have to be limited to this fixed order for their meaning to be clear.

People describe Croatian as having 'free word order' but this doesn't mean that it's totally random. Word order in Croatian can vary to emphasise different elements in a sentence, for example to highlight information that's new or particularly informative. So remember if you're trying to decipher or form a Croatian sentence, that word order in Croatian can be quite flexible.

Do you speak (English)?
Govorite/   gaw·vaw·ree·te/
Govoriš li   gaw·vaw·reesh lee
(engleski)? pol/inf   (en·gle·skee)

Does anyone speak (English)?
Da li itko govori   da lee eet·kaw gaw·vaw·ree
(engleski)?   (en·gle·skee)

Do you understand?
Da li razumijete/   da lee ra·zoo·mee·ye·te/
razumiješ? pol/inf   ra·zoo·mee·yesh

Yes, I understand.
Da, razumijem.   da, ra·zoo·mee·yem

No, I don't understand.
Ne, ja ne razumijem.   ne, ya ne ra·zoo·mee·yem

I (don't) understand.
Ja (ne) razumijem.   ya (ne) ra·zoo·mee·yem

I speak (English).
Ja govorim   ya gaw·vaw·reem
(engleski).   (en·gle·skee)

I don't speak (Croatian).
Ja ne govorim   ya ne gaw·vaw·reem
(hrvatski).   (hr·vat·skee)

I speak a little.
Ja govorim malo.   ya gaw·vaw·reem ma·law

What does 'dobro' mean?
Što znači 'dobro'?   shtaw zna·chee daw·braw

How do you …?	Kako se …?	*ka*·kaw se …
pronounce this	*izgovara*	eez·*gaw*·va·ra
write *'dobro'*	*piše 'dobro'*	*pee*·she *daw*·braw
Could you	**Možete li**	*maw*·zhe·te lee
please …?	**molim vas …?** pol	*maw*·leem vas …
	Možeš li	*maw*·zhesh lee
	molim te …? inf	*maw*·leem te …
repeat that	*to*	taw
	ponoviti	paw·*naw*·vee·tee
speak more	*govoriti*	gaw·*vaw*·ree·tee
slowly	*sporije*	*spaw*·ree·ye
write it down	*to napisati*	taw na·*pee*·sa·tee

---

tongue torture

Tongue twisters are called *jezikolomke* ye·zee·*kaw*·lawm·ke (lit: tongue breakers) in Croatian. You should have fun exercising your tongue with these little numbers, particularly as they're laced with 'r's between and before consonants. If you're having trouble negotiating these tricky syllables, refer to **pronunciation**, page 11.

Na vrh brda vrba mrda.
na vrh *br*·da *vr*·ba *mr*·da
(High on the hilltop, the willow sways.)

Cvrči cvrči cvrčak na čvoru crne smrče.
tsvr·chee *tsvr*·chee *tsvr*·chak na *chvaw*·roo *tsr*·ne *smr*·che
(A cricket chirps and chirps on the knotted branch of a black spruce.)

Crni jarac crnom trnu crn vrh grize.
Ne grizi mi crni jarče, crnom trnu crn vrh!
tsr·nee *ya*·rats *tsr*·nawm *tr*·noo tsrn vrh *gree*·ze.
ne *gree*·zee mee *tsr*·nee *yar*·che, *tsr*·nawm *tr*·noo tsrn vrh
(A black billy goat is chewing the black tip of a black thorny shrub. Don't you chew the top of my black thorny shrub off, you black billy goat!)

cardinal numbers

osnovni brojevi

0	*nula*	noo·la
1	*jedan/jedna/ jedno* m/f/n	ye·dan/yed·na/ yed·naw
2	*dva/dvije* m&n/f	dva/dvee·ye
3	*tri*	tree
4	*četiri*	che·tee·ree
5	*pet*	pet
6	*šest*	shest
7	*sedam*	se·dam
8	*osam*	aw·sam
9	*devet*	de·vet
10	*deset*	de·set
11	*jedanaest*	ye·da·na·est
12	*dvanaest*	dva·na·est
13	*trinaest*	tree·na·est
14	*četrnaest*	che·tr·na·est
15	*petnaest*	pet·na·est
16	*šesnaest*	shes·na·est
17	*sedamnaest*	se·dam·na·est
18	*osamnaest*	aw·sam·na·est
19	*devetnaest*	de·vet·na·est
20	*dvadeset*	dva·de·set
21	*dvadesetjedan/ dvadesetjedna/ dvadesetjedno* m/f/n	dva·de·set·ye·dan/ dva·de·set·yed·na/ dva·de·set·yed·naw
30	*trideset*	tree·de·set
40	*četrdeset*	che·tr·de·set
50	*pedeset*	pe·de·set
60	*šezdeset*	shez·de·set
70	*sedamdeset*	se·dam·de·set
80	*osamdeset*	aw·sam·de·set
90	*devedeset*	de·ve·de·set
100	*sto*	staw
1,000	*tisuću*	tee·soo·choo
1,000,000	*jedan milijun*	ye·dan mee·lee·yoon

ordinal numbers

1st	*prvi/a/o* m/f/n	pr·vee/a/aw
2nd	*drugi/a/o* m/f/n	droo·gee/a/aw
3rd	*treći/a/e* m/f/n	tre·chee/a/e
4th	*četvrti/a/o* m/f/n	chet·vr·tee/a/aw
5th	*peti/a/o* m/f/n	pe·tee/a/aw

fractions

a quarter	*četvrtina*	chet·vr·tee·na
a third	*trećina*	tre·chee·na
a half	*polovina*	paw·law·vee·na
three-quarters	*tri četvrtine*	tree chet·vr·tee·ne
all	*sve*	sve
none	*ništa*	neesh·ta

useful amounts

How much/many?	*Koliko?*	kaw·lee·kaw
Please give me ...	*Molim dajte mi ...*	maw·leem dai·te mee ...
a few	*nekoliko*	ne·kaw·lee·kaw
less	*manje*	ma·nye
(just) a little	*(samo) malo*	(sa·maw) ma·law
a lot	*puno*	poo·naw
many	*mnogo*	mnaw·gaw
more	*više*	vee·she
some	*malo*	ma·law

For more amounts, see **self-catering**, page 158.

TOOLS

32

telling the time

Official times are given according to the 24-hour clock. In conversation, though, Croatians mainly use the 12-hour clock.

What time is it?	*Koliko je sati?*	kaw·lee·kaw ye *sa*·tee
It's one o'clock.	*Jedan je sat.*	*ye*·dan ye sat
It's (ten) o'clock.	*(Deset) je sati.*	(*de*·set) ye *sa*·tee
Five past (ten).	*(Deset) i pet.*	(*de*·set) ee pet
Quarter past (ten).	*(Deset) i petnaest.*	(*de*·set) ee *pet*·na·est
Half-past (ten).	*(Deset) i po.*	(*de*·set) ee *paw*
Quarter to (ten).	*Petnaest do (deset).*	*pet*·na·est daw (*de*·set)
Twenty to (ten).	*Dvadeset do (deset).*	*dva*·de·set daw (*de*·set)
At what time?	*U koliko sati?*	oo kaw·lee·kaw *sa*·tee
am	*prijepodne*	*pree*·ye·*pawd*·ne
pm	*popodne*	paw·*pawd*·ne

the calendar

days

Monday	*ponedjeljak*	paw·*ne*·dye·lyak
Tuesday	*utorak*	oo·*taw*·rak
Wednesday	*srijeda*	sree·*ye*·da
Thursday	*četvrtak*	chet·*vr*·tak
Friday	*petak*	*pe*·tak
Saturday	*subota*	soo·*baw*·ta
Sunday	*nedjelja*	*ne*·dye·lya

months

January	*siječanj*	see·ye·chan'
February	*veljača*	ve·lya·cha
March	*ožujak*	aw·zhoo·yak
April	*travanj*	tra·van'
May	*svibanj*	svee·ban'
June	*lipanj*	lee·pan'
July	*srpanj*	sr·pan'
August	*kolovoz*	kaw·law·vawz
September	*rujan*	roo·yan
October	*listopad*	lee·staw·pad
November	*studeni*	stoo·de·nee
December	*prosinac*	praw·see·nats

nature's seasons

The names of the months look unrecognisable because, unlike the English months, they're not based on the Roman calendar. Instead they draw their meanings from ancient Slavic roots depicting the evolution of the seasons in the natural world. Some of these meanings are now obscure to Croatian speakers themselves but others retain delightfully poetic meanings. Here are a few of them:

January	*siječanj*	timber-cutting time
April	*travanj*	the season of growing grass
June	*lipanj*	linden-blossom time
July	*srpanj*	the time of the sickle (harvest time)
October	*listopad*	literally: leaf-fall

dates

What date is it today?
Koji je danas datum? kaw·yee ye da·nas da·toom

It's (18 October).
(Osamnaesti listopad). (aw·sam·na·e·stee lee·staw·pad)

seasons

spring	*proljeće* n	*praw*·lye·che
summer	*ljeto* n	*lye*·taw
autumn/fall	*jesen* f	*ye*·sen
winter	*zima* f	*zee*·ma

present

now	*sada*	*sa*·da
this ...		
afternoon	*ovog*	*aw*·vawg
	popodneva	paw·*pawd*·ne·va
month	*ovog mjeseca*	*aw*·vawg *mye*·se·tsa
morning	*ovog jutra*	*aw*·vawg *yoo*·tra
week	*ovog tjedna*	*aw*·vawg *tyed*·na
year	*ove godine*	*aw*·ve *gaw*·dee·ne
today	*danas*	*da*·nas
tonight	*večeras*	ve·*che*·ras

past

(three days) ago	*prije (tri dana)*	*pree*·ye (tree *da*·na)
day before yesterday	*prekjučer*	prek·*yoo*·cher
last ...		
month	*prošlog mjeseca*	*prawsh*·lawg *mye*·se·tsa
week	*prošlog tjedna*	*prawsh*·lawg *tyed*·na
year	*prošle godine*	*prawsh*·le *gaw*·dee·ne
last night	*sinoć*	*see*·nawch
since (May)	*od (svibnja)*	awd (*sveeb*·nya)

yesterday ...	jučer ...	yoo·cher ...
afternoon	popodne	paw·pawd·ne
evening	uvečer	oo·ve·cher
morning	ujutro	oo·yoo·traw

future

day after tomorrow	prekosutra	pre·kaw·soo·tra
in (six days)	za (šest dana)	za (shest da·na)
next ...		
month	idućeg mjeseca	ee·doo·cheg mye·se·tsa
week	idućeg tjedna	ee·doo·cheg tyed·na
year	iduće godine	ee·doo·che gaw·dee·ne
tomorrow ...	sutra ...	soo·tra ...
afternoon	popodne	paw·pawd·ne
evening	uvečer	oo·ve·cher
morning	ujutro	oo·yoo·traw
until (June)	do (lipnja)	daw (leep·nya)

during the day

afternoon	poslijepodne n	paw·slee·ye·pawd·ne
dawn	zora f	zaw·ra
day	dan m	dan
evening	večer f	ve·cher
midday	podne n	pawd·ne
midnight	ponoć f	paw·nawch
morning	jutro n	yoo·traw
night	noć f	nawch
sunrise	izlazak sunca m	eez·la·zak soon·tsa
sunset	zalazak sunca m	za·la·zak soon·tsa

How much is it?
Koliko stoji?   kaw·*lee*·kaw *stoy*·ee

Can you write down the price?
Možete li napisati   *maw*·zhe·te lee na·*pee*·sa·tee
cijenu?   tsee·*ye*·noo

Do you accept ...?	*Da li*	da lee
	prihvaćate ...?	pree·hva·cha·te ...
credit cards	*kreditne*	*kre*·deet·ne
	kartice	*kar*·tee·tse
debit cards	*debitne*	de·*beet*·ne
	kartice	*kar*·tee·tse
travellers	*putničke*	*poot*·neech·ke
cheques	*čekove*	*che*·kaw·ve
Where can I ...?	*Gdje mogu ...?*	gdye *maw*·goo ...
I'd like to ...	*Želio/Željela*	zhe·lee·aw/zhe·*lye*·la
	bih ... m/f	beeh ...
cash a cheque	*unovčiti*	oo·*nawv*·chee·tee
	ček	chek
change a	*zamijeniti*	za·mee·*ye*·nee·tee
travellers cheque	*putnički ček*	*poot*·neech·kee chek
change money	*zamijeniti*	za·mee·*ye*·nee·tee
	novac	*naw*·vats
get a cash	*uzeti*	oo·ze·tee
advance	*predujam u*	pre·*doo*·yam oo
	gotovini	gaw·taw·*vee*·nee
withdraw money	*podignuti*	paw·deeg·noo·tee
	novac	*naw*·vats

What's the charge for that?

Kolika je pristojba za to? kaw·*lee*·ka ye *pree*·stoy·ba za taw

What's the exchange rate?

Koji je tečaj razmjene? *koy*·ee ye *te*·chai *raz*·mye·ne

Could I have a receipt, please?

Mogu li dobiti račun, molim? *maw*·goo lee *daw*·bee·tee *ra*·choon *maw*·leem

Where's …?	*Gdje se nalazi …?*	gdye se *na*·la·zee …
an automated teller machine	*bankovni automat*	*ban*·kawv·nee a·oo·*taw*·mat
a foreign exchange office	*mjenjačnica za strane valute*	mye·*nyach*·nee·tsa za *stra*·ne va·*loo*·te
I'd like …, please.	*Želio/Željela bih …* m/f	zhe·lee·aw/zhe·lye·la beeh …
my change	*moj ostatak novca*	moy aw·*sta*·tak *nawv*·tsa
a refund	*povrat novca*	*pawv*·rat *nawv*·tsa

---

the colour of money

The currency in Croatia is the *kuna* (*koo*·na), which is divided into 100 *lipa* (*lee*·pa). Interestingly, the currency takes its name from the marten, a ferret-like animal whose pelt was used as a means of exchange in the Middle Ages. The word *lipa* means 'linden tree'. Though it has no obvious association with trade, the linden tree has a sacred significance in Slavic mythology as, among other things, a symbol of good luck and prosperity.

getting around

snalaženje

Which … goes to (Dubrovnik)?	Koji … ide za (Dubrovnik)?	koy·ee … ee·de za (doo·brawv·neek)
boat	brod	brawd
bus	autobus	a·oo·taw·boos
plane	zrakoplov	zra·kaw·plawv
tram	tramvaj	tram·vai
train	vlak	vlak

When's the … (bus)?	Kada ide … (autobus)?	ka·da ee·de … (a·oo·taw·boos)
first	prvi	pr·vee
last	zadnji	zad·nyee
next	slijedeći	slee·ye·de·chee

What time does it leave?
U koliko sati kreće? oo kaw·lee·kaw sa·tee kre·che

What time does it get to (Pula)?
U koliko sati stiže u (Pulu)? oo kaw·lee·kaw sa·tee stee·zhe oo (poo·loo)

Is this seat free?
Da li je ovo sjedište slobodno? da lee ye aw·vaw sye·deesh·te slaw·bawd·naw

That's my seat.
Ovo je moje sjedište. aw·vaw ye moy·e sye·deesh·te

Please tell me when we get to (Pula).
Molim vas recite mi kada stignemo u (Pulu). maw·leem vas re·tsee·te mee ka·da steeg·ne·maw oo (poo·loo)

Please stop here.
Molim vas stanite ovdje. maw·leem vas sta·nee·te awv·dye

transport

39

karte

Where do I buy a ticket?
Gdje mogu kupiti gdye *maw*·goo *koo*·pee·tee
kartu? *kar*·too

Do I need to book?
Trebam li rezervirati? *tre*·bam lee re·zer·*vee*·ra·tee

A ... ticket	*Jednu ... kartu*	*yed*·noo ... *kar*·too
(to Split).	*(do Splita).*	(daw *splee*·ta)
1st-class	*prvorazrednu*	pr·vaw·*raz*·red·noo
2nd-class	*drugorazrednu*	droo·gaw·*raz*·red·noo
child's	*dječju*	*dyech*·yoo
one-way	*jednosmjernu*	*yed*·naw·smyer·noo
return	*povratnu*	*paw*·vrat·noo
student's	*studentsku*	*stoo*·dent·skoo

I'd like a	*Želio/Željela*	*zhe*·lee·aw/*zhe*·lye·la
... seat.	*bih ... sjedište.* m/f	beeh ... *sye*·deesh·te
nonsmoking	*nepušačko*	ne·poo·shach·kaw
smoking	*pušačko*	poo·shach·kaw

I'd like a/an ...	*Želio/Željela bih*	*zhe*·lee·aw/*zhe*·lye·la beeh
seat.	*sjedište ...* m/f	*sye*·deesh·te ...
aisle	*u sredini*	oo sre·*dee*·nee
window	*do prozora*	daw *praw*·zaw·ra

I'd like to ... my	*Želio/Željela*	*zhe*·lee·aw/*zhe*·lye·la
ticket, please.	*bih ... svoju*	beeh ... *svoy*·oo
	kartu, molim. m/f	*kar*·too *maw*·leem
cancel	*poništiti*	*paw*·nee·shtee·tee
change	*promijeniti*	praw·mee·*ye*·nee·tee
confirm	*potvrditi*	pawt·*vr*·dee·tee

Is there (a) ...?	*Imate li ...?*	*ee*·ma·te lee ...
air-conditioning	*klima-uređaj*	*klee*·ma·oo·re·jai
blanket	*deku*	*de*·koo
toilet	*zahod*	*za*·hawd

How much is it?
Koliko stoji?   kaw·*lee*·kaw *stoy*·ee

How long does the trip take?
Koliko traje putovanje?   kaw·*lee*·kaw *trai*·e poo·taw·*va*·nye

Is it a direct route?
Je li to direktan pravac?   ye lee taw dee·*rek*·tan *pra*·vats

What time should I check in?
U koliko se sati   oo kaw·*lee*·kaw se *sa*·tee
trebam prijaviti?   *tre*·bam pree·*ya*·vee·tee

Can I get a sleeping berth?
Mogu li dobiti   *maw*·goo lee *daw*·bee·tee
kabinu s ležajem?   ka·*bee*·noo s *le*·zhai·em

---

listen for ...

aw·nai/*aw*·na/*aw*·naw	*Onaj/Ona/Ono.* m/f/n	**That one.**
aw·vai/*aw*·va/*aw*·vaw	*Ovaj/Ova/Ovo.* m/f/n	**This one.**
oo za·kash·*nye*·nyoo	*u zakašnjenju*	**delayed**
paw·neesh·te·naw	*poništeno*	**cancelled**
paw·poo·nye·naw	*popunjeno*	**full**

luggage

prtljaga

Where can I find ...?	*Gdje se nalazi ...?*	gdye se *na*·la·zee ...
the baggage claim	*šalter za podizanje prtljage*	*shal*·ter za *paw*·dee·za·nye prt·*lya*·ge
a luggage locker	*pretinac za odlaganje prtljage*	*pre*·tee·nats za awd·*la*·ga·nye prt·*lya*·ge

My luggage	*Moja prtljaga*	moy·a prt·*lya*·ga
has been ...	*je ...*	ye ...
damaged	*oštećena*	*awsh*·te·che·na
lost	*izgubljena*	eez·goob·lye·na
stolen	*ukradena*	oo·*kra*·de·na

That is/isn't mine.
To je/nije moje.   taw ye/*nee*·ye *moy*·e

Can I have some coins/tokens?
Mogu li dobiti   *maw*·goo lee *daw*·bee·tee
nekoliko kovanica/   ne·kaw·lee·kaw kaw·*va*·nee·tsa/
žetona?   zhe·*taw*·na

bus & coach

How often do buses come?
Koliko često   kaw·*lee*·kaw che·staw
dolaze autobusi?   *daw*·la·ze a·oo·*taw*·boo·see

Does it stop at (Split)?
Da li staje u (Splitu)?   da lee *stai*·e oo (*splee*·too)

What's the next stop?
Koja je slijedeća stanica?   *koy*·a ye slee·*ye*·de·cha *sta*·nee·tsa

I'd like to get off at (Split).
Želim izaći u (Splitu).   *zhe*·leem ee·*za*·chee oo (*splee*·too)

How long do we stop here?
Koliko dugo   kaw·*lee*·kaw *doo*·gaw
ostajemo ovdje?   aw·stai·e·maw *awv*·dye

city	*gradski*	*grad*·skee
inter-city	*međugradski*	me·joo·grad·skee
local	*mjesni*	*mye*·snee

train

What station is this?
Koja stanica je ovo?   koy·a sta·nee·tsa ye aw·vaw

What's the next station?
Koja je slijedeća stanica?   koy·a ye slee·ye·de·cha sta·nee·tsa

Does it stop at (Pula)?
Da li staje u (Puli)?   da lee stai·e oo (poo·lee)

Do I need to change?
Trebam li presjedati?   tre·bam lee pre·sye·da·tee

Which carriage is (for) ...?	Koja kola su za ...?	koy·a kaw·la soo za ...
(Dubrovnik)	(Dubrovnik)	(doo·brawv·neek)
1st class	prvi razred	prvee raz·red
dining	ručavanje	roo·cha·va·nye

Is it ...?	Da li je ...?	da lee ye ...
direct	direktan	dee·rek·tan
express	brzi	br·zee

you might read ...

brzi vlak	br·zee vlak	fast train
dolasci	daw·las·tsee	arrivals
lokalni vlak	law·kal·nee vlak	local train
ne vozi	ne vaw·zee	no service Sundays
nedjeljom	ne·dye·lyawm	and public holidays
i blagdanima	ee blag·da·nee·ma	
obvezatno	awb·ve·zat·naw	compulsory seat
rezerviranje	re·zer·vee·ra·nye	reservation
sjedišta	sye·deesh·ta	
odlasci	awd·las·tsee	departures
poslovni	paw·slawv·nee	executive train
vlak	vlak	(1st class only)
presjedanje	pre·sye·da·nye	change of trains
svakodnevno	sva·kawd·nev·naw	daily

tram

tramvaj

Is this the tram to (Arena)?
Je li ovo tramvaj   ye lee *aw*·vaw *tram*·vai
koji ide do (Arene)?   *koy*·ee ee·de daw (a·*re*·ne)

Could you tell me when we get to (Arena)?
Možete li mi reći kada   *maw*·zhe·te lee mee *re*·chee *ka*·da
stignemo kod (Arene)?   *steeg*·ne·maw kawd (a·*re*·ne)

boat

brod/čamac

The word *brod* (brawd) is generally used for a ship, whereas the word *čamac* (*cha*·mats) usually refers to a smaller private boat.

What's the sea like today?
Kakvo je danas more?   *kak*·vaw ye *da*·nas *maw*·re

Are there life jackets?
Postoje li prsluci   *paw*·stoy·e lee *pr*·sloo·tsee
za spašavanje?   za spa·*sha*·va·nye

What island is this?
Koji otok je ovo?   *koy*·ee *aw*·tawk ye *aw*·vaw

What beach is this?
Koja plaža je ovo?   *koy*·a *pla*·zha ye *aw*·vaw

I feel seasick.
Osjećam morsku bolest.   *aws*·ye·cham *mawr*·skoo *baw*·lest

anchor	*sidro* n	*see*·draw
anchorage	*sidrarina* f	see·*dra*·ree·na
cabin	*kabina* f	ka·*bee*·na
captain	*kapetan* m	ka·*pe*·tan
car deck	*platforma za*	plat·*fawr*·ma za
	vozila na brodu f	*vaw*·zee·la na *braw*·doo
car ferry	*trajekt za*	*trai*·ekt za
	prijevoz vozila m	pree·*ye*·vawz *vaw*·zee·la

charter yacht	*zakupljena jahta* f	*za*·koop·lye·na *yah*·ta
deck	*paluba* f	*pa*·loo·ba
ferry	*trajekt* m	*trai*·ekt
oar	*veslo* n	*ve*·slaw
port	*luka* f	*loo*·ka
sail	*jedro* n	*ye*·draw
speedboat	*gliser* m	*glee*·ser
yacht	*jahta* f	*yah*·ta

How much is the daily hire of your charter boats?
Koliki stoji dnevni — kaw·*lee*·kee *stoy*·ee *dnev*·nee
zakup vaših čamaca? — *za*·koop *va*·sheeh *cha*·ma·tsa

Is the skipper included?
Da li je u to uključen — da lee ye oo taw *ook*·lyoo·chen
i skipper? — ee *skee*·per

Where can I anchor a boat like this?
Gdje smijem usidriti — gdye *smee*·yem oo·*seed*·ree·tee
ovakav čamac? — aw·*va*·kav *cha*·mats

Which navigational devices is it equipped with?
Kojim navigacionim — *koy*·eem *na*·vee·ga·tsee·aw·neem
uređajima je opremljen? — oo·re·jai·ee·ma ye *aw*·prem·lyen

taxi

I'd like a taxi …	*Trebam taksi …*	*tre*·bam *tak*·see …
at (9am)	*u (devet*	oo (*de*·vet
	prijepodne)	*pree*·ye·*pawd*·ne)
now	*sada*	*sa*·da
tomorrow	*sutra*	*soo*·tra

Where's the taxi rank?
Gdje je taksi stanica? — gdye ye *tak*·see *sta*·nee·tsa

Is this taxi free?
Da li je ovaj taksi — da lee ye *aw*·vai *tak*·see
slobodan? — *slaw*·baw·dan

Please put the meter on.
Molim uključite taksimetar.	*maw·leem ook·lyoo·chee·te tak·see·me·tar*

How much is it to …?
Koliko stoji prijevoz do …?	*kaw·lee·kaw stoy·ee pree·ye·vawz daw …*

Please take me to (this address).
Molim da me odvezete na (ovu adresu).	*maw·leem da me awd·ve·ze·te na (aw·voo a·dre·soo)*

How much is it?
Koliko to stoji?	*kaw·lee·kaw taw stoy·ee*

Please …	*Molim vas …*	*maw·leem vas …*
slow down	*usporite*	*oo·spaw·ree·te*
stop here	*stanite ovdje*	*sta·nee·te awv·dye*
wait here	*pričekajte ovdje*	*pree·che·kai·te awv·dye*

car & motorbike

car & motorbike hire

I'd like to hire a/an …	*Želio/Željela bih iznajmiti …* m/f	*zhe·lee·aw/zhe·lye·la beeh eez·nai·mee·tee …*
4WD	*automobil sa pogonom na sva četiri kotača*	*a·oo·taw·maw·beel sa paw·gaw·nawm na sva che·tee·ree kaw·ta·cha*
automatic	*automobil sa automatskim mjenjačem*	*a·oo·taw·maw·beel sa a·oo·taw·mat·skeem mye·nya·chem*
manual	*automobil sa ručnim mjenjačem*	*a·oo·taw·maw·beel sa rooch·neem mye·nya·chem*
motorbike	*motocikl*	*maw·taw·tsee·kl*

With ...	*Sa ...*	sa ...
air-conditioning	*klima-uređajem*	klee·ma·*oo*·re·jai·em
a driver	*vozačem*	vaw·*za*·chem

How much for	*Koliko stoji*	kaw·*lee*·kaw *stoy*·ee
... hire?	*... najam?*	... *nai*·am
daily	*dnevni*	*dnev*·nee
weekly	*tjedni*	*tyed*·nee

Does that include insurance/mileage?
Da li to uključuje i   da lee taw ook·*lyoo*·choo·ye ee
osiguranje/   aw·see·goo·*ra*·nye/
kilometražu?   kee·law·me·*tra*·zhoo

on the road

What's the speed limit?
Koja je dozvoljena   *koy*·a ye *dawz*·vaw·lye·na
brzina?   br·zee·na

Is this the road to (Pazin)?
Je li ovo cesta za (Pazin)?   ye lee *aw*·vaw *tse*·sta za (*pa*·zeen)?

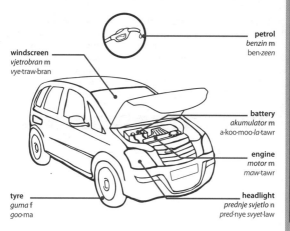

petrol
benzin m
ben·*zeen*

windscreen
vjetrobran m
vye·traw·bran

battery
akumulator m
a·koo·moo·*la*·tawr

engine
motor m
maw·tawr

tyre
guma f
goo·ma

headlight
prednje svjetlo n
pred·nye *svyet*·law

Is it a tollway?
> Da li se na ovom
> putu plaća cestarina?
>
> da lee se na *aw*·vawm
> *poo*·too pla·cha tse·*sta*·ree·na

(How long) Can I park here?
> (Koliko dugo) Mogu
> ovdje parkirati?
>
> (kaw·*lee*·kaw *doo*·gaw) *maw*·goo
> *awv*·dye par·*kee*·ra·tee

Where's a petrol station?
> Gdje je benzinska
> stanica?
>
> gdye ye *ben*·zeen·ska
> *sta*·nee·tsa

Can you check the …?	Možete li provjeriti …?	*maw*·zhe·te lee *praw*·vye·ree·tee …
oil	ulje	*oo*·lye
tyre pressure	tlak zraka u gumama	tlak *zra*·ka oo *goo*·ma·ma
water	vodu	*vaw*·doo
diesel	dizel gorivo n	*dee*·zel *gaw*·ree·vaw
leaded	olovni benzin m	*aw*·lawv·nee ben·*zeen*
LPG	tekući plin m	*te*·koo·chee pleen
regular	normalni benzin m	*nawr*·mal·nee ben·*zeen*
unleaded	bezolovni benzin m	*be*·zaw·lawv·nee ben·*zeen*

problems

I need a mechanic.
Trebam — tre·bam
automehaničara. — a·oo·taw·me·ha·nee·cha·ra

The car/motorbike has broken down (at Pazin).
Automobil/Motocikl — a·oo·taw·maw·beel/maw·taw·tsee·kl
se pokvario (u Pazinu). — se pawk·va·ree·aw (oo pa·zee·noo)

I've had an accident.
Imao/Imala sam — ee·ma·aw/ee·ma·la sam
prometnu nezgodu. m/f — praw·met·noo nez·gaw·doo

The car/motorbike won't start.
Automobil/Motocikl — a·oo·taw·maw·beel/maw·taw·tsee·kl
neće upaliti. — ne·che oo·pa·lee·tee

I have a flat tyre.
Imam probušenu — ee·mam praw·boo·she·noo
gumu. — goo·moo

I've lost my car keys.
Izgubio/Izgubila   eez·*goo*·bee·aw/eez·*goo*·bee·la
sam ključeve od   sam *klyoo*·che·ve awd
automobila. m/f   a·oo·taw·maw·*bee*·la

I've locked the keys inside.
Zaključao/Zaključala   *zak*·lyoo·cha·aw/*zak*·lyoo·cha·la
sam ključeve unutra. m/f   sam *klyoo*·che·ve oo·*noo*·tra

I've run out of petrol.
Nestalo mi je benzina.   *ne*·sta·law mee ye ben·*zee*·na

Can you fix it (today)?
Možete li ga   *maw*·zhe·te lee ga
popraviti (danas)?   *paw*·pra·vee·tee (*da*·nas)

How long will it take?
Koliko dugo će trebati?   kaw·*lee*·kaw *doo*·gaw che *tre*·ba·tee

bicycle

bicikl

I'd like ...	*Želio/Željela*	*zhe*·lee·aw/*zhe*·lye·la
	bih ... m/f	beeh ...
my bicycle	*popravak*	*paw*·pra·vak
repaired	*svoga bicikla*	*svaw*·ga bee·*tsee*·kla
to buy a bicycle	*kupiti bicikl*	*koo*·pee·tee bee·*tsee*·kl
to hire a	*iznajmiti*	eez·*nai*·mee·tee
bicycle	*bicikl*	bee·*tsee*·kl
I'd like a ...	*Želio/Željela bih*	*zhe*·lee·aw/*zhe*·lye·la beeh
bike.	*... bicikl.* m/f	... bee·*tsee*·kl
mountain	*brdski*	*brd*·skee
racing	*trkaći*	*tr*·ka·chee
second-hand	*polovni*	*paw*·lawv·nee

Do I need a helmet?
Treba li mi kaciga?   *tre*·ba lee mee *ka*·tsee·ga

Is there a bicycle-path map?
Da li postoji karta   da lee *paw*·stoy·ee *kar*·ta
biciklističkih staza?   bee·tsee·*klee*·steech·keeh *sta*·za

I'm …	*Ja sam ovdje …*	ya sam *awv*·dye …
in transit	*u prolazu*	oo *praw*·la·zoo
on business	*poslovno*	*paw*·slawv·naw
on holiday	*na odmoru*	na *awd*·maw·roo

I'm here for (three) …	*Ostajem ovdje na (tri) …*	aw·sta·yem *awv*·dye na (tree) …
days	*dana*	*da*·na
months	*mjeseca*	*mye*·se·tsa
weeks	*tjedna*	*tyed*·na

I'm going to (Zagreb).
Ja idem u (Zagreb).   ya *ee*·dem oo (*za*·greb)

I'm staying at (the Intercontinental).
Odsjesti ću u (Interkontinentalu).   awd·sye·stee choo oo (een·ter·kawn·tee·nen·*ta*·loo)

The children are on this passport.
Djeca su na ovoj putovnici.   *dye*·tsa soo na aw·voy poo·*tawv*·nee·tsee

I have nothing to declare.
Nemam ništa za
prijaviti.

ne·mam *neesh*·ta za
pree·*ya*·vee·tee

I have something to declare.
Imam nešto za
prijaviti.

ee·mam *nesh*·taw za
pree·*ya*·vee·tee

Do I have to declare this?
Trebam li ovo
prijaviti?

tre·bam lee *aw*·vaw
pree·*ya*·vee·tee

That's (not) mine.
To (nije) moje.

taw (*nee*·ye) *moy*·e

I didn't know I had to declare it.
Nisam znao/znala da
to treba prijaviti. m/f

nee·sam *zna*·aw/*zna*·la da
taw *tre*·ba pree·*ya*·vee·tee

signs		
Carinarnica	tsa·ree·*nar*·nee·tsa	**Customs**
Karantena	ka·ran·*te*·na	**Quarantine**
Oslobođeno od Carine	aw·*slaw*·baw·je·naw awd *tsa*·ree·ne	**Duty-Free**
Pregled Putovnica	*pre*·gled poo·*tawv*·nee·tsa	**Passport Control**
Ulazak u Zemlju	oo·la·zak oo zem·lyoo	**Immigration**

Where's (the market)?
Gdje je (tržnica)?   gdye ye (*tr*·zhnee·tsa)

How do I get there?
Kako mogu tamo stići?   ka·kaw *maw*·goo *ta*·maw *stee*·chee

How far is it?
Koliko je udaljeno?   kaw·*lee*·kaw ye *oo*·da·lye·naw

Can you show me (on the map)?
Možete li mi to   *maw*·zhe·te lee mee taw
pokazati (na karti)?   paw·*ka*·za·tee (na *kar*·tee)

It's ...	*Nalazi se ...*	na·*la*·zee se ...
behind ...	*iza ...*	*ee*·za ...
close	*nedaleko*	ne·da·le·kaw
here	*ovdje*	*awv*·dye
in front of ...	*ispred ...*	*ee*·spred ...
near ...	*blizu ...*	*blee*·zoo ...
next to ...	*pored ...*	*paw*·red ...
on the corner	*na uglu*	na *oo*·gloo
opposite ...	*nasuprot ...*	*na*·soo·prawt ...
straight ahead	*ravno naprijed*	*rav*·naw *na*·pree·yed
there	*tamo*	*ta*·maw

Turn ...	*Skrenite ...*	*skre*·nee·te ...
at the corner	*na uglu*	na *oo*·gloo
at the traffic lights	*na semaforu*	na *se*·ma·faw·roo
left	*lijevo*	*lee*·ye·vaw
right	*desno*	*de*·snaw

listen for ...		
... *kee*·law·me·ta·ra	... *kilometara*	... **kilometres**
... mee·*noo*·ta	... *minuta*	... **minutes**
... *me*·ta·ra	... *metara*	... **metres**

north	*sjever*	*sye*·ver
south	*jug*	yoog
east	*istok*	*ees*·tawk
west	*zapad*	*za*·pad

By …		
bus	*autobusom*	a·oo·*taw*·boo·sawm
foot	*pješke*	*pyesh*·ke
taxi	*taksijem*	*tak*·see·yem
train	*vlakom*	*vla*·kawm
tram	*tramvajem*	*tram*·vai·em

typical addresses

What's the address?
Koja je adresa?   koy·a ye a·*dre*·sa

avenue	*avenija* f	*a*·ve·nee·ya
lane	*prolaz* m	*praw*·laz
street	*ulica* f	oo·*lee*·tsa

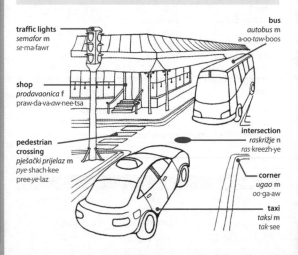

traffic lights
semafor m
se·ma·fawr

shop
prodavaonica f
praw·da·va·*aw*·nee·tsa

pedestrian crossing
pješački prijelaz m
pye·shach·kee pree·*ye*·laz

bus
autobus m
a·oo·*taw*·boos

intersection
raskrižje n
ras·kreezh·ye

corner
ugao m
oo·ga·aw

taxi
taksi m
tak·see

finding accommodation

Where's a …?	*Gdje se nalazi …?*	gdye se *na*·la·zee …
bed and	*konačište i*	*kaw*·na·cheesh·te ee
breakfast	*doručak*	*daw*·roo·chak
camping ground	*kamp*	kamp
guesthouse	*privatni*	*pree*·vat·nee
	smještaj	*smyesh*·tai
	za najam	za *nai*·am
hotel	*hotel*	*haw*·tel
nudist camping	*nudistički*	noo·*dee*·steech·kee
ground	*kamp*	kamp
pension	*pansion*	pan·*see*·awn
room for rent	*najmljena soba*	*nai*·mlye·na *saw*·ba
youth hostel	*prenoćište za*	*pre*·naw·cheesh·te za
	mladež	*mla*·dezh
Can you	*Možete li*	*maw*·zhe·te lee
recommend	*preporučiti*	pre·paw·*roo*·chee·tee
somewhere …?	*negdje …?*	*neg*·dye …
cheap	*jeftino*	*yef*·tee·naw
good	*dobro*	*daw*·braw
luxurious	*luksuzno*	*look*·sooz·naw
nearby	*blizu*	*blee*·zoo
romantic	*romantično*	raw·*man*·teech·naw

What's the address?
Koja je adresa? koy·a ye a·*dre*·sa

local talk		
dive	*ozloglašena*	aw·*zlaw*·gla·she·na
	gostionica f	gaw·stee·*aw*·nee·tsa
rat-infested	*ušljivo*	*oosh*·lyee·vaw
top spot	*odlično mjesto* n	*awd*·leech·naw *mye*·staw

booking ahead & checking in

rezervacije i prijava na recepciji

I'd like to book a ..., please.	*Želio/Željela bih rezervirati ..., molim.* m/f	zhe·lee·aw/zhe·lye·la beeh re·zer·*vee*·ra·tee ... *maw*·leem
campsite	*mjesto za kampiranje*	*mye*·staw za kam·*pee*·ra·nye
room	*sobu*	*saw*·boo

I have a reservation.
Imam rezervaciju. — ee·mam re·zer·*va*·tsee·yoo

My name's ...
Moje ime je ... — *moy*·e ee·me ye ...

For (three) nights/weeks.
Na (tri) noći/tjedna. — na (tree) *naw*·chee/*tyed*·na

From (2 July) to (6 July).
Od (2. srpnja) do (6. srpnja). — awd (*droo*·gawg srp·nya) daw (*she*·stawg srp·nya)

Do I need to pay upfront?
Trebam li platiti unaprijed? — *tre*·bam lee *pla*·tee·tee oo·*na*·pree·yed

Is breakfast included?
Da li je doručak uključen? — da lee ye *daw*·roo·chak ook·lyoo·chen

Do you offer half-board?
Da li nudite polu-pansion? — da lee *noo*·dee·te *paw*·loo·pan·*see*·awn

Do you have a swimming pool?
Imate li bazen za plivanje? — ee·ma·te lee ba·zen za *plee*·va·nye

listen for ...

kaw·*lee*·kaw *naw*·chee	*Koliko noći?*	**How many nights?**
paw·poo·nye·naw	*popunjeno*	**full**
poo·*tawv*·nee·tsa	*putovnica*	**passport**

PRACTICAL

56

How much is it per ...?	*Koliko je po ...?*	kaw·*lee*·kaw ye paw ...
night	*noći*	*naw*·chee
person	*osobi*	*aw*·saw·bee
week	*tjednu*	*tyed*·noo
Can I pay by ...?	*Mogu li platiti sa ...?*	maw·goo lee *pla*·tee·tee sa ...
credit card	*kreditnom karticom*	*kre*·deet·nawm *kar*·tee·tsawm
debit card	*debitnom karticom*	*de*·beet·nawm *kar*·tee·tsawm
travellers cheque	*putničkim čekom*	*poot*·neech·keem *che*·kawm

For other methods of payment, see **money**, page 37.

---

room at the inn

These local room classifications will come in handy if you're booking a room in a private home. This is one of the best accommodation options in Croatia. Not only is it cheaper than a hotel but interacting with your hosts will give you an opportunity to experience local culture.

jedna zvjezdica   *yed*·na *zvye*·zdee·tsa
  one-star (room with a bathroom shared between two rooms or with the owner)

dvije zvjezdice   *dvee*·ye *zvye*·zdee·tse
  two-star (room with a bathroom shared with one other room)

tri zvjezdice   tree *zvye*·zdee·tse
  three-star (room with a private bathroom)

Be sure to check when booking whether the price is per person or per room by asking:

Is this the price per ...?	*Da li je ovo cijena po ...?*	da lee ye *aw*·vaw tsee·*ye*·na paw ...
person	*osobi*	*aw*·saw·bee
room	*sobi*	*saw*·bee

Do you have a ... room?	Imate li ... sobu?	ee·ma·te lee ... saw·boo
double	dvokrevetnu	dvaw·kre·vet·noo
single	jednokrevetnu	yed·naw·kre·vet·noo

Do you have a twin room?

Imate li jednokrevetnu
sobu sa francuskim
ležajem?

ee·ma·te lee yed·naw·kre·vet·noo
saw·boo sa fran·tsoo·skeem
le·zhai·em

Can I see it?

Mogu li je vidjeti?   maw·goo lee ye vee·dye·tee

I'll take it.

Uzet ću ovu.   oo·zet choo aw·voo

requests & queries

When/Where is breakfast served?

Kada/Gdje služite
doručak?

ka·da/gdye sloo·zhee·te
daw·roo·chak

Please wake me at (seven).

Probudite me u
(sedam) molim.

praw·boo·dee·te me oo
(se·dam) maw·leem

Do you have a/an ...?	Imate li ...?	ee·ma·te lee ...
elevator/lift	dizalo	dee·za·law
laundry service	usluge pranja rublja	oo·sloo·ge pra·nya roob·lya
safe	sef	sef
swimming pool	bazen za plivanje	ba·zen za plee·va·nye

Can I use the ...?	Mogu li koristiti ...?	maw·goo lee kaw·ree·stee·te ...
kitchen	kuhinju	koo·hee·nyoo
laundry	praonicu	pra·aw·nee·tsoo
telephone	telefon	te·le·fawn

Do you … here?	*Da li … ovdje?*	da lee … *awv*·dye
arrange tours	*organizirate*	awr·ga·*nee*·zee·ra·te
	turistička	too·*ree*·steech·ka
	putovanja	poo·taw·*va*·nya
change money	*mijenjate*	mee·*ye*·nya·te
	novac	*naw*·vats

Could I have …, please?	*Mogu li dobiti … molim?*	*maw*·goo lee *daw*·bee·tee … *maw*·leem
an extra blanket	*jednu dodatnu deku*	*yed*·noo *daw*·dat·noo *de*·koo
a mosquito net	*mrežu za komarce*	*mre*·zhoo za kaw·*mar*·tse
a receipt	*račun*	*ra*·choon
my key	*moj ključ*	moy klyooch

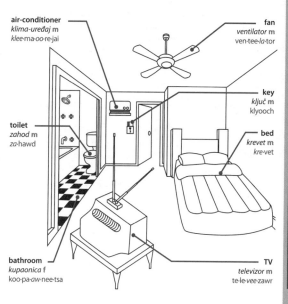

air-conditioner
klima-uređaj m
klee·ma·oo·re·jai

fan
ventilator m
ven·tee·*la*·tor

key
ključ m
klyooch

toilet
zahod m
za·hawd

bed
krevet m
kre·vet

bathroom
kupaonica f
koo·pa·*aw*·nee·tsa

TV
televizor m
te·le·*vee*·zawr

accommodation

59

Is there a message for me?

Ima li koja poruka za mene? — ee·ma lee *koy*·a *paw*·roo·ka za *me*·ne

Can I leave a message for someone?

Mogu li ostaviti poruku za nekoga? — *maw*·goo lee *aw*·sta·vee·tee *paw*·roo·koo za *ne*·kaw·ga

I'm locked out of my room.

Zaključao/Zaključala sam svoju sobu iznutra. m/f — zak·lyoo·cha·aw/zak·lyoo·cha·la sam *svoy*·oo *saw*·boo eez·*noo*·tra

complaints

prigovori

It's too ...	Suviše je ...	soo·vee·she ye ...
bright	osvijetljeno	aw·svee·*yet*·lye·naw
cold	hladno	*hlad*·naw
dark	tamno	*tam*·naw
expensive	skupo	*skoo*·paw
noisy	bučno	*booch*·naw
small	malo	*ma*·law

The ... doesn't work.	... je neispravan.	... ye ne·ee·spra·van
air-conditioning	Klima-uređaj	*klee*·ma·oo·re·jai
fan	Ventilator	ven·tee·*la*·tawr
toilet	Zahod	*za*·hawd

Can I get another ...?

Mogu li dobiti još jedan/jednu/jedno ...? m/f/n — *maw*·goo lee *daw*·bee·tee yawsh ye·dan/*yed*·noo/*yed*·naw ...

This ... isn't clean.

Ovaj/Ova/Ovo ... nije čist/čista/čisto. m/f/n — *aw*·vai/*aw*·va/*aw*·vaw ... *nee*·ye cheest/*chees*·ta/*chees*·taw

blanket	deka f	*de*·ka
sheet	plahta f	*plah*·ta
towel	ručnik m	*rooch*·neek

Who is it?	*Tko je?*	tkaw ye
Just a moment.	*Samo trenutak.*	sa·maw tre·noo·tak
Come in.	*Uđite.*	oo·jee·te
Come back later, please.	*Molim vas, vratite se kasnije.*	maw·leem vas vra·tee·te se ka·snee·ye

checking out

odlazak

What time is checkout?
U koliko sati treba napustiti sobu?
oo kaw·lee·kaw sa·tee tre·ba na·poo·stee·tee saw·boo

Can I have a late checkout?
Smijem li sobu napustiti kasnije od navedenog vremena?
smee·yem lee saw·boo na·poo·stee·tee ka·snee·ye awd na·ve·de·nawg vre·me·na

Can you call a taxi for me (for 11 o'clock)?
Možete li mi pozvati taksi (za 11 sati)?
maw·zhe·te lee mee paw·zva·tee tak·see (za ye·da·na·est sa·tee)

I'm leaving now.
Ja sada odlazim.
ya sa·da awd·la·zeem

Can I leave my bags here?
Mogu li ovdje ostaviti svoje torbe?
maw·goo lee awv·dye aw·sta·vee·tee svoy·e tawr·be

There's a mistake in the bill.
Ima jedna greška na računu.
ee·ma yed·na gresh·ka na ra·choo·noo

Could I have my ..., please?	*Mogu li dobiti ..., molim?*	maw·goo lee daw·bee·tee ... maw·leem
deposit	*svoj depozit*	svoy de·paw·zeet
passport	*svoju putovnicu*	svoy·oo poo·tawv·nee·tsoo
valuables	*svoje dragocjenosti*	svoy·e dra·gaw·tsye·naw·stee

I had a great stay, thank you.
*Moj boravak je bio
ugodan, hvala vam.*
moy *baw*·ra·vak ye *bee*·aw
oo·gaw·dan *hva*·la vam

I'll recommend it to my friends.
*Preporučit ću vas
svojim prijateljima.*
pre·paw·*roo*·cheet choo vas
svoy·eem *pree*·ya·te·lyee·ma

I'll be back …	*Vraćam se natrag …*	*vra*·cham se *na*·trag …
in (three) days	*za (tri) dana*	za (tree) *da*·na
on (Tuesday)	*u (utorak)*	oo (*oo*·taw·rak)

camping

kampiranje

Do you have …?	*Imate li …?*	ee·ma·te lee …
electricity	*struju*	stroo·yoo
a laundry	*praonicu*	pra·*aw*·nee·tsoo
shower facilities	*tuševe*	too·she·ve
a site	*mjesto za kampiranje*	mye·staw za kam·*pee*·ra·nye
tents for hire	*šatore za najam*	sha·taw·re za nai·am
How much is it per …?	*Koliko stoji po …?*	kaw·*lee*·kaw stoy·ee paw …
caravan	*kamp kućici*	kamp koo·chee·tsee
person	*osobi*	aw·saw·bee
tent	*šatoru*	sha·taw·roo
vehicle	*vozilu*	vaw·zee·loo

Can I ...? *Mogu li ...?* *maw·goo lee ...*
   camp here *ovdje kampirati* *awv·dye kam·pee·ra·tee*
   park next *parkirati pored* *par·kee·ra·tee paw·red*
    to my tent *svoga šatora* *svaw·ga sha·taw·ra*

Is it coin-operated?
  Treba li ubaciti *tre·ba lee oo·ba·tsee·tee*
  kovanice? *kaw·va·nee·tse*

Is the water drinkable?
  Da li je ova voda pitka? da lee ye aw·va vaw·da peet·ka

Who do I ask to stay here?
  Koga trebam pitati *kaw·ga tre·bam pee·ta·tee*
  da li mogu ostati ovdje? da lee maw·goo aw·sta·tee awv·dye

Could I borrow ...?
  Da li bih mogao/mogla da lee beeh maw·ga·aw/maw·gla
  posuditi ...? m/f paw·soo·dee·tee ...

renting

I'm here to	*Ja sam došao/*	ya sam *daw·sha·aw/*
see the ...	*došla vidjeti*	*daw·shla vee·dye·tee*
for rent.	*... za najam.* m/f	... za *nai·*am
Do you have	*Imate li ...*	*ee·*ma·te lee ...
a/an ...	*za najam?*	za *nai·*am
for rent?		
apartment	*stan*	stan
cabin	*kabinu*	ka·*bee·*noo
house	*kuću*	koo·choo
room	*sobu*	saw·boo
villa	*vilu*	vee·loo
furnished	*namješteno*	nam·yesh·te·naw
partly	*djelomično*	dye·law·meech·naw
furnished	*namješteno*	nam·yesh·te·naw
unfurnished	*nenamješteno*	ne·*nam·*yesh·te·naw

staying with locals

Can I stay at your place?
Mogu li ostati kod vas? maw·goo lee *aw*·sta·tee kawd vas

Is there anything I can do to help?
Mogu li vam pomoći maw·goo lee vam *paw*·maw·chee
na bilo koji način? na bee·law *koy*·ee na·cheen

Thanks for your hospitality.
Hvala vam na hva·la vam na
gostoprimstvu. gaw·staw·*preems*·tvoo

I have a (sleeping bag).
Ja imam (svoju vreću ya ee·mam (*svoy*·oo vre·choo
za spavanje). za spa·va·nye)

Can I …?	Mogu li …?	maw·goo lee …
bring anything	donijeti neku	daw·nee·ye·tee ne·koo
for the meal	hranu za naš	hra·noo za nash
	obrok	awb·rawk
do the dishes	oprati suđe	aw·pra·tee soo·je
set/clear	namjestiti/	na·mye·stee·tee/
the table	raščistiti stol	rash·chee·stee·tee stawl

the host with the most

Croatian hosts delight in regaling visitors with homemade delicacies and drinks. If you're fortunate enough to be invited to share a meal you can express your appreciation of your host's culinary prowess in the following manner:

Kako je ovo dobro i ukusno!
ka·kaw ye *aw*·vaw   This is so good and tasty!
daw·braw ee oo·koo·snaw

For their part, your hosts will implore you to eat to excess, possibly by saying:

Jedi sinko/kćeri, samo udri!
ye·dee *seen*·kaw/k·*che*·ree   Eat, my son/daughter. Let it rip!
sa·maw oo·dree

looking for ...

Where's ...?	*Gdje je ...?*	gdye ye ...
a department store	*robna kuća*	*rawb*·na *koo*·cha
the market	*tržnica*	*tr*·zhnee·tsa
a supermarket	*supermarket*	*soo*·per·*mar*·ket

Where can I buy (a padlock)?
Gdje mogu kupiti   gdye *maw*·goo *koo*·pee·tee
(lokot)?   (*law*·kawt)

For phrases on directions, see **directions**, page 53, and for additional shops and services, see the **dictionary**.

making a purchase

I'm just looking.
Ja samo razgledam.   ya *sa*·maw *raz*·gle·dam

I'd like to buy (an adaptor plug).
Želim kupiti   *zhe*·leem *koo*·pee·tee
(utikač za konverter).   (oo·*tee*·kach za kawn·*ver*·ter)

How much is it?
Koliko stoji?   kaw·*lee*·kaw *stoy*·ee

Can you write down the price?
Možete li napisati   *maw*·zhe·te lee na·*pee*·sa·tee
cijenu?   tsee·*ye*·noo

Do you have any others?
Imate li bilo kakve   ee·*ma*·te lee *bee*·law *kak*·ve
druge?   *droo*·ge

Can I look at it?
Mogu li to pogledati?   *maw*·goo lee taw *paw*·gle·da·tee

Could I have it wrapped?

Možete li mi to zamotati? — maw·zhe·te lee mee taw za·maw·ta·tee

Does it have a guarantee?

Ima li ovo garanciju? — ee·ma lee aw·vaw ga·ran·tsee·yoo

Can I have it sent abroad?

Možete li mi to poslati u inozemstvo? — maw·zhe·te lee mee taw paw·sla·tee oo ee·naw·zemst·vaw

Can you order it for me?

Možete li to naručiti za mene? — maw·zhe·te lee taw na·roo·chee·tee za me·ne

Can I pick it up later?

Mogu li doći po to kasnije? — maw·goo lee daw·chee paw taw ka·snee·ye

It's faulty.

Neispravno je. — ne·ees·prav·naw ye

Do you accept …?	*Da li prihvaćate …?*	da lee pree·hva·cha·te …
credit cards	*kreditne kartice*	kre·deet·ne kar·tee·tse
debit cards	*debitne kartice*	de·beet·ne kar·tee·tse
travellers cheques	*putničke čekove*	poot·neech·ke che·kaw·ve
Could I have a …, please?	*Mogu li dobiti …, molim?*	maw·goo lee daw·bee·tee … maw·leem
bag	*vrećicu*	vre·chee·tsoo
receipt	*račun*	ra·choon
I'd like …, please.	*Želio/Željela bih …* m/f	zhe·lee·aw/zhe·lye·la beeh …
my change	*moj ostatak novca*	moy aw·sta·tak nawv·tsa
a refund	*povrat novca*	pawv·rat nawv·tsa
to return this	*ovo vratiti*	aw·vaw vra·tee·tee

bargaining

Prices in shops are generally fixed but you could try bargaining at a market, *tržnica* (tr·zhnee·tsa).

That's too expensive.
To je preskupo. taw ye pre·skoo·paw

Do you have something cheaper?
Imate li nešto jeftinije? ee·ma·te lee nesh·taw yef·tee·nee·ye

I'll give you (five kuna).
Dati ću vam (pet kuna). da·tee choo vam (pet koo·na)

local talk		
bargain	*prigodna cijena* f	pree·gawd·na tsee·ye·na
rip-off	*prekomjerna*	pre·kaw·myer·na
	cijena f	tsee·ye·na
sale	*rasprodaja* f	ra·spraw·da·ya
specials	*posebne ponude* f pl	paw·seb·ne paw·noo·de

clothes

My size is ...	*Moja veličina je ...*	moy·a ve·lee·chee·na ye ...
(40)	*(četrdeset)*	(che·tr·de·set)
large	*krupna*	kroop·na
medium	*srednja*	sred·nya
small	*sitna*	seet·na

Can I try it on?
Mogu li to probati? maw·goo lee taw praw·ba·tee

It doesn't fit.
Ne odgovara mi to. ne awd·gaw·va·ra mee taw

For sizes, see **numbers & amounts**, page 31. For clothing items, see the **dictionary**.

verbal exchanges

Though it might relate to an outmoded item of apparel, the word 'cravat' has interesting origins. It's thought to stem from the word *Hrvat* (hr·vat) meaning 'a Croat'. These neck scarves were purportedly so named because they were worn by Croatian mercenaries serving in the French army during the Thirty Year's War of the early 17th century.

The black-and-white spotted dogs known as Dalmatians meanwhile, are thought not to have originated in the coastal province of Dalmatia but to have been brought there by Roma people for use as guard dogs.

repairs

popravci

Can I have my ... repaired here?

Mogu li popraviti		maw·goo lee *paw*·pra·vee·tee
svoj/svoju/svoje ...		svoy/*svoy*·oo/*svoy*·e ...
ovdje? m/f/n		awv·dye

When will my ... be ready?	*Kada će biti gotov/ gotove ...?* sg/pl	ka·da che bee·tee gaw·tawv/ gaw·taw·ve ...
backpack	*moj ranac* sg	moy *ra*·nats
camera	*moj foto-aparat* sg	moy faw·taw·a·*pa*·rat
(sun)glasses	*moje naočale (za sunce)* pl	*moy*·e na·aw·cha·le (za soon·tse)
shoes	*moje cipele* pl	*moy*·e tsee·pe·le
watch	*sat* sg	sat

hairdressing

I'd like (a) …	*Želio/Željela bih … m/f*	*zhe*·lee·aw/*zhe*·lye·la beeh …
blow wave	*feniranje*	fe·*nee*·ra·nye
colour	*bojenje kose*	*boy*·e·nye *kaw*·se
haircut	*šišanje*	*shee*·sha·nye
my beard trimmed	*podrezivanje brade*	paw·dre·*zee*·va·nye *bra*·de
shave	*brijanje*	*bree*·ya·nye
trim	*skraćivanje*	skra·*chee*·va·nye

Don't cut it too short.
Nemojte me ošišati ne·*moy*·te me aw·*shee*·sha·tee
prekratko. pre·*krat*·kaw

Please use a new blade.
Molim vas koristite *maw*·leem vas kaw·*ree*·stee·te
novi žilet. *naw*·vee *zhee*·let

Shave it all off!
Obrijte sve potpuno! aw·*breey*·te sve *pawt*·poo·naw

I should never have let you near me!
Nisam vam nikada trebao *nee*·sam vam *nee*·ka·da *tre*·ba·aw
ni dozvoliti blizu! nee dawz·*vaw*·lee·tee *blee*·zoo

For colours, see the **dictionary**.

books & reading

Do you have …?	*Imate li …?*	ee·*ma*·te lee …
a book by (August Senoa)	*knjigu (Augusta Šenoe)*	*knyee*·goo (*a*·oo·goo·sta *she*·naw·e)
an entertainment guide	*vodič o zbivanjima u svijetu razonode*	*vaw*·deech aw *zbee*·va·nyee·ma oo svee·*ye*·too ra·*zaw*·naw·de

Is there an English-language ...?	Postoji li ... za engleski jezik?	paw·stoy·ee lee ... za en·gle·skee ye·zeek
bookshop	knjižara	knyee·zha·ra
section	odjel	awd·yel

I'd like (a) ...	Želio/Željela bih ... m/f	zhe·lee·aw/zhe·lye·la beeh ...
dictionary	rječnik	ryech·neek
newspaper (in English)	novine (na engleskom)	naw·vee·ne (na en·gles·kawm)
notepad	bilježnicu	bee·lyezh·nee·tsoo

Can you recommend a book for me?

Možete li mi preporučiti jednu knjigu?	maw·zhe·te lee mee pre·paw·roo·chee·tee yed·noo knyee·goo

Do you have Lonely Planet guidebooks?

Imate li Lonely Planet priručnike?	ee·ma·te lee lawn·lee ple·net pree·rooch·nee·ke

listen for ...

maw·goo lee vam paw·maw·chee	
Mogu li vam pomoći?	**Can I help you?**
nesh·taw droo·gaw	
Nešto drugo?	**Anything else?**
ne ne·ma·maw taw·ga	
Ne, nemamo toga.	**No, we don't have any.**

music

glazba

I'd like a ...	Želio/Željela bih... m/f	zhe·lee·aw/zhe·lye·la beeh ...
blank tape	jednu praznu kazetu	yed·noo praz·noo ka·ze·too
CD	jedan CD	ye·dan tse de
DVD	jedan DVD	ye·dan de·ve·de

I'm looking for something by (Oliver Dragojevic).
Tražim nešto od — tra·zheem nesh·taw awd
(Olivera Dragojevića). — (aw·lee·ve·ra dra·goy·e·vee·cha)

What's their best recording?
Koji je njegov — koy·ee ye nye·gawv
najbolji album? — nai·baw·lyee al·boom

Can I listen to this?
Mogu li ovo — maw·goo lee aw·vaw
poslušati? — paw·sloo·sha·tee

photography

I need ... film	Trebam ... film	tre·bam ... feelm
for this	za ovaj	za aw·vai
camera.	foto-aparat.	faw·taw·a·pa·rat
APS	APS	a pe es
B&W	crno-bijeli	tsr·naw·bee·ye·lee
colour	kolor	kaw·lawr

I need ... film	Trebam film ...	tre·bam feelm ...
for this	za ovaj	za aw·vai
camera.	foto-aparat.	faw·taw·a·pa·rat
slide	za dijapozitive	za dee·ya·paw·zee·tee·ve
(200) speed	brzine (dvijesto)	br·zee·ne (dvee·ye·staw)

Can you ...?	Možete li ...?	maw·zhe·te lee ...
develop this	razviti ovaj	raz·vee·tee aw·vai
film	film	feelm
load my film	staviti moj film	sta·vee·tee moy feelm
	u foto-aparat	oo faw·taw·a·pa·rat

When will it be ready?
Kada će to biti — ka·da che taw bee·tee
gotovo? — gaw·taw·vaw

How much is it?
Koliko to stoji? — kaw·lee·kaw taw stoy·ee

I need a passport photo taken.

Trebam se slikati	tre·bam se slee·ka·tee
za putovnicu.	za poo·tawv·nee·tsoo

I'm not happy with these photos.

Nisam zadovoljan/	nee·sam za·daw·vaw·lyan/
zadovoljna sa ovim	za·daw·vawl'·na sa aw·veem
fotografijama. m/f	faw·taw·gra·fee·ya·ma

I don't want to pay the full price.

Ne želim platiti	ne zhe·leem pla·tee·tee
punu cijenu.	poo·noo tsee·ye·noo

souvenirs

embroidery	*vez* m	vez
folklore items	*folklorni*	fawl·klawr·nee
	predmeti m pl	pred·me·tee
handicrafts	*ručni rad* m	rooch·nee rad
lace	*čipka* f	cheep·ka
paintings	*slike* f pl	slee·ke
pottery	*grnčarija* f	grn·cha·ree·ya
silver jewellery	*srebrni nakit* m	sre·br·nee na·keet
sculptures	*skulpture* f pl	skoolp·too·re
stone carvings	*Bračanske*	bra·chan·ske
from Brač	*rezbarije*	rez·ba·ree·ye
	u kamenu f pl	oo ka·me·noo
woodcarvings	*drvorezi* m pl	dr·vaw·re·zee

books on historical and cultural heritage

knjige o povjesnoj	knyee·ge aw paw·vye·snoy
i kulturnoj baštini f pl	ee kool·toor·noy bash·tee·nee

jewellery and souvenirs made of shells, sea urchins etc

ukrasi iz mora m pl	oo·kra·see eez maw·ra

traditional folk costumes

tradicionalne narodne	tra·dee·tsee·aw·nal·ne na·rawd·ne
nošnje f pl	nawsh·nye

post office

poštanski ured

Postal services are catered for by HTP Hrvatska. If you just want to send a few postcards you can avoid going to the post office by buying stamps, *poštanske marke* (*pawsh·tan·ske mar·ke*), from any kiosk newsagent and dropping your mail into a yellow mailbox, *poštanski sandučić* (*pawsh·tan·ske san·doo·cheech*).

I want to send a ...	*Želim poslati ...*	*zhe·leem paw·sla·tee ...*
fax	*telefaks*	*te·le·faks*
letter	*pismo*	*pee·smaw*
parcel	*paket*	*pa·ket*
postcard	*dopisnicu*	*daw·pee·snee·tsoo*

I want to buy a/an ...	*Želim kupiti ...*	*zhe·leem koo·pee·tee ...*
aerogram	*avionski*	*a·vee·awn·skee*
	telegram	*te·le·gram*
envelope	*omotnicu*	*aw·mawt·nee·tsoo*
stamp	*jednu poštansku marku*	*yed·noo pawsh·tan·skoo mar·koo*

customs declaration	*prijava robe na carini* f	*pree·ya·va raw·be na tsa·ree·nee*
domestic	*domaće*	*daw·ma·che*
fragile	*lomljivo*	*lawm·lyee·vaw*
international	*međunarodno*	*me·joo·na·rawd·naw*
mail	*pošta* f	*pawsh·ta*
mailbox	*poštanski sandučić* m	*pawsh·tan·skee san·doo·cheech*
postcode	*poštanski broj* m	*pawsh·tan·skee broy*
post office	*poštanski ured* m	*pawsh·tan·skee oo·red*

airmail	*zračna pošta* f	*zrach*·na *pawsh*·ta
express mail	*ekspres pošta* f	*eks*·pres *pawsh*·ta
registered mail	*preporučena pošta* f	pre·*paw*·roo·che·na *pawsh*·ta
sea mail	*prekomorska pošta* f	pre·*kaw*·mawr·ska *pawsh*·ta
surface mail	*obična pošta* f	*aw*·beech·na *pawsh*·ta

Please send it by air/surface mail to (Australia).

Molim da pošaljete to zračnom/običnom poštom u (Australiju).

maw·leem da *paw*·sha·lye·te taw *zrach*·nawm/*aw*·beech·nawm *pawsh*·tawm oo (a·oo·*stra*·lee·yoo)

It contains (souvenirs).

Ovo sadrži (suvenire).

aw·vaw sa·dr·zhee (soo·ve·*nee*·re)

Where's the poste restante section?

Gdje se nalazi post restant odjel?

gdye se *na*·la·zee pawst re·*stant* *awd*·yel

Is there any mail for me?

Ima li bilo kakve pošte za mene?

ee·ma lee *bee*·law *kak*·ve *pawsh*·te za *me*·ne

phone

What's your phone number?

Koji je vaš/tvoj broj telefona? pol/inf

koy·ee ye vash/tvoy broy te·le·*faw*·na

Where's the nearest public phone?

Gdje je najbliži javni telefon?

gdye ye *nai*·blee·zhee *yav*·nee te·*le*·fawn

I want to ...	Želim ...	zhe·leem ...
buy a phonecard	kupiti telefonsku karticu	koo·pee·tee te·le·fawn·skoo kar·tee·tsoo
call (Singapore)	nazvati (Singapur)	naz·va·tee (seen·ga·poor)
make a (local) call	obaviti (lokalni) poziv	aw·ba·vee·tee (law·kal·nee) paw·zeev
reverse the charges	obaviti poziv na račun pozvanog	aw·ba·vee·tee paw·zeev na ra·choon pawz·va·nawg
speak for (three) minutes	govoriti (tri) minute	gaw·vaw·ree·tee (tree) mee·noo·te

How much does ... cost?	Koliko košta ...?	kaw·lee·kaw kawsh·ta ...
a (three)-minute call	poziv od (tri) minute	paw·zeev awd (tree) mee·noo·te
each extra minute	svaka naknadna minuta	sva·ka nak·nad·na mee·noo·ta

Can I look at a phone book?
Mogu li pogledati u imenik?
maw·goo lee paw·gle·da·tee oo ee·me·neek

The number is ...
Broj je ...
broy ye ...

What's the area/country code for (New Zealand)?
Koji je područni/ državni pozivni broj za (Novi Zeland)?
koy·ee ye paw·drooch·nee/ dr·zhav·nee paw·zeev·nee broy za (naw·vee ze·land)

Hello.	Halo.	ha·*law*
It's …	Ovdje …	awv·dye …
Is … there?	Da li je … tamo?	da lee ye … *ta*·maw
Can I speak to …?	Mogu li dobiti …?	*maw*·goo lee *daw*·bee·tee …
It's engaged.	Zauzeto je.	za·oo·ze·taw ye
I've been cut off.	Prekinuli su me.	pre·kee·noo·lee soo me
The connection is bad.	Veza je loša.	*ve*·za ye *law*·sha

Please tell (him/her) I called.
Molim da (mu/joj) kažete da sam zvao. m — *maw*·leem da moo/yoy *ka*·zhe·te da sam *zva*·aw
Molim da (mu/joj) kažete da sam zvala. f — *maw*·leem da moo/yoy *ka*·zhe·te da sam *zva*·la

Can I leave a message?
Mogu li ostaviti poruku? — *maw*·goo lee aw·sta·vee·tee *paw*·roo·koo

My number is …
Moj broj je … — moy broy ye …

I don't have a contact number.
Nemam broj na koji me možete dobiti. — *ne*·mam broy na *koy*·ee me *maw*·zhe·te *daw*·bee·tee

I'll call back later.
Nazvati ću kasnije. — *naz*·va·tee choo *ka*·snee·ye

mobile phone/cellphone

I'd like a …	Trebao/Trebala bih … m/f	tre·ba·aw/tre·ba·la beeh …
charger for my phone	punjač za moj telefon	poo·nyach za moy te·le·fawn
mobile phone/ cellphone	iznajmiti mobilni telefon	eez·nai·mee·tee maw·beel·nee te·le·fawn
for hire		
prepaid mobile phone/ cellphone	unaprijed plaćeni mobilni telefon	oo·na·pree·yed pla·che·nee maw·beel·nee te·le·fawn
SIM card	SIM karticu	seem kar·tee·tsoo

What are the rates?
Koje su cijene telefoniranja?
koy·ee soo tsee·ye·ne te·le·faw·nee·ra·nya

(3 kuna) per (30) seconds.
(3 kune) po (30) sekundi.
(tree koo·ne) paw (tree·de·set) se·koon·dee

the internet

Where's the local Internet café?
Gdje je mjesni internet kafić?
gdye ye mye·snee een·ter·net ka·feech

How do I log on?
Kako mogu pristupiti mreži?
ka·kaw maw·goo pree·stoo·pee·tee mre·zhee

Please change it to English-language setting.
Molim vas da promijenite jezičnu opciju na engleski jezik.
maw·leem vas da praw·mee·ye·nee·te ye·zeech·noo awp·tsee·yoo na en·gle·skee

I'd like to …	Želio/Željela bih … m/f	zhe·lee·aw/zhe·lye·la beeh …
check my email	provjeriti svoj email	praw·vye·ree·tee svoy ee·ma·eel
get Internet access	pristup internetu	pree·stoop een·ter·ne·too
use a printer	koristiti pisač	kaw·ree·stee·tee pee·sach
use a scanner	koristiti skener	kaw·ree·stee·tee ske·ner

Do you have …?	Imate li …?	ee·ma·te lee …
Macs	Macintosh računala	me·keen·tawsh ra·choo·na·la
PCs	PC-e	pe tse e
a Zip drive	pogon za Zip diskete	paw·gawn za zeep dee·ske·te

How much per …?	Koja je cijena po …?	koy·a ye tsee·ye·na paw …
hour	satu	sa·too
(five) minutes	(pet) minuta	(pet) mee·noo·ta
page	stranici	stra·nee·tsee

It's crashed.

Došlo je do prestanka rada računala.   dawsh·law ye daw pre·stan·ka ra·da ra·choo·na·la

I've finished.

Završio/Završila sam. m/f   za·vr·shee·aw/za·vr·shee·la sam

---

say I!

When you see a phrase containing the word 'I' in English, you'll notice that the Croatian translation often has two options to choose from. These are separated by a slash and are followed by the gender markers m/f, as in the phrase: *Želio/Željela bih … * m/f 'I'd like …'.

The two alternatives are masculine and feminine verb forms. Making the right selection is simple as it's based on the gender of the speaker – the person saying 'I'. If you're a man, you choose the first option and say *Želio bih*. If you're a woman, you say *Željela bih*. See the **a–z phrasebuilder**, page 19 for more on gender in Croatian.

PRACTICAL

78

Where can I ...?	Gdje mogu ...?	gdye *maw*·goo ...
I'd like to ...	Želio/Željela	zhe·lee·aw/zhe·lye·la
	bih ... m/f	beeh ...
cash a cheque	unovčiti ček	oo·*nawv*·chee·tee chek
change a	zamijeniti	za·mee·*ye*·nee·tee
travellers cheque	putnički ček	*poot*·neech·kee chek
change money	zamijeniti	za·mee·*ye*·nee·tee
	novac	*naw*·vats
get a cash	uzeti predujam	oo·ze·tee *pre*·doo·yam
advance	u gotovini	oo gaw·taw·*vee*·nee
withdraw money	podignuti	*paw*·deeg·noo·tee
	novac	*naw*·vats

Where's ...?	Gdje se	gdye se
	nalazi ...?	*na*·la·zee ...
an ATM	bankovni	*ban*·kawv·nee
	automat	a·oo·*taw*·mat
a foreign	mjenjačnica za	*mye*·nyach·nee·tsa za
exchange office	strane valute	*stra*·ne va·*loo*·te

What time does the bank open?

U koliko sati se   oo kaw·*lee*·kaw *sa*·tee se
otvara banka?   *awt*·va·ra *ban*·ka

The ATM took my card.

Bankovni automat mi   *ban*·kawv·nee a·oo·*taw*·mat mee
je oduzeo karticu.   ye aw·doo·ze·aw *kar*·tee·tsoo

I've forgotten my PIN.

Zaboravio/Zaboravila   za·*baw*·ra·vee·aw/za·*baw*·ra·vee·la
sam svoj osobni   sam svoy *aw*·sawb·nee
tajni broj. m/f   *tai*·nee broy

Can I use my credit card to withdraw money?

Mogu li koristiti   *maw*·goo lee *kaw*·ree·stee·tee
svoju kreditnu karticu   svoy·oo *kre*·deet·noo *kar*·tee·tsoo
za podizanje novca?   za *paw*·dee·za·nye *nawv*·tsa

What's the ...?	Koji/Kolika je ...? m/f	koy·ee/kaw·lee·ka ye ...
charge for that	*pristojba za to* f	*pree*·stoy·ba za taw
exchange rate	*tečaj razmjene* m	*te*·chai *raz*·mye·ne

Has my money arrived yet?

Da li je moj novac stigao?
da lee ye moy *naw*·vats *stee*·ga·aw

How long will it take to arrive?

Koliko će trebati da stigne?
kaw·*lee*·kaw che *tre*·ba·tee da *steeg*·ne

For other useful phrases, see **money**, page 37.

---

listen for ...

ee·den·tee·fee·*ka*·tsee·ya	*identifikacija*	**identification**
poo·*tawv*·nee·tsa	*putovnica*	**passport**

ee·ma·maw ye·dan *praw*·blem
Imamo jedan problem.   **There's a problem.**

mee taw ne *maw*·zhe·maw oo·*ra*·dee·tee
Mi to ne možemo uraditi.   **We can't do that.**

nee·ye vam *aw*·sta·law *neesh*·ta *nawv*·tsa
Nije vam ostalo ništa novca.   **You have no funds left.**

pawt·*pee*·shee·te *awv*·dye
Potpišite ovdje.   **Sign here.**

I'd like a/an ...	Želio/Željela bih ... m/f	zhe·lee·aw/zhe·lye·la beeh ...
audio set	set slušalica	set sloo·sha·lee·tsa
catalogue	katalog	ka·ta·log
guidebook	turistički	too·ree·steech·kee
in English	vodič na engleskom	vaw·deech na en·gles·kawm
(local) map	kartu (mjesta)	kar·too (mye·sta)

Do you have information on ... sights?	Da li imate informacije o ... znamenitostima?	da lee ee·ma·te een·fawr·ma·tsee·ye aw ... zna·me·nee·taw·stee·ma
cultural	kulturnim	kool·toor·neem
historical	povijesnim	paw·vee·ye·sneem
religious	vjerskim	vyer·skeem

I need a guide.
Trebam vodiča.   tre·bam vaw·dee·cha

I'd like to see ...
Želio/Željela bih vidjeti ... m/f   zhe·lee·aw/zhe·lye·la beeh vee·dye·tee ...

Could you take a photo of me?
Možete/Možeš li me slikati? pol/inf   maw·zhe·te/maw·zhesh lee me slee·ka·tee

Can I take a photo (of you)?
Mogu li ja slikati (vas/tebe)? pol/inf   maw·goo lee ya slee·ka·tee (vas/te·be)

I'll send you the photo.
Poslati ću vam/tebi tu fotografiju. pol/inf   paw·sla·tee choo vam/te·bee too faw·taw·gra·fee·yoo

Who made it?
 Tko je to napravio? tkaw ye taw *na*·pra·vee·aw

How old is it?
 Koliko je to staro? kaw·*lee*·kaw ye taw *sta*·raw

---

behold the grb!

On a sojourn in Croatia one thing that becomes imprinted upon your subconscious is the ubiquitous red-and-white checked emblem in the shape of a shield. It's known as the *Hrvatski grb* (hr·vat·skee grb) 'the Croatian coat of arms' or simply as *grb*. It's been around for hundreds of years and is about as potent a symbol of nationalism as you can find.

The origins of the *grb* are obscure but legend has it that a Croatian king defeated a Venetian prince at chess to maintain Croatia's freedom and so the chessboard was symbolically enshrined as a symbol of this freedom. Today, following the breakaway from the former Yugoslavia, the *grb* is proudly displayed everywhere to celebrate independence for which the Croats have yearned for over a millenium.

---

getting in

ulaz

What time does it open/close?
 U koliko sati se oo kaw·*lee*·kaw *sa*·tee se
 otvara/zatvara? *awt*·va·ra/*zat*·va·ra

What's the admission charge?
 Koliko stoji ulaznica? kaw·*lee*·kaw *stoy*·ee oo·laz·nee·tsa

Is there a	*Imate li*	*ee*·ma·te lee
discount for …?	*popust za …?*	*paw*·poost za …
children	*djecu*	*dye*·tsoo
families	*obitelji*	aw·*bee*·te·lyee
groups	*grupe*	*groo*·pe
seniors	*starije ljude*	*sta*·ree·ye *lyoo*·de
pensioners	*umirovljenike*	oo·mee·rawv·lye·*nee*·ke
students	*studente*	*stoo*·den·te

tours

Can you recommend a ...?	*Možete li mi preporučiti ...?*	*maw*·zhe·te lee mee pre·paw·*roo*·chee·tee ...
When's the next ...?	*Kada je idući/ iduća ...?* m/f	*ka*·da ye ee·*doo*·chee/ ee·doo·cha ...
boat trip	*izlet brodom* m	*eez*·let *braw*·dawm
day trip	*dnevni izlet* m	*dnev*·nee *eez*·let
tour	*turistička ekskurzija* f	too·*ree*·steech·ka ek·*skoor*·zee·ya
Is ... included?	*Da li je ... uključen/ uključena?* m/f	da lee ye ... *ook*·lyoo·chen/ *ook*·lyoo·che·na
accommodation	*smještaj* m	*smye*·shtai
food	*hrana* f	*hra*·na
transport	*prijevoz* m	pree·*ye*·vawz

The guide will pay.
   Vodič će platiti.   *vaw*·deech che *pla*·tee·tee

The guide has paid.
   Vodič je platio/platila. m/f   *vaw*·deech ye *pla*·tee·aw/*pla*·tee·la

How long is the tour?
   Koliko traje ekskurzija?   kaw·*lee*·kaw *trai*·e ek·*skoor*·zee·ya

What time should we be back?
   U koje bi se vrijeme   oo *koy*·e bee se vree·*ye*·me
   trebali vratiti?   *tre*·ba·lee *vra*·tee·tee

I'm with them.
   Ja sam s njima.   ya sam s *nyee*·ma

signs

Besplatan Ulaz	*be*·spla·tan *oo*·laz	**Free Admission**
Informacije	een·fawr·*ma*·tsee·ye	**Information**
Izlaz	*eez*·laz	**Exit**
Misa u Toku	*mee*·sa oo *taw*·koo	**Service (Mass) in Progress**
Muški	*moosh*·kee	**Men**
Ne Diraj	ne *dee*·rai	**Do Not Touch**
Otvoren	*awt* vawr·en	**Open**
Ulaz	*oo*·laz	**Entrance**
WC	ve·*tse*	**Toilets**
Zabranjen Ulaz	za·*bra*·nyen *oo*·laz	**No Entry**
Zabranjene Blic Kameri	za·bra·*nye*·ne bleets *ka*·me·ree	**No Flash Photography**
Zabranjeno Fotografirati	za·bra·*nye*·naw faw·taw·gra·*fee*·ra·tee	**No Photography**
Zabranjeno Pušenje	za·bra·*nye*·naw *poo*·she·nye	**No Smoking**
Zatvoren	zat vawr·en	**Closed**
Ženski	*zhen*·skee	**Women**

I'm attending a ...	Ja idem na ...	ya *ee*·dem na ...
conference	konferenciju	kon·fe·*ren*·tsee·yoo
course	tečaj	te·chai
meeting	sastanak	sa·sta·nak
trade fair	sajam	sai·am

Where's the ...?	Gdje je ...?	gdye ye ...
business centre	poslovni	*paw*·slawv·nee
(eg in hotel)	centar	tsen·tar
conference	konferencija	kon·fe·*ren*·tsee·ya
meeting	sastanak	sa·sta·nak

I'm with ...	Ovdje sam sa ...	*awv*·dye sam sa ...
(Kras)	(Krašem)	(kra·shem)
my colleague(s)	svojim kolegom/	*svoy*·eem kaw·*le*·gawm/
	kolegama sg/pl	kaw·*le*·ga·ma
(two) others	(dvoje) drugih	(*dvoy*·e) droo·geeh

I'm alone.
Ja sam sam/sama. m/f   ya sam sam/*sa*·ma

home alone

There's a little trick to the pronunciation of the above phrase *Ja sam sam*. It might look like simple repetition, but to be understood you'll need to say the first *sam* shorter than the second. You'll also need to pitch your voice a bit lower for the second *sam*. This aspect of Croatian is called pitch accent. See **pronunciation**, page 13, for an explanation of how it works if you're curious.

I have an appointment with ...
Ja imam sastanak sa ...   ya *ee*·mam sa·sta·nak sa ...

I'm staying at ..., room ...
Ostajem u ..., soba ...   aw·stai·em oo ... *saw*·ba ...

I need ...	*Treba mi ...*	*tre*·ba mee ...
a computer	*računalo*	ra·*choo*·na·law
an Internet connection	*priključak na internet*	*pree*·klyoo·chak na *een*·ter·net
an interpreter	*tumač*	*too*·mach
more business cards	*još posjetnica*	yosh *paw*·syet·nee·tsa
to send a fax	*da pošaljem telefaks*	da *paw*·sha·lyem te·le·faks

Here's my business card.
Evo vam moja posjetnica.   e·vaw vam *moy*·a paw·syet·nee·tsa

That went very well.
To je odlično prošlo.   taw ye *awd*·leech·naw *prawsh*·law

Thank you for your time.
Zahvaljujem na vašem vremenu.   za·hva·lyoo·yem na *va*·shem vre·me·noo

Shall we go for a drink/meal?
Hoćemo li na piće/večeru?   haw·che·maw lee na *pee*·che/ ve·che·roo

It's on me.
Ja častim.   ya *cha*·steem

---

down to business

Croatian business etiquette doesn't present any real peculiarities. One thing to be conscious of, though, is that Croatians in coastal areas have a more relaxed and flexible attitude to time than their Anglo-Saxon counterparts. Agitation about deadlines or punctuality might meet with the standard response:

Relax, we still have time.
Stani malo, imamo još vremena.   sta·nee ma·law ee·ma·maw yosh vre·me·na

Away from the coastal areas, Croatians see themselves as hard-working and efficient go-getters in the Central European mould. They tend to be more bureacratic and punctual in their business dealings than their Latin-influenced compatriots.

senior & disabled travellers

starjiji i onesposobljeni putnici

Because of the number of wounded war veterans, more attention is being paid to the needs of disabled travellers. In Zagreb, ZET Electric Tram Company (*Zagrebački Električni Tramvaj*) offers a service for disabled people.

I have a disability.
| *Ja sam onesposobljen/* | ya sam aw·ne·*spaw*·sawb·lyen/ |
| *onesposobljena.* m/f | aw·ne·*spaw*·sawb·lye·na |

I need assistance.
| *Ja trebam pomoć.* | ya *tre*·bam *paw*·mawch |

What services do you have for people with a disability?
| *Koje usluge nudite* | *koy*·e oo·sloo·ge *noo*·dee·te |
| *za onesposobljene?* | za aw·ne·*spaw*·sawb·lye·ne |

Are there disabled toilets?
| *Imate li zahod* | ee·ma·te lee *za*·hawd |
| *za onesposobljene?* | za aw·ne·*spaw*·sawb·lye·ne |

Are there disabled parking spaces?
| *Postoji li parkiralište* | paw·stoy·ee lee par·*kee*·ra·leesh·te |
| *za onesposobljene?* | za aw·ne·*spaw*·sawb·lye·ne |

Is there wheelchair access?
| *Imate li pristup za* | ee·ma·te lee *pree*·stoop za |
| *invalidska kolica?* | een·*va*·leed·ska kaw·*lee*·tsa |

How wide is the entrance?
| *Koje širine je ulaz?* | *koy*·e shee·*ree*·ne ye oo·laz |

I'm deaf.
| *Ja sam gluh/gluha.* m/f | ya sam glooh/*gloo*·ha |

I have a hearing aid.
| *Ja nosim slušni aparat.* | ya *naw*·seem *sloosh*·nee a·*pa*·rat |

Are guide dogs permitted?
Da li je dozvoljen	da lee ye *dawz*·vaw·lyen
pristup psima	*pree*·stoop *psee*·ma
vodičima?	vaw·*dee*·chee·ma

How many steps are there?
Koliko stepenica ima?   kaw·*lee*·kaw ste·pe·nee·tsa ee·ma

Is there a lift?
Da li postoji dizalo?   da lee *paw*·stoy·ee *dee*·za·law

Are there rails in the bathroom?
Imate li ručke za   ee·ma·te lee *rooch*·ke za
oslanjanje u kupaonici?   *aw*·sla·nya·nye oo koo·pa·*aw*·nee·tsee

Could you call me a disabled taxi?
Da li biste mi mogli   da lee *bee*·ste mee *maw*·glee
pozvati taksi za   *pawz*·va·tee *tak*·see za
onesposobljene?   aw·ne·*spaw*·sawb·lye·ne

Could you help me cross the street safely?
Da li biste mi mogli   da lee *bee*·ste mee *maw*·glee
pomoći sigurno   *paw*·maw·chee *see*·goor·naw
prijeći ulicu?   pree·*ye*·chee oo·lee·tsoo

Is there somewhere I can sit down?
Ima li negdje gdje   ee·ma lee *ne*·gdye gdye
mogu sjesti?   *maw*·goo sye·stee

guide dog	*pas vodič* m	pas *vaw*·deech
older person	*starija osoba* f	sta·ree·ya *aw*·saw·ba
person with a disability	*onesposobljena osoba* f	aw·ne·*spaw*·sawb·lye·na *aw*·saw·ba
ramp	*kosina za pristup kolicima* f	kaw·*see*·na za *pree*·stoop kaw·*lee*·tsee·ma
walking frame	*metalno pomagalo za hodanje* n	*me*·tal·naw paw·*ma*·ga·law za *haw*·da·nye
walking stick	*štap za hodanje* m	shtap za *haw*·da·nye
wheelchair	*invalidska kolica* f pl	een·*va*·leed·ska kaw·*lee*·tsa

travelling with children

putovanje sa djecom

Is there a ...?	Imate li ...?	ee·ma·te lee ...
baby change room	sobu za previjanjebeba	saw·boo za pre·vee·ya·nye be·ba
child-minding service	usluge čuvanja djece	oo·sloo·ge choo·va·nya dye·tse
child-sized portion	dječju porciju	dyech·yoo pawr·tsee·yoo
children's menu	dječji jelovnik	dyech·yee ye·lawv·neek
crèche	jaslice	ya·slee·tse
discount for children	popust za djecu	paw·poost za dye·tsoo
family ticket	kartu za cijelu obitelj	kar·too za tsee·ye·loo aw·bee·tel'
I need a/an ...	Treba mi ...	tre·ba mee ...
baby seat	sjedalo za dijete	sye·da·law za dee·ye·te
(English-speaking) baby-sitter	dadilja (koja govori engleski)	da·dee·lya (koy·a gaw·vaw·ree en·gle·skee)
booster seat	potporno dječje sjedalo	pawt·pawr·naw dyech·ye sye·da·law
cot	dječji krevet	dyech·yee kre·vet
highchair	visoka stolica za bebe	vee·saw·ka staw·lee·tsa za be·be
plastic bag	plastična vrećica	pla·steech·na vre·chee·tsa
potty	tuta	too·ta
sick bag	vrećica za povraćanje	vre·chee·tsa za paw·vra·cha·nye
stroller	dječja hodalica	dyech·ya haw·da·lee·tsa

Where's the	*Gdje je*	gdye ye
nearest ...?	*najbliži/a/e ...?* m/f/n	nai·blee·zhee/a/e ...
drinking	*izvor pitke*	eez·vawr peet·ke
fountain	*vode* m	vaw·de
park	*park* m	park
playground	*igralište* n	ee·gra·leesh·te
swimming	*bazen za*	ba·zen za
pool	*plivanje* m	plee·va·nye
tap	*slavina* f	sla·vee·na
theme park	*tematski*	te·mat·skee
	luna-park m	loo·na·park
toy shop	*prodavaonica*	praw·da·va·aw·nee·tsa
	igračaka f	ee·gra·cha·ka
Do you sell ...?	*Da li prodajete ...?*	da lee praw·dai·e·te ...
baby wipes	*vlažne*	vlazh·ne
	maramice	ma·ra·mee·tse
	za bebe	za be·be
painkillers	*dječje tablete*	dyech·ye ta·ble·te
for babies	*protiv bolova*	praw·teev baw·law·va
disposable	*pelene za*	pe·le·ne za
diapers/	*jednokratnu*	yed·naw·krat·noo
nappies	*upotrebu*	oo·paw·tre·boo
tissues	*papirnate*	pa·peer·na·te
	rupčiće	roop·chee·che
Do you	*Da li*	da lee
hire out ...?	*iznajmljujete ...?*	eez·naim·lyoo·ye·te ...
prams	*dječja kolica*	dyech·ya kaw·lee·tsa
strollers	*dječje hodalice*	dyech·ye haw·da·lee·tse

I need a pram.
Trebaju mi dječja   tre·bai·oo mee dyech·ya
kolica.   kaw·lee·tsa

Is there space for a pram?
Ima li mjesta za kolica?   ee·ma lee mye·sta za kaw·lee·tsa

Are there any good places to take children around here?
Ima li u okolini   ee·ma lee oo aw·kaw·lee·nee
dobrih mjesta za djecu?   daw·breeh mye·sta za dye·tsoo

Are children allowed?
Da li je dozvoljen   da lee ye *dawz*·vaw·lyen
pristup djeci?   *pree*·stoop dye·tsee

Where can I change a nappy?
Gdje mogu   gdye *maw*·goo
promijeniti pelene?   praw·mee·ye·nee·tee *pe*·le·ne

Do you mind if I breast-feed here?
Da li vam smeta   da lee vam *sme*·ta
ako ovdje dojim?   a·kaw awv·dye *doy*·eem

Could I have some paper and pencils, please?
Mogu li dobiti malo   *maw*·goo lee *daw*·bee·tee *ma*·law
papira i olovku molim?   pa·*pee*·ra ee aw·*lawv*·koo *maw*·leem

Is this suitable for (three)-year old children?
Da li je ovo pogodno   da lee ye *aw*·vaw *paw*·gawd·naw
za (tri) godine   za (tree) *gaw*·dee·ne
staru djecu?   *sta*·roo dye·tsoo

Do you know a dentist/doctor who is good with children?
Da li znate zubara/   da lee *zna*·te zoo·*ba*·ra/
liječnika koji je dobar   lee·*yech*·nee·ka *koy*·ee ye *daw*·bar
sa djecom?   sa dye·tsawm

For health issues, see **health**, page 177.

talking with children

When's your birthday?
Kada je tvoj rođendan?   *ka*·da ye tvoy *raw*·jen·dan

When's your name day?
Kada je tvoj imendan?   *ka*·da ye tvoy *ee*·men·dan

Do you go to school/kindergarten?
Ideš li u školu/   *ee*·desh lee oo *shkaw*·loo/
vrtić?   vr·teech

What grade are you in?
U kojem si razredu?   oo *koy*·em see *raz*·re·doo

Do you like …?	Voliš li …?	vaw·leesh lee …
school	školu	shkaw·loo
sport	sport	spawrt
your teacher	svog nastavnika	svawg na·stav·nee·ka

What do you do after school?

Čime se baviš nakon nastave?   chee·me se ba·veesh na·kawn na·sta·ve

Do you learn English?

Učiš li engleski?   oo·cheesh lee en·gle·skee

I come from very far away.

Ja dolazim iz   ya daw·la·zeem eez
jako daleke zemlje.   ya·kaw da·le·ke zem·lye

Are you lost?

Da li si se izgubio/   da lee see se eez·goo·bee·aw/
izgubila? **m/f**   eez·goo·bee·la

---

gender reminder

Throughout this book we've used the abbreviations **m**, **f** and **n** to indicate gender. The order of presentation is masculine, feminine and then neuter.

If a letter or letters have been added to a masculine form to denote a feminine or neuter form, these will appear in parentheses. Where the change involves more than the addition of a letter, different words are given separated by a slash. Sometimes, it's just a case of substituting the final letter of a word to make feminine or neuter forms as in this example: *mladi/a* (*mla*·dee/a) 'young' which has the masculine form *mladi* and the feminine form *mlada*.

Gender marking mostly applies to nouns and adjectives but it can apply to verb forms also. See gender in the **a–z phrasebuilder**, page 19 for more on gender in Croatian.

basics

osnove

Yes.	*Da.*	da
No.	*Ne.*	ne
Please.	*Molim.*	*maw*·leem
Thank you (very much).	*Hvala vam/ti (puno).* **pol/inf**	*hva*·la vam/tee (*poo*·no)
You're welcome.	*Nema na čemu.*	*ne*·ma na *che*·moo
Excuse me. (to get attention)	*Oprostite.*	aw·*praw*·stee·te
Excuse me. (to get past)	*Ispričavam se.*	ee·spree·*cha*·vam se
Sorry.	*Žao mi je.*	*zha*·aw mee ye

greetings & goodbyes

pozdravi dobrodošlice i oproštaja

It's usual for both men and women to shake hands when meeting for the first time and often on subsequent encounters too. Greeting someone with a kiss on each cheek is reserved for close friends.

Hello.	*Bog.*	bawg
Hi.	*Ćao.*	*cha*·aw
Good morning.	*Dobro jutro.*	*daw*·braw *yoo*·traw
Good afternoon/day.	*Dobar dan.*	*daw*·bar dan
Good evening.	*Dobra večer.*	*daw*·bra *ve*·cher

How are you?
Kako ste/si? pol/inf   ka·kaw ste/see

Fine. And you?
Dobro. A vi/ti? pol/inf   daw·braw, a vee/tee

What's your name?
Kako se zovete/zoveš? pol/inf   ka·kaw se zaw·ve·te/zaw·vesh

My name is …
Zovem se …   zaw·vem se …

I'd like to introduce you to …
Želim vas/te   zhe·leem vas/te
upoznati sa … pol/inf   oo·pawz·na·tee sa …

I'm pleased to meet you.
Drago mi je da   dra·gaw mee ye da
smo se upoznali.   smaw se oo·pawz·na·lee

This is my …	*Ovo je moj/moja/*	aw·vaw ye moy/moy·a/
	moje … m/f/n	moy·e …
child	*dijete* n	dee·ye·te
colleague	*kolega/*	kaw·le·ga/
	kolegica m/f	kaw·le·gee·tsa
friend	*prijatelj/*	pree·ya·tel'/
	prijateljica m/f	pree·ya·te·lyee·tsa
husband	*muž* m	moozh
partner	*suprug/*	soo·proog/
(intimate)	*supruga* m/f	soo·proo·ga
wife	*žena* f	zhe·na

For other family members, see **family**, page 101.

Bye.	*Ćao.*	cha·aw
Goodbye.	*Zbogom.*	zbaw·gawm
Good night.	*Laku noć.*	la·koo nawch
See you later.	*Doviđenja.*	daw·vee·je·nya

Croatian has two forms for the singular 'you', *ti* (tee) and *vi* (vee) though the pronouns themselves are not often used because verbs carry endings that indicate whether *ti* or *vi* is being referred to. With family, friends, children or peers, use the informal *ti* forms of the verb. The polite *vi* forms should be used when addressing strangers or people you've just met. Also use the polite forms to address a person considerably older than you, as to use *ti* forms could be seen as very disrespectful.

Phrases in this book are mostly given in the polite form but where you see inf you have a casual option to use where appopriate. If you feel (or someone else feels) that you're on a familiar-enough footing to use *ti* forms, the following phrase can be used:

You don't have to address me politely – we can use *ti*.

Nemorate mi persirati,	ne·maw·ra·te mee per·*see*·ra·tee
možemo prijeći na ti.	maw·*zhe*·maw pree·*ye*·chee na tee

addressing people

Croatians use a person's proper title when addressing an older person, an unfamiliar person, a someone in a position of authority or in other more formal contexts. The proper use of titles is seen as reflecting an individual's good upbringing. The convention is to write titles with an exclamation mark following them.

Mr/Sir	*Gospodine!*	gaw·*spaw*·dee·ne
Mrs/Madam	*Gospođo!*	gaw·spaw·jaw
Ms	*G'đo!*	g·jaw
Miss	*Gospođice!*	gaw·spaw·jee·tse
Doctor	*Doktore!*	dawk·*taw*·re
Professor	*Profesore!*	praw·fe·saw·re

In addition to these generic titles, you can address people by using one of the forms below, as appropriate. Some of these might seem a little odd or abrupt to English speakers but they're quite usual in Croatian. Again these titles are generally reserved for more formal contexts, including official situations or when a service is being rendered, such as in a shop or restaurant.

Boy	Dečko!	dech·kaw
Friend	Prijatelju!	pree·ya·te·lyoo
Girl	Djevojčice!	dye·voy·chee·tse
Young man	Momče!	mawm·che
Young woman	Djevojko!	dye·voy·kaw
An older female (lit: aunt)	Teta!	te·ta
An older male (lit: uncle)	Čiko!	chee·kaw

making conversation

Croatians are generally open and outgoing people so you shouldn't find it too hard to strike up a conversation. Good conversation topics to break the ice include football (soccer) and sports in general, food and wine and world events. Tread very lightly when discussing religion (in what is a profoundly Catholic country), politics and, most importantly, the war in the former Yugoslavia.

What a beautiful day!
 Kakav predivan dan! ka·kav pre·dee·van dan

It's so nice here.
 Predivno je ovdje. pre·deev·naw ye awv·dye

What are you up to?
 Što se radi? shtaw se ra·dee

What's up?
 Što ima? shtaw ee·ma

Nice/Awful weather, isn't it?
Lijepo/Užasno — lee·ye·paw/oo·zha·snaw ye
vrijeme, zar ne? — vree·ye·me zar ne

How are things?
Kako stoje stvari? — ka·kaw stoy·e stva·ree

Everything OK?
Sve u redu? — sve oo *re*·doo

Do you live here?
Vi živite ovdje? pol — vee zhee·vee·te *awv*·dye
Ti živiš ovdje? inf — tee zhee·veesh *awv*·dye

Where are you going?
Gdje idete/ideš? pol/inf — gdye ee·de·te/*ee*·desh

What are you doing?
Što radite/radiš? pol/inf — shtaw *ra*·dee·te/*ra*·deesh

Do you like it here?
Da li vam/ti se — da lee vam/tee se
sviđa ovdje? pol/inf — *svee*·ja *awv*·dye

I love it here.
Obožavam ovo mjesto. — aw·*baw*·zha·vam *aw*·vaw *mye*·staw

What's this called?
Kako se ovo zove? — ka·kaw se *aw*·vaw *zaw*·ve

Can I take a photo (of you)?
Mogu li (vas/te) — *maw*·goo lee (vas/te)
slikati? pol/inf — *slee*·ka·tee

That's (beautiful), isn't it?
To je (predivno), zar ne? — taw ye (*pre*·deev·naw) zar ne

Just joking.
Samo se šalim. — *sa*·maw se *sha*·leem

Are you here on holiday?
Jeste/Jesi li ovdje — *ye*·ste/*ye*·see lee *awv*·dye
na odmoru? pol/inf — na *awd*·maw·roo

I'm here … — *Ja sam ovdje …* — ya sam *awv*·dye …
  for a holiday — *na odmoru* — na *awd*·maw·roo
  on business — *poslovno* — *paw*·slawv·naw
  to study — *kao student* — ka·aw *stoo*·dent

How long are you here for?

Koliko dugo   kaw·*lee*·kaw doo·gaw
ste/si ovdje? pol/inf   ste/see *awv*·dye

I'm here for (four) weeks/days.

Ja sam ovdje na   ya sam *awv*·dye na
(četiri) tjedna/dana.   (che·tee·ree) *tyed*·na/*da*·na

nationalities

nacionalnosti

Where are you from?

Odakle ste/si? pol/inf   aw·*da*·kle ste/see

I'm from …   *Ja sam iz …*   ya sam eez …
  Australia   *Australije*   a·oo·*stra*·lee·ye
  England   *Engleske*   *en*·gles·ke
  the USA   *Amerike*   a·*me*·ree·ke

For more nationalities, see the **dictionary**.

age

godište

How old …?	*Koliko …*	kaw·*lee*·kaw …
	godina?	*gaw*·dee·na
are you	*imate/imaš* pol/inf	ee·ma·te/ee·mash
is your son	*vaš/tvoj* pol/inf	vash/tvoy
	sin ima	seen ee·ma
is your daughter	*vaša/tvoja* pol/inf	*va*·sha/*tvoy*·a
	kći ima	k·*chee* ee·ma

I'm ... years old.
  Imam ... godina. ee·mam ... gaw·dee·na

He/She is ... years old.
  On/Ona ima ... godina. awn/aw·na ee·ma ... gaw·dee·na

Too old!
  Prestar/Prestara! m/f pre·star/pre·sta·ra

I'm younger than I look.
  Mlađi/Mlađa sam nego mla·jee/mla·ja sam ne·gaw
  što izgledam. m/f shtaw eez·gle·dam

For your age, see **numbers & amounts**, page 31.

occupations & studies

What's your occupation?
  Čime se bavite/ chee·me se ba·vee·te/
  baviš? pol/inf ba·veesh

I'm a ...	*Ja sam ...*	ya sam ...
chef	*šef kuhinje/*	shef koo·hee·nye/
	šefica kuhinje m/f	shef·ee·tsa koo·hee·nye
journalist	*novinar/*	naw·vee·nar/
	novinarka m/f	naw·vee·nar·ka
manual	*fizički radnik/*	fee·zeech·kee rad·neek/
labourer	*fizička*	fee·zeech·ka
	radnica m/f	rad·nee·tsa
mechanical	*inženjer*	een·zhe·nyer
engineer	*strojarstva* m&f	stroy·ar·stvaw
musician	*muzičar/*	moo·zee·char/
	muzičarka m/f	moo·zee·char·ka
public servant	*službenik/*	sloozh·be·neek/
	službenica m/f	sloozh·be·nee·tsa
teacher	*nastavnik/*	na·stav·neek/
	nastavnica m/f	na·stav·nee·tsa
trades person	*zanatlija/*	za·nat·lee·ya/
	obrtnica m/f	aw·brt·nee·tsa

meeting people

Come in/Sit down.	Izvolite.	eez·vaw·lee·te
Come on then!	Daj ajde više!	dai ai·de vee·she
Great!	Super!	soo·per
Hey!	Hej!	hey
It's OK.	U redu je.	oo re·doo ye
Just a minute.	Trenutak.	tre·noo·tak
Maybe.	Možda.	mawzh·da
No problem.	Nema problema.	ne·ma praw·ble·ma
No way!	Nema šanse!	ne·ma shan·se
See you.	Vidimo se.	vee·dee·maw se
Sure.	Svakako!	sva·ka·kaw
Watch out!	Pazite/Pazi! pol/inf	pa·zee·te/pa·zee

I work in ...	Ja sam zaposlen/	ya sam za·paw·slen/
	zaposlena u ... m/f	za·paw·sle·na oo ...
administration	upravi	oo·pra·vee
health	zdravstvu	zdrav·stvoo
retail	trgovini	tr·gaw·vee·nee
	na malo	na ma·law

I'm ...	Ja sam ...	ya sam ...
retired	umirovljen/	oo·mee·rawv·lyen/
	umirovljena m/f	oo·mee·rawv·lye·na
self-employed	samostalno	sa·maw·stal·naw
	zaposlen/	za·paw·slen/
	zaposlena m/f	za·paw·sle·na
unemployed	nezaposlen/	ne·za·paw·slen/
	nezaposlena m/f	ne·za·paw·sle·na

I'm studying ...	Ja studiram ...	ya stoo·dee·ram ...
humanities	društvene	droosht·ve·ne
	znanosti	zna·naw·stee
Croatian	hrvatski	hr·vat·skee
science	znanost	zna·nawst

What are you studying?

| Što vi studirate? pol | shtaw vee stoo·dee·ra·te |
| Što ti studiraš? inf | shtaw tee stoo·dee·rash |

family

In Croatia, family is sacred and people you meet may well ask you about yours. It'll be appreciated if you reciprocate. Take care not to offend, however, by expressing surprise about aspects of family life that may seem unusual by the standards of your own culture (such as adult children still living at home).

Do you have a …?	*Imate/Imaš li …?* pol/inf	ee·ma·te/ee·mash lee …
I have a …	*Ja imam …*	ya ee·mam …
I don't have a …	*Ja nemam …*	ya ne·mam …
brother	*brata*	*bra*·ta
daughter	*ćerku*	*cher*·koo
family	*obitelj*	aw·*bee*·tel'
father	*oca*	*aw*·tsa
granddaughter	*unuku*	oo·*noo*·koo
grandfather	*djeda*	*dye*·da
grandmother	*baku*	*ba*·koo
grandson	*unuka*	oo·*noo*·ka
husband	*muža*	*moo*·zha
mother	*majku*	*mai*·koo
partner (intimate)	*supružnika*	soo·*proozh*·nee·ka
sister	*sestru*	*ses*·troo
son	*sina*	*see*·na
wife	*ženu*	*zhe*·noo
I'm …	*Ja sam …*	ya sam …
married	*u braku*	oo *bra*·koo
separated	*rastavljen/ rastavljena* m/f	ra·*stav*·lyen/ ra·*stav*·lye·na
single	*neoženjen/ neudata* m/f	ne·*aw*·zhe·nyen/ ne·oo·*da*·ta

Are you married?

Jeste li vi vjenčani? pol	ye·ste lee vee *vyen*·cha·nee
Jesi li ti vjenčan/ vjenčana? inf m/f	ye·see lee tee *vyen*·chan/ *vyen*·cha·na

farewells

Tomorrow is my last day here.
Sutra mi je zadnji   soo·tra mee ye *zad*·nyee
dan ovdje.   dan *awv*·dye

If you come to (Scotland) you can visit me.
Ako ikad dođete   a·kaw ee·kad *daw*·je·te
u (Škotsku), možete   oo (*shkawt*·skoo) *maw*·zhe·te
me posjetiti. **pol**   me *paw*·sye·tee·tee
Ako ikad dođeš   a·kaw ee·kad *daw*·jesh
u (Škotsku), možeš   oo (*shkawt*·skoo) *maw*·zhesh
me posjetiti. **inf**   me *paw*·sye·tee·tee

Keep in touch!
Ostanimo u vezi!   aw·sta·nee·maw oo *ve*·zee

It's been great meeting you.
Bilo je lijepo   *bee*·law ye lee·*ye*·paw
upoznati vas/te. **pol/inf**   oo·*pawz*·na·tee vas/te

Here's my ...	*Ovo je moj ...* m	*aw*·vaw ye moy ...
	Ovo je moja ... f	*aw*·vaw ye *moy*·a ...
What's your ...?	*Koji je tvoj ...?* m	*koy*·ee ye tvoy ...
	Koja je tvoja ...? f	*koy*·a ye *tvoy*·a ...
address	*adresa* f	a·*dre*·sa
email address	*email adresa* f	ee·ma·eel a·*dre*·sa
phone number	*broj telefona* m	broy te·le·*faw*·na

well wishing

Bless you!	*Nazdravlje!*	naz·*drav*·lye
Bon voyage!	*Sretan put!*	*sre*·tan poot
Congratulations!	*Čestitke!*	che·*steet*·ke
Good luck!	*Sretno!*	*sret*·naw
Happy birthday!	*Sretan rođendan!*	*sre*·tan *raw*·jen·dan
Merry Christmas!	*Sretan božić!*	*sre*·tan *baw*·zheech

In this chapter phrases are given in the informal *ti* forms. If you're not sure what this means, see the **a-z phrasebuilder**, page 24.

common interests

What do you do in your spare time?

Što radiš u slobodno vrijeme?		shtaw *ra*·deesh oo *slaw*·bawd·naw vree·*ye*·me

Do you like …?	*Voliš li …?*	*vaw*·leesh lee …
I (don't) like …	*Ja (ne) volim …*	ya (ne) *vaw*·leem …
card games	*kartanje*	*kar*·ta·nye
computer games	*kompjuterske igre*	kawm·*pyoo*·ter·ske ee·gre
cooking	*kuhanje*	*koo*·ha·nye
dancing	*ples*	ples
drawing	*crtanje*	*tsr*·ta·nye
films	*filmove*	*feel*·maw·ve
gardening	*vrtlarstvo*	vrt·*lars*·tvaw
hiking	*rekreaciono pješačenje*	re·kre·a·tsee·aw·naw pye·*sha*·che·nye
music	*glazbu*	*glaz*·boo
painting	*slikanje*	*slee*·ka·nye
photography	*fotografiju*	faw·taw·*gra*·fee·yoo
reading	*čitanje*	*chee*·ta·nye
shopping	*kupovanje*	koo·*paw*·va·nye
socialising	*druženje*	*droo*·zhe·nye
sport	*sport*	spawrt
travelling	*putovanja*	poo·taw·*va*·nya

For more sporting activities, see **sport**, page 129.

music

What music do you like?
Koju vrstu glazbe voliš?   *koy·oo vr·stoo glaz·be vaw·leesh*

What bands do you like?
Koje grupe voliš?   *koy·e groo·pe vaw·leesh*

Do you ...?	*Da li ...?*	da lee ...
dance	*plešeš*	*ple*·shesh
go to concerts	*ideš na*	ee·desh na
	koncerte	*kawn*·tser·te
listen to music	*slušaš glazbu*	*sloo*·shash *glaz*·boo
play an	*sviraš neki*	*svee*·rash ne·kee
instrument	*instrument*	een·stroo·*ment*
sing	*pjevaš*	*pye*·vash

blues	*bluz* m	blooz
classical music	*klasična glazba* f	*kla*·seech·na *glaz*·ba
electronic music	*elektronska*	e·*lek*·trawn·ska
	glazba f	*glaz*·ba
folk music	*folk glazba* f	fawlk *glaz*·ba
jazz	*džez* m	jez
opera	*opera* f	*aw*·pe·ra
operetta	*opereta* f	aw·pe·*re*·ta
pop	*pop* m	pawp
rock	*rock* m	rawk
traditional music	*tradicionalna*	*tra*·dee·tsee·aw·nal·na
	glazba f	*glaz*·ba
world music	*etno glazba* f	*et*·naw *glaz*·ba

Planning to go to a concert? See **going out**, page 113.

cinema & theatre

I feel like going to a …	Htio/Htjela bih otići na … m/f	htte·aw/htye·la beeh aw·tee·chee na …
Did you like the …?	Da li ti se dopao …?	da lee tee se daw·pa·aw …
ballet	balet	ba·let
film	film	feelm

I feel like going to a play.

Htio/Htjela bih otići na predstavu. m/f — htte·aw/htye·la beeh aw·tee·chee na pred·sta·voo

Did you like the play?

Da li ti se dopala predstava? — da lee tee se daw·pa·la pred·sta·va

What's showing at the cinema/theatre tonight?

Što se prikazuje u kinu/kazalištu večeras? — shtaw se pree·ka·zoo·ye oo kee·noo/ka·za·leesh·too ve·che·ras

Is it in English?

Da li je na engleskom? — da lee ye na en·gles·kawm

Does it have (English) subtitles?

Da li je film titlovan (na engleski)? — da lee ye feelm teet·law·van (na en·gle·skee)

Is this seat taken?

Je li ovo mjesto zauzeto? — ye lee aw·vaw mye·staw za·oo·ze·taw

This is my seat.

Ovo je moje mjesto. — aw·vaw ye moy·e mye·staw

Have you seen …?

Da li si pogledao/ pogledala …? m/f — da lee see paw·gle·da·aw/ paw·gle·da·la …

Who's in it?

Tko glumi u tome? — tkaw gloo·mee oo taw·me

It stars …

Glavnu ulogu igra … — glav·noo oo·law·goo ee·gra …

I thought it was …	Ja mislim	ya *mee*·sleem
	da je bio …	da ye *bee*·aw …
excellent	odličan	*awd*·lee·chan
long	dugačak	*doo*·ga·chak
OK	OK	aw·key

I (don't) like …	Ja (ne) volim …	ya (ne) *vaw*·leem …
action movies	akcione	ak·tsee·aw·ne
	filmove	*feel*·maw·ve
animated films	animirane	a·nee·*mee*·ra·ne
	filomove	*feel*·maw·ve
(Croatian) cinema	(hrvatski) film	(hr·vat·skee) feelm
comedies	komedije	*kaw*·me·dee·ye
documentaries	dokumentarce	daw·koo·men·*tar*·tse
drama	drame	*dra*·me
horror movies	filmove strave	*feel*·maw·ve *stra*·ve
	i užasa	ee *oo*·zha·sa
sci-fi	filmove	*feel*·maw·ve
	naučne	na·*ooch*·ne
	fantastike	fan·*ta*·stee·ke
short films	kratkometražne	krat·kaw·*me*·trazh·ne
	filmove	*feel*·maw·ve
thrillers	trilere	*tree*·le·re
war movies	ratne filmove	*rat*·ne *feel*·maw·ve

---

lost in translation

Croatians are proud of their rich literary heritage. It's a heritage that has absorbed the crosscurrents of Central European and Latin influence. Unfortunately though, little of Croatia's literary output is available in English translation.

The country's towering literary figure is undoubtedly the 20th-century novelist and playwright Miroslav Krleža. Always politcally active, Krleža broke with Tito in 1967 over the writer's campaign for equality between the Serbian and Croatian literary languages. He famously stated: 'Croatian and Serbian are one and the same language, which Croats call Croatian and Serbs Serbian'. His popular novel *The Return of Philip Latinovicz* which depicts the concerns of a changing Yugoslavia has been translated into English.

feelings

osjećaji

I'm (not) ...	Ja (ni)sam ...	ya (nee·)sam ...
annoyed	uznemiren/	ooz·ne·mee·ren/
	uznemirena m/f	ooz·ne·mee·re·na
disappointed	razočaran/	ra·zaw·cha·ran/
	razočarana m/f	ra·zaw·cha·ra·na
embarrassed	posramljen/	paw·sram·lyen/
	posramljena m/f	paw·sram·lye·na
happy	sretan/sretna m/f	sre·tan/sret·na
hungry	gladan/gladna m/f	gla·dan/glad·na
sad	tužan/tužna m/f	too·zhan/toozh·na
surprised	iznenađen/	eez·ne·na·jen/
	iznenađena m/f	eez·ne·na·je·na
thirsty	žedan/žedna m/f	zhe·dan/zhed·na
tired	umoran/	oo·maw·ran/
	umorna m/f	oo·mawr·na
worried	zabrinut/	za·bree·noot/
	zabrinuta m/f	za·bree·noo·ta

Are you hot/cold?
Je li vam toplo/hladno? pol ye lee vam *taw*·plaw/*hlad*·naw
Je li ti toplo/hladno? inf ye lee tee *taw*·plaw/*hlad*·naw

I'm (not) hot/cold.
Meni (ni)je toplo/hladno. me·nee (nee·)ye *taw*·plaw/*hlad*·naw

And how are you?
A kako ste vi? pol a *ka*·kaw ste vee
A kako si ti? inf a *ka*·kaw see tee

If feeling unwell, see **health**, page 177.

mixed emotions

a little	*malo*	*ma·*law
I'm a little sad.	*Malo sam tužan/ tužna.* m/f	*ma·*law sam *too·*zhan/ *toozh·*na
extremely	*krajnje*	*krai·*nye
I'm extremely sorry.	*Krajnje mi je žao.*	*krai·*nye mee ye *zha·*aw
very	*vrlo*	*vr·*law
I feel very lucky.	*Osjećam se vrlo sretno.*	*aw·*sye·cham se *vr·*law *sret·*naw

opinions

mišljenja

Did you like it?

| *Da li vam/ti se svidjelo?* pol/inf | da lee vam/tee se *svee·*dye·law |

I thought it was ...	*Mislio/Mislila sam da je bilo ...* m/f	*mee·*slee·aw/*mee·*slee·la sam da ye *bee·*law ...
It's ...	*Ovo je ...*	*aw·*vaw ye ...
awful	*užasno*	*oo·*zha·snaw
beautiful	*lijepo*	lee·*ye·*paw
boring	*dosadno*	*daw·*sad·naw
great	*odlično*	*awd·*leech·naw
interesting	*zanimljivo*	za·*neem·*lyee·vaw
OK	*OK*	*aw·*key
original	*originalno*	aw·ree·gee·*nal·*naw
strange	*neobično*	ne·aw·*beech·*naw

politics & social issues

You should anticipate being drawn into animated discussions on aspects of the recent conflict in the former Yugoslavia as the horrors of war are still very much alive in people's minds. Locals will seize the opportunity of converting you to the Croatian cause. Unless you enjoy very heated debates, you're best advised to stay in the role of nonjudgmental listener.

Who do you vote for?

Za koga glasate/	za *kaw*·ga *gla*·sa·te/	
glasaš? pol/inf	*gla*·sash	

I support the	*Ja sam pristaša*	ya sam *pree*·sta·sha
... party.	*... stranke.*	... *stran*·ke
I'm a member	*Ja sam član*	ya sam chlan
of the ... party.	*... stranke.*	... *stran*·ke
communist	*komunističke*	kaw·moo·*nee*·steech·ke
conservative	*konzervativne*	*kawn*·zer·va·teev·ne
democratic	*demokratske*	de·*maw*·krat·ske
farmers'	*seljačke*	se·lyach·ke
green	*zelene*	ze·le·ne
Istrian	*istarske*	ee·star·ske
regionalist	*regionalističke*	re·gee·aw·na·*lee*·steech·ke
liberal	*liberalne*	lee·be·ral·ne
(progressive)		
social	*socijal-*	saw·tsee·*yal*·
democratic	*demokratske*	de·*maw*·krat·ske
socialist	*socijalističke*	saw·tsee·ya·*lee*·steech·ke

Did you hear about ...?

Jeste li čuli za ...? pol	*ye*·ste lee *choo*·lee za ...
Jesi li čuo/čula za ...? inf m/f	*ye*·see lee *choo*·aw/*choo*·la za ...

Do you agree with it?

Da li podržavate/	da lee paw·*dr*·zha·va·te/
podržavaš to? pol/inf	paw·*dr*·zha·vash taw

I (don't) agree with ...

Ja (ne) podržavam ...	ya (ne) paw·*dr*·zha·vam ...

How do people	*Kako ljudi*	*ka·kaw lyoo·dee*
feel about …?	*gledaju na …?*	*gle·dai·oo na …*
abortion	*indicirani*	een·dee·*tsee*·ra·nee
	abortus	a·*bawr*·toos
admission	*primanje u*	*pree*·ma·nye oo
into the EU	*Europsku*	e·oo·rawp·skoo
	uniju	oo·nee·yoo
animal rights	*prava*	*pra*·va
	životinja	zhee·*vaw*·tee·nya
crime	*kriminal*	kree·*mee*·nal
the economy	*privredu*	*preev*·re·doo
education	*obrazovanje*	aw·bra·zaw·*va*·nye
equal	*jednake*	*yed*·na·ke
opportunity	*mogućnosti*	maw·*gooch*·naw·stee
euthanasia	*eutanaziju*	e·oo·ta·na·zee·yoo
globalisation	*globalizaciju*	glaw·ba·lee·*za*·tsee·yoo
human rights	*ljudska prava*	*lyood*·ska *pra*·va
immigration	*imigraciju*	ee·mee·*gra*·tsee·yoo
racism	*rasnu*	*ra*·snoo
	netrpeljivost	ne·tr·*pe*·lyee·vawst
the return of	*povratak ratnih*	*paw*·vra·tak *rat*·neeh
war refugees	*izbjeglica*	eez·bye·glee·tsa
sexism	*spolnu*	*spawl*·noo
	diskriminaciju	dee·skree·mee·*na*·tsee·yoo
unemployment	*nezaposlenost*	ne·*za*·paw·sle·nawst

hot topics

If you really have a burning curiosity to learn more about Croatian attitudes to the recent conflict in the former Yugoslavia and its aftermath, you could try out the phrase below. Best not to trot it out in a slivovitz-fuelled context as the passions aroused could be strong enough on their own.

How do people feel about the extradition of generals to the international war-crimes tribunal in the Hague?

Kako ljudi gledaju na   *ka·kaw lyoo·dee gle·dai·oo na*
isporuku generala   *ee·spaw·roo·koo* ge·ne·*ra*·la
međunarodnom sudu   me·joo·*na*·rawd·nawm *soo*·doo
za ratne zločine u Hagu?   za *rat*·ne zlaw·chee·ne oo *ha*·goo

the environment

Is there a … problem here?
Postoji li ovdje   paw·stoy·ee lee *awv*·dye
problem …?   *praw*·blem …

What should be done about …?
Što bi trebalo   shtaw bee *tre*·ba·law
učiniti u vezi …?   oo·*chee*·nee·tee oo *ve*·zee …

acid rain	*kisele kiše* f pl	kee·se·le *kee*·she
conservation	*zaštita*	zash·*tee*·ta
	okoliša f	aw·*kaw*·lee·sha
drought	*suša* f	*soo*·sha
ecosystem	*ekosustav* m	e·kaw·*soo*·stav
endangered	*ugrožene*	oo·*graw*·zhe·ne
species	*vrste* n	*vr*·ste
hunting	*lov na životinje* m	lawv na zhee·*vaw*·tee·nye
hydroelectricity	*hidroelektrane* n	hee·draw·e·lek·*tra*·ne
irrigation	*navodnjavanje* n	na·vawd·*nya*·va·nye
nuclear energy/	*nuklearna energija/*	noo·kle·ar·na e·*ner*·gee·ya/
testing	*testiranja* f	te·*stee*·ra·nya
ozone layer	*ozonski*	aw·*zawn*·skee
	omotač m	aw·maw·*tach*
pesticides	*pesticidi* m pl	pe·stee·*tsee*·dee
marine algae	*pošast morskih*	*paw*·shast *mawr*·skeeh
	algi m	*al*·gee
pollution	*zagađenje* n	za·ga·*je*·nye
protection of	*zaštita morske*	zash·tee·ta *mawr*·ske
marine flora	*flore i faune* f	*flaw*·re ee fa·*oo*·ne
and fauna		
recycling	*plan za preradu*	plan za *pre*·ra·doo
program	*otpadaka* m	*awt*·pa·da·ka
subterranean	*podzemne*	pawd·*zem*·ne
waterways	*vode* f pl	*vaw*·de
toxic waste	*toksični otpad* m	*tawk*·seech·nee *awt*·pad
water supply	*vodovod* m	*vaw*·daw·vawd
timber	*djelatnosti drvne*	dye·*lat*·naw·stee *drv*·ne
industry	*industrije* f pl	een·*doo*·stree·ye

Is this a protected ...?	Je li ovo ...?	ye lee *aw·*vaw ...
forest	*zaštićena šuma*	*zash·*tee·che·na *shoo·*ma
park	*zaštićen park*	*zash·*tee·chen park
species	*zaštićena vrsta*	*zash·*tee·che·na *vr·*sta

colourful Croatian

Croatian speakers can draw on a rich variety of swear words and obscene expressions to make their feelings plainly felt.

Swearing in any language tends to be very idiomatic and difficult to translate, but even the most hardened Anglophone might blanch at the graphic nature of Croatian swearing. However, what might sound like a string of unbelievable obscenities to an English speaker is not quite as bad as it sounds to Croatian speakers for whom colourful swearing is an intrinsic part of the language.

If you're exposed to some colourful Croatian you may even find it quite amusing and it's best not to take offence, as this may not be the swearer's intention.

In this chapter phrases are given in the informal *ti* forms. If you're not sure what this means, see the **a-z phrasebuilder**, page 24.

where to go

gdje izaći

What's there to do in the evenings?
Što se može raditi — shtaw se *maw*·zhe *ra*·dee·tee
uvečer? — oo·ve·cher

What's on …?	*Što se događa …?*	shtaw se *daw*·ga·ja …
locally	*u ovom mjestu*	oo *aw*·vawm *mye*·stoo
this weekend	*ovoga vikenda*	*aw*·vaw·ga *vee*·ken·da
today	*danas*	*da*·nas
tonight	*večeras*	ve·*che*·ras

Where can I find …?	*Gdje mogu pronaći …?*	gdye *maw*·goo praw·*na*·chee …
clubs	*noćne klubove*	*nawch*·ne *kloo*·baw·ve
gay venues	*'gay' lokale*	gey law·*ka*·le
places to eat	*ugostiteljske lokale*	oo·*gaw*·stee·tel'·ske law·*ka*·le
pubs	*gostionice*	gaw·stee·*aw*·nee·tse

Is there a local … guide?	*Postoji li mjesni vodič kroz …?*	paw·*stoy*·ee lee *mye*·snee *vaw*·deech krawz …
entertainment	*zbivanja u svijetu razonode*	*zbee*·va·nya oo svee·*ye*·too ra·*zaw*·naw·de
event	*predstojeća zbivanja*	pred·*stoy*·e·cha *zbee*·va·nya
film	*filmske novosti*	*feelm*·ske *naw*·vaw·stee
gay	*'gay' aktivnosti*	gey ak·*teev*·naw·stee
music	*glazbu*	*glaz*·boo

I feel like going to a ...	Želim otići ...	zhe·leem aw·tee·chee ...
ballet	na balet	na ba·let
bar	u bar	oo bar
café	u kafić	oo ka·feech
concert	na koncert	na kawn·tsert
disco	u disko	oo dee·skaw
festival	na festival	na fe·stee·val
film	na prikazivanje filma	na pree·ka·zee·va·nye feel·ma
hotel for terrace dancing	u hotel sa plesnom terasom	oo haw·tel sa ple·snawm te·ra·sawm
karaoke bar	u karaoke bar	oo ka·ra·aw·ke bar
nightclub	u noćni klub	oo nawch·nee kloob
party	na zabavu	na za·ba·voo
performance	na priredbu	na pree·red·boo
play	na predstavu	na pred·sta·voo
pub	u gostionicu	oo gaw·stee·aw·nee·tsoo
restaurant	u restoran	oo re·staw·ran

For more on eateries, bars and drinks, see **eating out**, page 145.

invitations

pozivanje nekoga na nešto

Would you like to go (for a/an) ...?	Da li bi htio/ htjela otići na ...? m/f	da lee bee htee·aw/ htye·la aw·tee·chee na ...
I feel like going (for a/an) ...	Ja želim otići na ...	ya zhe·leem aw·tee·chee na ...
coffee	kavu	ka·voo
dancing	ples	ples
drink	piće	pee·che
ice cream	sladoled	sla·daw·led
meal	ručak	roo·chak

What are you doing …?	Što radiš …?	shtaw *ra*·deesh …
now	*trenutno*	tre·*noot*·naw
this weekend	*ovoga vikenda*	aw·vaw·ga *vee*·ken·da
tonight	*večeras*	ve·*che*·ras

I feel like going out somewhere.
Ja želim ići   ya *zhe*·leem *ee*·chee
negdje vani.   ne·gdye *va*·nee

I feel like going for a walk.
Ja želim ići u šetnju.   ya *zhe*·leem *ee*·chee oo *shet*·nyoo

Do you know a good restaurant?
Da li znaš dobar   da lee znash *daw*·bar
restoran?   re·*staw*·ran

Do you want to come to the concert with me?
Da li bi htio/htjela ići   da lee bee *htee*·aw/*htye*·la *ee*·chee
samnom na koncert. m/f   sam·nawm na *kawn*·tsert

We're having a party.
Planiramo napraviti   *pla*·nee·ra·maw *na*·pra·vee·tee
zabavu.   za·ba·voo

You should come.
Ti si pozvan/pozvana. m/f   tee see *pawz*·van/*pawz*·va·na

responding to invitations

odgovaranje na poziv

Sure!
Svakako!   sva·ka·kaw

Yes, I'd love to.
Da, volio/voljela bih. m/f   da, *vaw*·lee·aw/*vaw*·lye·la beeh

That's very kind of you.
To je baš lijepo od tebe.   taw ye bash lee·*ye*·paw awd *te*·be

Where shall we go?
Gdje bismo mogli   gdye *bee*·smaw *maw*·glee
otići?   aw·tee·chee

No, I'm afraid I can't.
Ne, nažalost ne mogu.
ne, *na*·zha·lawst ne *maw*·goo

What about tomorrow?
A kako bi bilo sutra?
a *ka*·kaw bee *bee*·law *soo*·tra

Sorry, I can't sing/dance.
Oprosti, ali ja ne znam pjevati/plesati.
aw·*praw*·stee, *a*·lee ya ne znam *pye*·va·tee/*ple*·sa·tee

arranging to meet

ugovaranje sastanka

What time will we meet?
U koje vrijeme ćemo se naći?
oo *koy*·e vree·*ye*·me *che*·maw se *na*·chee

Where will we meet?
Gdje ćemo se naći?
gdye *che*·maw se *na*·chee

Let's meet …
Hajde da se nađemo …
hai·de da se *na*·je·maw …

  at (eight) o'clock
  u (osam) sati
  oo (*aw*·sam) *sa*·tee

  at (the entrance)
  na (ulazu)
  na (*oo*·la·zoo)

I'll pick you up.
Ja ću te pokupiti.
ya choo te *paw*·koo·pee·tee

Are you ready?
Jesi li spreman/spremna? m/f
ye·see lee *spre*·man/*sprem*·na

I'm ready.
Ja sam spreman/spremna. m/f
ya sam *spre*·man/*sprem*·na

I'll be coming later.
Ja ću ti se pridružiti kasnije.
ya choo tee se pree·*droo*·zhee·tee *ka*·snee·ye

Croatian rhythms

dalmatinska a
cappella klapa
dal·*ma*·teen·ska a
ka·*pe*·la *kla*·pa

male a cappella choral singing from the Dalmatian coast
whose main motifs are love, wine and love of homeland.
Klapa is still very much a living tradition and is often sung
in company over food and wine.

diple i mih
dee·ple ee meeh

traditional Istrian triangular bagpipes with a less piercing
sound than Scottish bagpipes

kolo
kaw·law

lively Slavic dance in which men and/or women hold hands
in either a circle or line and dance to the accompaniment of
an accordion, violins or the *tamburica*

roženice/sopile
raw·zhe·*nee*·tse/saw·*pee*·le

traditional Istrian two-stem reed pipe with a very pene-
trating oboe-like sound

tamburica
tam·boo·ree·tsa

type of three-string or five-string mandolin popular in
inland Croatia which has also given its name to a musical
style centred around idyllic themes of love and village life

zagorske i
međimurske popevke
za·*gawr*·ske ee
me·jee·moor·ske paw·*pev*·ke

traditional melancholic folk songs from the regions of
Zagorje and Međimurje, with alternating monophonic
and polyphonic segments

Where will you be?
Gdje ćeš ti biti?   gdye chesh tee *bee*·tee

If I'm not there by (nine), don't wait for me.
Ako ne budem tamo do   *a*·kaw ne *boo*·dem *ta*·maw daw
(devet), nemoj me čekati.   (*de*·vet) *ne*·moy me *che*·ka·tee

OK!
OK!   aw·*key*

I'll see you then.
Vidimo se tada.   *vee*·dee·maw se *ta*·da

See you later/tomorrow.
   Vidimo se kasnije/   *vee·*dee·maw se *ka·*snee·ye/
   sutra.   *soo·*tra

I'm looking forward to it.
   Jedva čekam.   *ye·*dva *che·*kam

Sorry I'm late.
   Oprosti što kasnim.   aw·*praw·*stee shtaw *ka·*sneem

Never mind.
   Nije važno.   *nee·*ye *vazh·*naw

drugs

droge

I don't take drugs.
   Ja ne koristim droge.   ya ne *kaw·*ree·steem *draw·*ge

I take ... occasionally.
   Ja koristim ... ponekad.   ya *kaw·*ree·steem ... *paw·*ne·kad

Do you want to have a smoke?
   Hoćeš zapaliti?   *haw·*chesh za·*pa·*lee·tee

Do you have a light?
   Imaš li vatre?   *ee·*mash lee *va·*tre

I'm high.
   Ja sam napljugan/   ya sam nap·*lyoo·*gan/
   napljugana. **m/f**   nap·*lyoo·*ga·na

In this chapter phrases are given in the informal *ti* forms. If you're not sure what this means, see the **a–z phrasebuilder**, page 24.

asking someone out

Where would you like to go (tonight)?
Gdje bi htio/htjela gdye bee *htee*·aw/*htye*·la
izaći (večeras)? m/f ee·*za*·chee (ve·*che*·ras)

Would you like to do something (tomorrow)?
Da li bi htio/htjela da lee bee *htee*·aw/*htye*·la
samnom nešto raditi *sam*·nawm *nesh*·taw *ra*·dee·tee
(sutra)? m/f (*soo*·tra)

Yes, I'd love to.
Da, to bih baš volio/ da, taw beeh bash *vaw*·lee·aw/
voljela. m/f *vaw*·lye·la

Sorry, I can't.
Žao mi je, ali ne mogu. zha·aw mee ye *a*·lee ne *maw*·goo

pick-up lines

Would you like a drink?
Mogu li ti kupiti *maw*·goo lee tee *koo*·pee·tee
piće? *pee*·che

You look like someone I know.
Ličiš na nekoga *lee*·cheesh na *ne*·kaw·ga
koga znam. *kaw*·ga znam

You're a fantastic dancer.
Krasno plešeš. *kra*·snaw *ple*·shesh

You were made for me.
Stvoren/Stvorena   stvaw·ren/stvaw·re·na
si za mene. m/f   see za me·ne

You blow me away.
Obaraš me s nogu.   aw·ba·rash me s naw·goo

Can I …?	Mogu li …?	maw·goo lee …
dance with you	dobiti ovaj ples	daw·bee·tee aw·vai ples
sit here	ovdje sjesti	awv·dye sye·stee
take you home	te ispratiti	te ee·spra·tee·tee
	kući	koo·chee

rejections

I'm here with my boyfriend.
Ovdje sam sa   awv·dye sam sa
svojom curom.   svoy·awm tsoo·rawm

I'm here with my girlfriend.
Ovdje sam sa   awv·dye sam sa
svojim dečkom.   svoy·eem dech·kawm

Excuse me, I have to go now.
Oprosti, ali sada   aw·praw·stee a·lee sa·da
stvarno žurim.   stvar·naw zhoo·reem

giving someone the flick

Leave me alone!
Ostavi me na miru!   aw·sta·vee me na mee·roo

Don't touch me!
Ne dodiruj me!   ne daw·dee·rooy me

Please control yourself.
Molim te obuzdaj se.   maw·leem te aw·booz·dai se

Piss off!
Odjebi!   aw·dye·bee

SOCIAL

local talk

He's a babe.
On je super frajer. awn ye *soo*·per *frai*·er

She's a babe.
Ona je super frajerica. *aw*·na ye *soo*·per *frai*·e·ree·tsa

He's hot.
On je privlačan. awn ye *preev*·lach·an

She's hot.
Ona je privlačna. *aw*·na ye *preev*·lach·na

He's a bastard.
On je nitkov. awn ye *neet*·kawv

She's a bitch.
Ona je pokvarena. *aw*·na ye *pawk*·va·re·na

He gets around.
On je kurver. awn ye *koor*·ver

She gets around.
Ona je drolja. *aw*·na ye *draw*·lya

I'd rather not.
Radije nebih. ra·dee·ye *ne*·beeh

No, thank you.
Ne, hvala ti. ne, *hva*·la tee

Who do you think you are?
Što si ti umišljaš? shtaw see tee oo·*meesh*·lyash

getting closer

I like you very much.
Jako mi se sviđaš. *ya*·kaw mee se *svee*·jash

You're great.
Super si. *soo*·per see

Can I kiss you?
Smijem li te poljubiti? *smee*·yem lee te paw·*lyoo*·bee·tee

Do you want to come inside for a while?
Da li želiš ući   da lee *zhe*·leesh *oo*·chee
na kratko?   na *krat*·kaw

Do you want a massage?
Hoćeš masažu?   *haw*·chesh ma·*sa*·zhoo

Can I stay over?
Mogu li ostati kod   *maw*·goo lee *aw*·sta·tee kawd
tebe večeras?   *te*·be ve·*che*·ras

sex

seks

Kiss me.
Poljubi me.   paw·*lyoo*·bee me

I want you.
Želim te.   *zhe*·leem te

Let's go to bed.
Idemo u krevet.   ee·de·maw oo *kre*·vet

Touch me here.
Dodirni me tu.   daw·*deer*·nee me too

Do you like this?
Da li ti se to sviđa?   da lee tee se taw *svee*·ja

I (don't) like that.
(Ne) sviđa mi se to.   (ne) *svee*·ja mee se taw

I think we should stop now.
Mislim da bi sada   *mee*·sleem da bee *sa*·da
trebali stati.   *tre*·ba·lee *sta*·tee

Do you have a (condom)?
Imaš li (prezervativ)?   *ee*·mash lee (pre·zer·va·*teev*)

Let's use a (condom).
Hajde da stavimo   *hai*·de da *sta*·vee·maw
(prezervativ).   (pre·zer·va·*teev*)

I won't do it without protection.
Ne želim dalje bez zaštite.   ne *zhe*·leem *da*·lye bez *zash*·tee·te

It's my first time.
Ovo mi je prvi put.   aw·vaw mee ye pr·vee poot

Don't worry, I'll do it myself.
Ne brini, sam/   ne bree·nee, sam/
sama ću. m/f   sa·ma choo

It helps to have a sense of humour.
Smisao za humor   smee·sa·aw za hoo·mawr
pomaže.   paw·ma·zhe

Oh my god!
O bože!   aw baw·zhe

That's great.
To je predivno.   taw ye pre·deev·naw

Easy tiger!
Lakše malo mačore!   lak·she ma·law ma·chaw·re

faster	brže	br·zhe
harder	jače	ya·che
slower	sporije	spaw·ree·ye
softer	nježnije	nyezh·nee·ye

That was …	Bilo je …	bee·law ye …
amazing	prekrasno	pre·kra·snaw
romantic	romantično	raw·man·teech·naw
wild	strastveno	strast·ve·naw

pillow talk

Whisper sweet nothings to your love with these terms of endearment. The words 'my fawn' and 'my little kitten' are usually reserved for women.

my candy	slatkišu	slat·kee·shoo
my dear	dragi/draga m/f	dra·gee/dra·ga
my fawn	lane moje	la·ne moy·e
my joy	srećo moja	sre·chaw moy·a
my little kitten	mače moje malo	ma·che moy·e ma·law
my love	ljubavi moja	lyoo·ba·vee moy·a
my soul	dušo moja	doo·shaw moy·a
my treasure	zlato moje	zla·taw moy·e

love

I love you.
Volim te.   vaw·leem te

I think we're good together.
Mislim da smo dobar par.   mee·sleem da smaw daw·bar par

Will you ...?	*Da li hoćeš ...?*	da lee *haw*·chesh ...
go out with me	*samnom*	sam·nawm
	izlaziti	eez·la·zee·tee
marry me	*udati se*	oo·da·tee se
	za mene	za me·ne
meet my	*upoznati*	oo·pawz·na·tee
parents	*moje roditelje*	moy·e raw·dee·te·lye

problems

Are you seeing someone else?
Viđaš li nekoga drugog?   vee·jash lee ne·kaw·ga droo·gawg

You're just using me for sex.
Ti me samo koristiš   tee me sa·maw kaw·ree·steesh
za seks.   za seks

I don't think it's working out.
Mislim da nam ne ide.   mee·sleem da nam ne ee·de

We'll work it out.
Riješit ćemo probleme.   ree·ye·sheet che·maw praw·ble·me

I never want to see you again.
Ne želim te više   ne zhe·leem te vee·she
nikada vidjeti.   nee·ka·da vee·dye·tee

beliefs & cultural differences

religion

vjera

What's your religion?
Koje ste/si vjere? pol/inf   kaw·ye ste/see vye·re

I'm ...	*Ja sam ...*	ya sam ...
agnostic	*agnostik* m&f	ag·naw·steek
Buddhist	*budist(kinja)* m/f	boo·deest(·kee·nya)
Catholic	*katolik/*	ka·taw·leek/
	katolkinja m/f	ka·tawl·kee·nya
Christian	*kršćanin/*	krsh·cha·neen/
	kršćanka m/f	krsh·chan·ka
Hindu	*hindu* m&f	heen·doo
Jewish	*Židov(ka)* m/f	zhee·dawv(·ka)
Muslim	*musliman(ka)* m/f	moo·slee·man(·ka)
Orthodox	*pravoslavac/*	pra·vaw·sla·vats/
	pravoslavka m/f	pra·vaw·slav·ka
Protestant	*protestant(kinja)* m/f	praw·te·stant(·kee·nya)
Roman	*rimski katolik/*	reem·skee ka·taw·leek/
Catholic	*rimska katolkinja* m/f	reem·ska ka·tawl·kee·nya
Greek	*grko-katolik/*	gr·kaw·ka·taw·leek/
Catholic	*grko-katolkinja* m/f	gr·kaw·ka·tawl·kee·nya

I (don't) believe in ...	*Ja (ne) vjerujem u ...*	ya (ne) vye·roo·yem oo ...
astrology	*astrologiju*	a·straw·law·gee·yoo
fate	*sudbinu*	sood·bee·noo
God	*boga*	baw·ga

Where can I attend ...?	*Gdje mogu otići ...?*	gdye maw·goo aw·tee·che ...
mass	*na misu*	na mee·soo
a service	*na obred*	na aw·bred

Where can I pray/worship?
    Gdje se mogu moliti?   gdye se *maw*·goo *maw*·lee·tee

Can I pray/worship here?
    Da li se mogu   da lee se *maw*·goo
    ovdje pomoliti?   awv·dye paw·*maw*·lee·tee

I didn't mean to do anything wrong.
    Nisam htio/htjela   nee·sam htee·aw/htye·la
    uraditi ništa krivo. m/f   oo·ra·dee·tee neesh·ta *kree*·vaw

cultural differences

Is this a local or national custom?
    Je li ovo mjesni ili   ye lee *aw*·vaw *mye*·snee *ee*·lee
    nacionalni običaj?   na·tsee·aw·nal·nee *aw*·bee·chai

I don't want to offend you.
    Ne želim vas/te   ne *zhe*·leem vas/te
    uvrijediti. pol/inf   oo·vree·*ye*·dee·tee

I'm not used to this.
    Nisam na ovo   nee·sam na *aw*·vaw
    navikao/navikla. m/f   na·vee·ka·aw/na·vee·kla

I'd rather not join in.
    Ja radije nebih   ya *ra*·dee·ye *ne*·beeh
    sudjelovao/   soo·dye·law·va·aw/
    sudjelovala. m/f   soo·dye·law·va·la

I'll try it.
    Ja ću to probati.   ya choo taw *praw*·ba·tee

I'm sorry, it's against my beliefs.
    Žao mi je, ali to   zha·aw mee ye *a*·lee taw
    je protivno mojim   ye *praw*·teev·naw *moy*·eem
    vjerovanjima.   vye·*raw*·va·nyee·ma

This is …	*Ovo je …*	*aw*·vaw ye …
different	*neobično*	*ne*·aw·beech·naw
fun	*zabavno*	za·bav·naw
interesting	*zanimljivo*	za·*neem*·lyee·vaw

When's the ...	Kada je ...	ka·da ye ...
open?	otvoren/	aw·tvaw·ren/
	otvorena? m/f	aw·tvaw·re·na
church	crkva f	tsr·kva
gallery	galerija f	ga·le·ree·ya
museum	muzej m	moo·zey

What kind of art are you interested in?

Koja vrsta umjetnosti	kaw·ya vr·sta oo·myet·naw·stee
vas/te zanima? pol/inf	vas/te za·nee·ma

What do you think of ...?

Kako doživljavate/	ka·kaw daw·zheev·lya·va·te/
doživljavaš ...? pol/inf	daw·zheev·lya·vash ...

What's in the collection?

Što sadrži ta zbirka?	shtaw sa·dr·zhee ta zbeer·ka

It's an exhibition of ...

Ova izložba je za ...	aw·va eez·lawzh·ba ye za ...

I'm interested in ...

Zainteresiran/	za·een·te·re·see·ran/
Zainteresirana sam za ... m/f	za·een·te·re·see·ra·na sam za ...

I like the works of ...

Sviđaju mi se djela	svee·ja·yoo mee se dye·la
koja spadaju pod ...	kaw·ya spa·dai·oo pawd ...

architecture	arhitektura f	ar·hee·tek·too·ra
artwork	umjetničko	oo·myet·neech·kaw
	djelo n	dye·law
curator	kurator m	koo·ra·tawr
design	dizajn m	dee·zain
etching	gravura f	gra·voo·ra
exhibit	izložak	eez·law·zhak
	predmet m	pred·met
exhibition hall	izložna	eez·lawzh·na
	dvorana f	dvaw·ra·na

installation	*instalacija* f	een·sta·*la*·tsee·ya
opening	*otvaranje* n	awt·*va*·ra·nye
painter	*slikar* m	*slee*·kar
painting (the art)	*slika* f	*slee*·ka
painting (canvas)	*slikanje* n	*slee*·ka·nye
period	*razdoblje* n	*raz*·dawb·lye
permanent collection	*stalna zbirka* f	*stal*·na *zbeer*·ka
print	*kopija* f	*kaw*·pee·ya
sculptor	*kipar* m	*kee*·par
sculpture	*skulptura* f	skoolp·*too*·ra
statue	*kip* m	keep
studio	*atelje* m	a·te·*lye*
style	*stil* m	steel
technique	*tehnika* f	*teh*·nee·ka

... art	... *umjetnost*	... oo·myet·nawst
baroque	*barokna*	ba·*rawk*·na
Byzantine	*bizantinska*	bee·*zan*·teen·ska
expressionist	*ekspresioni-stička*	eks·pre·see·aw·*nee*·steech·ka
Gothic	*gotička*	*gaw*·teech·ka
graphic	*grafička*	*gra*·feech·ka
impressionist	*impresioni-stička*	eem·pre·see·aw·*nee*·steech·ka
minimalist	*minimali-stička*	mee·nee·ma·*lee*·steech·ka
modern	*moderna*	*maw*·der·na
naive	*naivna*	*na*·eev·na
performance	*kazališna*	ka·za·*leesh*·na
pre-Romanesque	*pred-Romanička*	pred-raw·*ma*·neech·ka
Renaissance	*Renesansna*	re·ne·*san*·sna
Roman	*Rimska*	*reem*·ska
Romanesque	*Romanička*	raw·*ma*·neech·ka

In this chapter phrases are given in the informal *ti* forms. If you're not sure what this means, see the **a–z phrasebuilder**, page 24.

sporting interests

sportske zanimacije

What sport do you play?
Koji sport ti igraš?   koy·ee spawrt tee *ee*·grash

What sport do you follow?
Koji sport ti pratiš?   koy·ee spawrt tee *pra*·teesh

I play/do …	*Ja igram/*	ya *ee*·gram/
	treniram …	*tre*·nee·ram …
I follow …	*Ja pratim …*	ya *pra*·teem …
athletics	*atletiku*	at·*le*·tee·koo
basketball	*košarku*	*kaw*·shar·koo
football (soccer)	*nogomet*	*naw*·gaw·met
handball	*rukomet*	*roo*·kaw·met
scuba diving	*ronjenje sa*	*raw*·nye·nye sa
	bocama	*baw*·tsa·ma
tennis	*tenis*	*te*·nees
volleyball	*odbojku*	*awd*·boy·koo
water polo	*vaterpolo*	*va*·ter·paw·law
I …	*Ja …*	ya …
cycle	*vozim bicikl*	*vaw*·zeem bee·*tsee*·kl
run	*trčim*	*tr*·cheem
walk	*hodam*	*haw*·dam

For more sports, see the **dictionary**.

Who's your favourite team?
Koja je tvoja   koy·a ye tvoy·a
omiljena ekipa?   aw·mee·lye·na e·*kee*·pa

Who's your favourite sportsman?
Koji je tvoj omiljeni   *koy*·ee ye tvoy *aw*·mee·lye·nee
sportaš?   spawr·tash

Who's your favourite sportswoman?
Koja je tvoja omiljena   *koy*·a ye tvoy·a *aw*·mee·lye·na
sportašica ?   spawr·ta·shee·tsa

Do you like (basketball)?
Voliš li (košarku)?   *vaw*·leesh lee (*kaw*·shar·koo)

Yes, very much.
Da, vrlo.   da, *vr*·law

Not really.
Ne baš.   ne bash

I like watching it.
Ja ga volim gledati.   ya ga *vaw*·leem *gle*·da·tee

going to a game

odlazak na utakmicu

Would you like to go to a game?
Da li bi išao/išla   da lee bee ee·sha·aw/*eesh*·la
na utakmicu? m/f   na oo·tak·mee·tsoo

Who are you supporting?
Za koga navijaš?   za *kaw*·ga *na*·vee·yash

Who's playing/winning?
Tko igra/pobjeđuje?   tkaw *ee*·gra/paw·*bye*·joo·ye

---

scoring

What's the score?
Koji je rezultat?   *koy*·ee ye re·*zool*·tat

draw/even	*neodlučeno/*	ne·*awd*·loo·che·naw/
	neriješeno	*ne*·ree·ye·she·naw
match-point	*odlučujući*	awd·*loo*·choo·yoo·chee
	poen m	paw·*en*
nil (zero)	*nula* f	*noo*·la

That was a ...	Bila je to ...	bee·la ye taw ...
game!	utakmica!	oo·tak·mee·tsa
bad	loša	law·sha
boring	dosadna	daw·sad·na
great	sjajna	syai·na

sports talk

What a ...!	Kakav ...!	ka·kav ...
goal	gol	gawl
hit	pogodak	paw·gaw·dak
kick	šut	shoot
pass	dobačaj	daw·ba·chai
performance	nastup	na·stoop

playing sport

igranje sporta

Do you want to play?
Hoćeš igrati? — haw·ches ee·gra·te

Can I join in?
Mogu li se pridružiti? — maw·goo lee se pree·droo·zhee·tee

That would be great.
To bi bilo super. — taw bee bee·law soo·per

I can't.
Ja ne mogu. — ya ne maw·goo

My/Your point.
Mo/Tvoj poen. — moy/tvoy paw·en

Kick/Pass it to me!
Šutni/Dodaj meni! — shoot·nee/daw·dai me·nee

You're a good player.
Ti si dobar igrač. m — tee see daw·bar ee·grach
Ti si dobra igračica. f — tee see daw·bra ee·gra·chee·tsa

Thanks for the game.
Hvala na igri. — hva·la na ee·gree

Where's a good place to go …?	Gdje je dobro mjesto za …?	gdye ye *daw*·braw *mye*·staw za …
fishing	ribolov	*ree*·baw·lawv
horse riding	jahanje konja	*ya*·ha·nye *kaw*·nya
running	trčanje	*tr*·cha·nye
skiing	skijanje	*skee*·ya·nye
snorkeling	ronjenje s disalicom	*raw*·nye·nye s *dee*·sa·lee·tsawm
surfing	daskanje na valovima	*da*·ska·nye na *va*·law·vee·ma

Where's the nearest …?	Gdje je …	gdye ye …
golf course	najbliži teren za golf	*nai*·blee·zhee *te*·ren za gawlf
gym	najbliža teretana	*nai*·blee·zha te·re·*ta*·na
swimming pool	najbliži bazen za plivanje	*nai*·blee·zhee *ba*·zen za *plee*·va·nye
tennis court	najbliže tenisko igralište	*nai*·blee·zhe *te*·nee·skaw ee·*gra*·leesh·te

What's the charge per …?	Koja je cijena po …?	*koy*·a ye tsee·*ye*·na paw …
day	danu	*da*·noo
game	utakmici	oo·*tak*·mee·tsee
hour	satu	*sa*·too
visit	posjeti	*paw*·sye·tee

Can I hire a …?	Mogu li iznajmiti …?	*maw*·goo lee eez·*nai*·mee·tee …
ball	loptu	*lawp*·too
bicycle	bicikl	bee·*tsee*·kl
court	igralište	ee·*gra*·leesh·te
racquet	reket	*re*·ket

Do I have to be a member to attend?

	Da li moram biti član da bih prisustvovao/ prisustvovala? m/f	da lee *maw*·ram *bee*·tee chlan da beeh *pree*·soost·vaw·va·aw/ *pree*·soost·vaw·va·la

Is there a women-only session?
 Postoji li termin   paw·stoy·ee lee ter·meen
 samo za žene?   sa·maw za zhe·ne

Where are the changing rooms?
 Gdje su svlačionice?   gdye soo svla·chee·aw·nee·tse

diving

ronjenje

Is the visibility good?
 Da li je dobra vidljivost?   da lee ye daw·bra veed·lyee·vawst

How deep is the dive?
 Na koju se dubinu   na koy·oo se doo·bee·noo
 roni?   raw·nee

Is it a boat/shore dive?
 Da li je zaron sa   da lee ye za·rawn sa
 čamca/obale?   cham·tsa/aw·ba·le

I'd like to	*Želio/Željela*	zhe·lee·aw/zhe·lye·la
explore …	*bih … istražiti* m/f	beeh … ee·stra·zhee·tee
archaeological	*podvodna*	pawd·vawd·na
sites	*arheološka*	ar·he·aw·lawsh·ka
	nalazišta	na·la·zeesh·ta
caves/	*podvodne*	pawd·vawd·ne
wrecks	*spilje/olupine*	spee·lye/aw·loo·pee·ne
	brodova	braw·daw·va

I'd like to go …	*Želio/Željela*	zhe·lee·aw/zhe·lye·la
	bih ići … m/f	beeh ee·chee …
night	*na noćno*	na nawch·naw
diving	*ronjenje*	raw·nye·nye
scuba	*na ronjenje*	na raw·nye·nye
diving	*sa bocama*	sa baw·tsa·ma
snorkelling	*na ronjenje*	na raw·nye·nye
	sa disalicom	sa dee·sa·lee·tsawm
on a diving	*na ronilački*	na raw·nee·lach·kee
tour	*izlet*	eez·let

I'd like to ...	Želio/Željela bih ... m/f	zhe·lee·aw/zhe·lye·la beeh ...
learn to dive	naučiti roniti	na·oo·chee·tee raw·nee·tee
see sea walls	vidjeti morske nasipe	vee·dye·tee mawr·ske na·see·pe

I want to hire (a) ...	Želim iznajmiti ...	zhe·leem eez·nai·mee·tee ...
buoyancy vest	prsluk za spasavanje	pr·slook za spa·sa·va·nye
diving equipment	ronilačku opremu	raw·nee·lach·koo aw·pre·moo
flippers	peraje	pe·rai·e
mask	masku	ma·skoo
regulator	regulator	re·goo·la·tawr
snorkel	disalicu	dee·sa·lee·tsoo
tank	bocu	baw·tsoo
weight belt	olovni pojas	aw·lawv·nee poy·as
wetsuit	nepromočivo ronilačko odijelo	ne·praw·maw·chee·vaw raw·nee·lach·kaw aw·dee·ye·law

air fill	punjenje boca zrakom n	poo·nye·nye baw·tsa zra·kawm
dive (noun)	zaron m	za·rawn
dive (verb)	roniti	raw·nee·tee
diving boat	ronilački čamac m	raw·nee·lach·kee cha·mats
diving course	tečaj ronjenja m	te·chai raw·nye·nya

basketball

košarka

Who plays for (Cibona)?
Tko igra za (Cibonu)? tkaw ee·gra za (tsee·baw·noo)

He's a great (player).
On je odličan (igrač). awn ye awd·lee·chan (ee·grach)

Which team is the at the top of the league?
Koji je tim na čelu tablice? koy·ee ye teem na che·loo ta·blee·tse

back (position)	*bek* m	bek
ball	*lopta* f	*lawp*·ta
basket (structure)	*koš* m	kawsh
coach	*trener* m	*tre*·ner
double fault	*dupla greška* f	doo·pla *gresh*·ka
expulsion	*isključenje* n	ees·klyoo·*che*·nye
fan	*navijač* m	na·*vee*·yach
foul	*prekršaj* m	*pre*·kr·shai
free throw	*slobodno bacanje* n	*slaw*·bawd·naw *ba*·tsa·nye
jump-shot	*skok šut* m	skawk shoot
out	*aut* m	*a*·oot
player	*igrač* m	*ee*·grach
rebound	*odbitak* m	awd·*bee*·tak
referee	*sudac* m	*soo*·dats
skyhook shot	*horok* m	*haw*·rawk
slam-dunk	*zakucavanje* n	za·koo·*tsa*·va·nye
time-out	*pauza* f	*pa*·oo·za
travel	*koraci* m pl	*kaw*·ra·tsee

football/soccer

nogomet

Who plays for (Dinamo)?
Tko igra za (Dinamo)?   tkaw *ee*·gra za (*dee*·na·maw)

He's a great (goalkeeper).
On je odličan (vratar).   awn ye *awd*·lee·chan (*vra*·tar)

He played brilliantly in the match against (Italy).
On je sjajno odigrao utakmicu protiv (Italije).   awn ye *syai*·naw *aw*·dee·gra·aw oo·tak·mee·tsoo *praw*·teev (ee·*ta*·lee·ye)

What a great/terrible team!
Kakav sjajan/užasan tim! ka·kav syai·an/oo·zha·san teem

ball	lopta f	lawp·ta
coach	trener m	tre·ner
corner (kick)	korner m	kawr·ner
expulsion	isključenje f	ees·klyoo·che·nye
fan	navijač m	na·vee·yach
foul	prekršaj m	pre·kr·shai
free kick	slobodni udarac m	slaw·bawd·nee oo·da·rats
goal	gol m	gawl
goalkeeper	vratar m	vra·tar
offside	ofsaid m	awf·sa·eed
penalty	penal m	pe·nal
player	igrač m	ee·grach
red card	crveni karton m	tsr·ve·nee kar·tawn
referee	sudac m	soo·dats
striker	napadač m	na·pa·dach
yellow card	žuti karton m	zhoo·tee kar·tawn

tennis

tenis

I'd like to play tennis.
Želim igrati tenis. zhe·leem ee·gra·tee te·nees

Can we play at night?
Možemo li igrati maw·zhe·maw lee ee·gra·tee
noću? naw·choo

I need my racquet restrung.
Trebam promjenu tre·bam praw·mye·noo
struna na mom reketu. stroo·na na mawm re·ke·too

ace	*as* m	as
advantage	*prednost* f	*pred*·nawst
clay	*zemljana podloga* f	zem·lya·na *pawd*·law·ga
fault	*greška* f	*gresh*·ka
game, set, match	*gejm, set, meč* m	geym set mech
grass	*travnata podloga* f	*trav*·na·ta *pawd*·law·ga
hard court	*teniski teren sa tvrdom podlogom* m	te·nee·skee *te*·ren sa *tvr*·dawm *pawd*·law·gawm
net	*mreža* f	*mre*·zha
play doubles	*igrati u parovima*	*ee*·gra·tee oo pa·raw·vee·ma
racquet	*reket* m	*re*·ket
serve	*servis* m	*ser*·vees
set	*set* m	set
tennis ball	*teniska loptica* f	te·nee·ska *lawp*·tee·tsa

water sports

sportovi na vodi

Can I book a lesson?
Mogu li zakazati   maw·goo lee za·*ka*·za·tee
sat obuke?   sat *aw*·boo·ke

Can I hire (a) …?	*Mogu li iznajmiti …?*	maw·goo lee eez·*nai*·mee·tee …
boat	*čamac*	*cha*·mats
canoe	*kanu*	ka·*noo*
kayak	*kajak*	*kai*·ak
life jacket	*prsluk za spasavanje*	*pr*·slook za spa·*sa*·va·nye
sea kayak	*morski kajak*	*mawr*·skee *kai*·ak
snorkelling gear	*ronilačku masku i disalicu*	*raw*·nee·lach·koo *ma*·skoo ee *dee*·sa·lee·tsoo
water-skis	*skije za vodu*	*skee*·ye za *vaw*·doo
wetsuit	*nepromočivo podvodno odijelo*	ne·praw·*maw*·chee·vaw *pawd*·vawd·naw aw·dee·*ye*·law

Are there any …?	Da li ima kakvih …?	da lee *ee*·ma *kak*·veeh …
reefs	morskih grebenova	*mawr*·skeeh *gre*·be·naw·va
rips	jakih podvodnih struja	*ya*·keeh *pawd*·vawd·neeh *stroo*·ya
water hazards	opasnosti u vodi	aw·*pa*·snaw·stee oo *vaw*·dee

canoeing	kanuistika f	ka·noo·*ee*·stee·ka
guide	vodič m	*vaw*·deech
harbour master	lučki kapetan m	*looch*·kee ka·*pe*·tan
kayaking	kajakarenje n	kai·a·*ka*·re·nye
marina	marina f	ma·*ree*·na
motorboat	motorni čamac m	*maw*·tawr·nee *cha*·mats
oars	vesla n pl	*ve*·sla
port	luka f	*loo*·ka
sailing	jedrenje n	*ye*·dre·nye
sailing boat	jedrilica f	*ye*·*dree*·lee·tsa
surfboard	daska za surfanje f	*da*·ska za *soor*·fa·nye
surfing	daskanje na valovima n	*da*·ska·nye na *va*·law·vee·ma
swimming	plivanje n	*plee*·va·nye
wave	val m	val
water-skiing	skijanje na vodi n	*skee*·ya·nye na *vaw*·dee
windsurfing	jedrenje na dasci n	*ye*·dre·nye na *das*·tsee
yachting	krstarenje jahtom n	kr·*sta*·re·nye *yah*·tawm

For phrases about diving, see the **diving section**, page 133.
For phrases about hiking, see **outdoors**, page 139.

hiking

pješačenje

Where can I ...?	*Gdje mogu ...?*	gdye *maw*·goo ...
buy supplies	*kupiti*	*koo*·pee·tee
	namirnice	*na*·meer·nee·tse
find someone	*naći nekoga*	*na*·chee *ne*·kaw·ga
who knows	*tko zna ovo*	tkaw zna *aw*·vaw
this area	*područje*	*paw*·drooch·ye
get a map	*nabaviti kartu*	*na*·ba·vee·tee *kar*·too
hire hiking gear	*iznajmiti*	eez·*nai*·mee·tee
	opremu	*aw*·pre·moo
	za pješačenje	za pye·*sha*·che·nye

Do we need	*Trebamo li*	*tre*·ba·maw lee
to take ...?	*ponijeti ...?*	*paw*·nee·ye·tee ...
bedding	*krevetninu*	kre·vet·*nee*·noo
food	*hranu*	*hra*·noo
water	*vodu*	*vaw*·doo

How ...?	*Koliko ...?*	kaw·*lee*·kaw ...
high is the climb	*je visok uspon*	ye *vee*·sawk oo·spawn
long is the trail	*dugačka staza*	doo·gach·ka *sta*·za

Is there a hut?
Da li postoji   da lee *paw*·stoy·ee
planinarska koliba?   pla·*nee*·nar·ska *kaw*·lee·ba

When does it get dark?
Kada obično padne noć?   *ka*·da *aw*·beech·naw *pad*·ne nawch

Do we need a guide?
Treba li nam vodič?   *tre*·ba lee nam *vaw*·deech

Are there land mines in this area?
Da li ima mina   da lee *ee*·ma *mee*·na
na ovom području?   na *aw*·vawm *paw*·drooch·yoo

An unfortunate consequence of the recent war in the former Yugoslavia is the presence of land mines. Most mined areas are marked with warning signs which might have these words on them:

mine	*mee·ne*	**mines**
minirano	*mee·nee·ra·naw*	**mined**

Warning signs can be in the form of a red triangle with a black dot in the middle or depict a white skull and cross-bones against a red background. Unfortunately, warning signs are sometimes souvenired and mined areas may just be cordoned off with coloured plastic tape.

Less common improvised signs that you'll want to take close heed of if you venture off the beaten track include crossed tree branches or rock heaps by the road. Always be sure to check with the locals about the presence of land mines in their area and steer away from suspiciously deserted areas.

Is the track …?	*Je li staza …?*	ye lee *sta·*za …
dangerous	*opasna*	*aw·*pa·sna
marked	*označena*	*aw·*zna·che·na
open	*otvorena*	*awt·*vaw·re·na
scenic	*panoramska*	pa·naw·*ram·*ska

Which is the … route?	*Koji put je …?*	*koy·*ee poot ye …
easiest	*najlakši*	*nai·*lak·shee
shortest	*najkraći*	*nai·*kra·chee

Where can I find (a/the) …?	*Gdje se …?*	gdye se …
campsite	*nalazi kamp*	*na·*la·zee kamp
nearest	*nalazi najbliže*	*na·*la·zee *nai·*blee·zhe
village	*selo*	*se·*law
showers	*nalaze tuševi*	*na·*la·ze *too·*she·vee
toilets	*nalaze zahodi*	*na·*la·ze *za·*haw·dee

Where have you come from?
Odakle dolazite/   aw-*da*-kle *daw*-la-zee-te/
dolaziš? **pol/inf**   *daw*-la-zeesh

How long did it take?
Koliko dugo je trebalo?   kaw-*lee*-kaw *doo*-gaw ye *tre*-ba-law

Does this path go to …?
Da li ovaj put vodi do …?   da lee *aw*-vai poot *vaw*-dee daw …

Is the water OK to drink?
Je li ova voda pitka?   ye lee *aw*-va *vaw*-da *peet*-ka

I'm lost.
Ja sam izgubljen/   ya sam eez-*goob*-lyen/
izgubljena. **m/f**   eez-*goob*-lye-na

beach

plaža

You may see a beach referred to as a *žal* (zhal) but the most common word is *plaža* (pla-zha). Beaches are an important focus for social life both day and night during the warmer months. Terrace dancing, *ples na terasama* (ples na te-*ra*-sa-ma), at beachside hotels is also a favourite summer pastime.

Where's the … beach?	*Gdje se nalazi … plaža?*	gdye se *na*-la-zee … *pla*-zha
best	*najbolja*	*nai*-baw-lya
nearest	*najbliža*	*nai*-blee-zha
nudist	*nudistička*	noo-*dee*-steech-ka
public	*javna*	*yav*-na

signs

Zabranjen Ribolov		
za-bra-nyen *ree*-baw-lawv	**No Fishing**	
Zabranjeno Plivanje		
za-bra-nye-naw *plee*-va-nye	**No Swimming**	

bay	*uvala* f	oo·va·la
beach	*žal/plaža* f/m	zhal/*pla*·zha
cave	*spilja* f	*spee*·lya
channel	*kanal* m	*ka*·nal
cove	*dražica* f	*dra*·zhee·tsa
inlet	*draga* f	*dra*·ga
island	*otok* m	*aw*·tawk
lake	*jezero* n	*ye*·ze·raw
promontory	*rt* m	rt
reef	*morski greben* m	*mawr*·skee gre·ben

Is it safe to dive/swim here?

Da li je bezopasno 　da lee ye *bez*·aw·pa·snaw
skakati/plivati ovdje? 　*ska*·ka·tee/*plee*·va·tee *awv*·dye

What time is high/low tide?

U koliko sati je 　oo kaw·*lee*·kaw *sa*·tee ye
plima/oseka? 　*plee*·ma/*aw*·se·ka

Do we have to pay?

Trebamo li platiti? 　*tre*·ba·maw lee *pla*·tee·tee

Could you put some sunscreen on my back, please?

Možete/Možeš li mi 　*maw*·zhe·te/*maw*·zhesh lee mee
staviti kremu protiv 　*sta*·vee·tee *kre*·moo *praw*·teev
sunca na leđa, molim? pol/inf 　*soon*·tsa na *le*·ja *maw*·leem

How much for a/an …?	*Koliko stoji …?*	kaw·*lee*·kaw *stoy*·ee …
chair	*jedna stolica za sklapanje*	*yed*·na *staw*·lee·tsa za *skla*·pa·nye
hut	*jedna kućica*	*yed*·na koo·chee·tsa
umbrella	*jedan suncobran*	*ye*·dan *soon*·tsaw·bran

---

listen for …

aw·pa·snaw ye
Opasno je! 　　**It's dangerous!**

pa·zee·te na *pawd*·vawd·noo *pro*·too·stroo·yoo
Pazite na podvodnu 　**Be careful of**
protustruju! 　　**the undertow!**

weather

What's the weather like?
Kakvo je vrijeme?   *kak*·vaw ye vree·*ye*·me

What will the weather be like tomorrow?
Kakvo će vrijeme   *kak*·vaw che vree·*ye*·me
biti sutra?   *bee*·tee *soo*·tra

It's …	… je.	… ye
cloudy	*Oblačno*	*aw*·blach·naw
cold	*Hladno*	*hlad*·naw
fine	*Vedro*	*ve*·draw
freezing	*Ledeno*	*le*·de·naw
hot	*Vruće*	*vroo*·che
raining	*Kišovito*	kee·*shaw*·vee·taw
snowing	*Snjegovito*	snye·*gaw*·vee·taw
sunny	*Sunčano*	*soon*·cha·naw
warm	*Toplo*	*taw*·plaw
windy	*Vjetrovito*	vye·*traw*·vee·taw

flora & fauna

What ... is that?	... je to?	... ye taw
animal	*Koja životinja*	*koy*·a zhee·*vaw*·tee·nya
flower	*Koji cvijet*	*koy*·ee ts·vee·*yet*
plant	*Koja biljka*	*koy*·a *beel'*·ka
tree	*Koje stablo*	*koy*·e *sta*·blaw

Is it ...?	*Je li ...?*	ye lee ...
common	*često*	*che*·staw
dangerous	*opasno*	*aw*·pa·snaw
endangered	*ugroženo*	*oo*·graw·zhe·naw
poisonous	*otrovno*	*aw*·trawv·naw
protected	*zaštićeno*	*zash*·tee·che·naw

What is it used for?
Zašto se koristi?   *zash*·taw se *kaw*·ree·stee

local plants & animals

almond tree	*badem* m	*ba*·dem
black bear	*mrki medvjed* m	*mr*·kee *med*·vyed
rosehip shrub	*šipkov grm* m	*sheep*·kawv grm
stone/pine	*kuna bijelica/*	*koo*·na bee·ye·lee·tsa/
marten	*zlatica* f	*zla*·tee·tsa
white-headed	*bjeloglavi*	bye·*law*·gla·vee
vulture	*sup* m	soop
wild goat	*divokoza* f	*dee*·vaw·kaw·za

Breakfast, *doručak* (*daw*·roo·chak), typically consists of toast with butter and rosehip jam, ham or prosciutto omelettes or bread rolls with a choice of toppings. Lunch, *ručak* (*roo*·chak), is usually taken between midday and 1pm, and in coastal regions in the summer months, is often followed by a siesta. Dinner, *večera* (*ve*·che·ra), is the main meal of the day and the time it's taken varies between 6 and 9pm.

breakfast	*doručak* m	*daw*·roo·chak
lunch	*ručak* m	*roo*·chak
dinner	*večera* f	*ve*·che·ra
snack	*užina* f	*oo*·zhee·na
eat	*jesti*	*ye*·stee
drink	*piti*	*pee*·tee
I'd like ...	*Želim* ...	*zhe*·leem ...
I'm starving!	*Gladan/Gladna*	*gla*·dan/*glad*·na
	sam kao vuk. m/f	sam *ka*·aw vook

finding a place to eat

The word for café is both *kafić* (*ka*·feech) and *kavana* (ka·*va*·na), though *kafić* is much more commonly used. As restaurants don't usually display their menus outside you may need to go in and ask to have a look at the *jelovnik* (ye·*lawv*·neek).

Can you	*Možete/Možeš*	*maw*·zhe·te/*maw*·zhesh
recommend	*li preporučiti*	lee pre·pe·*paw*·roo·chee·tee
a ...	*neki ...* pol/inf	*ne*·kee ...
bar	*bar*	bar
café	*kafić*	*ka*·feech
restaurant	*restoran*	re·*staw*·ran

bistro   bee·*straw*

lively venue catering mainly to a young crowd and serving a variety of alcoholic drinks as well as a limited range of food – popular in beachside areas

buffet   bee·*fe*

small café – often with a lounge-style ambience including a TV – serving snacks and buffet-style foods, alcoholic and nonalcoholic beverages

gostionica   gaw·stee·*aw*·nee·tsa

inn or pub that also operates as a no-frills, cheap restaurant

kafić/kavana   ka·feech/ka·*va*·na

café – popular, usually licensed, social haunt that sometimes provides music and dancing in addition to a limited selection of dishes

konoba   kaw·*naw*·ba

rustic establishment that serves wine and local peasant-style specialities

menza/kantina   men·za/kan·tee·na

canteen usually for students or employees – for cheap eats as close to a home-cooked meal as one could hope

pekara   pe·ka·ra

bakery and pastry shop serving the full range of delectable Croatian pastries and bread

pivnica   peev·nee·tsa

pub or brewery-pub (pub attached to a brewery), often with an outdoor seating area during the warmer months, that sells a variety of draught and bottled beers and a limited selection of light meals

pizzeria   pee·tse·*ree*·a

restaurant that specialises in delicious, often wood-fired, pizzas that rival their Italian cousins as cheap and tasty fare

restoran   re·*staw*·ran

restaurant – serving a wide variety of dishes but often with a house speciality and usually licensed to sell alcohol

restoran sa   re·*staw*·ran sa
samoposluživanjem   sa·maw·paw·sloo·*zhee*·va·nyem
    quick and inexpensive self-service cafeteria with reasonably priced food of variable quality

slastičarnica   sla·stee·*char*·nee·tsa
    cake shop that serves ice cream, coffee, milk-based and other nonalcoholic drinks

taverna/birc   ta·*ver*·na/beerts
    tavern serving basic food as well as alcohol

Where would you go for …?	*Gdje se može otići na …?*	gdye se *maw*·zhe aw·*tee*·chee na …
a celebration	*proslavu*	*praw*·sla·voo
a cheap meal	*jeftini obrok*	*yef*·tee·nee *aw*·brawk
local specialities	*mjesne specijalitete*	*mye*·sne spe·tsee·ya·lee·*te*·te
I'd like to reserve a table for …	*Želim rezervirati stol za …*	zhe·leem re·zer·*vee*·ra·tee stawl za …
(two) people	*(dvoje) ljudi*	(*dvoy*·e) *lyoo*·dee
(eight) o'clock	*(osam) sati*	(*aw*·sam) *sa*·tee
I'd like …, please.	*Mogu li dobiti …, molim.*	*maw*·goo lee *daw*·bee·tee … *maw*·leem
a children's menu	*dječji jelovnik*	*dyech*·yee ye·*lawv*·neek
the drink list	*cjenik pića*	*tsye*·neek *pee*·cha
a half portion	*pola obroka*	*paw*·la *aw*·braw·ka
the menu	*jelovnik*	ye·*lawv*·neek
a menu in English	*jelovnik na engleskom*	ye·*lawv*·neek na *en*·gle·skawm
nonsmoking	*nepušačko mjesto*	ne·poo·*shach*·kaw *mye*·staw
smoking	*pušačko mjesto*	poo·*shach*·kaw *mye*·staw
a table for (five)	*stol za (petoro)*	stawl za (*pe*·taw·raw)

Are you still serving food?
   Da li još servirate hranu?   da lee yawsh *ser*·vee·ra·te *hra*·noo

How long is the wait?
   Koliko dugo se čeka?   kaw·*lee*·kaw *doo*·gaw se *che*·ka

at the restaurant

What would you recommend?
   Što biste nam   shtaw *bee*·ste nam
   preporučili?   pre·paw·*roo*·chee·lee

What's in that dish?
   Od čega se   awd *che*·ga se
   sastoji ovo jelo?   sa·stoy·ee *aw*·vaw *ye*·law

What's that called?
   Kako se ono zove?   *ka*·kaw se *aw*·naw *zaw*·ve

I'll have that.
   Ja bih to naručio/   ya beeh taw na·*roo*·chee·aw/
   naručila. m/f   na·*roo*·chee·la

---

listen for ...

zat·vaw·re·naw ye	
Zatvoreno je.	**We're closed.**
poo·nee smaw	
Puni smo.	**We're full.**
sam·aw tre·*noo*·tak	
Samo trenutak.	**One moment.**
gdye *zhe*·lee·te *sye*·stee	
Gdje želite sjesti?	**Where would you like to sit?**
shtaw vam *maw*·goo paw·noo·dee·tee	
Što vam mogu ponuditi?	**What can I get for you?**
eez·*vaw*·lee·te	
Izvolite!	**Here you go!**
pree·yat·naw/*daw*·bar tek	
Prijatno/Dobar tek.	**Enjoy your meal.**

Does it take long to prepare?

Da li priprema	da lee *pree*·pre·ma	
ovoga traje dugo?	aw·vaw·ga *trai*·e *doo*·gaw	

Is it self-serve?

Da li je ovdje	da lee ye *awv*·dye	
samoposluživanje?	sa·maw·paw·sloo·*zhee*·va·nye	

Is service included in the bill?

Da li je posluga	da lee ye *paw*·sloo·ga
uključena	oo·klyoo·che·na
u iznos na računu?	oo eez·naws na ra·*choo*·noo

Are these complimentary?

Da li su ovi	da lee soo *aw*·vee
besplatni?	be·splat·nee

I'd like …	*Želim …*	*zhe*·leem …
a local	*neki mjesni*	*ne*·kee *mye*·snee
speciality	*specijalitet*	spe·tsee·ya·*lee*·tet
a meal fit	*kraljevski*	*kra*·lyev·skee
for a king	*obrok*	*aw*·brawk
the menu	*jelovnik*	ye·*lawv*·neek
that dish	*ono jelo*	*aw*·naw ye·law

I'd like it with …	*Želim to sa …*	*zhe*·leem taw sa …
pepper	*paprom*	*pa*·prawm
salt	*soli*	*saw*·lee
tomato sauce/	*ketchupom*	ke·cha·pawm
ketchup		
vinegar	*ocatom*	*aw*·tsa·tawm

I'd like it without …	*Želim to bez …*	*zhe*·leem taw bez …
cheese	*sira*	*see*·ra
chilli	*čilija*	*chee*·lee·ya
garlic	*češnjaka*	chesh·*nya*·ka
nuts	*raznih oraha*	raz·neeh *aw*·ra·ha
oil	*ulja*	*oo*·lya

For other specific meal requests, see **vegetarian & special meals**, page 161.

predjela	*pre*·dye·la	appetisers
juhe	*yoo*·he	soups
salate	sa·*la*·te	salads
glavna jela	*glav*·na ye·la	main courses
prilozi	*pree*·law·zee	side dishes
poslastice	*paw*·sla·stee·tse	desserts
laki obroci	*la*·kee *aw*·braw·tsee	light meals
aperitivi	a·pe·ree·*tee*·vee	apéritifs
pića	*pee*·cha	drinks
bezalkoholna pića	be·zal·kaw·hawl·na *pee*·cha	soft drinks
topli napitci	*taw*·plee na·peet·tsee	hot drinks
žestoka pića	zhe·*staw*·ka pee·cha	spirits
piva	*pee*·va	beers
vinjaci	*vee*·nya·tsee	brandies
domaća vina	*daw*·ma·cha vee·na	local wines
pjenušava vina	pye·*noo*·sha·va vee·na	sparkling wines
bijela vina	bee·*ye*·la vee·na	white wines
crna vina	*tsr*·na vee·na	red wines
desertna vina	de·*sert*·na vee·na	dessert wines

For more words you might see on a menu, see the **culinary reader**, page 163.

talking food

I love this dish.
  Obožavam ovo jelo.   aw·*baw*·zha·vam *aw*·vaw ye·law

I love the local cuisine.
  Obožavam kuhinju   aw·*baw*·zha·vam *koo*·hee·nyoo
  ovoga područja.   aw·vaw·ga *paw*·drooch·ya

That was delicious!
  To je bilo izvrsno!   taw ye *bee*·law *eez*·vr·snaw

FOOD

My compliments to the chef.
Komplimenti   kawm·plee·*men*·tee
šefu kuhinje.   *she*·foo koo·hee·nye

I'm full.
Sit/Sita sam. m/f   seet/*see*·ta sam

This is ...	*Ovo je ...*	*aw*·vaw ye ...
(too) cold	*(pre)hladno*	(pre·)*hlad*·naw
spicy	*pikantno*	pee·*kant*·naw
superb	*odlično*	awd·leech·naw

at the table

Please bring ...	*Molim vas donesite ...*	*maw*·leem vas daw·*ne*·see·te ...
the bill	*račun*	*ra*·choon
a cloth	*stolnjak*	*stawl*·nyak
a menu	*jelovnik*	ye·*lawv*·neek
a serviette	*ubrus*	*oo*·broos

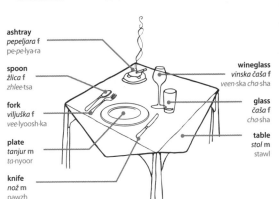

ashtray
pepeljara f
pe·*pe*·lya·ra

spoon
žlica f
zhlee·tsa

fork
viljuška f
vee·lyoosh·ka

plate
tanjur m
ta·nyoor

knife
nož m
nawzh

wineglass
vinska čaša f
veen·ska *cha*·sha

glass
čaša f
cha·sha

table
stol m
stawl

methods of preparation

način na koji je hrana pripremljena

I'd like it ...	*Želim da bude ...*	zhe·leem da *boo*·de ...
I don't want it ...	*Ne želim*	ne zhe·leem
	da bude ...	da *boo*·de ...
boiled	*obareno*	aw·*ba*·re·naw
deep-fried	*prženo u*	pr·zhe·naw oo
	dubokom ulju	doo·baw·kawm oo·lyoo
fried	*prženo*	pr·zhe·naw
grilled/broiled	*pečeno na*	pe·che·naw na
	roštilju	raw·*shtee*·lyoo
mashed	*zdrobljeno*	zdraw·blye·naw
	u kašu	oo ka·shoo
medium	*srednje pečeno*	sred·nye pe·che·naw
rare	*nepotpuno*	ne·pawt·poo·naw
	pečeno	pe·che·naw
reheated	*podgrijano*	pawd·gree·ya·naw
steamed	*kuhano na pari*	koo·ha·naw na *pa*·ree
well done	*dobro pečeno*	daw·braw pe·che·naw
with the dressing	*sa začinima sa*	sa za·chee·nee·ma sa
on the side	*strane*	stra·ne
without ...	*bez ...*	bez ...

in the bar

u baru

Excuse me!
Oprostite! — aw·*praw*·stee·te

I'm next.
Ja sam slijedeći/a. m/f — ya sam slee·ye·de·chee/a

I'll have ...
Želim naručiti ... — zhe·leem na·*roo*·chee·tee ...

Same again, please.
Opet isto, molim. — aw·pet ee·staw *maw*·leem

No ice, thanks.
Bez leda, hvala.   bez *le*·da *hva*·la

I'll buy you a drink.
Častim vas/te pićem. **pol/inf**   *cha*·steem vas/te *pee*·chem

What would you like?
Što želite/želiš? **pol/inf**   shtaw *zhe*·lee·te/*zhe*·leesh

It's my round.
Moj je red za čašćenje.   moy ye red za *chash*·che·nye

How much is that?
Koliko to stoji?   kaw·*lee*·kaw taw *stoy*·ee

Do you serve meals here?
Da li ovdje   da lee *awv*·dye
poslužujete obroke?   paw·*sloo*·zhoo·ye·te *aw*·braw·ke

nonalcoholic drinks

bezalkoholna pića

... (mineral) water	... (mineralna) voda f	... (*mee*·ne·ral·na) *vaw*·da
sparkling	*gazirana*	ga·*zee*·ra·na
still	*obična*	*aw*·beech·na
apricot juice with whipped cream	sok od marelice sa šlagom m	sawk awd ma·*re*·lee·tse sa *shla*·gawm
fizzy rosehip drink	pašareta f	pa·sha·*re*·ta
fresh lemonade	slatka limunada f	*slat*·ka lee·moo·*na*·da
(hot) water	(topla) voda f	(*taw*·pla) *vaw*·da
orange juice	sok od naranče m	sawk awd *na*·ran·che
rosehip and hibiscus tea	čaj od šipka i hibiscusa	chai awd *sheep*·ka ee hee·*bee*·skoo·sa
soft drink	bezalkoholno piće m	be·zal·*kaw*·hawl·naw *pee*·che
(cup of) tea ...	(šalica) čaja f ...	(*sha*·lee·tsa) *chai*·a ...
(cup of) coffee ...	(šalica) kave f ...	(*sha*·lee·tsa) *ka*·ve ...
with (milk)	*sa (mlijekom)*	sa (mlee·*ye*·kawm)
without (sugar)	*bez (šećera)*	bez (*she*·che·ra)

alcoholic drinks

alkoholna pića

beer	pivo n	pee·vaw
brandy	rakija f	ra·kee·ya
champagne	šampanjac m	sham·pa·nyats
cocktail	koktel m	kawk·tel
slivovitz (plum brandy)	šljivovica f	shlyee·vaw·vee·tsa

a shot of ...	jedna čašica ...	yed·na cha·shee·tsa ...
gin	džina	jee·na
rum	ruma	roo·ma
tequila	tekile	te·kee·le
vodka	vodke	vawd·ke
whisky	viskija	vee·skee·ya

a bottle/glass	boca/čaša	baw·tsa/cha·sha
of ... wine	... vina	... vee·na
dessert	desertnog	de·sert·nawg
red	crnog	tsr·nawg
rosé	rosea	raw·se·a
sparkling	pjenušavog	pye·noo·sha·vawg
white	bijelog	bee·ye·lawg
a ... of beer	jedna ... piva	yed·na ... pee·va
glass	čaša	cha·sha
large bottle	velika boca	ve·lee·ka baw·tsa
pint (500 ml)	krigla	kree·gla
small bottle	mala boca	ma·la baw·tsa

drinking up

If you're drinking in a threesome, don't at any price raise your thumb, index and middle finger all at once to signal another round. This is a Serbian gesture connected to Serbian nationalism and might see you swiftly ejected from your cosy bar-side nook.

Cheers!
Živjeli! zhee·vye·lee

This is hitting the spot.
Ovo mi baš prija. aw·vaw mee bash pree·ya

I feel fantastic!
Osjećam se fantastično! aw·sye·cham se fan·ta·steech·naw

I think I've had one too many.
Mislim da sam mee·sleem da sam
popio/popila paw·pee·aw/paw·pee·la
previše. m/f pre·vee·she

I'm feeling drunk.
Osjećam se pijano. aw·sye·cham se pee·ya·naw

I'm pissed.
Pijan/Pijana sam. m/f pee·yan/pee·ya·na sam

I feel ill.
Muka mi je. — moo·ka mee ye

Where's the toilet?
Gdje je zahod? — gdye ye za·hawd

Can you call a taxi for me?
Možete/Možeš li mi — maw·zhe·te/maw·zhesh lee mee
pozvati taksi? **pol/inf** — pawz·va·tee tak·see

I don't think you should drive.
Mislim da nebi trebali — mee·sleem da ne·bee tre·ba·lee
voziti. **pol** — vaw·zee·tee
Mislim da nebi trebao/ — mee·sleem da ne·bee tre·ba·aw/
trebala voziti. **m/f inf** — tre·ba·la vaw·zee·tee

---

brandy reader

Croatia produces a great variety of wines but dearest to the hearts of most Croatians are the home-made brandies collectively known as *rakije* (ra·kee·ye) that come in a profusion of herbal and fruit flavours.

kruškovac	kroosh·ko·vats	pear-flavoured brandy
lozovača	law·zhaw·va·cha	herb-flavoured wine brandy
maraskino	ma·ra·skee·naw	sour-cherry brandy
orahovac	aw·ra·haw·vats	walnut brandy
pelinkovac	pe·leen·kaw·vats	herbal digestif brandy
šljivovica	shlyee·vaw·vee·tsa	plum brandy
travarica	tra·va·ree·tsa	bitter herbal brandy
vinjak	vee·nyak	wine brandy

buying food

kupovina hrane

What's the local speciality?
Što je ovdje   shtaw ye *awv*·dye
područni specijalitet?   *paw*·drooch·nee spe·tsee·ya·*lee*·tet

What's that?
Što je to?   shtaw ye taw

Can I taste it?
Mogu li to probati?   *maw*·goo lee taw *praw*·ba·tee

Can I have a bag, please?
Mogu li dobiti   *maw*·goo lee *daw*·bee·tee
vrećicu toga, molim?   *vre*·chee·tsoo *taw*·ga *maw*·leem

How much is (a kilo of cheese)?
Koliko stoji (kila sira)?   kaw·*lee*·kaw *stoy*·ee (*kee*·la *see*·ra)

How much?
Koliko?   kaw·*lee*·kaw

how would you like that?		
cooked	*kuhano*	*koo*·ha·naw
cured	*prerađeno*	*pre*·ra·je·naw
dried	*sušeno*	*soo*·she·naw
fresh	*svježe*	*svye*·zhe
frozen	*zaleđeno*	*za*·le·je·naw
raw	*sirovo*	*see*·raw·vaw
smoked	*dimljeno*	*deem*·lye·naw

I'd like ...	Želim ...	zhe·leem ...
(200) grams	(dvijesto) grama	(dvee·ye·staw) gra·ma
half a dozen	pola tuceta	paw·la too·tse·ta
a dozen	tucet	too·tset
half a kilo	pola kile	paw·la kee·le
a kilo	kilu	kee·loo
(two) kilos	(dvije) kile	(dvee·ye) kee·le
a bottle	bocu	baw·tsoo
a jar	staklenku	sta·klen·koo
a packet	kutiju	koo·tee·yoo
a piece	komad	kaw·mad
(three) pieces	(tri) komada	(tree) kaw·ma·da
a slice	krišku	kreesh·koo
(six) slices	(šest) krišaka	(shest) kree·sha·ka
a tin	limenku	lee·men·koo
(just) a little	(samo) malo	(sa·maw) ma·law
more	više	vee·she
some ...	malo ...	ma·law ...
that one	onaj/onu/	aw·nai/aw·noo/
	ono m/f/n	aw·naw
this one	ovaj/ovu/	aw·vai/aw·voo/
	ovo m/f/n	aw·vaw

Less.	Manje.	ma·nye
A bit more.	Malo više.	ma·law vee·she
Enough.	Dosta.	daw·sta

listen for ...

maw·goo lee vam paw·maw·chee	
Mogu li vam pomoći?	**Can I help you?**
shtaw zhe·lee·te	
Što želite?	**What would you like?**
nesh·taw droo·gaw	
Nešto drugo?	**Anything else?**
ne·ma taw·ga	
Nema toga.	**There isn't any.**
taw ye (pet) koo·na	
To je (pet) kuna.	**That's (five) kuna.**

Do you have …?	*Da li imate …?*	da lee *ee*·ma·te …
anything	*nešto*	*nesh*·taw
cheaper	*jeftinije?*	yef·*tee*·nee·ye
other kinds	*druge vrste*	*droo*·ge vr·ste
Where can I find the … section?	*Gdje se nalazi dio prodavaonice za …?*	gdye se *na*·la·zee *dee*·aw praw·da·va·*aw*·nee·tse za …
dairy	*mliječne proizvode*	mlee·*yech*·ne praw·*eez*·vaw·de
fish	*ribu*	*ree*·boo
frozen goods	*zaleđenu hranu*	za·le·je·noo *hra*·noo
fruit and vegetable	*voće i povrće*	*vaw*·che ee *paw*·vr·che
meat	*meso*	*me*·saw
poultry	*meso od peradi*	*me*·saw awd pe·ra·dee

pekara f	*pe*·ka·ra	bakery
prodavaonica	praw·da·va·*aw*·nee·tsa	bottle shop/
alkohola f	*al*·kaw·haw·la	liquor store
mesnica f	*me*·snee·tsa	butcher's shop
delikatese f pl	de·lee·ka·*te*·se	delicatessen
trgovac	*tr*·gaw·vats	greengrocer
povrćem m	*paw*·vr·chem	
tržnica f	*trzh*·nee·tsa	market
supermarket m	soo·per·*mar*·ket	supermarket

cooking utensils

pribor i posuđe za kuhanje

Could I please	*Mogu li*	*maw*·goo lee
borrow a ...?	*posuditi jedan/*	paw·*soo*·dee·tee *ye*·dan/
	jednu ...	*yed*·noo ...
	molim? m/f	*maw*·leem
I need a ...	*Trebam jedan/*	*tre*·bam *ye*·dan/
	jednu ... m/f	*yed*·noo ...
chopping	*dasku za*	*da*·skoo za
board	*rezanje* f	*re*·za·nye
frying pan	*tavu* f	*ta*·voo
knife	*nož* m	nawzh
saucepan	*lonac* m	*law*·nats

For more cooking implements, see the **dictionary**.

ordering food

Is there a ...	Da li znate za ...	da lee *zna*·te za ...
restaurant near here?	restoran ovdje blizu?	re·*staw*·ran *awv*·dye *blee*·zoo
Do you have ... food?	Da li imate ... obrok?	da lee *ee*·ma·te ... *aw*·brawk
halal	halal	*ha*·lal
kosher	košer	*kaw*·sher
vegetarian	vegetarijanski	ve·ge·ta·*ree*·yan·skee

I don't eat ...
Ja ne jedem ...   ya ne *ye*·dem ...

Is it cooked in/with ...?
Je li to kuhano u/sa ...?   ye lee taw *koo*·ha·naw oo/sa ...

Could you prepare a meal without ...?	Možete li prirediti obrok koji ne sadrži ...?	*maw*·zhe·te lee pree·*re*·dee·tee *aw*·brawk *koy*·ee ne *sa*·dr·zhee ...
butter	maslac	*ma*·slats
eggs	jaja	*yai*·a
fish	ribu	*ree*·boo
fish stock	riblji bujon	*reeb*·lyee *boo*·yawn
meat stock	mesni bujon	*mes*·nee *boo*·yawn
oil	ulje	*oo*·lye
pork	svinjetinu	*svee*·nye·tee·noo
poultry	meso od peradi	*me*·saw awd *pe*·ra·dee
red meat	crveno meso	*tsr*·ve·naw *me*·saw

Is this ...?	*Da li je ovo ...?*	da lee ye *aw*·vaw ...
decaffeinated	*bez kafeina*	bez ka·fe·*ee*·na
free of	*bez*	bez
animal	*životinjskih*	zhee·*vaw*·teen'·skeeh
produce	*sastojaka*	sa·stoy·a·ka
free range	*domaće*	*daw*·ma·che
genetically	*genetski*	ge·net·skee
modified	*modificirano*	maw·dee·*fee*·tsee·ra·naw
gluten free	*bez glutena*	bez *gloo*·te·na
low fat	*s malo masnoće*	s *ma*·law ma·*snaw*·che
low in sugar	*s malo šećera*	s *ma*·law she·che·ra
organic	*organski*	*awr*·gan·skee
	proizvedeno	praw·eez·*ve*·de·naw
salt free	*bez soli*	bez *saw*·lee

special diets & allergies

posebna ishrana i alergije

I'm on a special diet.
Ja sam na posebnoj dijeti. ya sam na *paw*·seb·noy dee·*ye*·tee

I'm allergic	*Ja sam alergičan/*	ya sam a·*ler*·gee·chan/
to ...	*alergična na ... m/f*	a·*ler*·geech·na na ...
dairy	*mliječne*	mlee·*yech*·ne
produce	*proizvode*	praw·*eez*·vaw·de
eggs	*jaja*	*yai*·a
gelatine	*želatinu*	zhe·la·*tee*·noo
gluten	*gluten*	*gloo*·ten
honey	*med*	med
MSG	*glutaminat*	gloo·ta·mee·*nat*
nuts	*razne orahe*	*raz*·ne *aw*·ra·he
peanuts	*kikiriki*	kee·kee·*ree*·kee
seafood	*morske plodove*	*mawr*·ske *plaw*·daw·ve
shellfish	*školjke i rakove*	*shkawl'*·ke ee *ra*·kaw·ve

To explain your dietary restrictions with reference to religious
beliefs, see **beliefs & cultural differences**, page 125.

This miniguide to Croatian cuisine lists dishes and ingredients in alphabetical order in Croatian. It's designed to help you get the most out of your gastronomic experience by providing you with food terms that you may see on menus etc. Adjectives on their own are given in the masculine form only. For an explanation of how to form feminine and neuter adjectives see the **a–z phrasebuilder**, page 16.

A

ajvar ⓜ *ai*-var *relish made from minced roast eggplant & capsicum & flavoured with lemon juice, garlic, olive oil & parsley*
ananas ⓜ *a*-na-nas *pineapple*
arambašići ⓜ pl *a*-ram-ba-shee-chee *mincemeat parcels rolled in vine or silver beet leaves (also called **japraci**)*
artičoka ⓕ ar-tee-*chaw*-ka *artichoke*
artičoke na dalmatinski način ⓕ pl ar-tee-*chaw*-ke na dal-*ma*-teen-skee *na*-cheen *artichokes stuffed with bread-crumbs soaked in milk & lemon juice, seasoned with parsley & garlic then drizzled with olive oil & oven baked*

B

bakalar ⓜ ba-ka-*lar* *dried salted cod that is reconstituted in water before cooking*
— **s krumpirom** s kroom-*pee*-rawm *dried salted cod simmered with oil, bay leaves & lemon slices – served with diced boiled potatoes & parsley*
baklava ⓕ ba-*kla*-va *filo pastry squares stuffed with chopped nuts, sugar & cinnamon & drenched in melted butter & rose-water flavoured syrup*
banana ⓕ ba-*na*-na *banana*
bečki odrezak ⓜ *bech*-kee *aw*-dre-zak *Wiener schnitzel*
bijeli mekani sir ⓜ bee-*ye*-lee *me*-ka-nee seer *cottage cheese*
blatina ⓕ *bla*-tee-na *well-known red wine*
blitva ⓕ *bleet*-va *silver beet • Swiss chard – green leafy vegetable indigenous to Croatia*

— **s krumpirom** s kroom-*pee*-rawm *boiled potatoes served with silver beet fried in garlic & drizzled with olive oil*
bola ⓕ *baw*-la *refreshing chilled drink made from sugar & fruit or herbs soaked in white wine*
borgonja ⓕ bawr-*gaw*-nya *Istrian red wine*
borovnica ⓕ baw-*rawv*-nee-tsa *blueberry*
brancin ⓜ bran-*tseen* *sea bass*
breskva ⓕ *bres*-kva *peach*
brodet ⓜ braw-*det* *tasty fish stew often served with polenta*
— **na dalmatinski način** na dal-*ma*-teen-skee *na*-cheen *Dalmatian-style mixed fish stew with rice*
bubreg ⓜ *boo*-breg *kidney*
bučice ⓕ pl *boo*-chee-tse *courgette • zucchini*
burek ⓜ *boo*-rek *oily flaky pastry stuffed with cheese or minced meat – popular breakfast food or snack of Turkish origin*
— **s mesom** s me-*sawm* *fried minced beef & onion layered between filo pastry sheets then topped with beaten eggs & milk & baked*
— **sa sirom** sa see-*rawm* *filo pastry layered with a mixture of beaten eggs, cottage cheese, sour cream & dill then oven baked*
burgundac ⓜ boor-*goon*-dats *premium red wine*

C

celer ⓜ *tse*-ler *celery*
cikla ⓕ *tsee*-kla *beetroot*
crna maslina ⓕ *tsr*-na *ma*-slee-na *black olive*

crni rižoto ⓜ *tsr*-nee ree-*zhaw*-taw *'black risotto'* – highly prized risotto containing cuttlefish, squid, olive oil, onion, garlic, parsley & red wine & given its black colour by the addition of squid ink

crvena paprika ⓕ *tsr*-ve-na pa-*pree*-ka red capsicum • red bell pepper

cvjetača ⓕ *tsvye*-ta-cha cauliflower
— **s kiselim vrhnjem** s kee-se-leem *vrh*-nyem boiled cauliflower topped with sour cream, melted butter, cheese & breadcrumbs then oven baked

Č

čajno pecivo ⓝ *chai*-naw pe-*tsee*-vaw cookie • sweet biscuit

češnjak ⓜ chesh-*nyak* garlic

čevapčići ⓜ pl che-*vap*-chee-chee skinless minced beef & lamb sausages flavoured with garlic, parsley, pepper & salt – served grilled

čokoladna krema ⓕ chaw-kaw-*lad*-na *kre*-ma chocolate cream dessert

D

dagnja ⓕ *dag*-nya mussel

Dalmatinska salata od hobotnice ⓕ dal-*ma*-teen-ska sa-*la*-ta awd haw-*bawt*-nee-tse octopus salad – a Dalmatian speciality

dimljen *deem*-lyen smoked

dimljena riba ⓕ *deem*-lye-na *ree*-ba smoked fish

dimljeni losos ⓜ *deem*-lye-nee *law*-saws smoked salmon

dimljeni sir ⓜ *deem*-lye-nee seer smoked cheese

dingač ⓜ *deen*-gach Dalmatian red wine

dinja ⓕ *dee*-nya honeydew melon

divlji *deev*-lyee wild

divlja šparoga ⓕ *deev*-lya shpa-*raw*-ga wild asparagus

dnevni meni ⓜ *dnev*-nee me-*nee* daily special

doboš torta ⓕ *do*-bosh *tawr*-ta rich layered cake of Hungarian origin garnished with coffee cream & caramel

dobro pečen *daw*-braw pe-chen well done

domaći *daw*-ma-chee home-made • home-style

domaći rezanci ⓜ pl *daw*-ma-chee re-*zan*-tsee home-style egg noodles – often served in soups

dunja ⓕ *doo*-nya quince

Dž

džem ⓜ jem jam

đuveč ⓜ joo-vech casserole made from mixed vegetables pork cutlets & rice – flavoured with parsley, celery leaves, chilli & tomato paste

F

fazan ⓜ fa-zan pheasant

fileki ⓜ pl fee-*le*-kee tripe

francuska salata ⓕ fran-*tsoo*-ska sa-*la*-ta salad of diced potato, carrot & peas smothered in a lemony mayonnaise sauce

fuži ⓜ pl foo-zhee pasta twirls

G

gljiva ⓕ *glyee*-va mushroom

golub ⓜ *gaw*-loob pigeon

govedina ⓕ gaw-ve-dee-na beef

goveđa juha ⓕ *gaw*-ve-ja yoo-ha beef bouillon

goveđi gulaš ⓜ *gaw*-ve-jee goo-lash diced beef & pork braised with onion, sauerkraut, sour cream & paprika

grah ⓜ grah dried beans

graševina ⓕ gra-she-vee-na white riesling-style wine

grožđe ⓝ *grawzh*-je grape

gulaš od divljači ⓜ goo-lash od *deev*-lya-chee game goulash

gulaš-juha ⓕ goo-lash-yoo-ha *'goulash soup'* – thick hearty soup containing red pepper, potatoes, diced beef flavoured with red wine, bay leaf, tomato paste, caraway seed, chilli, onion & garlic

guska ⓕ goo-ska goose

H

heljda ⓕ *hel*-da buckwheat

hladetina ⓕ hla-de-tee-na brawn prepared from boiled pigs' hocks or trotters & cubed pork shoulder with the addition of

*vegetables, boiled eggs, garlic, parsley &
paprika – a special-occasion treat*

hladni pladanj ⓜ *hlad-nee pla-dan' cold
cuts – might include thin slices of delicious Istrian or Dalmatian pršut & goat's
cheese, all garnished with olives*

hobotnica ⓕ *haw-bawt-nee-tsa octopus*

hrenovka ⓕ *hre-nawv-ka frankfurter*

I

inćun ⓕ *een-choon anchovy*

Istarska jota ⓕ *ee-star-ska yaw-ta Istrian
stew prepared from sauerkraut, beans,
potatoes & smoked dried meats –
seasoned with garlic & bay leaves*

Istarski kaneloni ⓜ pl *ee-star-skee
ka-ne-law-nee pancakes filled with
a mixture of fried cubed prosciutto &
ham, cottage cheese & mushrooms then
dipped in beaten egg & breadcrumbs,
fried & topped with a tomato sauce*

Istarski lonac ⓜ *ee-star-skee law-nats
Istrian hotpot of diced lamb, carrot, cabbage, garlic, tomato, onion & olive
oil – flavoured with bay leaves &
sometimes white wine*

J

jabuka ⓕ *ya-boo-ka apple*

jagoda ⓕ *ya-gaw-da strawberry*

jaje ⓕ *yai-e egg*
  — na oko na *aw-kaw fried egg*

janjeća čorba ⓕ *ya-nye-cha chawr-ba
lamb stew of parsley root, celeriac,
Brussels sprouts & carrot – flavoured with
tomato paste, sour cream, paprika, bay
leaves, lemon juice & parsley*

janjeća juha ⓕ *ya-nye-cha yoo-ha soup
made from lamb, head vegetables, rice,
cabbage, egg yolk, garlic, onion, bay
leaf, peppercorns, lemon juice, sour
cream, parsley & spices*

janjetina ⓕ *ya-nye-tee-na lamb*
  — na ražnju na *razh-nyoo lamb cooked
on a spit*

japraci ⓜ pl *ya-pra-tsee mincemeat
parcels rolled in vine or silver beet leaves
(also called **arambašići**)*

jastog ⓜ *ya-stawg lobster*

ječam ⓜ *ye-cham barley*

jegulja ⓕ *ye-goo-lya eel*

jetrena pašteta ⓕ *ye-tre-na pash-te-ta
liverwurst (pâté)*

jogurt ⓜ *yaw-goort yoghurt*

juha ⓕ *yoo-ha soup*
  — od bujače awd *boo-ya-che pumpkin
soup*
  — od cvjetače awd *tsvye-ta-che
cauliflower soup with sour cream & egg
yolk – thickened with a roux*
  — od gljiva s heljdinom kašom awd
*glyee-va s hel'-dee-nawm ka-shawm
rich buckwheat & mushroom soup
containing beef stock & sour cream &
seasoned with cloves & parsley*
  — od graha awd *gra-ha soup made
from dried kidney or borlotti beans,
smoked bacon bones (or smoked pork
hock), onion, carrot, bay leaf & garlic*
  — od graška awd *grash-ka pea soup*
  — od heljdine kaše i krumpira awd
*hel'-dee-ne ka-she ee kroom-pee-ra
buckwheat & potato soup containing
sour cream, onion & minced parsley*
  — od kisele repe i graha awd *kee-se-le
re-pe ee gra-ha sour turnip & bean soup*
  — od kiselog kupusa i graha awd
*kee-se-lawg koo-poo-sa ee gra-ha
sauerkraut & bean soup*
  — od krastavca awd *kra-stav-tsa
cucumber soup*
  — od krumpira awd *kroom-pee-ra
potato soup containing smoked bacon,
garlic, sour cream, spices, marjoram, bay
leaves, parsley, vinegar & paprika*
  — od krumpira na Zagorski način
awd *kroom-pee-ra na za-gawr-skee
na-cheen Zagorje potato soup containing smoked bacon & onion – flavoured
with marjoram, bay leaves, paprika,
parsley & vinegar*
  — od mahuna awd *ma-hoo-na
runner-bean soup*
  — od piletine i povrća awd
*pee-le-tee-ne ee paw-vr-cha chicken
& vegetable soup with carrot, celery,
parsnip & peas – served with **noklice**
(dumplings)*
  — od povrća awd *paw-vr-cha
vegetable soup*
  — od rajčica awd *rai-chee-tsa
tomato soup*
  — od repe i kupusa awd *re-pe ee
koo-poo-sa turnip & cabbage soup*

juha od špinata i krumpira *yoo*-ha awd shpee-*na*-ta ee kroom-*pee*-ra spinach & potato soup containing puréed spinach, diced potatoes & beef bouillon – thickened with a sour cream & egg yolk roux

K

kajgana ① *kai*-ga-na scrambled eggs
kalamari ① pl ka-la-*ma*-ree calamari • squid
kapar ⓜ *ka*-par caper
kaša ① *ka*-sha gruel • porridge
— **od zobi** awd *zaw*-bee oatmeal porridge
kaštradina ① kash-tra-*dee*-na dried mutton soup with vegetables
kavijar ⓜ ka-vee-yar caviar
kesten ⓜ *ke*-sten chestnut
— **pire** pee-*re* dessert prepared from chestnut purée, sugar, vanilla, rum & cream & garnished with chocolate shavings
kiflice ① pl *kee*-flee-tse delicate crescent-shaped biscuits that come in a variety of flavours including vanilla
— **od badema** awd ba-*de*-ma almond biscuits dusted with icing sugar made from butter, flour, ground almonds & vanilla sugar
— **od oraha** awd *aw*-ra-ha biscuits made from a dough of butter, egg yolks, cream cheese, flour & sugar – stuffed with an egg white, sugar & ground-walnut filling
kiseli kupus ⓜ *kee*-se-lee koo-poos sauerkraut – dear to the hearts of Croatians, sauerkraut is prepared from whole cored cabbage heads layered with horseradish, bay leaves, garlic, dried red pepper & salt
klinčić ⓜ *kleen*-cheech clove
knedle ① pl *kned*-le dumplings made from butter, semolina flour, eggs & milk – often served in soups
kobasica ① kaw-*ba*-see-tsa sausage
kolač ⓜ *kaw*-lach cake
komorač ⓜ *kaw*-maw-rach fennel
kompot ⓜ *kawm*-pawt stewed fruit
kotlovina ① *kawt*-law-vee-na fried pork chops simmered in a piquant sauce containing onions, garlic, tomato, mustard,

chillies, white wine & paprika – traditionally prepared outdoors over an open fire
kozji sir ⓜ *kawz*-yee seer goat's milk cheese
krastavac ⓜ kra-*sta*-vats cucumber
krema ① *kre*-ma cream • filling
krempita ① krem-*pee*-ta layered puff pastry filled with a custard-like cream
krepka juha od mesa ① *krep*-ka yoo-ha awd me-sa broth • consommé
kroštule ① pl *krawsh*-too-le similar to Italian crostoli, these are bow-shaped pastries flavoured with lemon rind & vanilla then deep fried in oil & sprinkled with icing sugar
kruh ⓜ krooh bread
krumpir ⓜ kroom-peer potato
— **salata** sa-*la*-ta potato salad
kruška ① *kroosh*-ka pear
krvavica ① kr-*va*-vee-tsa blood sausage
kuglice od ruma ① pl koo-glee-tse awd roo-ma rum balls made from egg whites, ground walnuts, sugar, grated chocolate & rum – a rich treat
kuglof ⓜ koo-glawf ring-shaped sponge cake sometimes flavoured with lemon or containing raisins soaked in rum
kuhan koo-han boiled • cooked
— **na pari** na pa-ree steamed
kuhana govedina ① koo-ha-na gaw-ve-deena boiled beef
kuhana škrpina ① koo-ha-na shkr-pee-na boiled scorpion fish – a Dalmatian speciality
kuhana šunka ① koo-ha-na shoon-ka boiled ham
kuhani krumpir ⓜ koo-ha-nee kroom-peer boiled potatoes
kukuruz ⓜ koo-koo-rooz corn
kulen ⓜ koo-len paprika-flavoured sausage
kumin ⓜ koo-meen caraway – popular spice used in savoury dishes
kupina ① koo-pee-na blackberry
kupus ⓜ koo-poos cabbage

L

leća ① le-cha lentil
ledene kocke ① pl le-de-ne kawts-ke coffee-flavoured or chocolate-flavoured sponge cake layered with chocolate cream

lička kisela čorba ① *leech*-ka *kee*-se-la *chor*-ba 'Lika-style sour stew' – stew prepared with cubed meat, mixed vegetables & cabbage – flavoured with garlic, vinegar, sour cream & parsley

lignje ⓝ pl *leeg*-nye calamari • squid
— **s krumpirom** s kroom-*pee*-rawm traditional Dalmatian dish consisting of squid cooked between layers of potato seasoned with mixed herbs, garlic, parsley & doused with olive oil

limun ⓜ *lee*-moon lemon

lišće maslačka ⓝ *leesh*-che ma-*slach*-ka dandelion leaves – popular salad greens with a slightly bitter taste

losos ⓜ *law*-saws salmon

lovorov list ⓜ *law*-vaw-rawv leest bay leaf

lubenica ① *loo*-be-nee-tsa watermelon

lubin ⓜ *loo*-been sea bass

luk ⓜ look onion

M

mađarica ① ma-*ja*-ree-tsa layers of a rich sweet baked dough interspersed with a chocolate cream filling & topped with melted chocolate

mahuna ① ma-*hoo*-na green bean

majoneza ① mai-aw-*ne*-za mayonnaise

makov kolač ① ma-kawv *kaw*-lach poppy-seed cake

makovnjača ① ma-*kawv*-nya-cha poppy-seed roll

makovo sjeme ⓝ ma-kaw-vaw *sye*-me poppy seed – often used in pastries

malina ① ma-*lee*-na raspberry

malvazija ① mal-*va*-zee-ya white Istrian wine with a yellowy-gold colour

maneštra ① ma-*nesh*-tra vegetable & bean soup sometimes containing meat – similar to Italian minestrone
— **od bobi** awd *baw*-bee broad-bean soup with fresh maize

maraska voćna salata ① ma-*ra*-ska *vawch*-na sa-*la*-ta fruit salad containing sour & sweet cherries, pear & quince macerated in maraskino liqueur & dusted with sugar

maraskino ① ma-ra-*skee*-naw liqueur made from Dalmatian sour cherries & flavoured with the kernels, giving it a slightly bitter aftertaste – known in English as 'maraschino'

marelica ① ma-re-*lee*-tsa apricot

mariniran ma-*ree*-nee-ran marinated

maslac ⓜ *ma*-slats butter

maslina ① ma-*slee*-na olive

maslinovo ulje ⓝ ma-*slee*-naw-vaw *oo*-lye olive oil

masnoća ① ma-*snaw*-cha fat

med ⓜ med honey

medovina ① me-*daw*-vee-na mead (mildly alcoholic fermented honey drink)

Međimurska salata od luka ① me-jee-moor-ska sa-*la*-ta awd *loo*-ka salted onions with the excess liquid removed & dressed with pumpkinseed oil – served as a side dish

Međimurski gulaš ⓜ me-jee-moor-skee *goo*-lash veal stewed with onion, garlic, hot peppers, pickled peppers & ajvar

mesna jela ⓝ pl me-sna *ye*-la meat dishes

meso ⓝ me-saw meat

miješana salata ① mee-ye-sha-na sa-*la*-ta mixed salad

miješano meso ⓝ mee-ye-sha-naw me-saw mixed grill – popular menu item as Croatians love their meat

mlijeko ⓝ mlee-*ye*-kaw milk

mlinci ⓜ pl *mleen*-tsee pasta tatters made from flour, eggs & dripping & sometimes coated with butter, cream or cottage cheese – typical accompaniment to roasted meats or bakalar

mortadela ① mawr-ta-*de*-la mortadella – type of aromatic pork sausage with small squares of fat & served thinly sliced as an appetiser

moruna ① maw-*roo*-na sturgeon (fish)

musaka ① moo-*sa*-ka moussaka – layered lasagne-style dish containing meat & vegetables
— **od zeleni i crvenih paprika** awd ze-le-neeh ee tsr-ve-neeh *pa*-pree-ka moussaka made from peeled, grilled green & red capsicums layered with fried ground beef with onion & a sauce made from feta, sour cream & eggs
— **s patlidžanima i tikvicama** s pat-lee-ja-nee-ma ee teek-vee-tsa-ma eggplant & zucchini moussaka made from layered eggplant & zucchini interspersed with ground beef & a sauce made from feta, eggs & sour cream

muškatov oraščić ⓜ moosh-ka-tawv aw-*rash*-cheech nutmeg

N

na ražnju na *razh*-nyoo *roasted on a spit*

na žaru na *zha*-roo *barbecued • grilled (broiled)*

nabujak od riže ⓜ *na*-boo-yak awd *ree*-zhe *rice pudding*

nadjev ⓜ *nad*-yev *stuffing*

naranča ⓕ *na*-ran-cha *orange*

naravni odrezak ⓜ *na*-rav-nee *aw*-dre-zak *veal escalope*

narodna jela ⓕ pl *na*-rawd-na *ye*-la *traditional Croatian dishes*

nepotpuno pečen *ne*-pawt-poo-naw *pe*-chen *rare*

noklice ⓕ pl *naw*-klee-tse *dumplings for soup made from breadcrumbs, milk-soaked bread, eggs & parsley – there are variations containing minced liver & meat*

Nj

njoki ⓜ pl *nyaw*-kee *gnocchi (dumplings made from semolina or potato)*

O

ocat ⓜ *aw*-tsat *vinegar*

odojak na ražnju ⓜ *aw*-doy-ak na *razh*-nyoo *suckling pig roasted on a spit*

okruglice ⓕ pl aw-*kroo*-glee-tse *dumplings made from semolina or potato – served as a savoury accompaniment or, stuffed with plums or jam, as a dessert*

omlet ⓜ *aw*-mlet *omelette*
  — sa sirom sa *see*-rawm *cheese omelette*

opolo ⓕ *aw*-paw-law *Dalmatian red wine*

orada ⓕ aw-*ra*-da *gilthead (fish)*

orah ⓜ *aw*-rah *walnut*

orahnjača ⓕ aw-*rah*-nya-cha *walnut roll – ground walnut, butter, cinnamon & sugar mixture encased in a yeasty dough & then baked*

oslić ⓜ *aw*-sleech *hake*

oštriga ⓕ *awsh*-tree-ga *oyster*

ovčji sir awv-chyee seer *sheep's milk cheese*

P

palačinka ⓕ pa-la-*cheen*-ka *pancake – often served filled with jam or ground nuts then topped with chocolate, may also come with savoury fillings as a main course*
  — sa sirom sa *see*-rawm *dessert pancake filled with cottage cheese, sugar, raisins, egg & sour cream then oven baked*

palenta ⓕ pa-*len*-ta *polenta*

papar ⓜ *pa*-par *pepper*
  — od ljutih papričica awd *lyoo*-teeh pa-*pree*-chee-tsa *cayenne pepper*

paprika ⓕ *pa*-pree-ka *paprika*

paprikaš ⓜ *pa*-pree-kash *paprikash – beef or fish stew heavily flavoured with paprika*

pastičada ⓕ pa-stee-*cha*-da *Dalmatian speciality consisting of beef rounds larded with smoked bacon then stewed with fried vegetables flavoured with rosemary, bay leaves & peppercorns & served with a white wine, olive, lemon juice & beef stock sauce. Another version has a sauce made from dried fruit & apples, tomato paste & red wine.*

pastirska juha ⓕ pa-*steer*-ska yoo-ha *'shepherd's soup' – soup made from cubed lamb, veal chops & pork neck also containing onion, garlic, chilli, bay leaves, paprika, tomato, potato & wine*

pastrva ⓕ *pas*-tr-va *trout*

paški sir ⓜ *pash*-kee seer *sheep's milk cheese from the island of Pag*

pašta fažol ⓕ *pash*-ta fa-*zhawl* *bean soup with pasta*

patka ⓕ *pat*-ka *duck*
  — s maslinama s *ma*-slee-na-ma *duck rubbed with salt & garlic then marinated in a mixture of wine, lemon juice, thyme, oil & pepper & roasted in the oven*

patlidžan ⓜ pat-*lee*-jan *eggplant*

pečen *pe*-chen *baked • roasted*
  — na žaru na *zha*-roo *grilled*
  — u tavi oo *ta*-vee *pan-roasted*

pečena orada s prokulicom ⓕ *pe*-che-na aw-*ra*-da s *praw*-koo-lee-tsawm *roast gilthead (fish) with silver beet – a Dalmatian speciality*

pečena svinjetina ⓕ *pe*-che-na svee-nye-*tee*-na *roast pork*

pečurka ⓕ *pe*·choor·ka *field mushroom*
pečurke na žaru ⓕ pl *pe*·choor·ke na *zha*·roo *grilled field mushrooms*
peršin ⓜ *per*·sheen *parsley*
pikantan pee·*kan*·tan *hot (spicy) • savoury*
pile na dalmatinski način ⓝ *pee*·le na dal·*ma*·teen·skee *na*·cheen *'Dalmatian-style chicken' – boiled chicken pieces covered with a sauce of olive oil, onion, capers, parsley & anchovies then baked in the oven*
pileća krem-juha ⓕ *pee*·le·cha krem·*yoo*·ha *cream of chicken soup*
piletina ⓕ *pee*·le·tee·na *chicken*
pirjan *peer*·yan *stewed*
pita sa špinatom ⓕ *pee*·ta sa shpee·*na*·tawm *spinach pie made from flaky pastry & boiled seasoned spinach layered with cottage-style cheese*
pizza ⓕ *pee*·tsa *pizza – often wood-fired, Croatian pizzas rival their Italian cousins as cheap delicious meals*
plavac ⓜ *pla*·vats *Dalmatian red wine*
pljeskavice od blitve ⓕ pl *plye*·ska·vee·tse awd *bleet*·ve *patties made from silver beet, grated cheese, breadcrumbs, eggs & olive oil then seasoned with garlic & mint, fried & topped with sour cream*
podlanica ⓕ *pawd*·la·nee·tsa *gilthead seabream (fish)*
podravski lonac ⓜ *paw*·drav·skee *law*·nats *layer of cooked dried beans, topped with pork cubes (or pork chops), a layer of cabbage, a layer of capsicum, bacon, green beans & cabbage then baked in a sealed dish*
pohan *paw*·han *fried in a breadcrumb batter*
pomfrit ⓜ pawm·*freet* *French fries • chips*
poriluk ⓜ *paw*·ree·look *leek*
poslastice ⓕ pl *paw*·sla·stee·tse *desserts*
posutice ⓕ pl *paw*·soo·tee·tse *type of pasta served with various side dishes (eg, salted pilchards)*
poširan paw·*shee*·ran *poached*
povrće ⓝ *paw*·vr·che *vegetable(s)*
prepržen *pre*·pr·zhen *prepared au gratin*
prilozi ⓜ pl *pree*·law·zee *side dishes*
prokupac ⓜ *praw*·koo·pats *well-known red wine similar to Pinot Noir*
prošek ⓜ *praw*·shek *sweet Dalmatian dessert wine*
prstac ⓜ pr·*stats* *date mussel – popular on the Adriatic Coast*
pršut ⓜ *pr*·shoot *prized smoke-dried ham similar to Italian prosciutto*
pržen *pr*·zhen *fried*
pržen u dubokom ulju *pr*·zhen oo *doo*·baw·kawm *oo*·lyoo *deep-fried*
prženi krumpiri ⓜ pl *pr*·zhe·nee kroom·*pee*·ree *pan-fried potatoes*
pržolica s lukom ⓕ pr·*zhaw*·lee·tsa s *loo*·kawm *pan-fried steak with onions*
pšenica ⓕ *pshe*·nee·tsa *wheat*
puding ⓜ *poo*·deeng *pudding*
punjen *poo*·nyen *stuffed*
punjena teleća prsa ⓕ *poo*·nye·na *te*·le·cha *pr*·sa *stuffed breast of veal*
punjene paprike ⓕ pl *poo*·nye·ne *pa*·pree·ke *capsicums stuffed with rice, tomato paste, parsley, onion & mince-meat then oven baked*
punjene rajčice ⓕ pl *poo*·nye·ne *rai*·chee·tse *tomatoes stuffed with breadcrumbs, garlic & herbs then oven baked*
punjene sipe ⓕ pl *poo*·nye·ne *see*·pe *squid fried with onions & garlic, stuffed with a mixture of breadcrumbs, parsley & egg, then baked in the oven in a tomato, garlic, rosemary & wine sauce*
punjenje ⓝ *poo*·nye·nye *stuffing*
puran ⓜ *poo*·ran *turkey cock*
purica ⓕ *poo*·ree·tsa *turkey hen*
— **s mlincima** s *mleen*·tsee·ma *turkey with* **mlinci** *– a Zagorje speciality often served at festive gatherings*
puževi na Vrbovečki način ⓜ pl *poo*·zhe·vee na vr·baw·*vech*·kee *na*·cheen *snails sautéed with onions then cooked in a sauce made from flour, paprika, meat stock & sour cream*

R

rajčica ⓕ *rai*·chee·tsa *tomato*
rak ⓜ rak *crab*
rak (slatkovodni) ⓜ rak (*slat*·kaw·*vawd*·nee) *crayfish*
raž ⓕ razh *rye*
ražanj ⓜ *ra*·zhan' *grill with a spit*
ražnjići ⓜ pl *razh*·nyee·chee *shish kebabs*
rebarca ⓝ pl re·*bar*·tsa *ribs*
repa ⓕ *re*·pa *turnip*

restani krumpir ⓜ *re*-sta-nee kroom-*peer* roast potato

rezanci ⓜ pl re-*zan*-tsee *pasta*

riba ⓕ *ree*-ba *fish*

riblja juha ⓕ *reeb*-lya yoo-*ha fish chowder made with freshwater fish cooked with onion, chilli, bay leaves & peppercorns to which tomato paste, paprika, vinegar & chopped parsley are added*

riblji paprikaš ⓜ *reeb*-lyee pa-pree-kash *carp or pike stewed in a paprika sauce & served with home-made noodles*

ričet ⓜ *ree*-chet *hearty winter soup containing barley, kidney beans, smoked meat & vegetables – flavoured with parsley root, bay leaf & garlic*

riža ⓕ *ree*-zha *rice*

rižoto ⓜ ree-*zhaw*-taw *risotto – cooked rice dish made from arborio rice & often served with seafood dishes*

— **od liganja** awd lee-*ga*-nya *risotto containing squid, celery root, white wine, tomato paste, olive oil & fish stock – topped with parmesan cheese before serving*

rotkvica ⓕ *rawt*-kvee-tsa *radish*

rožata ⓕ *raw*-zha-ta *Croatian crème caramel with the zing of lemon zest*

Ruska salata ⓕ *roo*-ska sa-*la*-ta *'Russian salad' – salad of boiled potato, carrots, peas, chicken or ham, pickles & boiled eggs smothered in a sauce containing mayonnaise, lemon juice & parsley*

ruzmarin ⓜ *rooz*-ma-reen *rosemary*

S

salama ⓕ sa-*la*-ma *salami*

salata ⓕ sa-*la*-ta *salad*

— **od cikle i kupusa** awd *tsee*-kle ee *koo*-poo-sa *beetroot & cabbage salad containing horseradish, green capsicum, onion, garlic, oil & vinegar*

— **od krastavaca** awd *kra*-sta-va-tsa *cucumber salad*

— **od patlidžana i rajčica** awd *pat*-lee-*ja*-na ee *rai*-chee-tsa *eggplant & tomato salad*

— **od pečenih paprika** awd *pe*-che-neeh *pa*-pree-ka *peeled roasted red peppers sprinkled with garlic, parsley, oil & vinegar*

— **od prokulica** awd *praw*-koo-lee-tse *boiled Brussels sprouts tossed with minced garlic, oil, lemon juice & vinegar*

— **od rajčica** awd *rai*-chee-tsa *tomato salad*

salo ⓝ *sa*-law *lard*

— **na slavonski način** na *sla*-vawn-skee *na*-cheen *carp pieces layered with sliced potato, sprinkled with paprika, smoked bacon & parsley then baked in the oven*

sardela ⓕ sar-*de*-la *pilchard*

sardina ⓕ sar-*dee*-na *sardine*

sardine u ulju ⓕ pl sar-*dee*-ne oo oo-*lyoo sardines in oil*

sarma ⓕ *sar*-ma *sour cabbage leaves stuffed with a mixture of ground meat (beef, pork & bacon), rice & garlic & flavoured with paprika, chilli & bay leaves then topped with a roux*

— **od lišća od loze** awd *leesh*-cha awd *law*-ze *vine leaves wrapped around a filling of minced beef & lamb (or beef & pork), egg & rice flavoured with parsley, paprika & pepper then simmered in water, wine or beef consommé*

savijača ⓕ sa-vee-ya-cha *strudel see* **štrudla**

savijena teletina ⓕ sa-*vee*-ye-na *te*-le-tee-na *pounded veal cutlets rolled around a filling of bacon, carrot & dill pickles then coated in flour & fried*

seljački ručak ⓜ *se*-lyach-kee *roo*-chak *fried diced veal combined with eggplant, tomatoes, capsicum, mushrooms & parsley & seasoned with paprika*

sendvič ⓜ *send*-veech *sandwich*

senf ⓜ senf *mustard*

silvanac ⓜ *seel*-va-nats *well-known white wine from Orahovica*

sipa ⓕ *see*-pa *cuttlefish*

— **punjen pršutom i rižom** *poo*-nyen *pr*-shoo-tawm ee *ree*-zhawm *cuttlefish stuffed with prosciutto & rice – a Dalmatian speciality*

sipica ⓜ *see*-pee-tsa *squid*

sir ⓜ seer *cheese*

skuhan ⓜ *skoo*-han *done (cooked)*

skuša ⓕ *skoo*-sha *mackerel*

sladak *sla*-dak *sweet*

sladoled ⓜ *sla*-daw-led *ice cream*

— **od jagoda** od *ya*-gaw-da *strawberry ice cream*

— **sa šlagom** sa *shla*-gawm *ice cream with whipped cream*

slano ⓝ *sla*-naw salty • savoury

slanutak ⓜ sla-*noo*-tak chickpea

slastičarna ⓕ sla-stee-*char*-na cake shop

slatki kupus ⓜ *slat*-kee koo-poos sweet cabbage

slavonska riblja salata ⓕ *sla*-vawn-ska reeb-lya sa-*la*-ta Slavonian fish salad containing a number of different types of fish (pike, carp etc) poached with herbs & peppercorns then combined with vegetables sautéed in oil & white wine, lemon juice & parsley & served with sour cream

sleđ ⓜ slej herring

smokva ⓕ *smawk*-va fig

sok ⓜ sawk juice

sol ⓕ sawl salt

som ⓜ sawm catfish
— **na dunavski način** na *doo*-nav-skee na-cheen catfish fillets flavoured with lemon juice then rolled in flour, fried & baked with a mixture of fried onions, capsicum, chilli & tomato

sos ⓜ saws dip • gravy • sauce

srednje pečen ⓝ sred-nye pe-chen medium

srnetina ⓕ sr-ne-tee-na venison

stolno vino ⓝ stawl-naw vee-naw table wine

sušen soo-shen dried

sušena svinjska nožica ⓕ soo-she-na sveen'-ska naw-zhee-tsa dried pork hock

svinjetina ⓕ svee-nye-tee-na pork
— **na Đurđevački način** na joor-je-vach-kee na-cheen pork shanks cooked with tomato, green capsicum, smoked sausage, wine & sour cream & garnished with parsley

svinjski gulaš ⓜ sveen'-skee goo-lash pork goulash

svinjski kotlet ⓜ sveen'-skee kawt-let pork cutlet
— **na samoborski način** ⓜ na sa-maw-bawr-skee na-cheen pork chop served with garlic sauce & potato

svinjsko koljeno ⓝ sveen'-skaw kaw-lye-naw pork knuckle

svjež svyezh fresh

Š

šampinjon ⓜ sham-pee-*nyawn* button mushroom

šaran ⓜ sha-ran carp

šaumrole ⓕ pl sha-oom-*raw*-le puff pastry horns baked in the oven then filled with a mixture of whipped egg white, sugar & lemon juice

šećer ⓜ she-cher sugar

škampi ⓜ pl shkam-pee scampi (large prawns)
— **na buzaru** na boo-za-roo scampi stew – a Dalmatian speciality
— **na gradele** na gra-de-le grilled scampi – a Dalmatian speciality

školjke i rakovi ⓜ pl & ⓜ pl shkawl'-ke ee ra-kaw-vee 'shellfish & crabs' – equivalent to the collective term 'shellfish'

šljiva ⓕ shlyee-va plum

šljivovica ⓕ shlyee-vaw-vee-tsa slivovitz (plum brandy)

špageti ⓜ pl shpa-ge-tee spaghetti

šparoga ⓕ shpa-raw-ga asparagus

špinat ⓜ shpee-nat spinach

štrudla ⓕ shtroo-dla strudel – Croatian speciality containing a variety of sweet or savoury fillings such as cheese, buckwheat, potato, pumpkin, walnuts, poppy seed, nettles or fruit
— **s kupusom** s koo-poo-sawm savoury strudel-like pastry filled with shredded cabbage sautéed in oil

štrukle ⓕ pl shtroo-kle biscuit-sized boiled pastry parcels containing fruit fillings
— **s jabukama** s ya-boo-ka-ma **štrukle** filled with apple
— **s trešnjama** s tresh-nya-ma **štrukle** filled with sour cherries

štuka ⓕ shtoo-ka pike

šumska jagoda ⓕ shoom-ska ya-gaw-da wild strawberry

šunka ⓕ shoon-ka cured bacon

šunkarica ⓕ shoon-ka-ree-tsa type of salami made of rolled cured offal

T

tartuf ⓜ tar-*toof* truffle – delicacy from the region of Istria sometimes served shaved over scrambled eggs or risotto

teleća jetra na žaru ⓕ te-le-cha ye-tra na zha-roo grilled calf liver

teleća ragu-juha ⓕ te-le-cha ra-goo-yoo-ha veal ragout

teleće pečenje ⓝ te-le-che pe-che-nye roast veal

teletina ① te·le·tee·na *veal*

teran ⓜ te·ran *Istrian red wine*

tlačenica ① tla·che·nee·tsa *brawn • headcheese*

topljeni sir ⓜ taw·plye·nee seer *melted soft cheese*

torta od oraha ① tawr·ta awd aw·ra·ha *walnut layer cake*

traminac ⓜ tra·mee·nats *well-known dry white wine*

trapist ⓜ tra·peest *type of tasty cheese similar to Port Salut (French cheese)*

travarica ① tra·va·ree·tsa *herbal brandy purportedly with health giving properties*

trešnja ① tresh·nya *cherry*

tripice ① pl tree·pee·tse *tripe*

tučeno vrhnje ① too·che·naw vrh·nye *whipped cream*

tunjevina ① too·nye·vee·na *tuna*

turska kava ① toor·ska ka·va *Turkish coffee – strong brewed coffee popular in Croatia*

tvrdo kuhano jaje ⓝ tvr·daw koo·ha·no yai·ye *hard-boiled egg*

U

ukiseljena svinjetina ① oo·kee·se·lye·na svee·nye·tee·na *pickled pork*

umak ⓜ oo·mak *dip • gravy • sauce*
— **od hrena** awd hre·na *horseradish sauce with sour cream, egg yolk, mustard & lemon juice*
— **od rajčice** awd rai·chee·tse *tomato sauce*

uštipci ⓜ pl oosh·teep·tsee *savoury doughnuts*

V

voće ⓝ vaw·che *fruit*

voćna salata ⓜ vawch·na sa·la·ta *fruit salad*

voćni sladoled ⓜ vawch·nee sla·daw·led *fruit-flavoured ice cream*

Z

začin ⓜ za·cheen *seasoning*

Zagorska pita od tikvica s makom ①
za·gawr·ska pee·ta awd teek·vee·tsa
s ma·kawm *pumpkin pie with poppy seeds served in Zagorje*

Zagorska svatovska juha ① za·gawr·ska
sva·tawv·ska yoo·ha *'Zagorje-style wedding soup' – soup containing veal shanks, celery & parsley roots, kohlrabi, cabbage, onion & carrot flavoured with peppercorns & parsley, with rice, egg yolks & sour cream added*

Zagorske štrukle ① pl za·gawr·ske
shtroo·kle *strudel stuffed with a mixture of cottage cheese, butter, cream & eggs – an appetiser popular in the Zagorje region*

Zagorski džuveč ① za·gawr·skee
joo·vech *chicken pieces baked with mixed vegetables stewed in chicken stock, parsley, celery leaves, garlic, chilli & rice*

Zagorski pureći odrezak ① za·gawr·skee
poo·re·chee aw·dre·zak *turkey cutlets rolled around an omelette-like filling made from fried onions, mushrooms, turkey liver & eggs then dipped in beaten eggs & breadcrumbs & fried*

Zagrebački odrezak ⓜ za·gre·bach·kee
aw·dre·zak *veal stuffed with ham & cheese then fried in breadcrumbs*

zec na hvarski način ⓜ zets na hvar·skee
na·cheen *from the island of Hvar, this dish contains rabbit marinated in a mixture of vinegar, oil, red wine, celery, garlic, minced onion, thyme, rosemary, peppercorns & cloves then browned & braised in port*

zelena maslina ① ze·le·na ma·slee·na *green olive*

zelena paprika ① ze·le·na pa·pree·ka *green capsicum • green bell pepper*

zelena salata ① ze·le·na sa·la·ta *green salad • lettuce*

zubatac ⓜ zoo·ba·tats *dentex (fish)*

Ž

žaba ① zha·ba *frog – frogs legs are a popular delicacy sometimes found in a brodet or stew with eels*

žemička ① zhe·meech·ka *type of bread roll*

žgvacet od purana ⓜ zhgva·tset awd
poo·ra·na *fried cubed turkey combined with onion, garlic & tomato then simmered until tender in white wine, marjoram & basil – an Istrian specialty*

emergencies

hitni slučajevi

Help!	*Upomoć!*	oo·paw·mawch
Stop!	*Stanite!*	sta·nee·te
Go away!	*Maknite se!*	mak·nee·te se
Thief!	*Lopov!*	law·pawv
Fire!	*Požar!*	paw·zhar
Watch out!	*Pazite!*	pa·zee·te

It's an emergency.
Imamo hitan slučaj. — ee·ma·maw hee·tan sloo·chai

There's been an accident.
Desila se nezgoda. — de·see·la se nez·gaw·da

Call the police.
Nazovite policiju. — na·zaw·vee·te paw·lee·tsee·yoo

Call a doctor.
Zovite liječnika. — zaw·vee·te lee·yech·nee·ka

Call an ambulance.
Zovite hitnu pomoć. — zaw·vee·te heet·noo paw·mawch

Could you please help?
Molim vas, možete li mi pomoći? — maw·leem vas maw·zhe·te lee mee paw·maw·chee

Can I use your phone?
Mogu li koristiti vaš telefon? — maw·goo lee kaw·ree·stee·tee vash te·le·fawn

I'm lost.
Izgubio/Izgubila sam se. m/f — eez·goo·bee·aw/eez·goo·bee·la sam se

Where are the toilets?
Gdje se nalaze nužnici? — gdye se na·la·ze noozh·nee·tsee

Is it safe at night?
Je li bezopasno noću? — ye lee bez·aw·pa·snaw naw·choo

police

Where's the police station?
Gdje se nalazi   gdye se *na*·la·zee
policijska stanica?   paw·*lee*·tseey·ska *sta*·nee·tsa

I want to report an offence.
Želim prijaviti prekršaj.   *zhe*·leem pree·*ya*·vee·tee *pre*·kr·shai

It was him.
On je to uradio.   awn ye taw oo·*ra*·dee·aw

It was her.
Ona je to uradila.   *aw*·na ye taw oo·*ra*·dee·la

I've been ...	*Ja sam*	ya sam
	bio/bila ... m/f	*bee*·aw/*bee*·la ...
He's been ...	*On je bio ...*	awn ye *bee*·aw ...
She's been ...	*Ona je bila ...*	*aw*·na ye *bee*·la ...
assaulted	*napadnut/*	*na*·pad·noot
	napadnuta m/f	*na*·pad·noo·ta
raped	*silovan/*	*see*·law·van
	silovana m/f	*see*·law·va·na
robbed	*opljačkan/*	*awp*·lyach·kan
	opljačkana m/f	*awp*·lyach·ka·na

He tried to	*On me je*	awn me ye
... me.	*pokušao ...*	*paw*·koo·sha·aw ...
She tried to	*Ona me je*	*aw*·na me ye
... me.	*pokušala ...*	*paw*·koo·sha·la ...
assault	*napasti*	*na*·pa·stee
rape	*silovati*	see·*law*·va·tee
rob	*opljačkati*	*awp*·lyach·ka·tee

I've lost my ...	*Izgubio/*	eez·*goo*·bee·aw/
	Izgubila sam ... m/f	eez·*goo*·bee·la sam ...
backpack	*svoj ranac*	svoy *ra*·nats
bags	*svoje torbe*	svoy·e *tawr*·be
credit card	*svoju kreditnu*	svoy·oo kre·deet·noo
	karticu	kar·tee·tsoo
jewellery	*svoj nakit*	svoy *na*·keet
money	*svoj novac*	svoy *naw*·vats
passport	*svoju*	svoy·oo
	putovnicu	poo·*tawv*·nee·tsoo
travellers	*svoje putničke*	svoy·e *poot*·neech·ke
cheques	*čekove*	che·kaw·ve

My ... was/were stolen.
Ukrali su mi ...   oo·kra·lee soo mee ...

the police may say ...		
You're charged with ...	*Optuženi ste ...*	*awp*·too·zhe·nee ste ...
He/She is charged with ...	*On/Ona je optužen/ optužena ...* m/f	awn/*aw*·na ye *awp*·too·zhen/ *awp*·too·zhe·na ...
assault	*tvornim napadom*	*tvawr*·neem *na*·pa·dawm
disturbing the peace	*narušavanjem reda*	na·roo·*sha*·va·nyem *re*·da
not having a visa	*nedostatkom vize*	ne·daw·*stat*·kawm *vee*·ze
overstaying your visa	*ostankom u zemlji po isteku vize*	*aw*·stan·kawm oo *zem*·lyee paw ee·ste·koo *vee*·ze
possession (of illegal substances)	*posjedovanjem (ilegalnih tvari)*	*paw*·sye·daw·va·nyem (*ee*·le·gal·neeh *tva*·ree)
shoplifting	*krađom u prodavaonici*	*kra*·jawm oo praw·da·va·*aw*·nee·tsee
theft	*krađom*	*kra*·jawm

What am I accused of?
Čime me teretite?   chee·me me *te*·re·tee·te

I'm sorry.
Žao mi je.   zha·aw mee ye

I (don't) understand.
Ja (ne) razumijem.   ya (ne) ra·*zoo*·mee·yem

I didn't realise I was doing anything wrong.
Nisam bio svjesan   nee·sam bee·aw svye·san
da radim išta krivo. m   da *ra*·deem *eesh*·ta *kree*·vaw
Nisam bila svjesna   nee·sam bee·la svyes·na
da radim išta krivo. f   da *ra*·deem *eesh*·ta *kree*·vaw

I didn't do it.
Ja to nisam uradio/   ya taw nee·sam oo·*ra*·dee·aw/
uradila. m/f   oo·*ra*·dee·la

Can I pay an on-the-spot fine?
Mogu li platiti   maw·goo lee *pla*·tee·tee
novčanu globu na   nawv·cha·noo *glaw*·boo na
licu mjesta?   lee·tsoo mye·sta

I want to contact my embassy/consulate.
Želim stupiti u   zhe·leem stoo·pee·tee oo
kontakt sa svojom   kawn·takt sa svoy·awm
ambasadom/   am·ba·*sa*·dawm/
konzulatom.   kawn·zoo·*la*·tawm

Can I make a phone call?
Mogu li obaviti   maw·goo lee aw·ba·vee·tee
telefonski poziv?   te·*le*·fawn·skee paw·zeev

Can I have a lawyer (who speaks English)?
Mogu li dobiti   maw·goo lee daw·bee·tee
odvjetnika (koji   awd·vyet·nee·ka (koy·ee
govori engleski)?   gaw·vaw·ree en·gle·skee)

This drug is for personal use.
Ova droga je za   aw·va *draw*·ga ye za
osobnu upotrebu.   aw·sawb·noo oo·paw·tre·boo

I have a prescription for this drug.
Ja imam recept   ya ee·mam *re*·tsept
za ovaj lijek.   za aw·vai *lee*·yek

doctor

liječnik

Where's the	Gdje je	gdye ye
nearest ...?	najbliži/a ...? m/f	nai·blee·zhee/a ...
(night) chemist	(noćna)	(nawch·na)
	ljekarna f	lye·kar·na
dentist	zubar m	zoo·bar
doctor	liječnik m	lee·yech·neek
emergency	odjel hitne	aw·dyel heet·ne
department	pomoći m	paw·maw·chee
hospital	bolnica f	bawl·nee·tsa
medical centre	medicinski	me·dee·tseen·skee
	centar m	tsen·tar
optometrist	optičar m	awp·tee·char

I need a doctor (who speaks English).
Trebam liječnika   tre·bam lee·yech·nee·ka
(koji govori engleski).   (koy·ee gaw·vaw·ree en·gle·skee)

Could I see a female doctor?
Mogu li dobiti   maw·goo lee daw·bee·tee
ženskog liječnika?   zhen·skawg lee·yech·nee·ka

Could the doctor come here?
Može li liječnik   maw·zhe lee lee·yech·neek
doći ovamo?   daw·chee aw·va·maw

Is there an after-hours emergency number?
Postoji li noćni broj   paw·stoy·ee lee nawch·nee broy
telefona za hitne   te·le·faw·na za heet·ne
slučajeve?   sloo·chai·e·ve

I've run out of my medication.
Nestalo mi je lijekova.   ne·sta·law mee ye lee·*ye*·kaw·va

This is my usual medicine.
Ovo je moj   aw·vaw ye moy
uobičajeni lijek.   oo·aw·*bee*·chai·e·nee lee·*yek*

My child weighs (20 kilos).
Moje dijete teži   moy·e dee·*ye*·te te·zhee
(dvadeset kila).   (dva·de·set *kee*·la)

What's the correct dosage?
Koja je točna doza?   koy·a ye *tawch*·na *daw*·za

I don't want a blood transfusion.
Ne želim transfuziju krvi.   ne *zhe*·leem trans·*foo*·zee·yoo *kr*·vee

Please use a new syringe.
Molim upotrijebite   *maw*·leem oo·paw·tree·*ye*·bee·te
novu špricu.   *naw*·voo shpree·tsoo

I have my own syringe.
Ja imam svoju špricu.   ya *ee*·mam *svoy*·oo shpree·tsoo

I've been vaccinated against (tetanus).
Cijepljen/Cijepljena sam   tsee·*ye*·plyen/tsee·*ye*·plye·na sam
protiv (tetanusa). m/f   *praw*·teev (te·ta·noo·sa)

He's been vaccinated against (hepatitis A/B/C).
On je cijepljen protiv   awn ye tsee·*ye*·plyen *praw*·teev
(hepatitisa A/B/C).   (he·pa·*tee*·tee·sa a/be/tse)

She's been vaccinated against (typhoid).
Ona je cijepljena   *aw*·na ye tsee·*ye*·plye·na
protiv (tifusa).   *praw*·teev tee·foo·sa

My prescription is …
Moj recept je za …   moy *re*·tsept ye za …

How much will it cost?
Koliko će to stajati?   kaw·*lee*·kaw che taw *stai*·a·tee

Can I have a receipt for my insurance?
Mogu li dobiti račun   *maw*·goo lee *daw*·bee·tee *ra*·choon
za moje osiguranje?   za moy·e aw·see·goo·*ra*·nye

I need new …   *Trebam nove …*   *tre*·bam *naw*·ve …
   contact lenses   *kontakt leće*   *kawn*·takt *le*·che
   glasses   *naočale*   *na*·aw·cha·le

symptoms & conditions

I'm sick.
Ja sam bolestan/
bolesna. m/f

ya sam *baw*·le·stan/
baw·le·sna

My friend is (very) sick.
Moj prijatelj
je (vrlo) bolestan. m
Moja prijateljica
je (vrlo) bolesna. f

moy *pree*·ya·tel'
ye (*vr*·law) *baw*·le·stan
moy·a pree·ya·te·lyee·tsa
ye (*vr*·law) *baw*·les·na

My child is (very) sick.
Moje dijete
je (vrlo) bolesno.

moy·e dee·*ye*·te
ye (*vr*·law) *baw*·le·snaw

He/She is	On/Ona trenutno	awn/*aw*·na *tre*·noot·naw
having a/an …	ima …	*ee*·ma …
allergic	*alergičnu*	a·*ler*·geech·noo
reaction	*reakciju*	re·*ak*·tsee·yoo
asthma attack	*napad astme*	*na*·pad *ast*·me
baby	*trudove*	*troo*·daw·ve
epileptic fit	*napad epilepsije*	*na*·pad e·pee·*lep*·see·ye
heart attack	*srčani napad*	*sr*·cha·nee *na*·pad
I've been …	Ja sam …	ya sam …
He's been …	On je …	awn ye …
She's been …	Ona je …	*aw*·na ye …
injured	*povrijeđen/*	paw·vree·*ye*·jen
	povrijeđena m/f	paw·vree·*ye*·je·na
vomiting	*povraćao/*	paw·vra·cha·aw/
	povraćala m/f	paw·vra·cha·la

the doctor may say ...

What's the problem?
Što nije u redu?   shtaw *nee*·ye oo *re*·doo

Where does it hurt?
Gdje vas boli?   gdye vas *baw*·lee

Do you have a temperature?
Da li imate temperaturu?   da lee *ee*·ma·te tem·pe·ra·*too*·roo

How long have you been like this?
Koliko dugo ste   kaw·*lee*·kaw *doo*·gaw ste
u ovom stanju?   oo *aw*·vawm *sta*·nyoo

Have you had this before?
Da li ste patili od   da lee ste *pa*·tee·lee awd
ovoga u prošlosti?   *aw*·vaw·ga oo *prawsh*·law·stee

Are you sexually active?
Da li ste spolno aktivni?   da lee ste *spawl*·naw ak·teev·nee

Have you had unprotected sex?
Da li ste imali   da lee ste ee·ma·lee
nezaštićeni   ne·*zash*·tee·che·nee
spolni odnos?   *spawl*·nee *awd*·naws

How long are you travelling for?
Koliko dugo ćete   kaw·*lee*·kaw *doo*·gaw *che*·te
putovati?   poo·*taw*·va·tee

You need to be admitted to hospital.
Trebate ići u   *tre*·ba·te *ee*·chee oo
bolnicu.   *bawl*·nee·tsoo

Do you ...?	Da li ...?	da lee ...
drink	pijete	*pee*·ye·te
smoke	pušite	*poo*·shee·te
take drugs	uzimate droge	oo·zee·ma·te *draw*·ge

Are you ...?	Jeste li ...?	*ye*·ste lee ...
allergic to	alergični	a·*ler*·geech·nee
anything	na išta	na *eesh*·ta
on medication	na nekim	na *ne*·keem
	lijekovima	lee·ye·*kaw*·vee·ma

180

health

the doctor may say ...

You should have it checked when you go home.

Trebate otići na   tre·ba·te aw·tee·chee na
kontrolu kada   kawn·traw·loo ka·da
odete kući.   aw·dete koo·chee

You should return home for treatment.

Trebate se vratiti   tre·ba·te se vra·tee·tee
kući na liječenje.   koo·chee na lee·ye·che·nye

You're a hypochondriac.

Vi ste hipohondar.   vee ste hee·paw·hawn·dar

I feel ...	Osjećam se ...	aw·sye·cham se ...
anxious	napeto	na·pe·taw
better	bolje	baw·lye
depressed	potišteno	paw·teesh·te·naw
dizzy	ošamućeno	aw·sha·moo·che·naw
hot and cold	toplo i hladno	taw·plaw ee hlad·naw
nauseous	mučno u želudcu	mooch·naw oo zhe·lood·tsoo
shivery	drhtavo	drh·ta·vaw
strange	čudno	chood·naw
weak	slabo	sla·baw
worse	gore	gaw·re

It hurts here.

Boli me ovdje.   baw·lee me awv·dye

I'm dehydrated.

Ja sam dehidrirao/   ya sam de·hee·dree·ra·aw/
dehidrirala. m/f   de·hee·dree·ra·la

I can't sleep.

Ne mogu spavati.   ne maw·goo spa·va·tee

I think it's the medication I'm on.

Mislim da je to od   mee·sleem da ye taw awd
lijekova koje uzimam.   lee·ye·kaw·va koy·e oo·zee·mam

I'm on medication for ...

Ja sam na   ya sam na
lijekovima za ...   lee·ye·kaw·vee·ma za ...

He/She is on medication for …
On/Ona je na   awn/*aw*·na ye na
lijekovima za …   lee·*ye*·kaw·vee·ma za …

I have (a/an) …
Imam …   *ee*·mam …

He/She has (a/an) …
On/Ona ima …   awn/*aw*·na ee·ma …

I've recently had (a/an) …
Nedavno sam   *ne*·dav·naw sam
imao/imala … m/f   ee·ma·aw/*ee*·ma·la …

He/She has recently had (a/an) …
On/Ona je nedavno   awn/*aw*·na ye *ne*·dav·naw
imao/imala … m/f   ee·ma·aw/*ee*·ma·la …

asthma	*astma* f	*ast*·ma
cold (noun)	*prehlada* f	*pre*·hla·da
constipation	*zatvorenje* n	zat·vaw·*re*·nye
cough (noun)	*kašalj* m	*ka*·shal'
dehydration	*dehidratacija* f	de·hee·dra·*ta*·tsee·ya
diabetes	*dijabetes* m	dee·ya·*be*·tes
diarrhoea	*proljev* m	*pro*·lyev
ear infection	*upala uha* f	oo·pa·la *oo*·ha
fever	*groznica* f	*graw*·znee·tsa
flu	*gripa* f	*gree*·pa
headache	*glavobolja* f	gla·*vaw*·baw·lya
heatstroke	*sunčanica* f	sun·*cha*·nee·tsa
hypothermia	*hipotermija* f	hee·paw·*ter*·mee·ya
jellyfish sting	*opeklina od*	*aw*·pe·klee·na awd
	meduze f	me·*doo*·ze
muscle cramps	*grčenje mišića* n	gr·che·nye mee·*shee*·cha
nausea	*mučnina* f	mooch·*nee*·na
sore throat	*grlobolja* f	gr·*law*·baw·lya
sunburn	*opekline od*	*aw*·pe·klee·ne awd
	sunca f pl	*soon*·tsa

I've been ...	*Mene je ujela ...*	*me·ne ye oo·ye·la ...*
bitten by a snake	*zmija*	*zmee·ya*
stung by a bee	*pčela*	*pche·la*
stung by a wasp	*osa*	*aw·sa*

I ...	*Ja sam ...*	ya sam ...
removed a tick	*odstranio/ odstranila krpelja* m/f	*awd·stra·nee·aw/ awd·stra·nee·la kr·pe·lya*
stepped on a sea urchin	*stao/stala na morskog ježa* m/f	*sta·aw/sta·la na mawr·skawg ye·zha*

women's health

zdravlje žena

(I think) I'm pregnant.
Ja (mislim da) sam trudna.   ya (mee·sleem da) sam trood·na

I'm on the pill.
Ja sam na   ya sam na
antibaby-pilulama.   an·tee·bey·bee·pee·loo·la·ma

I haven't had my period for (six) weeks.
Nisam imala   nee·sam ee·ma·la
mjesečnicu već   mye·sech·nee·tsoo vech
(šest) tjedana.   (shest) tye·da·na

I've noticed a lump here.
Primjetila sam   pree·mye·tee·la sam
izraslinu ovdje.   eez·ra·slee·noo awv·dye

I need ...	*Trebam ...*	*tre·bam ...*
contraception	*sredstvo za sprječavanje trudnoće*	*sreds·tvaw za sprye·cha·va·nye trood·naw·che*
the morning-after pill	*hitnu kontracepciju*	*heet·noo kawn·tra·tsep·tsee·yoo*
a pregnancy test	*test na trudnoću*	test na trood·naw·choo

the doctor may say ...

Are you using contraception?
Da li koristite sredstva   da lee *kaw*·ree·stee·te *sreds*·tva
za sprječavanje   za sprye·*cha*·va·nye
trudnoće?   trood·*naw*·che

Are you menstruating?
Da li menstruirate?   da lee men·stroo·*ee*·ra·te

Are you pregnant?
Jeste li trudni?   *ye*·ste lee trood·nee

When did you last have your period?
Kada ste zadnji put   *ka*·da ste *zad*·nyee poot
imali mjesečnicu?   ee·ma·lee *mye*·sech·nee·tsoo

You're pregnant.
Vi ste trudni.   vee ste trood·nee

alternative treatments

alternativni oblici liječenja

I prefer ...	*Ja bih radije ...*	ya beeh *ra*·dee·ye ...
Can I see	*Mogu li*	*maw*·goo lee
someone who	*posjetiti*	*paw*·sye·tee·tee
practices ...?	*nekoga tko*	ne·*kaw*·ga tkaw
	vrši praksu ...?	*vr*·shee *prak*·soo ...
acupuncture	*akopunkture*	a·kaw·poonk·*too*·re
naturopathy	*naturopatije*	na·too·raw·pa·tee·ye
reflexology	*refleksologije*	re·flek·saw·*law*·gee·ye

I don't use (Western medicine).
Ja ne koristim   ya ne kaw·*ree*·steem
(Zapadnjačku medicinu).   (za·pad·nyach·koo me·dee·*tsee*·noo)

allergies

I'm allergic to ...	*Ja sam alergičan/*	ya sam a-*ler*-gee-chan/
	alergična na ... m/f	a-*ler*-geech-na na ...
He/She is	*On/Ona je*	awn/*aw*-na ye
allergic to ...	*alergičan/*	a-*ler*-gee-chan/
	alergična na ... m/f	a-*ler*-geech-na na ...
antibiotics	*antibiotike*	*an*-tee-bee-*aw*-tee-ke
anti-inflammatories	*lijekove protiv upale*	lee-*ye*-kaw-ve *praw*-teev oo-pa-le
aspirin	*aspirin*	a-*spee*-reen
bees	*pčele*	*pche*-le
codeine	*kodein*	kaw-*de*-een
penicillin	*penicilin*	pe-*nee*-*tsee*-leen
pollen	*pelud*	*pe*-lood
sulphur-based drugs	*lijekove koji sadrže sumpor*	lee-*ye*-kaw-ve *koy*-ee *sa*-dr-zhe *soom*-pawr

I have a skin allergy.
   Ja imam kožnu alergiju.   ya *ee*-mam *kawzh*-noo a-*ler*-gee-yoo

I'm on a special diet.
   Ja sam na posebnoj dijeti.   ya sam na *paw*-seb-noy dee-*ye*-tee

I'm allergic to (gluten).
   Ja sam alergičan/   ya sam a-*ler*-gee-chan/
   alergična na (gluten). m/f   a-*ler*-geech-na na (*gloo*-ten)

antihistamines	*antihistaminici* m pl	*an*-tee-hee-sta-*mee*-nee-tsee
inhaler	*inhalator* m	een-ha-*la*-tawr
injection	*injekcija* f	ee-*nyek*-tsee-ya

For more food-related allergies, see **vegetarian & special meals**, page 162.

parts of the body

My ... hurts.
Moj/Moja/Moje ... boli. m/f/n   moy/moy·a/moy·e ... baw·lee

I can't move my ...
Moj ... je nepomičan. m   moy ... ye ne·paw·mee·chan
Moja ... je nepomična. f   moy·a ... ye ne·paw·meech·na
Moje ... je nepomično. n   moy·e ... ye ne·paw·meech·naw

I have a cramp in my ...
Grči mi se ...   gr·chee mee se ...

My ... is swollen.
Moj ... je natekao. m   moy ... ye na·te·ka·aw
Moja ... je natekla. f   moy·a ... ye na·te·kla
Moje ... je nateklo. n   moy·e ... ye na·te·klaw

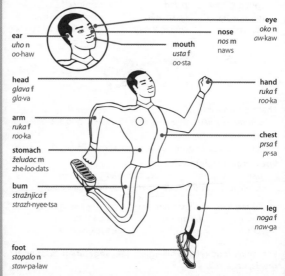

eye
oko n
aw·kaw

nose
nos m
naws

ear
uho n
oo·haw

mouth
usta f
oo·sta

head
glava f
gla·va

hand
ruka f
roo·ka

arm
ruka f
roo·ka

chest
prsa f
pr·sa

stomach
želudac m
zhe·loo·dats

bum
stražnjica f
strazh·nyee·tsa

leg
noga f
naw·ga

foot
stopalo n
staw·pa·law

chemist

I need something for (a headache).
Trebam nešto za   tre·bam nesh·taw za
(glavobolju).   (gla·vaw·baw·lyoo)

Do I need a prescription for (antihistamines)?
Da li mi treba recept   da lee mee tre·ba re·tsept
za (antihistaminike)?   za (an·tee·hee·sta·mee·nee·ke)

I have a prescription.
Ja imam recept.   ya ee·mam re·tsept

How many times a day?
Koliko puta na dan?   kaw·lee·kaw poo·ta na dan

Will it make me drowsy?
Hoće li me to napraviti   haw·che lee me taw na·pra·vee·tee
pospanim/pospanom? m/f   paw·spa·neem/paw·spa·nawm

antiseptic	*antiseptik* m	an·tee·sep·teek
contraceptives	*sredstva za*	sreds·tva za
	sprječavanje	sprye·cha·va·nye
	neželjene	ne·zhe·lye·ne
	trudnoće n pl	trood·naw·che
painkillers	*tablete protiv*	ta·ble·te praw·teev
	bolova f pl	baw·law·va
rehydration salts	*soli za*	saw·lee za
	rehidrataciju f	re·hee·dra·ta·tsee·yoo
thermometer	*toplomjer* m	taw·plaw·myer

---

listen for ...

dva poo·ta dnev·naw (ooz hra·noo)
Dva puta dnevno (uz hranu).   **Twice a day (with food).**

maw·ra·te oo·ze·tee chee·ta·voo praw·pee·sa·noo daw·zoo
lee·ye·ka paw oo·poo·ta·ma
Morate uzeti čitavu propisanu   **You must complete**
dozu lijeka po uputama.   **the course.**

dentist

I have a ...	Ja imam ...	ya ee·mam ...
broken tooth	razbijen zub	ra·zbee·yen zoob
cavity	karijes	ka·ree·yes
toothache	zubobolju	zoo·baw·baw·lyoo

I've lost a filling.
Ispala mi je plomba.   ee·spa·la mee ye *plawm*·ba

My dentures are broken.
Razbilo mi se   ra·zbee·law mee se
umjetno zubalo.   oo·myet·naw zoo·ba·law

My gums hurt.
Bole me desni.   *baw*·le me *de*·snee

I don't want it extracted.
Ne želim da ga vadite.   ne *zhe*·leem da ga va·dee·te

Ouch!
Jao!   ya·aw

I need (a/an) ...	Treba mi ...	tre·ba mee ...
anaesthetic	anestetik	a·ne·ste·teek
filling	plomba	plawm·ba

---

listen for ...

shee·rawm awt·vaw·ree·te oo·sta
Širom otvorite usta.   **Open wide.**

aw·vaw ne·che nee·ma·law baw·lye·tee
Ovo neće nimalo boljeti.   **This won't hurt a bit.**

za·gree·zee·te aw·vaw
Zagrizite ovo.   **Bite down on this.**

ne·moy·te se mee·tsa·tee
Nemojte se micati.   **Don't move.**

ee·spe·ree·te
Isperite!   **Rinse!**

A

Nouns in the dictionary have their gender indicated by ⓜ, ① or ⑪. If it's a plural noun you'll also see pl. When a word that could be either a noun or a verb has no gender indicated, it's a verb.

Nouns and adjectives are in the nominative case. You'll be understood if you just pick words out of this dictionary, but if you'd like to know more about case, see the **a–z phrasebuilder**, page 21.

Adjectives in the dictionary are given in the masculine form only. For an explanation of how to form feminine and neuter adjectives, refer to the **a–z phrasebuilder**, page 16.

Verbs are mostly given in two forms: perfective and imperfective. See the **a–z phrasebuilder**, page 17 for an explanation of these terms and when to use which form. Perfective and imperfective forms are either separated by a slash (with the perfective form given first) or consist of a root imperfective form to which a bracketed prefix is added to form the perfective. For example, the verb 'give' has the forms *dati/ davati* da·tee/da·va·tee with the first form being the perfective form and the second the imperfective. The verb 'call' is represented as *(po)zvati* (paw·)zva·tee which has the perfective form *pozvati* and the imperfective form *zvati*. Where two syllables are stressed in the transliteration, eg *(paw·)zva·tee* it means that once you add the prefix to form the perfective, the stress shifts to the prefix.

Where only one form of a verb is given (not all verbs have both forms) the abbreviations perf and imp have been used to identify whether they are perfective or imperfective.

A

aboard (boat, plane) *ukrcan na* oo·kr·tsan na
aboard (train, bus) *u* oo
abortion *pobačaj* ⓜ paw·ba·chai
about *o • oko • u vezi • zbog* aw • aw·kaw • oo ve·zee • zbawg
above *iznad* eez·nad
abroad *u inozemstvu* oo ee·naw·zemst·voo
accident *nezgoda* ① nez·gaw·da
accommodation *smještaj* ⓜ smye·shtai
account (bank) *račun* ⓜ ra·choon
across *kroz • preko* krawz • pre·kaw
activist *aktivist* ⓜ ak·tee·veest
actor *glumac* ⓜ gloo·mats
acupuncture *akopunktura* ① a·kaw·poonk·too·ra
adaptor *konverter* ⓜ kawn·ver·ter
addiction *ovisnost* ① aw·vee·snawst
address *adresa* ① a·dre·sa

administration *uprava* ① oo·pra·va
admission (price) *ulaznica (cijena)* ① oo·laz·nee·tsa (tsee·ye·na)
admit (allow) *dozvoliti/dozvoljavati* dawz·vaw·lee·tee/ dawz·vaw·lya·va·tee
admit (confess) *priznati/priznavati* pree·zna·tee/pree·zna·va·tee
Adriatic Coast *Jadranska obala* ① ya·dran·ska aw·ba·la
Adriatic Sea *Jadransko more* ⑪ ya·dran·skaw maw·re
adult *odrasla osoba* ① aw·dra·sla aw·saw·ba
advertisement *oglas* ⓜ aw·glas
advice *savjet* ⓜ sa·vyet
aerobics *aerobik* ⓜ a·e·raw·beek
aeroplane *zrakoplov* ⓜ zra·kaw·plawv
Africa *Afrika* ① a·free·ka
after *iza • po • poslije* ee·za • paw • paw·slee·ye

(this) afternoon *(ovo) poslijepodne* ⓝ
(aw·vaw) paw·slee·ye·pawd·ne
aftershave *losion za upotrebu poslije
brijanja* ⓜ law·see·awn za
oo·paw·tre·boo paw·slee·ye bree·ya·nya
again *opet* aw·pet
age (person) *uzrast* ⓜ ooz·rast
(three days) ago *(tri dana) prije* (tree
da·na) pree·ye
agree *složiti/slagati se*
slaw·zhee·tee/sla·ga·tee se
agriculture *poljodjelstvo* ⓝ
paw·lyaw·dyel·stvaw
ahead *naprijed* na·pree·yed
AIDS *SIDA* ⓕ see·da
air *zrak* ⓜ zrak
air-conditioned *klimatiziran*
klee·ma·tee·zee·ran
air-conditioning *klima* ⓕ klee·ma
airline *zrakoplovna tvrtka* ⓕ
zra·kaw·plawv·na tvr·tka
airmail *zračna pošta* ⓕ zrach·na pawsh·ta
airplane *zrakoplov* ⓜ zra·kaw·plawv
airport *zračna luka* ⓕ zrach·na loo·ka
airport tax *porez na zračni prijevoz* ⓜ
paw·rez na zrach·nee pree·ye·vawz
aisle (plane etc) *prolaz između sjedišta* ⓜ
praw·laz eez·me·joo sye·deesh·ta
alarm clock *budilica* ⓕ boo·dee·lee·tsa
alcohol *alcohol* ⓜ al·kaw·hawl
all *sve* sve
allergy *alergija* ⓕ a·ler·gee·ya
alley *uska ulica* ⓕ oo·ska oo·lee·tsa
almond *badem* ⓜ ba·dem
almost *skoro* skaw·raw
alone *sam* sam
already *već* vech
also *također* ta·kaw·jer
altar *oltar* ⓜ awl·tar
altitude *visina* ⓕ vee·see·na
always *uvijek* oo·vee·yek
ambassador *veleposlanik* ⓜ
ve·le·paw·sla·neek
ambulance *hitna pomoć* ⓕ
heet·na paw·mawch
American football *američki nogomet* ⓜ
a·me·reech·kee naw·gaw·met
amphitheatre *amfiteatar* ⓜ am·fee·te·a·tar
anaemia *anemija* ⓕ a·ne·mee·ya
anarchist *anarhist* ⓜ a·nar·heest
ancient *antički* an·teech·kee
and *i* ee
angry *ljutit* lyoo·teet

animal *životinja* ⓕ zhee·vaw·tee·nya
ankle *gležanj* ⓜ gle·zhan'
another *drugi* droo·gee
answer *odgovor* ⓜ awd·gaw·vawr
ant *mrav* ⓜ mrav
antibiotics *antibiotici* ⓜ pl
an·tee·bee·aw·tee·tsee
antinuclear *antinuklearni*
an·tee·noo·kle·ar·nee
antique *antikvitet* ⓜ an·tee·kvee·tet
antiseptic *antiseptik* ⓜ an·tee·sep·teek
any *bilo koji* bee·law koy·ee
apartment *stan* ⓜ stan
appendix (body) *slijepo crijevo* ⓝ
slee·ye·paw tsree·ye·vaw
apple *jabuka* ⓕ ya·boo·ka
appointment *sastanak* ⓜ sa·sta·nak
apricot *kajsija* ⓕ kai·see·ya
April *travanj* ⓜ tra·van'
apse *apsida* ⓕ a·psee·da
archaeological *arheološki* ⓜ
ar·he·aw·lawsh·kee
architect *arhitekt* ⓜ ar·hee·tekt
architecture *arhitektura* ⓕ ar·hee·tek·too·ra
argue *(po)svađati se* (paw')sva·ja·tee se
arm *ruka* ⓕ roo·ka
aromatherapy *aromaterapija* ⓕ
a·raw·ma·te·ra·pe·ya
arrest *uhititi* perf oo·hee·tee·tee
arrivals *dolasci* ⓜ pl daw·las·tsee
arrive *stići/stizati* stee·chee/stee·za·tee
art *umjetnost* ⓕ oo·myet·nawst
art gallery *galerija* ⓕ ga·le·ree·ya
artist *umjetnik/umjetnica* ⓜ/ⓕ
oo·myet·neek/oo·myet·nee·tsa
ashtray *pepeljara* ⓕ pe·pe·lya·ra
Asia *Azija* ⓕ a·zee·ya
ask (a question) *(u)pitati* (oo·)pee·ta·tee
ask (for something) *(za)tražiti*
(za·)tra·zhee·tee
asparagus *šparoga* ⓕ shpa·raw·ga
aspirin *aspirin* ⓜ a·spee·reen
asthma *astma* ⓕ ast·ma
at *kod · pri · na · u* kawd · pree · na · oo
athletics *atletika* ⓕ at·le·tee·ka
atmosphere *atmosfera* ⓕ at·maw·sfe·ra
aubergine *patlidžan* ⓜ pa·tlee·jan
August *kolovoz* ⓜ kaw·law·vawz
aunt *tetka* ⓕ tet·ka
Australia *Australija* ⓕ a·oo·stra·lee·ya
Australian Rules Football *Australski nogomet* ⓜ a·oo·stral·skee
naw·gaw·met

Austria *Austrija* ① *a*-oo-stree-ya
Austro-Hungarian Empire
Austru-Ugarsko carstvo ⑩
a-oo-straw-oo-gar-skaw *tsar*-stvaw
automated teller machine (ATM)
bankovni automat ⑩ *ban*-kawv-nee
a-oo-*taw*-mat
autumn *jesen* ① *ye*-sen
avenue *avenija* ① *a*-ve-*nee*-ya
awful *užasan* oo-zha-san

B

B&W (film) *crno-bijeli (film)*
tsr-naw-*bee*-*ye*-lee (feelm)
baby *beba* ① *be*-ba
baby food *hrana za bebe* ① *hra*-na za *be*-be
baby powder *puder za bebe* ⑩ *poo*-der
za *be*-be
baby-sitter *dadilja* ① *da*-dee-lya
back (body) *leđa* ① *le*-ja
back (position) *pozadina* ①
paw-za-dee-na
backpack *ranac* ⑩ *ra*-nats
bacon *slanina* ① *sla*-nee-na
bad *loš* lawsh
bag *torba* ① *tawr*-ba
baggage *prtljaga* ① prt-*lya*-ga
baggage allowance *dozvoljena*
količina prtljage ① *dawz*-vaw-lye-na
kaw-lee-chee-na prt-*lya*-ge
baggage claim *šalter za podizanje*
prtljage ⑩ *shal*-ter za *paw*-dee-za-nye
prt-*lya*-ge
bakery *pekara* ① *pe*-ka-ra
balance (account) *saldo* ⑩ *sal*-daw
balcony *balkon* ⑩ *bal*-kawn
(the) Balkans *Balkan* ⑩ *bal*-kan
ball *lopta* ① *lawp*-ta
ballet *balet* ⑩ ba-*let*
banana *banana* ① ba-*na*-na
band (music) *grupa* ① *groo*-pa
bandage *zavoj* ⑩ *za*-voy
Band-aid *flaster* ⑩ *fla*-ster
bank (institution) *banka* ① *ban*-ka
bank account *bankovni račun* ⑩
ban-kawv-nee *ra*-choon
banknote *novčanica* ① nawv-*cha*-nee-tsa
baptism *krštenje* ① krsh-*te*-nye
bar *bar* ⑩ bar
barber *brijač* ⑩ *bree*-yach
baseball *bejzbol* ⑩ *beyz*-bawl

basket *koš* ⑩ kawsh
basketball *košarka* ① *kaw*-shar-ka
bath *kupka* ① *koop*-ka
bathing suit *kupaći kostim* ⑩
koo-pa-chee *kaw*-steem
bathroom *kupaonica* ①
koo-pa-*aw*-nee-tsa
battery (for car) *akumulator* ⑩
a-koo-moo-*la*-tawr
battery (general) *baterija* ① ba-*te*-ree-ya
bay *uvala* ① *oo*-va-la
be *biti/bivati* *bee*-tee/*bee*-va-tee
beach *plaža* ① *pla*-zha
beach volleyball *odbojka na pjesku* ①
awd-boy-ka na *pye*-skoo
bean *grah* ⑩ grah
beansprout *klica graha* ① *klee*-tsa *gra*-ha
beautiful *lijep* lee-*yep*
beauty salon *kozmetički salon* ⑩
kawz-me-*teech*-kee *sa*-lawn
because *zato* *za*-taw
bed *krevet* ⑩ *kre*-vet
bed linen *posteljina* ① paw-ste-*lyee*-na
bedding *krevetnina* ① kre-vet-*nee*-na
bedroom *spavaća soba* ① *spa*-va-cha
saw-ba
bee *pčela* ① *pche*-la
beef *govedina* ① *gaw*-ve-dee-na
beer *pivo* ⑩ *pee*-vaw
beer hall *pivnica* ① *peev*-nee-tsa
beetroot *cikla* ① *tsee*-kla
before *prije* *pree*-ye
beggar *prosjak* ⑩ *praw*-syak
behind *iza* ee-za
Belgium *Belgija* ① *bel*-gee-ya
bell pepper *paprika* ① *pa*-pree-ka
below *ispod* ee-spawd
beside *pored* • *kraj* • *do* • *uz* *paw*-red • kraj
• *daw* • ooz
best *najbolji* nai-*baw*-lyee
bet *oklada* ① *aw*-kla-da
better *bolji* *baw*-lyee
between *između* ee-*zme*-joo
Bible *biblija* ① *bee*-blee-ya
bicycle *bicikl* ⑩ *bee*-tsee-kl
big *velik* *ve*-leek
bigger *veći* *ve*-chee
biggest *najveći* nai-*ve*-chee
bike *bicikl* ⑩ *bee*-tsee-kl
bike chain *lanac na biciklu* ⑩ *la*-nats na
bee-tsee-kloo
bike lock *lokot na biciklu* ⑩ *law*-kawt na
bee-tsee-kloo

bike path *biciklistička staza* ①
bee·tsee·*klee*·steech·ka *sta*·za

bike shop *prodavaonica bicikala* ①
praw·da·va·*aw*·nee·tsa bee·*tsee*·ka·la

bill (account) *račun* ⓜ *ra*·choon

binoculars *dalekozor* ⓜ *da*·le·kaw·zawr

bird *ptica* ① *ptee*·tsa

birth certificate *izvod iz matične knjige
rođenih* ⓜ *eez*·vawd eez *ma*·teech·ne
knyee·ge *raw*·je·neeh

birthday *rođendan* ⓜ *raw*·jen·dan

biscuit *keks* ⓜ keks

bite (dog) *ugriz* ⓜ oo·greez

bite (insect) *ubod* ⓜ oo·bawd

bitter *gorak* gaw·rak

black *crn* tsrn

bladder *mjehur* ⓜ mye·hoor

blanket *deka* ① *de*·ka

blind *slijep* slee·*yep*

blister *žulj* ⓜ zhool'

blocked *zaglavljen* za·glav·lyen

blood *krv* ① krv

blood group *krvna grupa* ① *krv*·na groo·pa

blood pressure *tlak krvi* tlak kr·vee

blood test *krvne pretrage* ① pl
krv·ne *pre*·tra·ge

blue *plav* ⓜ plav

board (a plane, ship etc) *ukrcati/ukrca-
vati se* oo·kr·tsa·tee/oo·kr·*tsa*·va·tee se

boarding house *pansion* ⓜ pan·*see*·awn

boarding pass *zrakoplovna ulaznica* ①
zra·kaw·plawv·na oo·laz·nee·tsa

boat (ship) *brawd* ⓜ brawd

boat (smaller/private) *čamac* ⓜ *cha*·mats

body *tijelo* ① tee·ye·law

boiled *obaren* aw·*ba*·ren

bone *kost* ① kawst

book *knjiga* ① knyee·ga

book (make a booking) *rezervirati* perf
re·zer·*vee*·ra·tee

booked out *popunjen* paw·poo·nyen

bookshop *knjižara* ① knyee·zha·ra

boot(s) (footwear) *čizma/e* ⓜ sg/① pl
chee·zma/e

border *granica* ① *gra*·nee·tsa

bored *koji se dosađuje* koy·ee se
daw·*sa*·joo·ye

boring *dosadan* daw·sa·dan

borrow *posuditi/posuđivati*
paw·soo·dee·tee/paw·soo·*jee*·va·tee

Bosnia-Herzegovina *Bosna i
Hercegovina* ① *baw*·sna ee
her·tse·gaw·vee·na

botanic garden *botanički vrt* ⓜ
baw·*ta*·neech·kee vrt

both *oba/obje* ⓜ&ⓕ/① *aw*·ba/*aw*·bye

bottle *boca* ① *baw*·tsa

bottle opener *otvarač za boce* ⓜ
awt·*va*·rach za *baw*·tse

bottle shop *prodavaonica alkohola* ①
praw·da·va·*aw*·nee·tsa al·kaw·haw·la

bottom (body) *stražnjica* ①
strazh·nyee·tsa

bottom (position) *dno* ⓜ dnaw

bowl *zdjela* ① zdye·la

box *kutija* ① koo·tee·ya

boxer shorts *bokserice* ① pl
bawk·se·ree·tse

boxing *boks* ⓜ bawks

boy *dječak* ⓜ dye·chak

boyfriend *dečko* ⓜ dech·kaw

bra *grudnjak* ⓜ grood·nyak

brakes *kočnice* ① pl kawch·nee·tse

brandy *rakija* ① *ra*·kee·ya

brave *hrabar* hra·bar

bread *kruh* ⓜ krooh

bread rolls *žemičke* ① pl zhe·*meech*·ke

break *(s)lomiti* (s)*law*·mee·tee

break down (po)kvariti se
(paw·)*kva*·ree·tee se

breakfast *doručak* ⓜ *daw*·roo·chak

breast (body) *prsa* ① *pr*·sa

breathe *dahnuti/disati* dah·noo·tee/
dee·sa·tee

bribe *mito* ⓜ *mee*·taw

bridge *most* ⓜ mawst

briefcase *aktovka* ① *ak*·tawv·ka

brilliant *briljantan* bree·*lyan*·tan

bring *donijeti/donositi* daw·nee·ye·tee/
daw·*naw*·see·tee

broccoli *brokula* ① *braw*·koo·la

brochure *brošura* ① braw·shoo·ra

broken *razbijen* ra·zbee·yen

broken down *pokvaren* paw·*kva*·ren

bronchitis *bronhitis* ⓜ brawn·*hee*·tees

brother *brat* ⓜ brat

brown *smeđ* smej

bruise *modrica* ① *maw*·dree·tsa

brush *četka* ① *chet*·ka

bucket *kanta* ① *kan*·ta

Buddhist *Budist* ⓜ boo·*deest*

budget *budžet* ⓜ boo·jet

buffet *bife* ⓜ bee·fe

bug (insect) *stjenica* ① stye·nee·tsa

build *(iz)graditi* (eez·)*gra*·dee·tee

builder *građevinar* ⓜ gra·je·vee·nar

building *zgrada* ① *zgra*-da
bumbag *torbica nošena oko struka* ①
tawr-bee-tsa naw-she-na aw-kaw stroo-ka
burn *opeklina* ① *aw*-pe-klee-na
burnt *izgoren* eez-gaw-ren
bus (city) *gradski autobus* ⓜ *grad*-skee
a-oo-taw-boos
bus (intercity) *međugradski autobus* ⓜ
me-joo-grad-skee a-oo-taw-boos
bus station *autobuska stanica* ①
a-oo-taw-boo-ska *sta*-nee-tsa
bus stop *autobuska stanica* ①
a-oo-taw-boo-ska *sta*-nee-tsa
business *biznis* ⓜ beez-nees
business class *prvi razred* ⓜ *pr*-vee *ra*-zred
business man/woman *biznismen* ⓜ&①
beez-nees-men
business person *poslovna osoba* ①
paw-slawv-na aw-saw-ba
business trip *službeno putovanje* ⓝ
sloozh-be-naw poo-taw-*va*-nye
busker *ulični zabavljač* ⓜ oo-leech-nee
za-*bav*-lyach
busy *zauzet* za-oo-zet
but *osim* aw-seem
butcher *mesar* ⓜ me-sar
butcher's shop *mesnica* ① *me*-snee-tsa
butter *maslac* ⓜ *ma*-slats
butterfly *leptir* ⓜ *le*-pteer
button *dugme* ⓝ *doog*-me
buy *kupiti/kupovati* koo-pee-tee/
koo-*paw*-va-tee

C

cabbage *kupus* ⓜ *koo*-poos
cable car *uspinjača* ① oo-*spee*-nya-cha
café *kafić/kavana* ⓜ/① *ka*-feech/ka-*va*-na
cake *kolač* ⓜ *kaw*-lach
cake shop *slastičarnica* ①
sla-stee-*char*-nee-tsa
calculator *digitron* ⓜ dee-gee-trawn
calendar *kalendar* ⓜ *ka*-len-dar
call *(po)zvati* (*paw*-)zva-tee
camera *foto-aparat* ⓜ faw-taw-*a*-pa-rat
camera shop *prodavaonica foto-aparata* ①
praw-da-va-*aw*-nee-tsa faw-taw-a-pa-*ra*-ta
camp *kampirati* imp kam-*pee*-ra-tee
camping ground *kamp* ⓜ kamp
camping store *prodavaonica opreme za
kampiranje* ① praw-da-va-*aw*-nee-tsa
aw-pre-me za kam-*pee*-ra-nye

campsite *mjesto za kampiranje* ⓝ
mye-staw za kam-*pee*-ra-nye
can (be able) *moći* imp *maw*-chee
can (have permission) *smjeti* imp smye-tee
can (tin) *limenka* ① *lee*-men-ka
can opener *otvarač za limenke* ⓜ
awt-va-rach za *lee*-men-ke
Canada *Kanada* ① *ka*-na-da
cancel *poništiti/poništavati*
paw-nee-shtee-tee/paw-nee-*shta*-va-tee
cancer *rak* ⓜ rak
candle *svijeća* ① svee-*ye*-cha
candy *slatkiši* ⓜ pl slat-*kee*-shee
cantaloupe *dinja* ① *dee*-nya
cape (promontory) *rt* ⓜ rt
capsicum *paprika* ① *pa*-pree-ka
car *automobil* ⓜ a-oo-taw-*maw*-beel
car hire *najam automobila* ⓜ *nai*-am
a-oo-taw-maw-*bee*-la
car owner's title *potvrda vlasništva automobila* ① *paw*-tvr-da *vlas*-neesh-tva
a-oo-taw-maw-*bee*-la
car park *parkiralište* ⓝ par-*kee*-ra-leesh-te
car registration *registracija*
re-gee-*stra*-tsee-ya
caravan *karavana* ① ka-ra-*va*-na
cardiac arrest *srčani udar* ⓜ
sr-cha-nee oo-dar
cards (playing) *karte za igranje* ① pl
kar-te za ee-*gra*-nye
care (for someone) *(po)brinuti se*
(*paw*-)bree-noo-tee se
Careful! *Oprez!* aw-prez
carpenter *tesar* ⓜ *te*-sar
carrot *mrkva* ① mrk-va
carry *nositi* imp naw-see-tee
carton *kartonska kutija* ① *kar*-tawn-ska
koo-tee-ya
cash *gotovina* ① gaw-taw-*vee*-na
cash (a cheque) *unovčiti/unovčavati*
oo-nawv-chee-tee/oo-nawv-*cha*-va-tee
cash register *blagajna* ① bla-gai-na
cashier *blagajnik* ⓜ bla-*gai*-neek
casino *kasino* ⓜ ka-see-naw
cassette *kazeta* ① ka-ze-ta
castle *dvorac* ⓜ *dvaw*-rats
casual work *povremeni posao* ⓜ
paw-vre-me-nee paw-sa-aw
cat *mačka* ① *mach*-ka
cathedral *katedrala* ① ka-te-*dra*-la
Catholic *katolik* ⓜ *ka*-taw-leek
Catholicism *Katoličanstvo* ⓝ
ka-taw-lee-*chan*-stvaw

cauliflower *cvjetača* ① tsvye·ta·cha
cave *spilja* ① spee·lya
CD *CD* ⑩ tse de
celebration *proslava* ① praw·sla·va
cemetery *groblje* ⑩ graw·blye
cent *cent* ⑩ tsent
centimetre *centimetar* ⑩ tsen·tee·me·tar
centre *centar* ⑩ tsen·tar
ceramics *keramika* ① ke·ra·mee·ka
cereal *žitarica* ① zhee·ta·ree·tsa
certificate *svjedodžba* ① svye·dawj·ba
chain *lanac* ⑩ la·nats
chair *stolica za sklapanje* ① staw·lee·tsa
   za *skla*·pa·nye
chairlift (skiing) *žičara* ① zhee·cha·ra
champagne *šampanjac* ⑩ sham·pa·nyats
championships *prvenstvo* ⑪ pr·vens·tvaw
chance *šansa* ① shan·sa
change *promjena* ① praw·mye·na
change (coins) *kusur* ⑫ koo·soor
change (money) *zamijeniti/*
   zamijenjivati za·mee·ye·nee·tee/
   za·mee·ye·nyee·va·tee
changing room *kabina za*
   presvlačenje ⑪ pl ka·bee·na za
   pres·vla·che·nye
charming *šarmantan* shar·man·tan
chat up *udvarati se* imp oo·dva·ra·tee se
cheap *jeftino* ⑪ yef·tee·naw
cheat *varalica* ① va·ra·lee·tsa
check (bill) *račun* ⑫ ra·choon
check *provjeriti/provjeravati*
   praw·vye·ree·tee/praw·vye·ra·va·tee
check-in (airport) *prijemni šalter* ⑫
   pree·yem·nee shal·ter
checkpoint *mjesto kontrole* ⑪ mye·staw
   kawn·traw·le
cheese *sir* ⑫ seer
cheese shop *prodavaonica sira* ①
   praw·da·va·aw·nee·tsa see·ra
chef *šef kuhinje* ⑫ shef koo·hee·nye
chemist (pharmacist) *ljekarnik* ①
   lye·kar·neek
chemist (pharmacy) *ljekarna* ① lye·kar·na
cheque *ček* ⑫ chek
cherry *trešnja* ① tresh·nya
chess *šah* ⑫ shah
chess board *šahovska ploča* ①
   sha·hawv·ska plaw·cha
chest (body) *prsa* ⑪ pr·sa
chestnut *kesten* ⑫ ke·sten
chewing gum *žvakača guma* ①
   zhva·ka·cha goo·ma

chicken (as food) *piletina* ① pee·le·tee·na
chickenpox *vodene kozice* ① pl
   vaw·de·ne kaw·zee·tse
chickpea *slanutak* ⑫ sla·noo·tak
child *dijete* ⑪ dee·ye·te
child seat *sjedalo za dijete* ⑪ sye·da·law
   za dee·ye·te
childminding *čuvanje djece* ⑪
   choo·va·nye dye·tse
children *djeca* ⑪ pl dye·tsa
chilli *čili* ⑫ chee·lee
chilli sauce *umak od čilija* ⑫ oo·mak awd
   chee·lee·ya
chiropractor *kiropraktor* ⑫
   kee·raw·prak·tawr
chocolate *čokolada* ① chaw·kaw·la·da
choose *izabrati/izabirati* ee·za·bra·tee/
   ee·za·bee·ra·tee
chopping board *daska za sjeckanje* ①
   da·ska za syets·ka·nye
chopsticks *štapići za jelo* ⑫ pl
   shta·pee·chee za ye·law
Christian *kršćanin/kršćanka* ⑫/①
   krsh·cha·neen/krsh·chan·ka
Christmas *božić* ⑫ baw·zheech
Christmas Day *božićni dan* ⑫
   baw·zheech·nee dan
Christmas Eve *badnjak* ⑫ bad·nyak
church *crkva* ① tsr·kva
cider *jabukovača* ① ya·boo·kaw·va·cha
cigar *cigara* ① tsee·ga·ra
cigarette *cigareta* ① tsee·ga·re·ta
cigarette lighter *upaljač* ⑫ oo·pa·lyach
cinema *kino* ⑪ kee·naw
circle dance *kolo* ⑪ kaw·law
circus *cirkus* ⑫ tseer·koos
citizenship *državljanstvo* ⑪
   dr·zhav·lyan·stvaw
city *grad* ⑫ grad
city centre *gradski centar* ⑫ grad·skee
   tsen·tar
civil rights *građanska prava* ⑪ pl
   gra·jan·ska pra·va
class (category) *klasa* ① kla·sa
classical *klasičan* kla·see·chan
clean *čist* cheest
clean *(o)čistiti (aw·)chee·stee·tee*
cleaning *čišćenje* ⑪ cheesh·che·nye
client *stranka* ① stran·ka
cliff *litica* ① lee·tee·tsa
climb *popeti/penjati se* paw·pe·tee/
   pe·nya·tee se
cloakroom *garderoba* ① gar·de·raw·ba

clock *sat* ⑩ sat
close (nearby) *blizak* blee·zak
close (shut) *zatvoriti/zatvarati* zat·vaw·ree·tee/zat·va·ra·tee
closed *zatvoren* zat·vaw·ren
clothesline *konop za sušenje rublja* ⑩ kaw·nawp za soo·she·nye roob·lya
clothing *odjeća* ① awd·ye·cha
clothing store *prodavaonica odjeće* ① praw·da·va·aw·nee·tsa aw·dye·che
cloud *oblak* ⑩ aw·blak
cloudy *oblačan* aw·bla·chan
clutch (car) *kvačilo* ⑩ kva·chee·law
coach (sports) *trener* ⑩ tre·ner
coast *obala* ① aw·ba·la
coat *kaput* ⑩ ka·poot
cocaine *kokain* ⑩ kaw·ka·een
cockroach *žohar* ⑩ zhaw·har
cocktail *koktel* ⑩ kawk·tel
cocoa *kakao* ⑩ ka·ka·aw
coffee *kava* ① ka·va
coins *novčići* ⑩ pl nawv·chee·chee
cold *prehlada* ① pre·hla·da
cold *hladan* hla·dan
(have a) cold *imati prehladu* imp ee·ma·tee pre·hla·doo
colleague *kolega/kolegica* ⑩/① kaw·le·ga/kaw·le·gee·tsa
collect call *poziv na račun nazvane osobe* ⑩ paw·zeev na ra·choon naz·va·ne aw·saw·be
college *koledž* ⑩ kaw·lej
colour *boja* ① bo·ya
comb *češalj* ⑩ che·shal'
come *doći/dolaziti* daw·chee/daw·la·zee·tee
comedy *komedija* ① kaw·me·dee·ya
comfortable *ugodan* oo·gaw·dan
commission *komisija* ① kaw·mee·see·ya
communications (profession) *komunikacije* ① pl kaw·moo·nee·ka·tsee·ye
communion *pričest* ① pree·chest
communism *komunizam* ⑩ kaw·moo·nee·zam
communist *komunista* ⑩ kaw·moo·nee·sta
companion *drug* ⑩ droog
company *društvo* ⑩ droosh·tvaw
compass *kompas* ⑩ kawm·pas
complain *(po)žaliti se* (paw·)zha·lee·tee se
complaint *prigovor* ⑩ pree·gaw·vawr
complimentary (free) *besplatan* be·spla·tan
computer *računalo* ⑩ ra·choo·na·law

computer game *kompjuterska igra* ① kawm·pyoo·ter·ska ee·gra
concert *koncert* ⑩ kawn·tsert
concussion *potres mozga* ⑩ paw·tres maw·zga
conditioner (hair) *omekšivač (za kosu)* ⑩ aw·mek·shee·vach (za kaw·soo)
condom *prezervativ* ⑩ pre·zer·va·teev
conference (big) *konferencija* ① kon·fe·ren·tsee·ya
conference (small) *vječanje* ① vye·cha·nye
confession (admission) *priznanje* ⑩ pree·zna·nye
confession (at church) *ispovijed* ① ee·spaw·vee·yed
confirm (a booking) *potvrditi/potvrđivati* pawt·vr·dee·tee/pawt·vr·jee·va·tee
congratulations *čestitke* ① pl che·steet·ke
conjunctivitis *konjunktivitis* ⑩ kaw·nyoonk·tee·vee·tees
connection *veza* ① ve·za
conservative *konzervativan* kawn·zer·va·tee·van
constipation *zatvorenje* ⑩ zat·vaw·re·nye
consulate *konzulat* ⑩ kawn·zoo·lat
contact-lens solution *tekućina za kontakt leće* ① te·koo·chee·na za kawn·takt le·che
contact lenses *kontakt leće* ① pl kawn·takt le·che
contraceptives *sredstva za sprječavanje neželjene trudnoće* ⑩ pl sreds·tva za sprye·cha·va·nye ne·zhe·lye·ne trood·naw·che
contract *ugovor* ⑩ oo·gaw·vawr
convenience store *prodavaonica sa produženim radnim vremenom* ① praw·da·va·aw·nee·tsa sa praw·doo·zhe·neem rad·neem vre·me·nawm
convent *samostan* ⑩ sa·maw·stan
cook *kuhar/kuharica* ⑩/① koo·har/koo·ha·ree·tsa
cook *(s)kuhati* (s)koo·ha·tee
cookie *keks* ⑩ keks
cooking *kuhanje* ⑩ koo·ha·nye
cool *hladan* hla·dan
coral *koralj* ⑩ kaw·ral'
corkscrew *vadičep* ⑩ va·dee·chep
corn *kukuruz* ⑩ koo·koo·rooz
corner *ugao* ⑩ oo·ga·aw
cornflakes *kukuruzne pahuljice* ① pl koo·koo·rooz·ne pa·hoo·lyee·tse

corrupt *pokvaren* paw·kva·ren

cost *stajati* imp *staj·*a·tee

cotton *pamuk* ⑩ pa·mook

cotton balls *kuglice vate* ① pl koo·glee·tse va·te

cotton buds *vatene čačkalice za uši* ① pl va·te·ne chach·ka·lee·tse za oo·shee

cough *(za)kašljati* (za·)kash·lya·tee

cough medicine *sirup za kašalj* ⑩ see·roop za ka·shal'

count *(iz)brojati* (eez·)broy·a·tee

counter (at bar) *šank* ⑩ shank

country (land) *zemlja* ① zem·lya

country (nation state) *država* ① dr·zha·va

countryside *seosko područje* ⑩ se·aw·skaw paw·drooch·ye

county *okrug* ⑩ aw·kroog

coupon *kupon* ⑩ koo·pawn

courgette *bučice* ① pl boo·chee·tse

court (legal) *sud* ⑩ sood

court (tennis) *igralište* ⑩ ee·gra·leesh·te

cove *dražica* ① dra·zhee·tsa

cover charge (nightclub) *cijena ulaznice* ① tsee·ye·na oo·laz·nee·tse

cow *krava* ① kra·va

crafts (handicrafts) *umjetnički obrti* ⑩ pl oo·myet·neech·kee aw·br·tee

crash *sudar* ⑩ soo·dar

crazy *lud* lood

cream (cosmetic) *krema* ① kre·ma

cream (food) *vrhnje* ⑩ vrh·nye

creche *jaslice* ① pl ya·slee·tse

credit *kredit* ⑩ kre·deet

credit card *kreditna kartica* ① kre·deet·na kar·tee·tsa

cricket (sport) *kriket* ⑩ kree·ket

Croat *Hrvat/Hrvatica* ⑩/① hr·vat/ hr·va·tee·tsa

Croatia *Hrvatska* ① hr·vat·ska

crop *urod* ⑩ oo·rawd

cross *križ* ⑩ kreezh

crowded *prepun* pre·poon

cucumber *krastavac* ⑩ kra·sta·vats

cup *šalica* ① sha·lee·tsa

cupboard *ormar* ⑩ awr·mar

currency exchange *tečaj stranih valuta* ⑩ te·chai stra·neeh va·loo·ta

current (electricity) *struja* ① stroo·ya

current affairs *aktualna zbivanja* ⑩ pl ak·too·el·na zbee·va·nya

custom *običaj* ⑩ aw·bee·chai

customs *carinarnica* ① tsa·ree·nar·nee·tsa

cut *(na)rezati* (na·)re·za·tee

cutlery *pribor za jelo* ⑩ pree·bawr za ye·law

CV *kratak životopis* ⑩ kra·tak zhee·vaw·taw·pees

cycle *voziti bicikl* imp vaw·zee·tee bee·tsee·kl

cycling *vožnja biciklom* ① vawzh·nya bee·tsee·klawm

cyclist *biciklist* ⑩ bee·tsee·kleest

cystitis *cistitis* ⑩ tsee·stee·tees

D

dad *tata* ⑩ ta·ta

daily *dnevni* dnev·nee

dance *ples* ⑩ ples

dance *(za)plesati* (za·)ple·sa·tee

dancing *plesanje* ⑩ ple·sa·nye

dangerous *opasan* aw·pa·san

dark *mračan* mra·chan

dark (of colour) *taman* ta·man

date (appointment) *spoj* ⑩ spoy

date (day) *datum* ⑩ da·toom

date (fruit) *datulja* ① da·too·lya

date (a person) *izaći/izlaziti* ee·za·chee/ ee·zla·zee·tee

date of birth *datum rođenja* ⑩ da·toom raw·je·nya

daughter *kći* ① kchee

dawn *zora* ① zaw·ra

day *dan* ⑩ dan

day after tomorrow *prekosutra* ⑩ pre·kaw·soo·tra

day before yesterday *prekjučer* ⑩ prek·yoo·cher

dead *mrtav* mr·tav

deaf *gluh* glooh

deal (cards) *(po)dijeliti* (paw·)dee·ye·lee·tee

December *prosinac* ⑩ praw·see·nats

decide *odlučiti/odlučivati* awd·loo·chee·tee/awd·loo·chee·va·tee

deck chairs *ležaljka* ① le·zhal'·ka

deep *dubok* ⑩ doo·bawk

deforestation *krčenje šuma* ⑩ kr·che·nye shoo·ma

degrees (temperature) *stupnjevi* ⑩ pl stoop·nye·vee

delay *zakašnjenje* ⑩ za·kash·nye·nye

delicatessen *delikatese* ① de·lee·ka·te·se

deliver *dostaviti/dostavljati* daw·sta·vee·tee/daw·stav·lya·tee

democracy *demokracija* ① de·maw·kra·tsee·ya

demonstration (protest) *demonstracija* ⓕ
dee·mawn·*stra*·tsee·ya

Denmark *Danska* ⓕ *dan*·ska

dental floss *konac za čišćenje zubi* ⓜ
kaw·nats za *cheesh*·che·nye zoo·bee

dentist *zubar* ⓜ zoo·bar

deodorant *dezodorans* ⓜ de·zaw·*daw*·rans

depart (leave) *otići/odlaziti* aw·*tee*·chee/
awd·la·zee·tee

department store *robna kuća* ⓕ *rawb*·na
koo·cha

departure *odlazak* ⓜ *awd*·la·zak

departure gate *izlaz* ⓜ *eez*·laz

deposit (bank) *depozit* ⓜ de·*paw*·zeet

deposit (surety) *jamstvo* ⓝ *yam*·stvaw

derailleur *mjenjač brzina na biciklu* ⓜ
mye·nyach br·*zee*·na na bee·*tsee*·kloo

descendant *potomak* ⓜ *paw*·taw·mak

desert *pustinja* ⓕ *poo*·stee·nya

design *dizajn* ⓜ dee·*zain*

dessert *poslastice* ⓕ pl *paw*·sla·stee·tse

destination *odredište* ⓝ *aw*·dre·deesh·te

details *podatci* ⓜ pl *paw*·dat·tsee

diabetes *dijabetes* ⓜ dee·ya·*be*·tes

dial tone *znak slobodnog biranja na
telefonu* ⓜ *znak slaw*·bawd·nawg
bee·ra·nya na te·le·*faw*·noo

diaper *pelene* ⓕ pl *pe*·le·ne

diaphragm (body part) *dijafragma* ⓕ
dee·ya·*frag*·ma

diarrhoea *proljev* ⓜ *praw*·lyev

diary *dnevnik* ⓜ *dnev*·neek

dice *kockice* ⓕ pl *kawts*·kee·tse

dictionary *rječnik* ⓜ *ryech*·neek

die *umrijeti/umirati* oo·*mree*·ye·tee/
oo·*mee*·ra·tee

diet *dijeta* ⓕ dee·*ye*·ta

different (not this one) *drugačiji*
droo·*ga*·chee·yee

difficult *težak* *te*·zhak

dining car *kola za ručavanje* ⓕ *kaw*·la za
roo·cha·va·nye

dinner *večera* ⓕ *ve*·che·ra

direct *direktan* dee·*rek*·tan

direct-dial *direktan poziv* ⓜ dee·*rek*·tan
paw·zeev

direction *smjer* ⓜ smyer

director *director* ⓜ dee·*rek*·tawr

dirty *prljav* *pr*·lyav

disabled *onesposobljen*
aw·ne·*spaw*·sawb·lyen

disco *disko* ⓜ *dee*·skaw

discount *popust* ⓜ *paw*·poost

discrimination *diskriminacija* ⓕ
dee·skree·mee·*na*·tsee·ya

disease *bolest* ⓕ *baw*·lest

dish (food item) *jelo* ⓝ *ye*·law

dish (plate) *posuda* ⓕ *paw*·soo·da

disk (CD-ROM) *disk (CD-ROM)* ⓜ deesk
(tse de rawm)

disk (floppy) *disketa* ⓕ dee·*ske*·ta

diving (underwater) *ronjenje* ⓝ
raw·nye·nye

diving equipment *ronilačka oprema* ⓕ
raw·nee·lach·ka aw·*pre*·ma

divorced (of man) *razveden* raz·*ve*·den

divorced (of woman) *razvedena*
raz·ve·*de*·na

dizzy *ošamućen* aw·*sha*·moo·chen

do *(u)činiti* (oo·)*chee*·nee·tee

doctor (medical) *liječnik* ⓜ lee·*yech*·neek

documentary *dokumentarac* ⓜ
daw·koo·men·*ta*·rats

dog *pas* ⓜ pas

dole (unemployment benefit) *potpora
za nezaposlene* ⓕ *pawt*·paw·ra za
ne·*za*·paw·sle·ne

doll *lutka* ⓕ *loot*·ka

dollar *dolar* ⓜ *daw*·lar

door *vrata* ⓝ *vra*·ta

dope (drugs) *trava* ⓕ *tra*·va

double *dvostruk* *dvaw*·strook

double bed *dupli krevet* ⓜ *doo*·plee *kre*·vet

double room *dvokrevetna soba* ⓕ
dvaw·kre·vet·na *saw*·ba

down *dolje* *daw*·lye

downhill *nizbrdo* *neez*·br·daw

dozen *tucet* ⓜ *too*·tset

drama *drama* ⓕ *dra*·ma

dream *san* ⓜ san

dress *haljina* ⓕ *ha*·lyee·na

dried *sušeni* soo·*she*·nee

drink *piće* ⓝ *pee*·che

drink (alcoholic) *alkoholno piće* ⓝ
al·kaw·hawl·naw *pee*·che

drink *(po)piti* *(paw·)pee*·tee

drive *voziti* imp *vaw*·zee·tee

driving licence *vozačka dozvola* ⓕ
vaw·zach·ka *dawz*·vaw·la

drug (illicit) *droga* ⓕ *draw*·ga

drug addiction *ovisnost o drogama* ⓕ
aw·*vee*·snawst aw *draw*·ga·ma

drug dealer *trgovac drogama* ⓜ
tr·gaw·vats *draw*·ga·ma

drug trafficking *trgovina drogama* ⓕ
tr·*gaw*·vee·na *draw*·ga·ma

drug user *korisnik droga* ⓜ
kaw-ree-sneek draw-ga
drugs (illicit) *droge* ① pl *draw-ge*
drum (instrument) *bubanj* ⓜ *boo-ban'[]*
drunk *pijan pee-yan*
dry *suh* sooh
dry (o)sušiti (aw-)*soo-shee-tee*
duck *patka* ① *pa-tka*
dummy (pacifier) *duda* ① *doo-da*
DVD *DVD* ⓜ *de ve de*

E

each *svaki* ⓜ *sva-kee*
ear *uho* ⓝ *oo-haw*
early *rani ra-nee*
earn *zaraditi/zarađivati za-ra-dee-tee/
za-ra-jee-va-tee*
earplugs *čepovi za uši* ⓜ pl *che-paw-vee
za oo-shee*
earrings *naušnice* ① pl *na-oosh-nee-tse*
Earth *zemlja* ① *zem-lya*
earthquake *potres* ⓜ *paw-tres*
east *istok* ⓜ *ee-stawk*
Easter *uskrs oos-krs*
easy *jednostavan yed-naw-sta-van*
eat *(po)jesti* (paw-)*ye-stee*
economy class *drugi razred* ⓜ *droo-gee
raz-red*
ecstasy (drug) *ekstasi* ⓜ *ek-sta-see*
eczema *ekcem* ⓜ *ek-tsem*
editor *urednik* ⓜ *oo-red-neek*
education *obrazovanje* ⓝ
aw-bra-zaw-va-nye
egg *jaje* ① *yai-e*
eggplant *patlidžan* ⓜ *pat-lee-jan*
election *izbori* ⓜ pl *eez-baw-ree*
electricity *struja* ① *stroo-ya*
elevator *dizalo* ⓝ *dee-za-law*
email *e-mail* ⓝ *ee-me-eel*
embarrassed *posramljen paw-sram-lyen*
embassy *ambasada* ① *am-ba-sa-da*
emergency *hitan slučaj* ⓜ *hee-tan sloo-chai*
emergency department (hospital)
Odjel hitne pomoći ⓜ *aw-dyel heet •ne
paw-maw-chee*
emotional *emocionalan*
e-maw-tsee-aw-na-lan
employee *zaposlenik/zaposlenica* ⓜ/①
za-paw-sle-neek/za-paw-sle-nee-tsa
employer *poslodavac* ⓜ
paw-slaw-da-vats

empty *prazan pra-zan*
end *kraj* ⓜ krai
endangered species *ugrožene vrste* ① pl
oo-graw-zhe-ne vr-ste
engaged (marriage) *vjeren vye-ren*
engaged (phone) *zauzet za-oo-zet*
engagement *vjerenje* ① *vye-re-nye*
engine *motor* ⓜ *maw-tawr*
engineer *inženjer* ⓜ *een-zhe-nyer*
engineering *inženjerstvo* ⓝ
een-zhe-nyer-stvaw
England *Engleska* ① *en-gle-ska*
English *engleski en-gle-skee*
enjoy (oneself) *provesti/provoditi se
praw-ve-stee/praw-vaw-dee-tee se*
enough *dosta daw-sta*
enter *ući/ulaziti oo-chee/oo-la-zee-tee*
entertainment guide *vodič o zbivan-
jima u svijetu razonode* ⓜ *vaw-deech
aw zbee-va-nyee-ma oo svee-ye-too
ra-zaw-naw-de*
entry *ulaz* ⓜ *oo-laz*
envelope *omotnica* ① *aw-mawt-nee-tsa*
environment *prirodna okolina* ①
pree-rawd-na aw-kaw-lee-na
epilepsy *padavica* ① *pa-da-vee-tsa*
equal opportunity *jednake
mogućnosti* ① pl *yed-na-ke
maw-gooch-naw-stee*
equality *ravnopravnost* ①
rav-naw-prav-nawst
equipment *oprema* ① *aw-pre-ma*
escalator *pokretne stepenice* ① pl
paw-kret-ne ste-pe-nee-tse
estate agency *agencija za prodaju
nekretnina* ① *a-gen-tsee-ya za
praw-dai-oo ne-kret-nee-na*
euro *euro* ⓜ *e-oo-raw-pa*
Europe *Europa* ① *e-oo-raw-pa*
evening *večer* ① *ve-cher*
every *svaki* ⓜ *sva-kee*
everyone *svatko svat-kaw*
everything *sve* sve
exactly *točno tawch-naw*
excellent *odličan awd-lee-chan*
excess (baggage) *višak prtljage* ⓜ
vee-shak prt-lya-ge
exchange *razmjena* ① *raz-mye-na*
exchange *razmijeniti/razmjenjivati
raz-mee-ye-nee-tee/raz-mye-nyee-va-tee*
exchange rate *tečaj razmjene* ⓜ *te-chai
raz-mye-ne*
excluded *isključen ees-klyoo-chen*

exhaust (car) *ispušni plinovi* ⓜ
ee-spoosh-nee plee-naw-vee
exhibition *izložba* ⓕ eez-lawzh-ba
exit *izlaz* ⓜ eez-laz
expensive *skup* skoop
experience *iskustvo* ⓝ ees-koost-vaw
exploitation *iskorištavanje* ⓝ
ee-skaw-reesh-ta-va-nye
express *brzi* br-zee
express (mail) *ekspres pošta* ⓕ eks-pres
pawsh-ta
express mail *poslano expres poštom* ⓝ
paw-sla-naw eks-pres pawsh-tawm
extension (visa) *produženje* ⓝ
praw-doo-zhe-nye
eye *oko* ⓝ aw-kaw
eye drops *kapi za oči* ⓕ pl ka-pee za
aw-chee
eyes *oči* ⓕ pl aw-chee

F

fabric *tkanina* ⓕ tka-nee-na
face *lice* lee-tse
face cloth *ručnik za lice* ⓜ rooch-neek
za lee-tse
factory *tvornica* ⓕ tvawr-nee-tsa
factory worker *radnik u tvornici* ⓜ
rad-neek oo tvawr-nee-tsee
fall *pad* ⓜ pad
fall (autumn) *jesen* ⓕ ye-sen
family *obitelj* ⓕ aw-bee-tel'
family name *prezime* ⓝ pre-zee-me
fan (machine) *ventilator* ⓜ ven-tee-la-tawr
fan (sport, etc) *navijač* ⓜ na-vee-yach
fanbelt *remen za ventilator* ⓜ re-men za
ven-tee-la-tawr
far *daleko* da-le-kaw
fare *cijena vožnje* ⓕ tsee-ye-na vawzh-nye
farm *farma* ⓕ far-ma
farmer *poljodjelac* ⓜ paw-lyaw-dye-lats
fashion *moda* ⓕ maw-da
fast *brz* brz
fat *debeo* de-be-aw
father *otac* ⓜ aw-tats
father-in-law (of husband) *punac* ⓜ
poo-nats
father-in-law (of wife) *svekar* sve-kar
faucet *slavina* ⓕ sla-vee-na
faulty *pokvaren* pawk-va-ren
fax machine *telefaks* ⓜ te-le-faks
February *veljača* ⓕ ve-lya-cha

feed *(na)hraniti* (na-)hra-nee-tee
feel (touch) *dirnuti/dirati* deer-noo-tee/
dee-ra-tee
feeling *osjećaj* ⓜ aw-sye-chai
feelings *osjećaji* ⓜ pl aw-sye-chai-ee
female *ženski* zhen-skee
fence *ograda* ⓕ aw-gra-da
fencing (sport) *mačevanje* ⓝ
ma-che-va-nye
ferry *trajekt* ⓜ trai-ekt
festival *festival* ⓜ fe-stee-val
fever *groznica* ⓕ graw-znee-tsa
few *nekoliko* ne-kaw-leek-aw
fiancé *vjerenik* ⓜ vye-re-neek
fiancée *vjerenica* ⓕ vye-re-nee-tsa
fiction (genre) *fikcija* ⓕ feek-tsee-ya
fig *smokva* ⓕ smaw-kva
fight (battle) *borba* ⓕ bawr-ba
fight (fisticuffs) *tuča* ⓕ too-cha
fill *(na)puniti* (na-)poo-nee-tee
film (cinema) *film* ⓜ feelm
film (for camera) *film za foto-aparat* ⓜ
feelm za faw-taw-a-pa-rat
film speed *brzina filma* ⓕ br-zee-na feel-ma
filtered *filtriran* feel-tree-ran
find *naći/nalaziti* na-chee/na-la-zee-tee
fine (penalty) *novčana globa* ⓕ
nawv-cha-na glaw-ba
fine (delicate) *sitan* see-tan
fine (weather) *vedar* ve-dar
finger *prst* ⓜ prst
finish *završiti/završavati* za-vr-shee-tee/
za-vr-sha-va-tee
Finland *Finska* ⓕ feen-ska
fire *požar* ⓜ paw-zhar
firewood *drvo za ogrjev* ⓝ dr-vaw za
aw-gryev
first *prvi* pr-vee
first class *prvi razred* ⓜ pr-vee raz-red
first-aid kit *pribor za prvu pomoć* ⓜ
pree-bawr za pr-voo paw-mawch
fish *riba* ⓕ ree-ba
fish shop *prodavaonica ribe* ⓕ
praw-da-va-aw-nee-tsa ree-be
fisherman *ribar* ⓜ ree-bar
fishing *ribolov* ⓜ ree-baw-lawv
fishing village *ribarsko selo* ⓝ
ree-bar-skaw se-law
fishmonger *trgovac ribom* ⓜ tr-gaw-vats
ree-bawm
flag *zastava* ⓕ za-sta-va
flannel *flanel* ⓜ fla-nel
flash (camera) *blic* ⓜ bleets

flashlight *(ručna) svjetiljka* ① *(rooch·na) svye·teel'·ka*
flat *plosnat plaw·snat*
flat (apartment) *stan* ⓜ *stan*
flea *buha* ① *boo·ha*
flea market *buvljak* ⓜ *boov·lyak*
flight *let* ⓝ *let*
flood *poplava* ① *paw·pla·va*
floor (ground) *pod* ⓜ *pawd*
floor (storey) *kat* ⓝ *kat*
florist *cvjećara* ① *tsvye·cha·ra*
flour *brašno* ⓝ *brash·naw*
flower *cvijet* ⓜ *tsvee·yet*
flu *gripa* ① *gree·pa*
fly *(po)letjeti (paw·)let·ye·tee*
foggy *maglovit ma·glaw·veet*
follow *pratiti* imp *pra·tee·tee*
food *hrana* ① *hra·na*
food supplies *zalihe hrane* ⓝ pl *za·lee·he hra·ne*
foot *stopalo* ⓝ *staw·pa·law*
football (soccer) *nogomet* ⓜ *naw·gaw·met*
footpath *pločnik* ⓜ *plawch·neek*
foreign *strani stra·nee*
forest *šuma* ① *shoo·ma*
forever *zauvijek za·oo·vee·yek*
forget *zaboraviti/zaboravljati za·baw·ra·vee·tee/za·baw·rav·lya·tee*
forgive *oprostiti/opraštati aw·praw·stee·tee/aw·prash·ta·tee*
fork *viljuška* ① *vee·lyoosh·ka*
fortnight *dva tjedna* ① *dva tyed·na*
fortune-teller *vrač* ⓜ *vrach*
foul *prekršaj* ⓜ *pre·kr·shai*
foyer *foaje* ① *faw·ai·e*
fragile *lomljiv lawm·lyeev*
France *Francuska* ① *fran·tsoo·ska*
free (available) *slobodan slaw·baw·dan*
free (gratis) *besplatan be·spla·tan*
free (not bound) *nevezan ne·ve·zan*
freeze *zamrznuti/zamrzavati za·mr·znoo·tee/za·mr·za·va·tee*
fresh *svjež svyezh*
Friday *petak* ⓜ *pe·tak*
fridge *hladnjak* ⓜ *hlad·nyak*
fried *prženi pr·zhe·nee*
friend *prijatelj/prijateljica* ⓜ/① *pree·ya·tel'/pree·ya·te·lyee·tsa*
from *iz · od eez · awd*
frost *mraz* ⓜ *mraz*
frozen *zaleđen za·le·jen*
fruit *voće* ⓝ *vaw·che*

fruit picking *branje voća* ⓝ *bra·nye vaw·cha*
fry *(is)pržiti (ees·)pr·zhee·tee*
frying pan *tava* ① *ta·va*
full *pun poon*
full-time *punim radnim vremenom poo·neem rad·neem vre·me·nawm*
fun *zabavan za·ba·van*
(have) fun *uživati* imp *oo·zhee·va·tee*
funeral *pogreb* ⓜ *paw·greb*
funny *smješan smye·shan*
furniture *namještaj* ⓜ *na·mye·shtai*
future *budućnost* ① *boo·dooch·nawst*

G

game *igra* ① *ee·gra*
game (football) *utakmica* ① *oo·tak·mee·tsa*
garage *garaža* ① *ga·ra·zha*
garbage *smeće* ⓝ *sme·che*
garbage can *kanta za smeće* ① *kan·ta za sme·che*
garden *vrt* ⓜ *vrt*
gardener *vrtlar* ⓜ *vrt·lar*
gardening *vrtlarstvo* ⓝ *vrt·lars·tvaw*
garlic *češnjak* ⓜ *chesh·nyak*
gas (for cooking) *plin* ⓜ *pleen*
gas (petrol) *benzin* ⓜ *ben·zeen*
gas cartridge *plinski uložak* ⓜ *pleen·skee oo·law·zhak*
gastroenteritis *gastroenteritis* ⓜ *ga·straw·en·te·ree·tees*
gate (airport, etc) *izlaz* ⓜ *eez·laz*
gauze *gaza* ① *ga·za*
gay *homoseksualan haw·maw·sek·soo·a·lan*
Germany *Njemačka* ① *nye·mach·ka*
get *dobiti/dobivati daw·bee·tee/ daw·bee·va·tee*
get off (a train, etc) *sići/silaziti sa see·chee/see·la·zee·tee sa*
gift *dar* ⓜ *dar*
gig *nastup* ⓜ *na·stoop*
gin *džin* ⓜ *jeen*
girl *djevojčica* ① *dye·voy·chee·tsa*
girlfriend *cura* ① *tsoo·ra*
give *dati/davati da·tee/da·va·tee*
given name *krsno ime* ⓝ *kr·snaw ee·me*
glandular fever *mononukleoza* ① *maw·naw·nook·le·aw·za*
glass (material) *staklo* ⓝ *sta·klo*
glass (receptacle) *čaša* ① *cha·sha*

glasses (spectacles) *naočale* ① pl
na-aw-cha-le

glove(s) *rukavica/e* ① sg/① pl
roo-ka-vee-tsa/e

glue *ljepilo* ① lye-pee-law

go *ići* imp ee-chee

go out *izaći/izlaziti* ee-za-chee/eez-la-zee-tee

go out with *izaći/izlaziti sa* ee-za-chee/
eez-la-zee-tee sa

goal *gol* ⑩ gawl

goalkeeper *vratar* ⑩ vra-tar

goat *jarac* ⑩ ya-rats

god (general) *bog* ⑩ bawg

goggles (skiing) *naočale za skijanje* ① pl
na-aw-cha-le za skee-ya-nye

goggles (swimming) *zaštitne naočale za
plivanje* ① pl zash-teet-ne na-aw-cha-le
za plee-va-nye

gold *zlato* ⑩ zla-taw

golf *golf* ⑩ gawlf

golf ball *loptica za golf* ① lawp-tee-tsa
za gawlf

golf course *teren za golf* ⑩ te-ren za gawlf

good *dobar* daw-bar

Goodbye. *Zbogom.* zbaw-gawm

government *vlada* ① vla-da

gram *gram* ⑩ gram

grandchild *unuk/unuka* ⑩/①
oo-nook/oo-noo-ka

grandfather *djed* ⑩ dyed

grandmother *baka* ① ba-ka

grapefruit *grejpfrut* ⑩ greyp-froot

grapes *grožđe* ⑩ grawzh-je

grass (lawn) *trava* ① tra-va

grateful *zahvalan* za-hva-lan

grave (tomb) *grob* ⑩ grawb

gray *siv* seev

great (fantastic) *krasno* kra-snaw

green *zelen* ze-len

greengrocer *trgovac povrćem* ⑩
tr-gaw-vats paw-vr-chem

grey *siv* seev

grocery *namirnica* ① na-meer-nee-tsa

groundnut *kikiriki* ⑩ kee-kee-ree-kee

grow (po)rasti (paw-)ra-stee

g-string *g-string* ⑩ ge-streeng

guaranteed *garantiran* ga-ran-tee-ran

guess *pogoditi/pogađati*
paw-gaw-dee-tee/paw-ga-ja-tee

guesthouse *privatni smještaj za najam* ⑩
pree-vat-nee smyesh-tai za nai-am

guide (audio) *audio vodič* ⑩ a-oo-dee-aw
vaw-deech

guide (person) *vodič* ⑩ vaw-deech

guide dog *pas vodič* ⑩ pas vaw-deech

guidebook *vodič* ⑩ vaw-deech

guided tour *ekskurzija s vodičem* ①
ek-skoor-zee-ya s vaw-dee-chem

guilty *kriv* kreev

guitar *gitara* ① gee-ta-ra

gums (teeth) *desni* ① pl de-snee

gun *puška* ① poosh-ka

gym (place) *teretana* ① te-re-ta-na

gymnastics *gimnastika* ① geem-na-stee-ka

gynaecologist *ginekolog* ⑩
gee-ne-kaw-lawg

H

hair (body) *dlaka* ① dla-ka

hair (head) *kosa* ① kaw-sa

hairbrush *četka za kosu* ① chet-ka za
kaw-soo

haircut *šišanje* ① shee-sha-nye

hairdresser *frizer* ⑩ free-zer

halal *halal* ha-lal

half *polovina* ① paw-law-vee-na

ham *šunka* ① shoon-ka

hammer *čekić* ⑩ che-keech

hammock *viseća mreža za ležanje* ①
vee-se-cha mre-zha za le-zha-nye

hand *ruka* ① roo-ka

handbag *ručna torbica* ① rooch-na
tawr-bee-tsa

handball *rukomet* ⑩ roo-kaw-met

handicrafts *ručni radovi* ⑩ pl rooch-nee
ra-daw-vee

handkerchief *rupčić* ⑩ roop-cheech

handlebars *volan bicikla* ⑩ vaw-lan
bee-tsee-kla

handmade *ručno izrađen* rooch-naw
eez-ra-jen

handsome *zgodan* zgaw-dan

happy *sretan* sre-tan

harassment *uznemiravanje* ⑩
ooz-ne-mee-ra-va-nye

harbour *luka* ① loo-ka

hard (not easy) *težak* te-zhak

hard (not soft) *tvrd* tvrd

hardware store *prodavaonica metalne i
tehničke robe* ① praw-da-va-aw-nee-tsa
me-tal-ne ee teh-neech-ke raw-be

hash *hašiš* ⑩ ha-sheesh

hat *šešir* ⑩ she-sheer

have *imati* imp ee-ma-tee

hay fever *peludna groznica* ① *pe*-lood-na grawz-nee-tsa
hazelnut *lješnjak* ⑩ *lyesh*-nyak
he *on* ⑩ awn
head *glava* ① *gla*-va
headache *glavobolja* ① gla-*vaw*-baw-lya
headlights *prednje svjetlo* ⑩ *pred*-nye svyet-law
health *zdravlje* ⑪ zdrav-lye
hear *čuti* perf choo-tee
hearing aid *slušni aparat* ⑩ sloosh-nee a-*pa*-rat
heart *srce* ⑪ sr-tse
heart attack *srčani udar* ⑩ sr-cha-nee oo-dar
heart condition *poremećaj srca* ⑩ paw-re-me-chai sr-tsa
heat *vrućina* ① vroo-chee-na
heated *zagrijan* za-gree-yan
heater *grijač* ⑩ gree-yach
heating *grijanje* ⑪ gree-ya-nye
heavy *težak* te-zhak
Hello. (answering telephone) *Halo.* ha-law
Hello. (not answering telephone) *Zdravo.* zdra-vaw
helmet *kaciga* ① *ka*-tsee-ga
help *pomoć* ① paw-mawch
help *pomoći/pomagati* paw-maw-chee/ paw-ma-ga-tee
Help! *Upomoć!* oo-paw-mawch
hepatitis *hepatitis* ⑩ he-pa-*tee*-tees
her *njen/njena/njeno* ⑩/①/⑩ nyen/ nye-na/nyen-naw
herb *biljka* ① *beel*-ka
herbalist *travar* ⑩ *tra*-var
here *ovdje* awv-dye
heroin *heroin* ⑩ he-*raw*-een
high *visok* vee-sawk
high school *srednja škola* ① *sred*-nya shkaw-la
highchair *visoka stolica za bebe* ① vee-saw-ka staw-lee-tsa za *be*-be
highway *autoput* ⑩ a-oo-taw-*poot*
hike *(pro)pješačiti* (praw-)pye-sha-chee-tee
hiking *pješačenje* ⑩ pye-*sha*-che-nye
hiking boots *gležnjače* ① pl glezh-nya-che
hiking route *pješački put* ⑩ pye-*shach*-kee poot
hill *brežuljak* ⑩ bre-zhoo-lyak
hire *iznajmiti/iznajmljivati* eez-*nai*-mee-tee/eez-naim-*lyee*-va-tee
his *njegov/njegova/negovo* ⑩/①/⑩ nye-gawv/nye-gawv-va/nye-gawv-vaw

historical *povijesni* paw-vee-ye-snee
history *povijest* ① paw-vee-yest
hitchhike *stopirati* imp staw-*pee*-ra-tee
HIV *HIV* ⑩ heev
hockey *hokej* ⑩ haw-key
holiday (day off) *blagdan* ⑩ blag-dan
holidays *praznici* ⑩ pl praz-nee-tsee
Holy Week *veliki tjedan* ⑩ ve-lee-kee tye-dan
home *dom* ⑩ dawm
(at) home *kući* koo-chee
homeless *koji je bez doma* ⑩ *koy*-ee ye bez daw-ma
homemaker *domaćica* ① daw-*ma*-chee-tsa
homeopathy *homeopatija* ① haw-me-aw-*pa*-tee-ya
homosexual *homoseksualac/ homoseksualka* ⑩/① haw-maw-sek-soo-*a*-lats/ haw-maw-sek-soo-*al*-ka
honey *med* ⑩ med
honeymoon *medeni mjesec* ⑩ me-de-nee mye-sets
horoscope *horoskop* ⑩ haw-raw-skawp
horse *konj* ⑩ kawn'
horse riding *jahanje konja* ① ya-ha-nye kaw-nya
hospital *bolnica* ① bawl-nee-tsa
hospitality *gostoprimstvo* gaw-staw-*preems*-tvaw
hot *vruć* vrooch
hot water *topla voda* ① *taw*-pla vaw-da
hotel *hotel* ⑩ haw-*tel*
hour *sat* ⑩ sat
house *kuća* ① koo-cha
housework *kućni poslovi* ⑩ pl *kooch*-nee paw-slaw-vee
how *kako* ka-kaw
how much *koliko* kaw-*lee*-kaw
hug *(za)grliti* (za-)gr-lee-tee
huge *ogroman* aw-graw-man
human resources *ljudski resursi* ⑩ pl *lyood*-skee re-*soor*-see
human rights *ljudska prava* ⑩ pl *lyood*-ska pra-va
humanities *društvene znanosti* ① pl *droosht*-ve-ne zna-naw-stee
hundred *sto* staw
Hungary *Mađarska* ① *ma*-jar-ska
hungry (to be) *biti gladan/gladna* ⑩/① *bee*-tee gla-dan/gla-dna
hunting *lov na životinje* ⑩ lawv na zhee-*vaw*-tee-nye

hurt (emotionally) *uvrijediti/vrijeđati* oo·vree·ye·dee·tee/vree·ye·ja·tee
hurt (physically) *raniti/ranjavati* ra·nee·tee/ra·nya·va·tee
husband *muž* ⓜ moozh

I

I *ja* ya
ice *led* ⓜ led
ice cream *sladoled* ⓜ sla·daw·led
ice hockey *hokej na ledu* ⓜ haw·key na le·doo
ice-cream parlour *sladoledarna* ⓕ sla·daw·le·dar·na
identification *identifikacija* ⓕ ee·den·tee·fee·ka·tsee·ya
identification card (ID) *osobna iskaznica* ⓕ aw·sawb·na ee·skaz·nee·tsa
idiot *budala* ⓕ boo·da·la
if *ako* a·kaw
ill *bolestan* baw·le·stan
Illyrians *Iliri* ⓜ pl ee·lee·ree
immigration *imigracija* ⓕ ee·mee·gra·tsee·ya
important *važan* va·zhan
impossible *nemoguć* ne·maw·gooch
in *u · na · po · kroz* oo · na · paw · krawz
in a hurry *užurban* oo·zhoor·ban
in front of *pred* pred
included *uključen* ook·lyoo·chen
income tax *porez na dohodak* ⓜ paw·rez na daw·haw·dak
independence *nezavisnost* ⓕ ne·za·vee·snawst
India *Indija* ⓕ een·dee·ya
indicator (car) *žmigavac* ⓜ zhmee·ga·vats
indigestion *probavne smetnje* ⓕ pl praw·bav·ne smet·nye
indoor *unutrašnji* oo·noo·trash·nyee
industry *industrija* ⓕ een·doo·stree·ya
infection *zaraza* ⓕ za·ra·za
inflammation *upala* ⓕ oo·pa·la
influenza *gripa* ⓕ gree·pa
information *informacije* ⓕ pl een·fawr·ma·tsee·ye
ingredient *sastojak* ⓜ sa·stoy·ak
inject *ubrizgati/ubrizgavati* oo·breez·ga·tee/oo·breez·ga·va·tee
injection *injekcija* ⓕ ee·nyek·tsee·ya
injured *povrijeđen* ⓜ paw·vree·ye·jen
injury *povreda* ⓕ paw·vre·da

inner tube *zračnica* ⓕ zrach·nee·tsa
innocent *nevin* ⓜ ne·veen
inside *unutra* oo·noo·tra
instructor *instruktor* ⓜ een·strook·tawr
insurance *osiguranje* ⓕ aw·see·goo·ra·nye
interesting *zanimljiv* za·neem·lyeev
intermission *prekid* ⓜ pre·keed
international *međunarodan* me·joo·na·raw·dan
Internet *internet* ⓜ een·ter·net
Internet café *internet kafić* ⓜ een·ter·net ka·feech
interpreter *tumač* ⓜ too·mach
interview *intervju* ⓜ een·ter·vyoo
invite *pozvati/pozivati* pawz·va·tee/paw·zee·va·tee
Ireland *Irska* ⓕ eer·ska
iron (for clothes) *pegla* ⓕ pe·gla
island *otok* ⓜ aw·tawk
Israel *Izrael* ⓜ ee·zra·el
it *ovo/to* ⓝ aw·vaw/taw
IT *Informacijska tehnologija* ⓕ een·fawr·ma·tseey·ska teh·naw·law·gee·ya
Italy *Italija* ⓕ ee·ta·lee·ya
itch *svrbež* ⓜ svr·bezh
itemised *nabrojan* ⓜ na·broy·an
itinerary *plan puta* ⓜ plan poo·ta
IUD *spirala* ⓕ spee·ra·la

J

jacket *jakna* ⓕ yak·na
jail *zatvor* ⓜ zat·vawr
jam *džem* ⓜ jem
January *siječanj* ⓜ see·ye·chan'
Japan *Japan* ⓜ ya·pan
jar *staklenka* ⓕ sta·klen·ka
jaw *čeljust* ⓕ che·lyoost
jealous *ljubomoran* lyoo·baw·maw·ran
jeans *traperice* ⓕ pl tra·pe·ree·tse
jeep *džip* ⓜ jeep
jet lag *umor poslije dugog leta* oo·mawr paw·slee·ye doo·gawg le·ta
jewellery *nakit* ⓜ na·keet
Jewish *Židovski* zhee·dawv·skee
job *posao* ⓜ paw·sa·aw
jogging *trčanje* ⓕ tr·cha·nye
joke *šala* ⓕ sha·la
journalist *novinar/novinarka* ⓜ/ⓕ naw·vee·nar/naw·vee·nar·ka
journey *putovanje* ⓝ poo·taw·va·nye

judge *sudac* ⓜ *soo*-dats
juice *sok* ⓜ sawk
July *srpanj* ⓜ sr-pan'
jump *skočiti/skakati* skaw-chee-tee/ska-ka-tee
jumper (sweater) *džemper* ⓜ *jem*-per
jumper leads *kablovi za punjenje akumulatora* pl *ka*-blaw-vee za poo-nye-nye a-koo-moo-*la*-taw-ra
June *lipanj* ⓜ *lee*-pan'

K

karst *krš* ⓜ krsh
ketchup *ketchup* ⓜ *ke*-chap
key *ključ* ⓜ klyooch
keyboard (computer) *tastatura* ⓕ ta-sta-*too*-ra
keyboard (instrument) *klavijatura* ⓕ kla-vee-ya-*too*-ra
kick *šutnuti/šutirati shoot*-noo-tee/shoo-tee-ra-tee
kidney *bubreg* ⓜ *boo*-breg
kilo *kila* ⓕ *kee*-la
kilogram *kilogram* ⓜ kee-law-*gram*
kilometre *kilometar* ⓜ kee-law-me-tar
kind (nice) *prijazan* pree-ya-zan
kindergarten *vrtić za djecu* ⓜ *vr*-teech za dye-tsoo
king *kralj* ⓜ kral'
kiosk *kiosk* ⓜ *kee*-awsk
kiss *poljubac* ⓜ paw-*lyoo*-bats
kiss *(po)ljubiti* (paw-)*lyoo*-bee-tee
kitchen *kuhinja* ⓕ *koo*-hee-nya
knee *koljeno* ⓝ *kaw*-lye-naw
knife *nož* ⓜ nawzh
know (sa)znati (sa-)*zna*-tee
kosher *košer* ⓜ *kaw*-sher

L

labourer *radnik* ⓜ *rad*-neek
lace *čipka* ⓕ *cheep*-ka
lake *jezero* ⓝ *ye*-ze-raw
lamb (animal) *janje* ⓝ *ya*-nye
lamb (meat) *janjetina* ⓕ *ya*-nye-tee-na
land *zemlja* *zem*-lya
landlady *gazdarica* ⓕ *gaz*-da-ree-tsa
landlord *gazda* ⓜ *gaz*-da
language *jezik* ⓜ *ye*-zeek
laptop *prenosivi računar* ⓜ pre-*naw*-see-vee ra-*choo*-nar

large *krupan* kroo-pan
last (previous) *predhodni* pred-*hawd*-nee
last (week) *prošli* prawsh-lee
late *kasan* ka-san
later *kasnije* ka-snee-ye
laugh *(na)smijati se* (na-)*smee*-ya-tee se
laundrette *automatska praonica* ⓕ a-oo-*taw*-mat-ska pra-*aw*-nee-tsa
laundry (clothes) *pranje rublja* ⓝ *pra*-nye *roob*-lya
laundry (place) *praonica* ⓕ pra-*aw*-nee-tsa
laundry (room) *soba za pranje rublja* ⓕ *saw*-ba za *pra*-nye *roob*-lya
law *zakon* ⓜ za-kawn
law (study, professsion) *pravo* ⓝ *pra*-vaw
lawyer *pravnik* ⓜ *prav*-neek
laxative *laksativ* ⓜ *lak*-sa-teev
lazy *lijen* lee-yen
leader *čelnik* ⓜ *chel*-neek
leaf *list* ⓜ leest
learn *(na)učiti* (na-)*oo*-chee-tee
leather *koža* ⓕ *kaw*-zha
lecturer *nastavnik* ⓜ *na*-stav-neek
ledge *izbočina* ⓕ *eez*-baw-chee-na
leek *poriluk* ⓜ *paw*-ree-look
left (direction) *lijevi* lee-*ye*-vee
left luggage *odložena prtljaga* ⓕ awd-*law*-zhe-na prt-*lya*-ga
left luggage (office) *ured za odlaganje prtljage* ⓜ oo-red za *awd*-la-ga-nye prt-*lya*-ge
left-wing *ljevičarski* ⓜ *lye*-vee-char-skee
leg *noga* ⓕ *naw*-ga
legal *zakonit* za-kaw-neet
legislation *zakonodavstvo* ⓝ za-kaw-naw-*davs*-tvaw
legume *mahunar* ⓜ *ma*-hoo-nar
lemon *limun* ⓜ *lee*-moon
lemonade *limunada* ⓕ lee-moo-*na*-da
lens *leća* ⓕ *le*-cha
Lent *post* ⓜ pawst
lentil *leća* ⓕ *le*-cha
lesbian *lezbijka* ⓕ *lez*-beey-ka
less *manje* *ma*-nye
letter (mail) *pismo* ⓝ *pee*-smaw
lettuce *zelena salata* ⓕ *ze*-le-na *sa*-la-ta
liar *lažljivac/lažljivica* ⓜ/ⓕ *lazh*-lyee-vats/lazh-*lyee*-vee-tsa
library *knjižnica* ⓕ *knyeezh*-nee-tsa
lice *uši* ⓕ pl oo-shee
licence *dozvola* ⓕ *dawz*-vaw-la
licence-plate number *broj registarske tablice* ⓜ broy re-gee-star-ske *ta*-blee-tse

lie (not stand) *leći/ležati* le·chee/le·zha·tee
life *život* ⓜ zhee·vawt
life jacket *prsluk za spasavanje* ⓜ
  pr·slook za spa·sa·va·nye
lift (elevator) *dizalo* ⓝ dee·za·law
light (illumination) *svjetlost* ① svyet·lawst
light (lamp) *svjetiljka* ① svye·teel′·ka
light (not heavy) *lagan* la·gan
light (of colour) *svjetao* svye·ta·aw
light bulb *žarulja* ① zha·roo·lya
light meter *svjetlomjer* ⓜ svyet·law·myer
lighter *peniša* ⓜ pe·nee·sha
lighter (cigarette) *upaljač* ⓜ oo·pa·lyach
like (appeal to) *dopasti/dopadati se*
  daw·pa·stee/daw·pa·da·tee se
like (a person) *voljeti* imp vaw·lye·tee
like (want) *(po)željeti* (paw·)zhe·lye·tee
linen (material) *laneno platno* ⓝ
  la·ne·naw plat·naw
linen (sheets etc) *posteljina* ①
  paw·ste·lyee·na
lip balm *balzam za usne* ⓜ bal·zam za
  oo·sne
lips *usne* ① pl oo·sne
lipstick *ruž za usne* ⓜ roozh za oo·sne
liquor store *prodavaonica alkohola* ①
  praw·da·va·aw·nee·tsa al·kaw·haw·la
listen (to) *(po)slušati* (paw·)sloo·sha·tee
little *mali* ma·lee
little (not much) *malo* ma·law
live (somewhere) *stanovati* imp
  sta·naw·va·tee
liver *jetra* ① ye·tra
lizard *gušter* ⓜ goosh·ter
local *mjesni* mye·snee
lock *brava* ① bra·va
lock *zaključati/zaključavati*
  zak·lyoo·cha·tee/zak·lyoo·cha·va·tee
locked *zaključan* zak·lyoo·chan
lollies *bomboni* ⓜ pl bawm·baw·nee
long *dugačak* doo·ga·chak
look *(po)gledati* (paw·)gle·da·tee
look after *(po)brinuti se za*
  (paw·)bree·noo·tee se za
look for *(po)tražiti* (paw·)tra·zhee·tee
lookout *vidik* ⓜ vee·deek
loose *labav* la·bav
loose change *sitniš* ⓜ seet·neesh
lose *(iz)gubiti* (eez·)goo·bee·tee
lost *izgubljen* eez·goob·lyen
lost property office *ured za izgubljene
  stvari* ⓜ oo·red za eez·goob·lye·ne
  stva·ree

(a) lot *puno* ⓝ poo·naw
loud *glasan* gla·san
love *ljubav* ① lyoo·bav
love *voljeti* imp vaw·lye·tee
lover *ljubavnik/ljubavnica* ⓜ/①
  lyoo·bav·neek/lyoo·bav·nee·tsa
low *nizak* nee·zak
lubricant *lubrikant* ⓜ loo·bree·kant
luck *sreća* ① sre·cha
lucky *sretan* sre·tan
luggage *prtljaga* ① prt·lya·ga
luggage lockers *pretinac za
  odlaganje prtljage* ⓜ pre·tee·nats za
  awd·la·ga·nye prt·lya·ge
luggage tag *etiketa za prtljagu* ①
  e·tee·ke·ta za prt·lya·goo
lump *grumen* ⓜ groo·men
lunch *ručak* ⓜ roo·chak
lung *pluća* ⓝ pl ploo·cha
luxury *raskošan* ra·skaw·shan

M

Macedonia *Makedonija* ①
  ma·ke·daw·nee·ya
machine *stroj* ⓜ stroy
magazine *magazin* ⓜ ma·ga·zeen
mail (letters, postal system) *pošta* ①
  pawsh·ta
mailbox *poštanski sandučić* ⓜ
  pawsh·tan·skee san·doo·cheech
main *glavni* glav·nee
main road *glavna ulica* ① glav·na oo·lee·tsa
make (bring about) *(na)praviti*
  (na·)pra·vee·tee
make (fabricate) *(u)činiti* (oo·)chee·nee·tee
make-up *šminka* ① shmen·ka
mammogram *mamogram* ⓜ
  ma·maw·gram
man (human) *čovjek* ⓜ chaw·vyek
man (male person) *muškarac* ⓜ
  moosh·ka·rats
manager *menadžer* ⓜ me·na·jer
mandarin *mandarina* ① man·da·ree·na
mandolin *mandolina* ① man·daw·lee·na
manual worker *fizički radnik* ⓜ
  fee·zeech·kee rad·neek
many *mnogi* mnaw·gee
map (of country) *karta* ① kar·ta
map (of town) *plan grada* ⓜ plan gra·da
March *ožujak* ⓜ aw·zhoo·yak
margarine *margarin* ⓜ mar·ga·reen

marijuana *marihuana* ① ma-ree-hoo-*a*-na
marina *marina* ① ma-*ree*-na
marital status *bračno stanje* ⑩ *brach*-naw *sta*-nye
market *tržnica* ① *trzh*-nee-tsa
marmalade *marmelada* ① mar-me-*la*-da
marriage *brak* ⑩ brak
married (of man) *vjenčan* vyen-chan
married (of woman) *vjenčana* vyen-cha-na
marry *udati/udavati se* oo-da-tee/ oo-*da*-va-tee se
martial arts *borilačke vještine* ① pl baw-ree-lach-ke vye-*shtee*-ne
mass (Catholic) *misa* ① *mee*-sa
massage *masaža* ① ma-*sa*-zha
masseur/masseuse *maser/maserka* ⑩/① ma-*ser*/ma-*ser*-ka
mat *otirač* ⑩ aw-*tee*-rach
match (sports) *utakmica* ① oo-*tak*-mee-tsa
matches (for lighting) *šibice* ① pl *shee*-bee-tse
mattress *madrac* ⑩ *mad*-rats
May *svibanj* ⑩ *svee*-ban'
maybe *možda* *mawzh*-da
mayonnaise *majoneza* ① mai-aw-*ne*-za
mayor *gradonačelnik* ⑩ gra-daw-*na*-chel-neek
me *me* mee
meal *ručak* ⑩ *roo*-chak
measles *ospice* ① pl *aw*-spee-tse
meat *meso* ⑩ *me*-saw
mechanic *automehaničar* ⑩ a-oo-taw-me-*ha*-nee-char
media *mediji* ⑩ pl *me*-dee-yee
medicine (medication) *lijekovi* ⑩ pl *lee*-ye-kaw-vee
medicine (profession) *medicina* ① me-dee-*tsee*-na
meditation *meditacija* ① me-dee-*ta*-tsee-ya
meet (for first time) *upoznati/upoznavati* oo-*pawz*-na-tee/oo-pawz-*na*-va-tee
meet (run into) *sresti/sretati* *sre*-stee/ *sre*-ta-tee
melon *dinja* ① *dee*-nya
member *član/članica* ⑩/① chlan/ *chlan*-ee-tsa
menstruation *mjesečnica* ① *mye*-sech-nee-tsa
menu *jelovnik* ⑩ ye-*lawv*-neek
message *poruka* ① *paw*-roo-ka
metal *metal* ⑩ *me*-tal
metre *metar* ⑩ *me*-tar
metro (train) *metro* ⑩ *me*-traw

metro station *metro stanica* ① *me*-traw *sta*-nee-tsa
microwave (oven) *mikrovalna pećnica* ① *mee*-kraw-val-na *pech*-nee-tsa
midday *podne* ⑩ *pawd*-ne
midnight *ponoć* ① *paw*-nawch
migraine *migrena* ① *me*-gre-na
military *vojska* ① *voy*-ska
military service *vojna obveza* ① *voy*-na *awb*-ve-za
milk *mlijeko* ⑩ mlee-*ye*-kaw
millimetre *milimetar* ⑩ mee-lee-*me*-tar
million *milijun* ⑩ mee-*lee*-yoon
mince *mljeveno meso* ⑩ *mlye*-ve-naw *me*-saw
mineral water *mineralna voda* ① *mee*-ne-ral-na *vaw*-da
minute *minuta* ① *mee*-noo-ta
mirror *ogledalo* ⑩ aw-*gle*-da-law
miscarriage *pobačaj* ⑩ *paw*-ba-chai
Miss *Gospođica* ① *gaw*-spaw-jee-tsa
miss (feel absence of) *nedostajati* imp *ne*-daw-stai-a-tee
mistake *pogreška* ① *paw*-gresh-ka
mix *(po)miješati* (paw-)mee-ye-*sha*-tee
mobile phone *mobilni telefon* ⑩ *maw*-beel-nee te-le-fawn
modem *modem* ⑩ *maw*-dem
modern *suvremen* soo-*vre*-men
moisturiser *hidratantna krema* ① hee-dra-*tant*-na *kre*-ma
monastery *samostan* ⑩ *sa*-maw-stan
Monday *ponedjeljak* ⑩ *paw*-ne-dye-lyak
money *novac* ⑩ *naw*-vats
monk *redovnik* ⑩ re-*dawv*-neek
Montenegro *Crna Gora* ① *tsr*-na *gaw*-ra
month *mjesec* ⑩ *mye*-sets
monument *spomenik* ⑩ *spaw*-me-neek
moon *mjesec* ⑩ *mye*-sets
more *više* *vee*-she
morning *jutro* ⑩ *yoo*-traw
morning sickness *trudnička jutarnja mučnina* ① *trood*-neech-ka *yoo*-tar-nya *mooch*-nee-na
mosque *džamija* ① *ja*-mee-ya
mosquito *komarac* ⑩ *kaw*-ma-rats
mosquito coil *zapaljivo sredstvo protiv komaraca* ① *za*-pa-lyee-vaw *sreds*-tvaw *praw*-teev kaw-*ma*-ra-tsa
mosquito net *mreža za komarce* ① *mre*-zha za kaw-*mar*-tse
motel *motel* ⑩ *maw*-tel
mother *majka* ① *mai*-ka

mother-in-law (of husband) *punica* ① poo-nee-tsa

mother-in-law (of wife) *svekrva* ① sve-kr-va

motorbike *motocikl* ⓜ maw-taw-*tsee*-kl

motorboat *motorni čamac* ⓜ maw-tawr-nee cha-mats

motorcycle *motocikl* ⓜ maw-taw-*tsee*-kl

motorway (tollway) *autoput na kojem se plaća cestarina* ⓜ a-oo-taw-poot na koy-em se *pla*-cha tse-sta-ree-na

mountain *planina* ① pla-*nee*-na

mountain bike *brdski bicikl* ⓜ brd-skee bee-*tsee*-kl

mountain path *brdska staza* ① brd-ska sta-za

mountain range *gorski lanac* ⓜ gawr-skee *la*-nats

mountaineering *alpinizam* ⓜ al-pee-*nee*-zam

mouse *miš* ⓜ meesh

mouth *usta* ① oo-sta

movie *film* ⓜ feelm

Mr *Gospodin* ⓜ gaw-*spaw*-deen

Mrs *Gospođa* ① gaw-*spaw*-ja

Ms *G'đa* ① g-ja

mud *blato* ⓝ bla-taw

muesli *muesli* ⓜ pl moo-zlee

mum *mama* ① ma-ma

mumps *zaušnjaci* pl za-oosh-nya-tsee

murder *ubojstvo* ① oo-*boys*-tvaw

murder *ubiti/ubijati* oo-bee-tee/ oo-*bee*-ya-tee

muscle *mišić* ⓜ mee-sheech

museum *muzej* ⓜ moo-zey

mushroom *gljiva* ① glyee-va

music *glazba* ① glaz-ba

music shop *prodavaonica muzike* ① praw-da-va-*aw*-nee-tsa moo-zee-ke

musician *muzičar* ⓜ moo-zee-char

Muslim *musliman/muslimanka* ⓜ① moo-*slee*-man/moo-*slee*-man-ka

mussel *dagnja* ① dag-nya

mustard *senf* ⓜ senf

mute *nijem* nee-*yem*

my *moj/moja/moje* ⓜ/①/ⓝ moy/moy-a/ moy-e

N

nail clippers *škarice za nokte* ① pl shka-ree-tse za *nawk*-te

name (given) *ime* ⓝ ee-me

napkin *salveta* ① sal-*ve*-ta

nappy *pelene* ① pl pe-le-ne

nappy rash *osip od pelena* ⓜ aw-seep awd pe-le-na

national park *nacionalni park* ⓜ na-tsee-aw-nal-nee park

nationality *nacionalnost* ① na-tsee-aw-*nal*-nawst

nature *priroda* ① pree-raw-da

naturopathy *naturoterapije* ① pl na-too-raw-te-ra-pee-ye

nausea *mučnina* ① mooch-*nee*-na

nave *srednja lađa crkve* ① sred-nya la-ja tsr-kve

navigation *navigacija* ① na-vee-ga-tsee-ya

near *blizu* blee-zoo

nearby *obližnji* aw-bleezh-nyee

nearest *najbliži* nai-blee-zhee

necessary *potreban* paw-tre-ban

necklace *ogrlica* ① aw-gr-lee-tsa

nectarine *nektarinka* ① nek-ta-*reen*-ka

need *(za)trebati* (za-)tre-ba-tee

needle (sewing) *igla za šivenje* ① ee-gla za shee-ve-nye

needle (syringe) *igla injekcije* ① ee-gla ee-*nyek*-tsee-ye

negative *negativan* ne-ga-tee-van

neither *niti* nee-tee

net *mreža* ① mre-zha

Netherlands *Nizozemska* ① nee-zaw-zem-ska

never *nikada* nee-ka-da

new *nov* nawv

New Year's Day *novogodišnji dan* ⓜ naw-vaw-*gaw*-deesh-nyee dan

New Year's Eve *doček nove godine* ⓜ daw-chek naw-ve gaw-dee-ne

New Zealand *Novi Zeland* ⓜ naw-vee ze-land

news *vijesti* ① pl vee-ye-stee

newsstand *kiosk za prodaju novina* ⓜ kee-awsk za praw-dai-oo naw-vee-na

newsagency *prodavaonica novina i časopisa* ① praw-da-va-aw-nee-tsa naw-vee-na ee cha-saw-pee-sa

newspaper *novine* ① pl naw-vee-ne

next (month) *slijedeći* slee-ye-de-chee

next to *pored* paw-red

nice *lijep* lee-yep

nickname *nadimak* ⓜ na-dee-mak

night *noć* ① nawch

nightclub *noćni klub* ⓜ nawch-nee kloob

no (response) *ne* ne

no (absence of something) *ništa* neesh·ta
no vacancy *bez slobodnih mjesta*
  bez slaw·bawd·neeh mye·sta
noisy *bučan* boo·chan
none *nikakav* nee·ka·kav
nonsmoking *nepušački* ⓜ
  ne·poo·shach·kee
noodles *rezanci* ⓜ pl re·zan·tsee
noon *podne* ⓝ pawd·ne
north *sjever* ⓜ sye·ver
Norway *Norveška* ⓕ nawr·vesh·ka
nose *nos* ⓜ naws
not *ne* ne
notebook *bilježnica* ⓕ bee·lyezh·nee·tsa
nothing *ništa* ⓝ neesh·ta
November *studeni* ⓜ stoo·de·nee
now *sada* sa·da
nuclear energy *nuklearna energija* ⓕ
  noo·kle·ar·na e·ner·gee·ya
nuclear testing *nuklearna testiranja* ⓝ pl
  noo·kle·ar·na te·stee·ra·nya
nuclear waste *nuklearni otpad* ⓜ
  noo·kle·ar·nee awt·pad
number (figure) *broj* ⓜ broy
number (quantity) *količina* ⓕ
  kaw·lee·chee·na
numberplate *registarska tablica* ⓕ
  re·gee·star·ska ta·blee·tsa
nun *opatica* ⓕ aw·pa·tee·tsa
nurse *medicinska sestra* ⓕ
  me·dee·tseen·ska se·stra
nut *orah* ⓜ aw·rah

O

oats *zob* ⓕ zawb
ocean *ocean* ⓜ aw·tse·an
October *listopad* ⓜ lee·staw·pad
off (spoiled) *pokvaren* pawk·va·ren
office *ured* ⓜ oo·red
office worker *službenik/službenica* ⓜ/ⓕ
  sloozh·be·neek/sloozh·be·nee·tsa
often *često* che·staw
oil *ulje* ⓝ oo·lye
oil (petrol) *nafta* ⓕ naf·ta
old *star* star
olive *maslina* ⓕ ma·slee·na
olive oil *maslinovo ulje* ⓝ ma·slee·naw·vaw
  oo·lye
Olympic Games *Olimpijske igre* ⓕ pl
  aw·leem·peey·ske ee·gre
omelette *omlet* ⓜ aw·mlet

on *na · pri · o · u* na · pree · aw · oo
on time *na vrijeme* na vree·ye·me
once *jednom* yed·nawm
one *jedan* ⓜ ye·dan
one-way (ticket) *jednosmjeran*
  yed·naw·smye·ran
onion *luk* ⓜ look
only *samo* sa·maw
open *otvoren* awt·vaw·ren
open *otvoriti/otvarati* awt·vaw·ree·tee/
  awt·va·ra·tee
opening hours *početak radnog vremena* ⓜ
  paw·che·tak rad·nawg vre·me·na
opera *opera* ⓕ aw·pe·ra
opera house *operna dvorana* ⓕ
  aw·per·na dvaw·ra·na
operation *operacija* ⓕ aw·pe·ra·tsee·ya
operator *operator* ⓜ aw·pe·ra·tawr
opinion *mišljenje* ⓝ meesh·lye·nye
opposite *nasuprot* na·soo·prawt
optometrist *optičar* ⓜ awp·tee·char
or *ili* ee·lee
orange (colour) *narančast* na·ran·chast
orange (fruit) *naranča* ⓕ na·ran·cha
orange juice *sok od naranče* ⓜ sawk awd
  na·ran·che
orchestra *orkestar* ⓜ awr·ke·star
order *poredak* ⓜ paw·re·dak
order (demand) *narediti/naređivati*
  na·re·dee·tee/na·re·jee·va·tee
order (request) *naručiti/naručivati*
  na·roo·chee·tee/na·roo·chee·va·tee
ordinary *običan* ⓜ aw·bee·chan
orgasm *orgazam* ⓜ awr·ga·zam
original *originalan* aw·ree·gee·na·lan
other *drugi* droo·gee
our *naš/naša/naše* ⓜ/ⓕ/ⓝ nash/nash·a/
  na·she
out of order *pokvaren* ⓜ pawk·va·ren
outside *vani* va·nee
ovarian cyst *cista na jajniku* ⓕ tsee·sta na
  yai·nee·koo
ovary *jajnik* ⓜ yai·neek
oven *pećnica* ⓕ pech·nee·tsa
overcoat *zimski kaput* ⓜ zeem·skee ka·poot
overdose *prevelika doza* ⓕ pre·ve·leeka
  daw·za
overnight *preko noći* pre·kaw naw·chee
overseas *inostranstvo* ⓕ
  ee·naw·strans·tvaw
owe *dugovati* imp doo·gaw·va·tee
owner *vlasnik* ⓜ vla·sneek
oxygen *kisik* ⓜ kee·seek

oyster *oštrige* ① pl *awsh*-tree-ge
ozone layer *ozonski omotač* ⑩
aw-zawn-skee aw-*maw*-tach

P

pacemaker *elekronski stimulator srca* ⑩
e-*lek*-trawn-skee stee-moo-*la*-tawr sr-tsa
pacifier *duda* ① *doo*-da
package *paket* ⑩ *pa*-ket
packet (general) *kutija* ① *koo*-tee-ya
padlock *lokot* ⑩ *law*-kawt
page *stranica* ① *stra*-nee-tsa
pain *bol* ① bawl
painful *bolan* *baw*-lan
painkiller *tableta protiv bolova* ①
ta-ble-ta *praw*-teev baw-*law*-va
painter *slikar* ① *slee*-kar
painting (a work) *slika* ① *slee*-ka
painting (the art) *slikarstvo* ⑩
slee-*kars*-tvaw
pair (couple) *par* ⑩ par
Pakistan *Pakistan* ① *pa*-kee-stan
palace *palača* ① *pa*-la-cha
pan *tava* ① *ta*-va
pants (trousers) *hlače* ① pl *hla*-che
panty liners *ulošci za žensko donje
rublje* ⑩ pl oo-*lawsh*-tsee za *zhen*-skaw
daw-nye roob-lye
pantyhose *hulahopke* ① pl hoo-la-*hawp*-ke
pap smear *PAPA test* ⑩ *pa*-pa test
paper *papir* ⑩ *pa*-peer
paperwork *dokumentacija* ①
daw-koo-men-*ta*-tsee-ya
paraplegic *paraplegičar* ⑩
pa-ra-*ple*-gee-char
parcel *paket* ⑩ *pa*-ket
parents *roditelji* ⑩ pl *raw*-dee-te-lyee
park *park* ⑩ park
park (a car) *parkirati* imp par-*kee*-ra-tee
parliament *sabor* ⑩ *sa*-bawr
part (component) *dio* ⑩ *dee*-aw
part-time *honorarni* ⑩ *haw*-naw-rar-nee
party (night out) *provod* ⑩ *praw*-vawd
party (politics) *stranka* ① *stran*-ka
pass *dobaciti/dobacivati* daw-*ba*-tsee-tee/
daw-*ba*-tsee-va-tee
passenger *putnik* ⑩ *poot*-neek
passport *putovnica* ① poo-*tawv*-nee-tsa
passport number *broj putovnice* ⑩ broy
poo-*tawv*-nee-tse
past *prošlost* ① *prawsh*-lawst

pasta *tjestenina* ① tye-ste-*nee*-na
pastry *fino pecivo* ⑩ *fee*-naw pe-*tsee*-vaw
path *staza* ① *sta*-za
pay *(u)platiti* (oo)*pla*-tee-tee
payment (by someone) *uplata* ① oo-*pla*-ta
payment (to someone) *isplata* ① ees-*pla*-ta
pea *grašak* ② *gra*-shak
peace *mir* ⑩ meer
peach *breskva* ① *bresk*-va
peak (mountain) *vrh* ⑩ vrh
peanut *kikiriki* ① *kee*-kee-*ree*-kee
pear *kruška* ① *kroosh*-ka
pedal *pedala* ① pe-*da*-la
pedestrian *pješak* ⑩ *pye*-shak
pen (ballpoint) *kemijska* ① *ke*-meey-ska
pencil *olovka* ① *aw*-lawv-ka
penis *penis* ⑩ *pe*-nees
penknife *džepni nožić* ⑩ *jep*-nee
naw-zheech
pensioner *umirovljenik* ⑩
oo-mee-rawv-*lye*-neek
people *ljudi* ⑩ pl *lyoo*-dee
pepper *papar* ⑩ *pa*-par
pepper (bell) *paprika* ① *pa*-pree-ka
per (day) *na* na
per cent *postotak* ⑩ paw-*staw*-tak
perfect *savršen* sa-*vr*-shen
performance *priredba* ① *pree*-red-ba
perfume *parfem* ⑩ par-*fem*
period pain *menstrualni bolovi* ⑩ pl
men-*stroo*-al-nee baw-*law*-vee
permission *dopuštenje* ⑩ daw-*poosh*-te-nye
permit *dozvola* ① *dawz*-vaw-la
person *osoba* ① *aw*-saw-ba
petrol *benzin* ⑩ ben-*zeen*
petrol station *benzinska stanica* ①
ben-*zeen*-ska *sta*-nee-tsa
pharmacy *ljekarna* ① lye-*kar*-na
phone book *telefonski imenik* ⑩
te-*le*-fawn-skee ee-me-neek
phone box *telefonska govornica* ①
te-*le*-fawn-ska *gaw*-vawr-nee-tsa
phonecard *telefonska kartica* ①
te-*le*-fawn-ska *kar*-tee-tsa
photo *fotografija* ① faw-*taw*-*gra*-fee-ya
photograph *slikati* perf *slee*-ka-tee
photographer *fotograf* ⑩ faw-*taw*-graf
photography *fotografija* ①
faw-*taw*-*gra*-fee-ya
phrasebook *zbirka fraza* ① *zbeer*-ka *fra*-za
pickaxe *pijuk* ⑩ *pee*-yook
pickles *kiseli krastavci* ⑩ pl *kee*-se-lee
kra-stav-tsee

picnic *piknik* ① peek·neek

pie *pita* ① pee·ta

piece *komad* ⓜ kaw·mad

pig *svinja* ① svee·nya

pill *tableta* ① ta·ble·ta

(the) Pill (contraceptive) *antibaby-pilula* ① an·tee·bey·bee·pee·loo·la

pillow *jastuk* ⓜ ya·stook

pillowcase *jastučnica* ① ya·stooch·nee·tsa

pineapple *ananas* ⓜ a·na·nas

pink *ružičast* roo·zhee·chast

pistachio *trišlja* ① treesh·lya

place *mjesto* ⓝ mye·staw

place of birth *mjesto rođenja* ⓝ mye·staw raw·je·nya

plaited ornamentation *pletenasti ukras* ⓜ ple·te·na·stee oo·kras

plane *zrakoplov* ⓜ zra·kaw·plawv

planet *planeta* ① pla·ne·ta

plant *biljka* ① beel'·ka

plastic *plastičan* pla·stee·chan

plate *tanjur* ⓜ ta·nyoor

plateau *plato* ⓜ pla·taw

platform *peron* ⓜ pe·rawn

play (board games) *igrati* imp ee·gra·tee

play (instrument) *(od)svirati (awd·)svee·ra·tee*

play (theatre) *predstava* ① pred·sta·va

plug (bath) *čep* ⓜ chep

plug (electricity) *utikač* ⓜ oo·tee·kach

plum *šljiva* ① shlyee·va

poached *poširan* paw·shee·ran

pocket *džep* ⓜ jep

pocket knife *džepni nožić* ⓜ jep·nee naw·zheech

poetry *poezija* ① paw·e·zee·ya

point (logic) *svrha* ① svr·ha

point (direction) *pokazati/pokazivati* paw·ka·za·tee/ paw·ka·zee·va·tee

poisonous *otrovan* aw·traw·van

police *policija* ① paw·lee·tsee·ya

police officer *policajac* ⓜ paw·lee·tsai·ats

police station *policijska stanica* ① paw·lee·tsey·ska sta·nee·tsa

politician *političar* ⓜ paw·lee·tee·char

politics *politika* ① paw·lee·tee·ka

pollen *pelud* ⓜ pe·lood

pollution *zagađenje* ⓝ za·ga·je·nye

pool (game) *bilijar* ⓜ bee·lee·yar

pool (swimming) *bazen za plivanje* ⓜ ba·zen za plee·va·nye

poor *siromašan* see·raw·ma·shan

popular *popularan* paw·poo·la·ran

pork *svinjetina* ① svee·nye·tee·na

pork sausage *svinjska kobasica* ① sveen'·ska kaw·ba·see·tsa

port (sea) *luka* ① loo·ka

positive *pozitivan* paw·zee·tee·van

possible *moguć* maw·gooch

post office *poštanski ured* ⓜ pawsh·tan·skee oo·red

postage *poštarina* ① pawsh·ta·ree·na

postcard *dopisnica* ① daw·pee·snee·tsa

postcode *poštanski broj* ⓜ pawsh·tan·skee broy

poster *poster* ⓜ paw·ster

pot (ceramics) *posuda* ① paw·soo·da

pot (dope) *trava* ① tra·va

potato *krumpir* ⓜ kroom·peer

pottery *grnčarija* ① grn·cha·ree·ya

pound (money, weight) *funta* ① foon·ta

poverty *siromaštvo* ⓝ see·raw·mash·tvaw

powder *prah* ⓜ prah

power *snaga* ① sna·ga

prawn *škamp* ⓜ shkamp

prayer *molitva* ① maw·leet·va

prefer *pretpostaviti/pretpostavljati* pret·paw·sta·vee·tee/ pret·paw·stav·lya·tee

pregnancy test kit *test na trudnoću* ⓜ test na trood·naw·choo

pregnant *trudna* ① trood·na

premenstrual tension *predmenstrualna napetost* ① pred·men·stroo·al·na na·pe·tawst

prepare *pripremiti/pripremati* pree·pre·mee·tee/pree·pre·ma·tee

prescription *recept za lijekove* ⓜ re·tsept za lee·ye·kaw·ve

present (gift) *poklon* ① paw·klawn

present (time) *sadašnjost* ① sa·dash·nyawst

president *predsjednik* ⓜ pred·syed·neek

pressure *pritisak* ⓜ pree·tee·sak

pretty *zgodan* zgaw·dan

price *cijena* ① tsee·ye·na

priest *svećenik* ⓜ sve·che·neek

prime minister *ministar predsjednik* ⓜ mee·nee·star pred·syed·neek

printer (computer) *pisač* ⓜ pee·sach

prison *zatvor* ⓜ zat·vawr

prisoner *zatvorenik* ① zat·vaw·re·neek

private *privatan* pree·va·tan

profit *dobitak* ⓜ daw·bee·tak

program *program* ⓜ praw·gram

projector *projektor* ⓜ proy·ek·tawr

promise *obećati/obečavati*
aw·be·cha·tee/aw·be·cha·va·tee
promontory *rt* ⓜ rt
prostitute *prostitutka* ⓕ praw·stee·*toot*·ka
protect *(za)štititi* (za·)shtee·tee·tee
protected (species) *zaštićen* zash·tee·chen
protest *prosvjed* ⓜ *praws*·vyed
protest *prosvjedovati* imp
praw·svye·daw·va·tee
provisions *namirnice* ⓕ pl na·meer·nee·tse
pub (bar) *gostionica* ⓕ gaw·stee·aw·nee·tsa
public gardens *javni parkovi* ⓜ pl
yav·nee par·kaw·vee
public relations *odnosi s javnošću* ⓜ pl
awd·naw·see s yav·nawsh·choo
public telephone *javni telefon* ⓜ yav·nee
te·*le*·fawn
public toilet *javni zahod* ⓜ yav·nee za·hawd
publishing *izdavanje* ⓝ eez·da·va·nye
pull *(po)vući* (paw·)voo·chee
pump *pumpa* ⓕ *poom*·pa
pumpkin *bundeva* ⓕ *boon*·de·va
puncture *(pro)bušiti* (praw·)*boo*·shee·tee
pure *čist* cheest
purple *ljubičast* lyoo·bee·chast
purse *novčarka* ⓕ nawv·*char*·ka
push *gurnuti/gurati* goor·noo·tee/*goo*·ra·tee
put *staviti/stavljati* sta·vee·tee/*stav*·lya·tee

Q

quadriplegic *potpuno paralizirana
osoba* ⓕ *pawt*·poo·naw
pa·ra·le·zee·ra·na aw·saw·ba
qualifications *kvalifikacije* ⓕ pl
kva·lee·fee·*ka*·tsee·ye
quality *kvaliteta* ⓕ kva·lee·*te*·ta
quarantine *karantena* ⓕ ka·ran·*te*·na
quarter *četvrtina* ⓕ chet·vr·*tee*·na
queen *kraljica* ⓕ *kra*·lyee·tsa
question *pitanje* ⓝ *pee*·ta·nye
queue *red* ⓜ red
quick *brz* brz
quiet *tih* teeh
quit *ostaviti/ostavljati* aw·sta·vee·tee/
aw·*stav*·lya·tee

R

rabbit *zec* ⓜ zets
race (sport) *utrka* ⓕ *oo*·tr·ka
racetrack *trkalište* ⓝ *tr*·ka·leesh·te

racing bike *trkaći bicikl* ⓜ *tr*·ka·chee
bee·tsee·kl
racism *rasna netrpeljivost* ⓕ *ra*·sna
ne·tr·pe·lyee·vawst
racquet *reket* ⓜ *re*·ket
radiator *radijator* ⓜ ra·dee·*ya*·tawr
radio *radio* ⓜ *ra*·dee·aw
radish *rotkva* ⓕ *rawt*·kva
railway station *željeznička stanica* ⓕ
zhe·lyez·nee·chka sta·nee·tsa
rain *kiša* ⓕ *kee*·sha
raincoat *kabanica* ⓕ ka·ba·nee·tsa
raisin *grožđica* ⓕ grawzh·jee·tsa
rape *silovanje* ⓝ see·law·va·nye
rape *silovati* perf see·law·va·tee
rare (uncommon) *rijedak* ree·ye·dak
rare (meat) *nepotpuno pečen*
ne·pawt·poo·naw pe·chen
rash *osip* ⓜ *aw*·seep
raspberry *malina* ⓕ *ma*·lee·na
rat *štakor* ⓜ *shta*·kawr
rave *rejv parti* ⓜ reyv *par*·tee
raw *sirov* ⓜ see·*rawv*
razor *brijač* ⓜ *bree*·yach
razor blade *britva* ⓕ *breet*·va
read *(pro)čitati* (praw·)*chee*·ta·tee
reading *čitanje* ⓝ *chee*·ta·nye
ready *spreman* spre·man
real-estate agent *posrednik za prodaju
nekretnina* ⓜ paw·sred·neek za
praw·dai·oo ne·kret·nee·na
rear (seat etc) *stražnji* strazh·nyee
reason *razlog* ⓜ *raz*·lawg
receipt *račun* ⓜ ra·choon
recently *nedavno* ne·dav·naw
recommend *preporučiti/preporučivati*
pre·paw·roo·chee·tee/
pre·paw·roo·chee·va·tee
record (music etc) *snimiti/snimati*
snee·mee·tee/*snee*·ma·tee
recording *snimak* ⓜ *snee*·mak
recyclable *koji se može reciklirati* ⓜ
koy·ee se *maw*·goo re·tsee·*klee*·ra·tee
recycle *reciklirati* perf re·tsee·*klee*·ra·tee
red *crven* tsr·ven
referee *sudac* ⓜ *soo*·dats
reference *preporuka* ⓕ pre·paw·roo·ka
reflexology *refleksologija* ⓕ
re·flek·saw·*law*·gee·ya
refrigerator *hladnjak* ⓜ *hlad*·nyak
refugee *izbjeglica* ⓕ eez·byeg·lee·tsa
refund *povrat novca* ⓜ *pawv*·rat
nawv·tsa

refuse *odbiti/odbijati* awd·bee·tee/ awd·bee·ya·tee
regional *područni* paw·drooch·nee
registered mail (by) *preporučenom poštom* pre·paw·roo·che·nawm pawsh·tawm
rehydration salts *soli za rehidrataciju* ① saw·lee za re·hee·dra·ta·tsee·yoo
reiki *reiki* ① re·ee·kee
relationship (not family) *odnos* ⑩ awd·naws
relationship (family) *srodstvo* ⑩ srawd·stvaw
relax *opustiti/opuštati se* aw·poo·stee·tee/ aw·poosh·ta·tee se
relic *relikvija* ① re·leek·vee·ya
religion *vjera* ① vye·ra
religious (concerning religion) *vjerski* vyer·skee
religious (person) *pobožan* paw·baw·zhan
remote *udaljen* oo·da·lyen
remote control *daljinski upravljač* ⑩ da·lyeen·skee oo·prav·lyach
rent *iznajmiti/iznajmljivati* eez·nai·mee·tee/eez·naim·lyee·va·tee
repair *popraviti/popravljati* paw·pra·vee·tee/paw·prav·lya·tee
republic *republika* ① re·poo·blee·ka
reservation (booking) *rezervacija* ① re·zer·va·tsee·ya
rest *odmoriti/odmarati se* awd·maw·ree·tee/awd·ma·ra·tee se
restaurant *restoran* ⑩ re·staw·ran
restaurant (family run) *gostiona* ① gaw·stee·aw·na
résumé *rezime* ⑩ re·zee·me
retired *umirovljen* oo·mee·rawv·lyen
return (come back) *vratiti/vraćati se* vra·tee·tee/vra·cha·tee se
return (ticket) *povratan* paw·vra·tan
reverse charge call *poziv na račun nazvane osobe* ⑩ paw·zeev na ra·choon naz·va·ne aw·saw·be
review (article) *pregled* ⑩ pre·gled
rhythm *ritam* ⑩ ree·tam
rib *rebro* ⑩ re·braw
rice *riža* ① ree·zha
rich (wealthy) *bogat* baw·gat
ride (trip) *vožnja* ① vawzh·nya
ride (horse) *jahati* imp ya·ha·tee
right (correct) *ispravan* ee·spra·van
right (direction) *desno* de·snaw
right-wing *desničarski* de·snee·char·skee

ring (on finger) *prsten* ⑩ pr·sten
ring (of phone) *nazvati/nazivati* naz·va·tee/na·zee·va·tee
rip-off *prekomjerna cijena* ① pre·kawm·yer·na tsee·ye·na
river *rijeka* ① ree·ye·ka
road *cesta* ① tse·sta
road map *putna karta* ① poot·na kar·ta
rob *(o)pljačkati* (aw)·plyach·ka·tee
rock *stijena* ① stee·ye·na
rock (music) *rock* rawk
rock climbing *alpinističko penjanje* ⑩ al·pee·nee·steech·kaw pe·nya·nye
rock group *rock grupa* ① rawk groo·pa
rockmelon *dinja* ① dee·nya
roll (bread) *žemička* ① zhe·meech·ka
rollerblading *rošulanje* ⑩ raw·shoo·la·nye
romantic *romantičan* raw·man·tee·chan
room *soba* ① saw·ba
room number *broj sobe* ⑩ broy saw·be
rope *uže* ⑩ oo·zhe
round *okrugao* aw·kroo·ga·aw
roundabout *kružni tok* ⑩ kroozh·nee tawk
route *put* ⑩ poot
rowing *veslanje* ⑩ ve·sla·nye
rubbish *smeće* ⑩ sme·che
rubbish bin *kanta za smeće* ① kan·ta za sme·che
rubella *rubeola* ① roo·be·aw·la
rug *tepih* ⑩ te·peeh
rugby *ragbi* ⑩ rag·bee
ruins *ruševine* ① pl roo·she·vee·ne
rule *pravilo* ① pra·vee·law
rum *rum* ⑩ room
run *(po)trčati* (paw·)tr·cha·tee
running *trčanje* ⑩ tr·cha·nye
runny nose *šmrkav nos* ⑩ shmr·kav naws

S

sad *tužan* too·zhan
saddle *sedlo* ⑩ sed·law
safe *sef* sef
safe *siguran* see·goo·ran
safe sex *siguran seks* ⑩ see·goo·ran seks
saint *svetac/svetica* ⑩/① sve·tats/sve·tee·tsa
salad *salata* ① sa·la·ta
salami *salama* ① sa·la·ma
salary *plaća* ① pla·cha
sale *rasprodaja* ① ra·spraw·dai·a
sales tax *porez na promet* ⑩ paw·rez na praw·met

salmon *losos* ⓜ *law*·saws
salt *sol* ⓕ *sawl*
same *isti* ⓜ *ee*·stee
sand *pijesak* ⓜ *pee*·ye·sak
sandal *sandala* ⓕ *san·da*·la
sanitary napkin *higijenski uložak* ⓜ *hee·gee·yen·skee oo·law·zhak*
sardine *sardina* ⓕ *sar·dee*·na
Saturday *subota* ⓕ *soo·baw*·ta
sauce *umak* ⓜ *oo*·mak
saucepan *lonac* ⓜ *law*·nats
sauna *sauna* ⓕ *sa·oo*·na
sausage *kobasica* ⓕ *kaw·ba·see·tsa*
say *kazati/kazivati* ka·za·tee/ka·zee·va·tee
scalp *skalp* ⓜ skalp
scarf *šal* ⓜ shal
school *škola* ⓕ *shkaw·*la
science *znanost* ⓕ *zna*·nawst
scientist *znanstvenik* ⓜ *znanst*·ve·neek
scissors *škare* ⓕ pl *shka*·re
score *postići/postizati* paw·stee·chee/ paw·stee·za·tee
scoreboard *semafor* ⓜ *se*·ma·fawr
Scotland *Škotska* ⓕ *shkawt*·ska
scuba diving *ronjenje sa bocama* ⓝ *raw·nye·nye sa baw·tsa*·ma
sculpture *skulptura* ⓕ *skoolp·too·ra*
sea *more* ⓝ *maw*·re
seasick *koji pati od morske bolesti koy·ee pa·tee awd mawr·ske baw·le·stee*
seaside *primorje* ⓝ *pree·mawr*·ye
season (winter etc) *godišnje doba* ⓝ *gaw·deesh·nye daw*·ba
season (for activities) *sezona* ⓕ *se·zaw*·na
seat (place) *sjedište* ⓝ *sye·deesh*·te
seatbelt *sigurnosni pojas* ⓜ *see·goor·naw·snee poy*·as
second (clock) *sekunda* ⓕ *se·koon*·da
second *drugi droo*·gee
second class *drugi razred* ⓜ *droo·gee raz*·red
second-hand *polovni paw·lawv*·nee
second-hand shop *prodavaonica polovne robe* ⓕ *praw·da·va·aw·nee·tsa paw·lawv·ne raw*·be
secretary *tajnik/tajnica* ⓜ/ⓕ *tai·neek/ tai·nee*·tsa
see *vidjeti/viđati vee·dye·tee/vee*·ja·tee
self-service *samoposluga* ⓕ *sa·maw·paw·sloo*·ga
self-employed *samostalno zaposlen* *sa·maw·stal·naw za·paw*·slen
selfish *sebičan* ⓜ *se·bee*·chan

sell *prodati/prodavati praw·da·tee/ praw·da·va·tee*
send *(po)slati (paw·)sla*·tee
sensible *razuman* ra·zoo·man
sensual *razbludan* raz·bloo·dan
separate *odvojen* awd·voy·en
September *rujan* ⓜ *roo·yan'*
Serbia *Srbija* ⓕ *sr·*be·ya
serious *ozbiljan* aw·zbee·lyan
service *usluga* ⓕ *oo·sloo*·ga
service charge *naplata za usluge* ⓕ *na·pla·ta za oo·sloo·ge*
service station *benzinska stanica* ⓕ *ben·zeen·ska sta·nee·tsa*
serviette *salveta* ⓕ *sal·ve*·ta
several *nekoliko* ne·kaw·lee·kaw
sew *sašiti/šivati sa·shee·tee/shee·va·tee*
sex *seks* ⓜ seks
sexism *spolna diskriminacija* ⓕ *spawl·na dee·skree·mee·na·tsee·ya*
sexy *privlačan* pree·vla·chan
shade *hladovina* ⓕ *hla·daw·vee*·na
shadow *sjena* ⓕ *sye*·na
shampoo *šampon* ⓜ sham·pawn
shape *oblik* ⓜ *aw·*bleek
share (a dorm etc) *dijeliti* imp dee·ye·lee·tee
share (with) *podijeliti* perf paw·dee·ye·lee·tee
shave *(o)brijati se (aw·)bree·ya·tee se*
shaving cream *pjena za brijanje* ⓕ *pye·na za bree·ya·nye*
she *ona* ⓕ *aw·*na
sheep *ovca* ⓕ *awv·*tsa
sheet (bed) *plahta* ⓕ *pla·*hta
shelf *polica* ⓕ *paw·lee*·tsa
shiatsu *shiatsu* ⓝ shee·a·tsoo
shingles (illness) *osip u struku* ⓜ *aw·seep oo stroo·koo*
ship *brod* ⓜ brawd
shirt *košulja* ⓕ *kaw·shoo·*lya
shoe(s) *cipela/e* ⓕ sg/ⓕ pl *tsee·pe·la/e*
shoe shop *prodavaonica cipela* ⓕ *praw·da·va·aw·nee·tsa tsee·pe·la*
shoot *(u)pucati (oo·)poo·tsa·tee*
shop *prodavaonica* ⓕ *praw·da·va·aw·nee·tsa*
shop *kupovati* imp koo·paw·va·tee
shopping *kupovina* ⓕ *koo·paw·vee·na*
shopping centre *trgovački centar* ⓜ *tr·gaw·vach·kee tsen·tar*
short (duration) *kratak kra·*tak
short (height) *nizak nee·*zak
shortage *nedostatak* ⓜ *ne·daw·sta·tak*

shorts *kratke hlače* ① pl *krat*·ke *hla*·che
shoulder *rame* ① *ra*·me
shout *viknuti/vikati* *veek*·noo·tee/*vee*·ka·tee
show *predstava* ① *pred*·sta·va
show *pokazati/pokazivati* *paw·ka·za·tee*/
  paw·ka·zee·va·tee
shower (bathroom) *tuš* ⓜ toosh
shrine *moćnica* ① *mawch*·nee·tsa
shut *zatvoren* *zat*·vaw·ren
shy *stidljiv* *steed*·lyeev
sick *bolestan* *baw*·les·tan
side *strana* ① *stra*·na
sign *znak* ① znak
signature *potpis* ⓜ *pawt*·pees
silk *svila* ① *svee*·la
silver *srebro* ⓝ *sre*·braw
similar *sličan* *slee*·chan
simple *jednostavan* *yed*·naw·sta·van
since (May etc) *od* • *otkako* awd •
  awt·ka·kaw
sing (za)pjevati (za·)*pye*·va·tee
Singapore *Singapur* ⓜ *seen*·ga·poor
singer *pjevač/pjevačica* ⓜ/① *pye*·vach/
  pye·va·chee·tsa
single (man) *neoženjen* ne·*aw*·zhen·yen
single (woman) *neudata* ne·oo·da·ta
single room *jednokrevetna soba* ①
  yed·naw·kre·vet·na *saw*·ba
singlet *potkošulja* ① *pawt*·kaw·shoo·lya
sister *sestra* ① *se*·stra
sit *sjesti/sjedati* *sye*·stee/*sye*·da·tee
size (general) *veličina* ① *ve*·lee·*chee*·na
skate *rošulati se* imp *raw*·shoo·la·tee se
skateboarding *vožnja na skateboardu* ①
  vawzh·nya na *skeyt*·bawr·doo
ski *skijati* imp *skee*·ya·tee
skiing *skijanje* ① *skee*·ya·nye
skim milk *obrano mlijeko* ⓝ *aw*·bra·naw
  mlee·*ye*·kaw
skin *koža* ① *kaw*·zha
skirt *suknja* ① *sook*·nya
skull *lubanja* ① *loo*·ba·nya
sky *nebo* ⓝ *ne*·baw
sleep (od)spavati (awd·)*spa*·va·tee
sleeping bag *vreća za spavanje* ①
  vre·cha za *spa*·va·nye
sleeping berth *spavaća kola* ①
  spa·va·cha *kaw*·la
sleeping car *spavaći kupe* ⓜ *spa*·va·chee
  koo·pe
sleeping pills *tableta za spavanje* ①
  tab·*le*·ta za *spa*·va·nye
(to be) sleepy *pospan* *paw*·span

slice *kriška* ① *kreesh*·ka
slide (film) *dijapozitiv* ⓜ
  dee·ya·paw·zee·teev
Slovakia *Slovačka* ① *slaw*·vach·ka
Slovenia *Slovenija* ① slaw·ve·nee·ya
slow *spor* spawr
slowly *sporo* *spaw*·raw
small *mali* *ma*·lee
smaller *manji* *ma*·nyee
smallest *najmanji* *nai*·ma·nyee
smell (pleasant) *miris* ⓜ *mee*·rees
smell (unpleasant) *smrad* ⓜ smrad
smile *(na)smiješiti se* (na·)smee·*ye*·shee·tee se
smoke *(is)pušiti* (ees·)*poo*·shee·tee
snack *laki obrok* ⓜ *la*·kee *aw*·brawk
snail *puž* ⓜ poozh
snake *zmija* ① *zmee*·ya
snorkelling *ronjenje s disalicom* ①
  raw·nye·nye s *dee*·sa·lee·tsawm
snow *snijeg* ⓜ snee·*yeg*
snowboarding *daskanje na snijegu* ①
  da·ska·nye na snee·*ye*·goo
soap *sapun* ⓜ *sa*·poon
soccer *nogomet* ⓜ *naw*·gaw·met
social welfare *socijalna skrb* ①
  saw·tsee·yal·na skrb
socialist *socijalistički* saw·tsee·ya·*lee*·st
  eech·kee
sock(s) *čarapa/e* ① sg/① pl *cha*·ra·pa/e
soft drink *bezalkoholno piće* ⓝ
  be·zal·kaw·hawl·naw *pee*·che
soldier *vojnik* ⓜ *voy*·neek
some *malo* *ma*·law
someone *netko* *net*·kaw
something *nešto* *nesh*·taw
sometimes *ponekad* *paw*·ne·kad
son *sin* ⓜ seen
song *pjesma* ① *pye*·sma
soon *uskoro* oo·*skaw*·raw
sore *bolan* *baw*·lan
soup *juha* ① *yoo*·ha
sour cream *kiselo vrhnje* ⓝ *kee*·se·law
  vrh·nye
south *jug* ⓜ yoog
souvenir *suvenir* ⓜ soo·ve·*neer*
souvenir shop *prodavaonica suvenira* ①
  praw·da·va·aw·nee·tsa soo·ve·*nee*·ra
soy milk *sojino mlijeko* ⓝ *soy*·ee·naw
  mlee·*ye*·kaw
soy sauce *soja* ① *soy*·a
spa *toplice* ① pl *taw*·plee·tse
space *prostor* ⓜ *praw*·stawr
Spain *Španjolska* ① shpa·*nyawl*·ska

sparkling wine *pjenušavo vino* ⓝ
pye·noo·sha·vaw *vee*·naw

speak *(pro)govoriti* (praw·)gaw·*vaw*·ree·tee

special *poseban* ⓜ *paw*·se·ban

specialist *stručnjak* ⓜ *strooch*·nyak

speed *brzina* ⓕ br·*zee*·na

speed limit *brzinsko ograničenje* ⓝ
br·zeen·skaw aw·gra·nee·che·nye

speedometer *brzinomjer* ⓜ
br·*zee*·naw·myer

spider *pauk* ⓜ *pa*·ook

spinach *špinat* ⓜ *shpee*·nat

spoiled *razmažen* raz·*ma*·zhen

spoke *žbica* ⓕ *zhbee*·tsa

spoon *žlica* ⓕ *zhlee*·tsa

sport *sport* ⓜ spawrt

sports store *prodavaonica sportske robe* ⓕ
praw·da·va·*aw*·nee·tsa spawrt·ske *raw*·be

sportsperson *sportaš/sportašica* ⓜ/ⓕ
spawr·tash/spawr·*ta*·shee·tsa

sprain *uganuće* ⓝ oo·ga·*noo*·che

spring (coil) *opruga* ⓕ *aw*·proo·ga

spring (season) *proljeće* ⓝ *praw*·lye·che

square (town) *trg* ⓜ trg

stadium *stadion* ⓜ *sta*·dee·awn

stairway *stepenište* ⓝ *ste*·pe·neesh·te

stale *ustajao* oo·stai·a·aw

stamp (mail) *poštanska marka* ⓕ
pawsh·tan·ska *mar*·ka

stand-by ticket *uvjetna karta* ⓕ
oo·*vyet*·noo *kar*·ta

star *zvjezda* ⓕ *zvyez*·da

(four-)star *(sa četiri) zvjezdice* ⓕ pl
(sa *che*·tee·ree) zvye·*zdee*·tse

start *početak* ⓜ *paw*·che·tak

start *započeti/započinjati* za·*paw*·che·te/
za·*paw*·chee·nya·tee

station *stanica* ⓕ *sta*·nee·tsa

stationer's (shop) *prodavaonica uredskog
materijala* ⓕ praw·da·va·*aw*·nee·tsa
oo·reds·kawg ma·te·ree·*ya*·la

statue *kip* ⓜ keep

stay (at a hotel) *odsjesti/odsjedati*
awd·*sye*·stee/awd·sye·*da*·tee

stay (in one place) *ostati/ostajati* imp
aw·*sta*·tee/aw·sta·*ya*·tee

steak (beef) *odrezak* ⓜ aw·*dre*·zak

steal *(u)krasti* (oo·)*kra*·stee

steep *strm* strm

step *stepenica* ⓕ *ste*·pe·nee·tsa

stereo *linija* ⓕ *lee*·nee·ya

still water *obična voda* ⓕ *aw*·beech·na
vaw·da

stock (food) *bujon* ⓜ *boo*·yawn

stockings *visoke čarape* ⓕ pl *vee*·saw·ke
cha·ra·pe

stolen *ukraden* ⓜ oo·*kra*·den

stomach *želudac* ⓜ zhe·*loo*·dats

stomachache (to have a) *imati trbobolju*
ee·ma·tee tr·baw·*bah*·lyoo

stone *kamen* ⓜ *ka*·men

stoned (drugged) *napljugan* nap·*lyoo*·gan

stop (bus, tram) *stanica* ⓕ *sta*·nee·tsa

stop (cease) *zaustaviti/zaustavljati*
za·oo·sta·vee·tee/za·oo·stav·lya·tee

stop (prevent) *spriječiti/sprječavati*
spree·ye·chee·tee/spree·ye·*cha*·va·tee

Stop! *Stanite/Stani!* pol/inf *sta*·nee·te/*sta*·nee

storm *oluja* ⓕ aw·*loo*·ya

story *priča* ⓕ *pree*·cha

stove *pećnica* ⓕ *pech*·nee·tsa

straight (not crooked) *ravan* *ra*·van

strange *neobičan* ne·aw·bee·chan

stranger *stranac* ⓜ *stra*·nats

strawberry *jagoda* ⓕ *ya*·gaw·da

stream *struja* ⓕ *stroo*·ya

street *ulica* ⓕ oo·*lee*·tsa

street market *ulična tržnica* ⓕ oo·leech·na
trzh·nee·tsa

strike *štrajk* ⓜ shtraik

string *struna* ⓕ *stroo*·na

stroke (health) *moždani udar* ⓜ
mawzh·da·nee oo·dar

stroller *dječja hodalica* ⓕ *dyech*·ya
haw·da·lee·tsa

strong (physically) *jak* yak

stubborn *tvrdoglav* tvr·*daw*·glav

student *student* ⓜ *stoo*·dent

studio *atelje* ⓝ a·*te*·lye

stupid *glup* gloop

style *stil* ⓜ steel

subtitles *titlovi* ⓜ pl *teet*·law·vee

suburb *predgrađe* ⓝ *pred*·gra·je

subway *podzemna željeznica* ⓕ
pawd·zem·na zhe·lye·znee·tsa

sugar *šećer* ⓜ *she*·cher

suitcase *kofer* ⓜ *kaw*·fer

sultana *vrsta velikih grožđica* ⓕ vr·sta
ve·lee·keeh *grawzh*·jee·tsa

summer *ljeto* ⓝ *lye*·taw

summit *vrh* ⓜ vrh

sun *sunce* ⓝ *soon*·tse

sunblock *losion za zaštitu od sunca* ⓝ
law·see·awn za *zash*·tee·too awd *soon*·tsa

sunburn *opekline od sunca* ⓕ pl
aw·pe·klee·ne awd *soon*·tsa

Sunday *nedjelja* ① ne-dye-lya
sunglasses *naočale za sunce* ① pl na-aw-cha-le (za soon-tse)
sunny *sunčan* soon-chan
sunrise *izlazak sunca* ⓜ eez-la-zak soon-tsa
sunset *zalazak sunca* ⓜ za-la-zak soon-tsa
sunstroke *sunčanica* ① soon-cha-nee-tsa
supermarket *supermarket* ⓜ soo-per-mar-ket
superstition *praznovjerje* ① praz-naw-vyer-ye
supporter (politics) *pristaša* ⓜ pree-sta-sha
supporter (sport) *navijač* ⓜ na-vee-yach
surf *daskati na valovima* da-ska-tee na va-law-vee-ma
surface mail (land) *obična pošta* ① aw-beech-na pawsh-ta
surface mail (sea) *prekomorska pošta* ① pre-kaw-mawr-ska pawsh-ta
surfboard *daska za surfanje* ① da-ska za soor-fa-nye
surfing *daskanje na valovima* ⓝ da-ska-nye na va-law-vee-ma
surname *prezime* ⓝ pre-zee-me
surprise *iznenađen* ⓜ eez-ne-na-jen
sweater *džemper* ⓜ jem-per
Sweden *Švedska* ① shved-ska
sweet *sladak* sla-dak
sweets *bomboni* ⓜ pl bawm-baw-nee
swelling *oteklina* ① aw-te-klee-na
swim *(za)plivati* (za-)plee-va-tee
swimming (sport) *plivanje* ⓝ plee-va-nye
swimming pool *bazen za plivanje* ⓜ ba-zen za plee-va-nye
swimsuit *kupaći kostim* ⓜ koo-pa-chee kaw-steem
Switzerland *Švicarska* ① shvee-tsar-ska
synagogue *sinagoga* ① see-na-gaw-ga
synthetic *sintetičan* ⓜ seen-te-te-chan
syringe *štrcaljka* ① shtr-tsal'-ka

T

table *stol* ⓜ stawl
table tennis *stolni tenis* ⓜ stawl-nee te-nees
tablecloth *stolnjak* ⓜ stawl-nyak
tail *rep* ⓜ rep
tailor *krojač* ⓜ kroy-ach
take *uzeti/uzimati* oo-ze-tee/oo-zee-ma-tee
talk *(pro)govoriti* (praw-)gaw-vaw-ree-tee
tall *visok* vee-sawk
tampon *tampon* ⓜ tam-pawn

tanning lotion *losion za dobijanje tena* ⓜ law-see-awn za daw-bee-ya-nye te-na
tap *slavina* ① sla-vee-na
tap water *obična voda* ① aw-beech-na vaw-da
tasty *ukusan* oo-koo-san
tax *porez* ⓜ paw-rez
taxi *taksi* ⓜ tak-see
taxi stand *taksi stanica* ① tak-see sta-nee-tsa
tea *čaj* ⓜ chai
teacher *učitelj* ⓜ oo-chee-tel'
team *momčad* ① mawm-chad
teaspoon *žličica* ① zhlee-chee-tsa
technique *tehnika* ① teh-nee-ka
teeth *zubi* ⓝ pl zoo-bee
telegram *telegram* ⓜ te-le-gram
telephone *telefon* ⓜ te-le-fawn
telephone *telefonirati* imp te-le-faw-nee-ra-tee
telephone box *telefonska govornica* ① te-le-fawn-ska gaw-vawr-nee-tsa
telephone centre *telefonska centrala* ① te-le-fawn-ska tsen-tra-la
telescope *teleskop* ⓜ te-le-skawp
television (general) *televizija* ① te-le-vee-zee-ya
television set *televizor* ⓜ te-le-vee-zawr
tell *reći* perf re-chee
temperature (fever) *groznica* ① grawz-nee-tsa
temperature (weather) *temperatura* ① tem-pe-ra-too-ra
temple *hram* ⓜ hram
tennis *tenis* ⓜ te-nees
tennis court *teniski igralište* ⓝ te-nee-skaw ee-gra-leesh-te
tent *šator* ⓜ sha-tawr
tent peg *šatorski kolčić* ⓜ sha-tawr-skee kawl-cheech
terrible *strašan* stra-shan
test *test* ⓜ test
thank *zahvaliti/zahvaljivati* za-hva-lee-tee/za-hva-lyee-va-tee
thank you *hvala vam/ti* pol/inf hva-la vam/tee
that (one) *ono* ⓝ aw-naw
theatre *kazalište* ⓝ ka-za-leesh-te
their *njihov/njihova/njihovo* ⓜ/①/ⓝ nyee-hawv/nyee-haw-va/nyee-haw-vaw
there *tamo* ta-maw
they *oni/one/ona* ⓜ/①/ⓝ aw-nee/aw-ne/aw-na

thick (liquid) *gust* goost

thick (object) *debeo* de-be-aw

thief *lopov* ⓜ law-pawv

thin *tanak* ⓜ ta-nak

think (po)misliti (paw-)mee-slee-tee

third *treći* tre-chee

(to be) thirsty *žedan* zhe-dan

this *ovaj/ova/ovo* ⓜ/①/① aw-vai/aw-va/aw-vaw

this (one) *ovo* ① aw-vaw

thread *konac* ⓜ kaw-nats

throat *grlo* ① gr-law

thrush (illness) *infekcija kandide* ① een-fek-tsee-ya kan-dee-de

thunderstorm *grmljavina* ① grm-lya-vee-na

Thursday *četvrtak* ⓜ chet-vr-tak

ticket *karta* ① kar-ta

ticket collector *osoblje koje uzima odrezak karte* ① aw-sawb-lye koy-e oo-zee-ma aw-dre-zak kar-te

ticket machine *automat za prodaju karata* ⓜ a-oo-taw-mat za praw-dai-oo ka-ra-ta

ticket office *šalter* ⓜ shal-ter

tide *plima i oseka* ① plee-ma ee aw-se-ka

tight *tijesan* tee-ye-san

time *vrijeme* ① vree-ye-me

time difference *razlika u vremenu* ① raz-lee-ka oo vre-me-noo

timetable *vozni red* ⓜ vawz-nee red

tin *limenka* ① lee-men-ka

tin opener *otvarač za limenke* ⓜ awt-va-rach za lee-men-ke

tiny *sićušan* ⓜ see-choo-shan

tip (gratuity) *bakšiš* bak-sheesh

tire (car) *guma na automobile* ① goo-ma na a-oo-taw-maw-bee-le

tire (general) *guma* ① goo-ma

tired *umoran* oo-maw-ran

tissues *papirnati rupčići* ⓜ pl pa-peer-na-tee roop-chee-chee

to do • nad • prema • u • za daw • nad • pre-ma • oo • za

toast *tost* ⓜ tawst

toaster *toster* ⓜ taw-ster

tobacco *duhan* ⓜ doo-han

tobacconist *prodavač duhana* ⓜ praw-da-vach doo-ha-na

today *danas* da-nas

toe *nožni prst* ⓜ nawzh-nee prst

together *zajedno* zai-ed-naw

toilet *zahod* ⓜ za-hawd

toilet paper *toaletni papir* ⓜ taw-a-let-nee pa-peer

tomato *rajčica* ① rai-chee-tsa

tomato sauce *umak od rajčica* ⓜ oo-mak awd rai-chee-tsa

tomorrow *sutra* soo-tra

tomorrow afternoon *sutra popodne* soo-tra paw-pawd-ne

tomorrow evening *sutra uvečer* soo-tra oo-ve-cher

tomorrow morning *sutra ujutro* soo-tra oo-yoo-traw

tonight *večeras* ve-che-ras

too (expensive etc) *suviše* soo-vee-she

tooth *zub* ⓜ zoob

toothache *zubobolja* ① zoo-baw-baw-lya

toothbrush *četkica za zube* ① chet-kee-tsa za zoo-be

toothpaste *pasta za zube* ① pa-sta za zoo-be

toothpick *čačkalica* ① chach-ka-lee-tsa

torch (flashlight) *ručna svjetiljka* ① (rooch-na) svye-teel'-ka

touch (sense) *dirnuti/dirati* deer-noo-tee/dee-ra-tee

tour *ekskurzija* ① ek-skoor-zee-ya

tourist *turist* ⓜ too-reest

tourist office *turistička agencija* ① too-ree-steech-ka a-gen-tsee-ya

towards (direction) *prema* pre-ma

towel *ručnik* ⓜ rooch-neek

tower *toranj* ⓜ taw-ran'

toxic waste *toksični otpad* ⓜ tawk-seech-nee awt-pad

toy shop *prodavaonica igračaka* ① praw-da-va-aw-nee-tsa ee-gra-cha-ka

track (path) *put* ⓜ poot

track (sport) *staza* ① sta-za

trade *trgovina* ① tr-gaw-vee-na

tradesperson *obrtnik* ⓜ aw-brt-neek

traffic *promet* ⓜ praw-met

traffic light *semafor* ⓜ se-ma-fawr

trail *put* ⓜ poot

train *vlak* ⓜ vlak

train station *željeznička stanica* ① zhe-lyez-neech-ka sta-nee-tsa

tram *tramvaj* ⓜ tram-vai

transit lounge *tranzitna čekaonica* ① tran-zeet-na che-ka-aw-nee-tsa

translate *prevesti/prevoditi* pre-ve-stee/pre-vaw-dee-tee

transport *prijevoz* ⓜ pree-ye-vawz

travel *(pro)putovati* (praw-)poo-taw-va-tee

travel agency *putna agencija* ① *poot*·na a·*gen*·tsee·ya

travel sickness *mučnina od vožnje* ① mooch·*nee*·na awd *vawzh*·nye

travellers cheque *putnički čekovi* ⓜ pl *poot*·neech·kee *che*·kaw·vee

tree *stablo* ⓝ *sta*·blaw

trip (journey) *izlet* ① *eez*·let

trolley *kolica za prtljagu* ① kaw·*lee*·tsa za prt·*lya*·goo

trousers *hlače* ① pl *hla*·che

truck *kamion* ⓜ *ka*·mee·awn

trust *(po)vjerovati (paw)*·vye·*raw*·va·tee

try *probati/probavati praw*·ba·tee/ praw·*ba*·va·tee

try (attempt) *pokušati/pokušavati paw*·koo·sha·tee/paw·koo·*sha*·va·tee

T-shirt *majica* ① *mai*·ee·tsa

tube (tyre) *zračnica* ① *zrach*·nee·tsa

Tuesday *utorak* ⓜ *oo*·taw·rak

tumour *tumor* ⓜ *too*·mawr

tuna (as food) *tunjevina* ① *too*·nye·vee·na

tuna (fish) *tuna* ① *too*·na

tune *melodija* ① *me*·law·dee·ya

turkey *puran* ⓜ *poo*·ran

turn *okrenuti/okretati* aw·kre·noo·tee/ aw·kre·ta·tee

TV (set) *televizor* ⓜ te·le·*vee*·zawr

tweezers *pinceta* ① *peen·tse*·ta

twice *dvaput* dva·poot

twin room *dvokrevetna soba* ① *dvaw*·kre·vet·na *saw*·ba

twins *blizanci* ⓜ pl blee·*zan*·tsee

two *dva* dva

type *vrsta* ① *vr*·sta

typical *tipičan* tee·pee·chan

tyre (car) *guma na automobile* ① *goo*·ma na a·oo·taw·maw·*bee*·le

tyre (general) *guma* ① *goo*·ma

U

ultrasound *ultrazvuk* ⓜ *ool*·tra·zvook

umbrella *suncobran* ⓜ *soon*·tsaw·bran

uncomfortable *neudoban* ne·oo·daw·ban

underground railway *podzemna željeznica* ① *pawd*·zem·na zhe·lye·znee·tsa

understand *razumjeti/razumijevati* ra·zoo·mye·tee/ra·zoo·mee·ye·va·tee

underwear *donje rublje* ⓝ *daw*·nye roob·lye

unemployed *nezaposlen* ne·*za*·paw·slen

unfair *nepravedan* ne·pra·ve·dan

uniform *uniforma* ① oo·nee·fawr·ma

universe *svemir* ⓜ *sve*·meer

university *sveučilište* ⓝ sve·oo·chee·leesh·te

unleaded *bezolovni* be·zaw·lawv·nee

unsafe *nesiguran* ne·see·goo·ran

until (Friday, etc) *do* daw

unusual *neobičan* ne·aw·bee·chan

up *gore* gaw·re

urgent *hitan* hee·tan

urinary infection *infekcija mokraćnih kanala* ① een·*fek*·tsee·ya maw·krach·neeh ka·*na*·la

USA *SAD* ⓜ pl es a de

useful *koristan* kaw·ree·stan

V

vacancy *slobodno mjesto* ⓝ *slaw*·bawd·naw mye·staw

vacant *prazan* pra·zan

vacation *praznici* ⓜ pl *praz*·nee·tsee

vaccination *cijepljenje* ⓝ tsee·*yep*·lye·nye

vagina *vagina* ① va·*gee*·na

validate *potvrditi/potvrđivati* pawt·vr·dee·tee/pawt·vr·*jee*·va·tee

valley *dolina* ① daw·lee·na

valuable *dragocjen* dra·*gaw*·tsyen

value (price) *vrijednost* ① vree·*yed*·nawst

van *kombi* ⓜ kawm·bee

veal *teletina* ① te·le·tee·na

vegetable *povrće* ⓝ *paw*·vr·che

vegetarian *vegetarijanac* ① ve·ge·ta·ree·*ya*·nats

vein *vena* ① ve·na

venereal disease *spolna bolesta* ① spawl·na baw·les·ta

Venetian *venecijanski* ve·ne·tsee·yan·skee

Venice *Venecija* ① ve·ne·tsee·ya

venue *lokal* ⓜ law·kal

very *vrlo* vr·law

video recorder *video rekorder* ⓜ vee·de·aw re·kawr·der

video tape *video kazeta* ① vee·de·aw ka·ze·ta

view *prizor* ⓜ pree·zawr

village *selo* ⓝ se·law

vine *vinova loza* ① vee·naw·va law·za

vinegar *ocat* ⓜ aw·tsat

vineyard *vinograd* ⓜ vee·naw·grad

virus *virus* ⓜ vee·roos

visa *viza* ① vee·za

visit *posjetiti/posjećivati* paw·sye·tee·tee/paw·sye·chee·va·tee
vitamins *vitamini* ⓜ pl vee·ta·*mee*·nee
vodka *vodka* ① *vawd*·ka
voice *glas* ⓜ glas
volleyball (sport) *odbojka* ① *awd*·boy·ka
volume *ton* ⓜ tawn
vote *glasovati* imp gla·saw·va·tee

W

wage *plaća* ① *pla*·cha
wait (for) *(pri)čekati nekoga* (pree·)che·ka·tee ne·kaw·ga
waiter *konobar* ⓜ kaw·naw·bar
waiting room *čekaonica* ① che·ka·*aw*·nee·tsa
wake (someone) up *(pro)buditi nekoga* (praw·)boo·dee·tee ne·kaw·ga
walk *hodati* imp *haw*·da·tee
walkway *hodnik* ⓜ *hawd*·neek
wall (outer) *zid* ⓜ zeed
walled city *citadela* ① tsee·ta·*de*·la
want *(po)željeti* (paw·)*zhe*·lye·tee
war *rat* ⓜ rat
wardrobe *ormar za odjeću* ⓜ *awr*·mar za *aw*·dye·choo
warm *topao* ⓜ *taw*·pa·aw
warn *upozoriti/upozoravati* oo·paw·zaw·*ree*·tee/oo·paw·zaw·*ra*·va·tee
wash (oneself) *(o)prati se* (aw·)*pra*·tee se
wash (something) *(o)prati* (aw·)*pra*·tee
wash cloth (flannel) *ručnik* ⓜ *rooch*·neek
washing machine *stroj za pranje rublja* ⓜ stroy za *pra*·nye roob·lya
watch *(po)gledati* (paw·)*gle*·da·tee
watch *sat* ⓜ sat
water *voda* ① *vaw*·da
water bottle *boca za vodu* ① *baw*·tsa za *vaw*·doo
water bottle (hot) *termofor* ⓜ *ter*·maw·fawr
water taxi *taksi na vodi* ⓜ *tak*·see na *vaw*·dee
waterfall *vodopad* ⓜ *vaw*·daw·pad
waterfront *riva* ① *ree*·va
watermelon *lubenica* ① loo·be·*nee*·tsa
waterproof *nepromočiv* ne·*praw*·maw·cheev
water-skiing *skijanje na vodi* ⓜ *skee*·ya·nye na *vaw*·dee
wave *val* ⓜ val

way (manner) *način* ⓜ *na*·cheen
we *mi* mee
weak *slab* slab
wealthy *bogat* baw·gat
wear *nositi* imp *naw*·see·tee
weather *vremenski uvjeti* ⓜ pl *vre*·men·skee oo·vye·tee
wedding *vjenčanje* ① vyen·*cha*·nye
wedding cake *svadbena torta* ① *svad*·be·na *tawr*·ta
wedding present *svadbeni dar* ⓜ *svad*·be·nee dar
Wednesday *srijeda* ① sree·*ye*·da
week *tjedan* ① *tye*·dan
(this) week *(ovaj) tjedan* (aw·vai) *tye*·dan
weekend *vikend* ⓜ *veek*·end
weigh *(iz)vagati* (eez·)*va*·ga·tee
weight *težina* ① te·*zhee*·na
weights *tegovi* ⓜ pl te·gaw·vee
welcome *dočekati/dočekivati* daw·che·ka·tee/daw·che·*kee*·va·tee
welfare *socijalna skrb* ① *saw*·tsee·yal·na skrb
well *dobro* daw·braw
west *zapad* ⓜ *za*·pad
wet *mokar* ⓜ *maw*·kar
what *koji/koja/koje* ⓜ/①/ⓝ *koy*·ee/*koy*·a/*koy*·e
wheel *kotač* ⓜ *kaw*·tach
wheelchair *invalidska kolica* ① pl een·va·leed·ska kaw·*lee*·tsa
when *kada* ka·da
where *gdje* gdye
which *koji* koy·ee
whisky *viski* ⓜ *vee*·skee
white *bijel* bee·yel
who *tko* tkaw
wholemeal bread *crni kruh* ⓜ *tsr*·nee krooh
why *zašto* zash·taw
wide *širok* shee·rawk
wife *žena* ① *zhe*·na
win *pobijediti/pobjeđivati* paw·bee·ye·dee·tee/paw·bye·*jee*·va·tee
wind *vjetar* ⓜ *vye*·tar
window *prozor* ⓜ *praw*·zawr
windscreen *vjetrobran* ⓜ *vye*·traw·bran
windsurfing *jedrenje na dasci* ⓝ *ye*·dre·nye na *das*·tsee
wine *vino* ⓝ *vee*·naw
wings *krila* ⓝ pl *kree*·la
winner *pobjednik* ⓜ *paw*·byed·neek
winter *zima* ① *zee*·ma

wire *žica* ① *zhee*·tsa
wish *(po)željeti* (paw·)*zhe*·lye·tee
with *kod · od · sa · za·* kawd · awd · sa · za
within (an hour) *u roku od* oo *raw*·koo awd
without *bez* bez
wok *duboka posuda za prženje* ①
  doo·baw·ka *paw·soo*·da za *pr*·zhe·nye
woman *žena* ① *zhe*·na
wonderful *divan* dee·van
wood *drvo* ⑩ dr·vaw
wool *vuna* ① *voo*·na
word *riječ* ① ree·yech
work *rad* ⑩ rad
work *raditi* imp *ra*·dee·tee
work experience *radno iskustvo* ⑩
  rad·naw ee·*skoos*·tvaw
work permit *radna dozvola* ① *rad*·na
  dawz·vaw·la
workout *tjelovježba* ① tye·law·*vyezh*·ba
workshop *radionica* ① ra·dee·*aw*·nee·tsa
world *svijet* ⑩ svee·yet
World Cup *svjetski kup* ⑩ *svyet*·skee koop
worried *zabrinut* ⑩ za·*bree*·noot
worship *(po)moliti se* (paw·)*maw*·lee·tee
  (se)
wrist *ručni zglob* ⑩ rooch·nee zglawb
write *(na)pisati* (na·)*pee*·sa·tee
writer *pisac* ⑩ *pee*·sats
wrong *kriv* kreev

Y

yacht *jahta* ① *yah*·ta
year *godina* ① *gaw*·dee·na
(this) year *(ova) godina* ① (*aw*·va)
  gaw·dee·na
yellow *žut* ⑩ zhoot
yes *da* da
yesterday *jučer* yoo·cher
(not) yet *(ne) još* (ne) yawsh
yoga *joga* ① *yaw*·ga
yogurt *jogurt* ⑩ *yaw*·goort
you inf *ti* tee
you pol sg & pl *vi* vee
young *mlad* mlad
your *tvoj/tvoja/tvoje* ⑩/①/⑩ *tvoy*/
  tvoy·a/*tvoy*·e
youth hostel *prenoćište za mladež* ⑩
  pre·*naw*·cheesh·te za *mla*·dezh
Yugoslavia *Jugoslavija* ①
  yoo·gaw·*sla*·vee·ya

Z

zip/zipper *šlic* ⑩ shleets
zodiac *zodijak* ⑩ *zaw*·dee·yak
zoo *zološki vrt* ⑩ *zaw*·lawsh·kee vrt
zucchini *bučice* ① pl *boo*·chee·tse

Nouns in the dictionary have their gender indicated by ⓜ, ⓕ or ⓝ. If it's a plural noun you'll also see pl. When a word that could be either a noun or a verb has no gender indicated, it's a verb.

Nouns and adjectives are in the nominative case. You'll be understood if you just pick words out of this dictionary, but if you'd like to know more about case, see the **a–z phrasebuilder,** page 21.

Adjectives in the dictionary are given in the masculine form only. For an explanation of how to form feminine and neuter adjectives, refer to the **a–z phrasebuilder,** page 16.

Verbs are mostly given in two forms: perfective and imperfective. See the **a–z phrasebuilder,** page 17 for an explanation of these terms and when to use which form. Perfective and imperfective forms are either separated by a slash (with the perfective form given first) or consist of a root imperfective form to which a bracketed prefix is added to form the perfective. For example, the verb 'give' has the forms *dati/ davati* da·tee/da·va·tee with the first form being the perfective form and the second the imperfective. The verb 'call' is represented as *(po)zvati* (paw·)zva·tee which has the perfective form *pozvati* and the imperfective form *zvati*. Where two syllables are stressed in the transliteration, eg *(paw·)zva*·tee it means that once you add the prefix to form the perfective, the stress shifts to the prefix. Verbs are listed alphabetically according to their root (unprefixed) form.

Where only one form of a verb is given (not all verbs have both forms) the abbreviations perf and imp have been used to identify whether they are perfective or imperfective.

A

adresa ⓕ a·dre·sa *address*
aerobik ⓜ a·e·raw·beek *aerobics*
Afrika ⓕ a·free·ka *Africa*
agencija za prodaju nekretnina ⓕ
  a·gen·tsee·ya za praw·dai·oo
  ne·kret·nee·na *estate agency*
ako a·kaw *if*
akopunktura ⓕ a·kaw·poonk·too·ra
  acupuncture
aktivist ⓜ ak·tee·veest *activist*
aktovka ⓕ ak·tawv·ka *briefcase*
aktuelna zbivanja ⓝ pl ak·too·el·na
  zbee·va·nya *current affairs*
akumulator ⓜ a·koo·moo·la·tawr
  battery (for car)
alcohol ⓜ al·kaw·hawl *alcohol*
alergija ⓕ a·ler·gee·ya *allergy*
alkoholno piće ⓝ al·kaw·hawl·naw
  pee·che *drink (alcoholic)*

alpinističko penjanje ⓝ
  al·pee·nee·steech·kaw pe·nya·nye *rock
  climbing*
alpinizam ⓜ al·pee·nee·zam
  mountaineering
ambasada ⓕ am·ba·sa·da *embassy*
amfiteatar ⓜ am·fee·te·a·tar
  amphitheatre
amfora ⓕ am·faw·ra *amphora*
ananas ⓜ a·na·nas *pineapple*
anarhist ⓜ a·nar·heest *anarchist*
anemija ⓕ a·ne·mee·ya *anaemia*
antibaby-pilula ⓕ an·tee·bey·bee·pee·
  loo·la *the Pill (contraceptive)*
antibiotici ⓜ pl an·tee·bee·aw·tee·tsee
  antibiotics
antički an·teech·kee *ancient*
antikvitet ⓜ an·tee·kvee·tet *antique*
antinuklearni an·tee·noo·kle·ar·nee
  antinuclear
antiseptik ⓜ an·tee·sep·teek *antiseptic*

arheološki ⓜ ar·he-*aw*-lawsh·kee *archaeological*

arhitekt ⓜ ar·hee-*tekt* *architect*

arhitektura ⓕ ar·hee-tek-*too*·ra *architecture*

aromaterapija ⓕ a·*raw*·ma·te·*ra*·pee·ya *aromatherapy*

aspirin ⓜ a·*spee*·reen *aspirin*

astma ⓕ *ast*·ma *asthma*

atelje ⓜ a·*te*·lye *studio*

atletika ⓕ at·*le*·tee·ka *athletics*

atmosfera ⓕ at·maw·*sfe*·ra *atmosphere*

audio vodič ⓜ a·oo·dee·aw *vaw*·deech *guide (audio)*

Australija ⓕ a·oo·*stra*·lee·ya *Australia*

Austrija ⓕ a·oo·*stree*·ya *Austria*

Austru-Ugarsko carstvo ⓜ a·oo·*straw*·oo·gar·skaw *tsar*·stvaw *Austro-Hungarian Empire*

autobus a·oo-*taw*·boos *bus*

autobuska stanica ⓕ a·oo-*taw*·boo·ska *sta*·nee·tsa *bus station • bus stop*

automat za prodaju karata ⓜ a·oo·*taw*·mat za *praw*·dai·oo *ka*·ra·ta *ticket machine*

automatska praonica ⓕ a·oo·*taw*·mat·ska pra·*aw*·nee·tsa *launderette*

automehaničar ⓜ a·oo·taw·me·*ha*·nee·char *mechanic*

automobil ⓜ a·oo·taw·*maw*·beel *car*

autoput ⓜ a·oo·taw·*poot* *highway*

avenija ⓕ a·*ve*·nee·ya *avenue*

Azija ⓕ a·*zee*·ya *Asia*

B

badem ⓜ *ba*·dem *almond*

badnjak ⓜ *bad*·nyak *Christmas Eve*

baka ⓕ *ba*·ka *grandmother*

bakšiš *bak*·sheesh *tip (gratuity)*

balet ⓜ ba·*let* *ballet*

Balkan ⓜ *bal*·kan *the Balkans*

balkon ⓜ *bal*·kawn *balcony*

banana ⓕ ba·*na*·na *banana*

banka ⓕ *ban*·ka *bank (institution)*

bankovni automat ⓜ *ban*·kawv·nee a·oo·*taw*·mat *automated teller machine (ATM)*

bankovni račun ⓜ *ban*·kawv·nee *ra*·choon *bank account*

bar ⓜ bar *bar*

baterija ⓕ ba·te·*ree*·ya *battery (general)*

bazen za plivanje ⓜ *ba*·zen za *plee*·va·nye *swimming pool*

beba ⓕ *be*·ba *baby*

bejzbol ⓜ *beyz*·bawl *baseball*

Belgija ⓕ *bel*·gee·ya *Belgium*

benzin ⓜ ben·*zeen* *gasoline • petrol*

benziska stanica ⓕ ben·*zeen*·ska *sta*·nee·tsa *gas station • petrol station*

besplatan be·*spla*·tan *free (gratis)*

bez bez *without*

— **slobodnih mjesta** *slaw*·bawd·neeh *mye*·sta *no vacancy*

bezalkoholno piće ⓝ be·zal·kaw·*hawl*·naw *pee*·che *soft drink*

bezolovni be·*zaw*·lawv·nee *unleaded*

biblija ⓕ *bee*·blee·ya *Bible*

bicikl ⓜ bee·*tsee*·kl *bicycle*

biciklist ⓜ bee·tsee·*kleest* *cyclist*

bife ⓜ bee·*fe* *buffet*

bijel bee·*yel* *white*

bilijar ⓜ bee·lee·*yar* *pool (game)*

bilježnica ⓕ bee·*lyezh*·nee·tsa *notebook*

biljka ⓕ *beel*'·ka *herb • plant*

biti/bivati *bee*·tee/*bee*·va·tee *be*

biznis ⓜ *beez*·nees *business*

biznismen ⓜ&ⓕ *beez*·nees·men *business man/woman*

blagajna ⓕ bla·*gai*·na *cash register*

blagajnik ⓜ bla·*gai*·neek *cashier*

blagdan ⓜ *blag*·dan *holiday (day off)*

blato ⓝ *bla*·taw *mud*

blic ⓜ bleets *flash (camera)*

blizak *blee*·zak *close (nearby)*

blizanci ⓜ pl blee·*zan*·tsee *twins*

blizu *blee*·zoo *near*

boca ⓕ *baw*·tsa *bottle*

— **za vodu** za *vaw*·doo *water bottle*

bog ⓜ bawg *god (general)*

bogat *baw*·gat *wealthy*

boja ⓕ *boy*·a *colour*

boks ⓜ bawks *boxing*

bokserice ⓕ pl *bawk*·se·ree·tse *boxer shorts*

bol ⓕ bawl *pain*

bolan *baw*·lan *painful*

bolest ⓕ *baw*·lest *disease*

bolestan *baw*·les·tan *sick*

bolji *baw*·lyee *better*

bolnica ⓕ *bawl*·nee·tsa *hospital*

bomboni ⓜ pl bawm·*baw*·nee *candy • lollies • sweets*

borba ⓕ *bawr*·ba *fight (battle)*

borilačke vještine ⓕ pl baw·ree·lach·ke vye·shtee·ne *martial arts*

Bosna i Hercegovina ⓕ baw·sna ee her·tse·gaw·vee·na *Bosnia-Hercegovina*

botanički vrt ⓜ baw·ta·neech·kee vrt *botanic garden*

božić ⓜ baw·zheech *Christmas*

božićni dan ⓜ baw·zheech·nee dan *Christmas Day*

bračno stanje ⓝ brach·naw sta·nye *marital status*

brak ⓜ brak *marriage*

brašno ⓝ brash·naw *flour*

brat ⓜ brat *brother*

brava ⓕ bra·va *lock*

brdska staza ⓕ brd·ska sta·za *mountain path*

brdski bicikl ⓜ brd·skee bee·tsee·kl *mountain bike*

breskva ⓕ bresk·va *peach*

brežuljak ⓜ bre·zhoo·lyak *hill*

brijač ⓜ bree·yach *barber • razor*

(o)brijati se (aw·)bree·ya·tee se *shave*

briljantan bree·lyan·tan *brilliant*

(po)brinuti se (paw·)bree·noo·tee se *care (for someone)*

(po)brinuti se za (paw·)bree·noo·tee se za *look after*

britva ⓕ breet·va *razor blade*

brod ⓜ brawd *ship*

broj ⓜ broy *number (figure)*
— **putovnice** poo·tawv·nee·tse *passport number*
— **registarske tablice** re·gee·star·ske ta·blee·tse *licence-plate number*
— **sobe** saw·be *room number*

(iz)brojati (eez·)broy·a·tee *count*

brokula ⓕ braw·koo·la *broccoli*

bronhitis ⓜ brawn·hee·tees *bronchitis*

brošura ⓕ braw·shoo·ra *brochure*

brz brz *fast*

brzi br·zee *express*

brzina ⓕ br·zee·na *speed*
— **filma** feel·ma *film speed*

brzinomjer ⓜ br·zee·naw·myer *speedometer*

brzinsko ograničenje ⓝ br·zeen·skaw aw·gra·nee·che·nye *speed limit*

bučan boo·chan *noisy*

bučice ⓕ pl boo·chee·tse *courgette • zucchini*

budala ⓕ boo·da·la *idiot*

budilica ⓕ boo·dee·lee·tsa *alarm clock*

Budist ⓜ boo·deest *Buddhist*

(pro)buditi nekoga (praw·)boo·dee·tee ne·kaw·ga *wake (someone) up*

budućnost ⓕ boo·dooch·nawst *future*

budžet ⓜ boo·jet *budget*

buha ⓕ boo·ha *flea*

bundeva ⓕ boon·de·va *pumpkin*

(pro)bušiti (praw·)boo·shee·tee *puncture*

buvljak ⓜ boov·lyak *flea market*

C

carinarnica ⓕ tsa·ree·nar·nee·tsa *customs*

CD ⓜ tse de *CD*

cent ⓜ tsent *cent*

centar ⓜ tsen·tar *centre*

centimetar ⓜ tsen·tee·me·tar *centimetre*

cesta ⓕ tse·sta *road*

cigara ⓕ tsee·ga·ra *cigar*

cigareta ⓕ tsee·ga·re·ta *cigarette*

cijena ⓕ tsee·ye·na *price*
— **ulaznice** oo·laz·nee·tse *cover charge (nightclub etc)*
— **vožnje** vawzh·nye *fare*

cijepljenje ⓝ tsee·yep·lye·nye *vaccination*

cipela/e ⓕ sg/ⓕ pl tsee·pe·la/e *shoe(s)*

cirkus ⓜ tseer·koos *circus*

cistitis ⓕ tsee·stee·tees *cystitis*

citadela ⓕ tsee·ta·de·la *walled city*

crkva ⓕ tsr·kva *church*

crn tsrn *black*

Crna Gora ⓕ tsr·na gaw·ra *Montenegro*

crno-bijeli (film) tsr·naw·bee·ye·lee (feelm) *B&W (film)*

crven tsr·ven *red*

crvi ⓜ pl tsr·vee *worms*

cura ⓕ tsoo·ra *girlfriend*

cvijet ⓜ tsvee·yet *flower*

cvjećara ⓕ tsvye·cha·ra *florist*

Č

čačkalica ⓕ chach·ka·lee·tsa *toothpick*

čaj ⓜ chai *tea*

čamac ⓜ cha·mats *boat*

čarapa/e ⓕ sg/ⓕ pl cha·ra·pa/e *sock(s)*

čaša ⓕ cha·sha *glass (receptacle)*

ček ⓜ chek *cheque*

čekaonica ⓕ che·ka·aw·nee·tsa *waiting room*

(pri)čekati nekoga (pree-)che-ka-tee ne-kaw-ga *wait (for)*
čekić ⓜ che-keech *hammer*
čeljust ⓕ che-lyoost *jaw*
čelnik ⓜ chel-neek *leader*
čep ⓜ chep *plug (bath)*
čepovi za uši ⓜ pl che-paw-vee za oo-shee *earplugs*
čestitke ⓕ pl che-steet-ke *congratulations*
često che-staw *often*
češalj ⓜ che-shal' *comb*
češnjak ⓜ chesh-nyak *garlic*
četka ⓕ chet-ka *brush*
  — za kosu ⓕ za kaw-soo *hairbrush*
četkica za zube ⓕ chet-kee-tsa za zoo-be *toothbrush*
četvrtak ⓜ chet-vr-tak *Thursday*
četvrtina ⓕ chet-vr-tee-na *quarter*
(u)činiti (oo-)chee-nee-tee *do • make*
čipka ⓕ cheep-ka *lace*
čist cheest *clean • pure*
(o)čistiti (aw-)chee-stee-tee *clean*
čišćenje ⓝ cheesh-che-nye *cleaning*
čitanje ⓝ chee-ta-nye *reading*
(pro)čitati (praw-)chee-ta-tee *read*
čizma/e ⓕ sg/ⓕ pl chee-zma/e *boot(s) (footwear)*
član(ica) ⓜ/ⓕ chlan(-ee-tsa) *member*
čokolada ⓕ chaw-kaw-la-da *chocolate*
čovjek ⓜ chaw-vyek *man (human)*
čuti perf choo-tee *hear*
čuvanje djece ⓝ choo-va-nye dye-tse *childminding*

D

da da *yes*
dadilja ⓕ da-dee-lya *baby-sitter*
dahnuti/disati dah-noo-tee/dee-sa-tee *breathe*
daleko da-le-kaw *far*
dalekozor ⓜ da-le-kaw-zawr *binoculars*
daljinski upravljač ⓜ da-lyeen-skee oo-prav-lyach *remote control*
dan ⓜ dan *day*
danas da-nas *today*
Danska ⓕ dan-ska *Denmark*
dar ⓜ dar *gift*
daska ⓕ da-ska *board*
  — za surfanje za soor-fa-nye *surfboard*

daskanje na snijegu ⓝ da-ska-nye na snee-ye-goo *snowboarding*
daskanje na valovima ⓝ da-ska-nye na va-law-vee-ma *surfing*
dati/davati da-tee/da-va-tee *give*
datulja ⓕ da-too-lya *date (fruit)*
datum ⓜ da-toom *date (day)*
  — rođenja raw-je-nya *date of birth*
debeo de-be-aw *fat • thick (object)*
dečko ⓜ dech-kaw *boyfriend*
deka ⓕ de-ka *blanket*
delikatese ⓕ pl de-lee-ka-te-se *delicatessen*
demokracija ⓕ de-maw-kra-tsee-ya *democracy*
demonstracija ⓕ de-mawn-stra-tsee-ya *demonstration (protest)*
depozit ⓜ de-paw-zeet *deposit (bank)*
desni ⓕ pl de-snee *gum (teeth)*
desničarski de-snee-char-skee *right-wing*
desno de-snaw *right (direction)*
dezodorans ⓜ de-zaw-daw-rans *deodorant*
digitron ⓜ dee-gee-trawn *calculator*
dijabetes ⓜ dee-ya-be-tes *diabetes*
dijafragma ⓕ dee-ya-frag-ma *diaphragm (body part)*
dijapozitiv ⓜ dee-ya-paw-zee-teev *slide (film)*
dijeliti imp dee-ye-lee-tee *share (a dorm etc)*
(po)dijeliti (paw-)dee-ye-lee-tee *deal (cards)*
dijeta ⓕ dee-ye-ta *diet*
dijete ⓝ dee-ye-te *child*
dinja ⓕ dee-nya *cantaloupe • melon • rockmelon*
dio ⓜ dee-aw *part (component)*
director ⓜ dee-rek-tawr *director*
direktan dee-rek-tan *direct*
  — poziv paw-zeev *direct-dial*
dirnuti/dirati deer-noo-tee/dee-ra-tee *feel • touch*
disk (CD-ROM) ⓜ deesk (tse de rawm) *disk (CD-ROM)*
disketa ⓕ dee-ske-ta *disk (floppy)*
disko ⓜ dee-skaw *disco*
diskriminacija ⓕ dee-skree-mee-na-tsee-ya *discrimination*
divan dee-van *wonderful*
dizajn ⓜ dee-zain *design*
dizalo ⓝ dee-za-law *elevator • lift*

djeca ⓝ pl *dye*·tsa *children*

djećak ⓜ *dye*·chak *boy*

dječja hodalica ⓕ *dyech*·ya *haw*·da·lee·tsa *stroller*

djed ⓜ dyed *grandfather*

djevojčica ⓕ dye·*voy*·chee·tsa *girl*

dlaka ⓕ *dla*·ka *hair (body)*

dnevni *dnev*·nee *daily*

dnevnik ⓜ *dnev*·neek *diary*

dno ⓝ dnaw *bottom (position)*

do daw *beside • to*

dobaciti/dobacivati daw·*ba*·tsee·tee/ daw·ba·*tsee*·va·tee *pass*

dobar ⓜ daw·bar *good*

dobitak ⓜ daw·*bee*·tak *profit*

dobiti/dobivati *daw*·bee·tee/ daw·*bee*·va·tee *get*

dobro *daw*·braw *well*

doček nove godine ⓜ *daw*·chek *naw*·ve *gaw*·dee·ne *New Year's Eve*

dočekati/dočekivati daw·che·ka·tee/ daw·che·*kee*·va·tee *welcome*

doći/dolaziti daw·chee/daw·*la*·zee·tee *come*

dokumentacija ⓕ daw·koo·men·*ta*·tsee·ya *paperwork*

dokumentarac ⓜ daw·koo·men·*ta*·rats *documentary*

dolar ⓜ *daw*·lar *dollar*

dolasci ⓜ pl daw·*las*·tsee *arrivals*

dolina ⓕ daw·*lee*·na *valley*

dolje *daw*·lye *down*

dom ⓜ dawm *home*

donijeti/donositi daw·nee·ye·tee/ daw·*naw*·see·tee *bring*

donje rublje ⓝ *daw*·nye roob·lye *underwear*

dopasti/dopadati se daw·pa·stee/ *daw*·pa·da·tee se *like (appeal to)*

dopisnica ⓕ *daw*·pee·snee·tsa *postcard*

dopuštenje ⓝ daw·poosh·*te*·nye *permission*

doručak ⓜ *daw*·roo·chak *breakfast*

dosadan *daw*·sa·dan *boring*

dosta *daw*·sta *enough*

dostaviti/dostavljati daw·sta·vee·tee/ *daw*·stav·lya·tee *deliver*

dozvola ⓕ *dawz*·vaw·la *licence • permit*

dozvoliti/dozvoljavati dawz·*vaw*·lee·tee/ dawz·*vaw*·lya·va·tee *admit (allow)*

dozvoljena količina prtljage ⓕ *dawz*·vaw·lye·na kaw·lee·*chee*·na prt·*lya*·ge *baggage allowance*

dragocjen dra·*gaw*·tsyen *valuable*

drama ⓕ *dra*·ma *drama*

dražica ⓕ *dra*·zhee·tsa *cove*

droga/e ⓕ sg/ⓕ pl *draw*·ga/e *drug(s) (illicit)*

drug ⓜ droog *companion*

drugačiji droo·*ga*·chee·yee *different (another)*

drugi *droo*·gee *another • other • second* — **razred** *raz*·red *economy class • second class*

društvene znanosti ⓕ pl *droosht*·ve·ne zna·naw·stee *humanities*

društvo ⓝ *droosh*·tvaw *company*

drvo ⓝ *dr*·vaw *wood* — **za ogrjev** za *aw*·gryev *firewood*

država ⓕ *dr*·zha·va *country (nation state)*

državljanstvo ⓝ dr·zhav·lyan·stvaw *citizenship*

dubok ⓜ doo·bawk *deep*

dugačak doo·ga·chak *long*

dugme ⓝ *doog*·me *button*

dugovati imp doo·*gaw*·va·tee *owe*

duhan ⓜ *doo*·han *tobacco*

dupli krevet ⓜ *doo*·plee *kre*·vet *double bed*

dva dva *two* — **tjedna** ⓕ *tyed*·na *fortnight*

dvaput dva·poot *twice*

DVD ⓜ de ve de *DVD*

dvokrevetna soba ⓕ *dvaw*·kre·vet·na *saw*·ba *double room • twin room*

dvorac ⓜ *dvaw*·rats *castle*

dvostruk *dvaw*·strook *double*

Dž

džamija ⓕ *ja*·mee·ya *mosque*

džem ⓜ jem *jam*

džemper ⓜ *jem*·per *jumper • sweater*

džep ⓜ jep *pocket*

džepni nožić ⓜ *jep*·nee *naw*·zheech *pocket knife*

džin ⓜ jeen *gin*

džip ⓜ jeep *jeep*

E

ekcem ⓜ ek·*tsem* *eczema*

ekskurzija ⓕ ek·*skoor*·zee·ya *tour* — **s vodičem** ⓕ s vaw·*dee*·chem *guided tour*

ekspres pošta ① *eks·pres pawsh·ta express (mail)*
ekstasi ⑩ *ek·sta·see ecstasy (drug)*
e-mail ⑩ *ee·me·eel email*
emocionalan *e·maw·tsee·aw·na·lan emotional*
Engleska ① *en·gle·ska England*
engleski *en·gle·skee English*
euro ⑩ *e·oo·raw euro*
Europa ① *e·oo·raw·pa Europe*

F

farma ① *far·ma farm*
festival ⑩ *fe·stee·val festival*
fikcija ① *feek·tsee·ya fiction (genre)*
film ⑩ *feelm film • movie*
— **za foto-aparat** *za faw·taw·a·pa·rat film (for camera)*
filtriran *feel·tree·ran filtered*
fino pecivo ⑩ *fee·naw pe·tsee·vaw pastry*
Finska ① *feen·ska Finland*
fizički radnik ⑩ *fee·zeech·kee rad·neek manual worker*
flanel ⑩ *fla·nel flannel*
flaster ⑩ *fla·ster Band-aid*
foaje ⑩ *faw·a·i·e foyer*
foto-aparat ⑩ *faw·taw·a·pa·rat camera*
fotograf ⑩ *faw·taw·graf photographer*
fotografija ① *faw·taw·gra·fee·ya photo • photography*
Francuska ① *fran·tsoo·ska France*
frizer ⑩ *free·zer hairdresser*
funta ① *foon·ta pound (money, weight)*

G

galerija ① *ga·le·ree·ya art gallery*
garantiran *ga·ran·tee·ran guaranteed*
garaža ① *ga·ra·zha garage*
garderoba ① *gar·de·raw·ba cloakroom*
gastroenteritis ⑩ *ga·straw·en·te·ree·tees gastroenteritis*
gazda ⑩ *gaz·da landlord*
gazdarica ① *gaz·da·ree·tsa landlady*
gdje *gdye where*
G'đa *g·ja Ms*
gimnastika ① *geem·na·stee·ka gymnastics*
ginekolog ⑩ *gee·ne·kaw·lawg gynaecologist*
gitara ① *gee·ta·ra guitar*

gladan/gladna ⑩/① *gla·dan/gla·dna hungry*
glas ⑩ *glas voice*
glasan ⑩ *gla·san loud*
glasovati imp *gla·saw·va·tee vote*
glava ① *gla·va head*
— **ulica** *oo·lee·tsa main road*
glavni *glav·nee main*
glavobolja ① *gla·vaw·baw·lya headache*
glazba ① *glaz·ba music*
(po)gledati *(paw·)gle·da·tee look • watch*
gležanj ⑩ *gle·zhan' ankle*
gležnjače ① pl *glezh·nya·che hiking boots*
gljiva ① *glyee·va mushroom*
gluh *glooh deaf*
glumac ⑩ *gloo·mats actor*
glup *gloop stupid*
godišnje doba ⑩ *gaw·deesh·nye daw·ba season (winter etc)*
gol ⑩ *gawl goal*
golf ⑩ *gawlf golf*
gorak *gaw·rak bitter*
gore *gaw·re up*
gorski lanac ⑩ *gawr·skee la·nats mountain range*
Gospodin ⑩ *gaw·spaw·deen Mr*
Gospođa ① *gaw·spaw·ja Mrs*
Gospođica ① *gaw·spaw·jee·tsa Miss*
gostiona ① *gaw·stee·aw·na restaurant (family run)*
gostionica ① *gaw·stee·aw·nee·tsa pub (bar)*
gostoprimstvo *gaw·staw·preems·tvaw hospitality*
gotovina ① *gaw·taw·vee·na cash*
govedina ① *gaw·ve·dee·na beef*
(pro)govoriti *(praw·)gaw·vaw·ree·tee speak • talk*
grad ⑩ *grad city*
(iz)graditi *(eez·)gra·dee·tee build*
gradski autobus ⑩ *grad·skee a·oo·taw·boos bus (city)*
gradski centar ⑩ *grad·skee tsen·tar city centre*
građanska prava ⑩ pl *gra·jan·ska pra·va civil rights*
građevinar ⑩ *gra·je·vee·nar builder*
gram ⑩ *gram gram*
granica ① *gra·nee·tsa border*
grijač ⑩ *gree·yach heater*
grijanje ⑩ *gree·ya·nye heating*
gripa ① *gree·pa influenza*

(za)grliti (*za-*)*gr*·lee·tee *hug*
grlo ⓝ *gr*·law *throat*
grmljavina ① *grm*·lya·vee·na *thunderstorm*
grnčarija ① grn·*cha*·ree·ya *pottery*
grob ⓜ grawb *grave (tomb)*
groblje ⓝ *graw*·blye *cemetery*
groznica ① *grawz*·nee·tsa *fever*
grožđica ① *grawzh*·jee·tsa *raisin*
grudnjak ⓜ *grood*·nyak *bra*
grumen ⓜ *groo*·men *lump*
grupa ① *groo*·pa *band (music)*
g-string ⓝ ge·streeng *g-string*
guma ① *goo*·ma *gum (substance)* •
tire • *tyre*
— na automobile na
a·oo·taw·*maw*·bee·le *tire (car)*
gurnuti/gurati *goor*·noo·tee/*goo*·ra·tee
push
gust goost *thick (liquid)*
gušter ⓜ *goosh*·ter *lizard*

H

halal *ha*·lal *halal*
haljina ① *ha*·lyee·na *dress*
Halo. ha·*law* Hello. *(answering telephone)*
halucinacija ① ha·loo·tsee·*na*·tsee·ya
hallucination
hašiš ⓜ *ha*·sheesh *hash*
hepatitis ⓜ he·pa·*tee*·tees *hepatitis*
heroin ⓜ he·*raw*·een *heroin*
hidratantna krema ① hee·dra·*tant*·na
kre·ma *moisturiser*
higijenski uložak ⓜ *hee*·gee·yen·skee
oo·*law*·zhak *sanitary napkin*
Hinduist ⓜ heen·doo·*eest* *Hindu*
hitan *hee*·tan *urgent*
— slučaj *sloo*·chai *emergency*
hitna pomoć ① *heet*·na *paw*·mawch
ambulance
HIV ⓜ heev *HIV*
hlače ① pl *hla*·che *trousers*
hladan *hla*·dan *cold* • *cool*
hladnjak ⓜ *hlad*·nyak *refrigerator*
hladovina ① hla·*daw*·vee·na *shade*
hodati imp *haw*·da·tee *walk*
hodnik ⓜ *hawd*·neek *walkway*
hokej ⓜ *haw*·key *hockey*
— na ledu na *le*·doo *ice hockey*
homeopatija ① *haw*·me·aw·*pa*·tee·ya
homeopathy

homoseksualac/homoseksualka ⓜ/①
haw·maw·sek·soo·*a*·lats/
haw·maw·sek·soo·*al*·ka *homosexual*
homoseksualan *haw*·maw·sek·soo·a·lan *gay*
honorarni ⓜ *haw*·naw·rar·nee *part-time*
horoskop ⓜ *haw*·raw·skawp *horoscope*
hotel ⓜ *haw*·*tel* *hotel*
hrabar *hra*·bar *brave*
hram ⓜ hram *temple*
hrana ① *hra*·na *food*
— za bebe za *be*·be *baby food*
(na)hraniti (na·)*hra*·nee·tee *feed*
Hrvat/Hrvatica ⓜ/① *hr*·vat/hr·*va*·tee·tsa
Croat
Hrvatska ① *hr*·vat·ska *Croatia*
hvala vam/ti pol/inf *hva*·la vam/tee
thank you

I

i ee *and*
ići imp ee·*chee* *go*
— u kupovinu imp oo
koo·*paw*·vee·noo *go shopping*
identifikacija ① ee·den·tee·fee·*ka*·tsee·ya
identification
igla injekcije ① ee·gla ee·*nyek*·tsee·ye
syringe
igla za šivenje ① ee·gla za *shee*·ve·nye
sewing needle
igra ① ee·gra *game*
igralište ⓝ ee·gra·*leesh*·te *court (tennis)*
igrati imp ee·*gra*·tee *play (board games)*
ili ee·lee *or*
Iliri ⓜ pl ee·*lee*·ree *Illyrians*
imati imp ee·*ma*·tee *have*
ime ⓝ *ee*·me *name (given)*
imigracija ① ee·mee·*gra*·tsee·ya
immigration
Indija ① een·*dee*·ya *India*
indijski oraščić ⓜ *een*·deey·skee
aw·*rash*·cheech *cashew*
industrija ① een·*doo*·stree·ya *industry*
infekcija ① een·*fek*·tsee·ya *infection*
— kandide kan·*dee*·de *thrush (illness)*
— mokraćnih kanala *maw*·krach·neeh
ka·*na*·la *urinary infection*
informacije ① pl een·*fawr*·ma·tsee·ye
information
Informacijska tehnologija ①
een·*fawr*·ma·tseey·ska
teh·*naw*·law·gee·ya *IT*

injekcija ① ee-*nyek*-tsee-ya *injection*
inostranstvo ⓝ ee-*naw*-strans-tvaw
   overseas
instruktor ⓜ een-*strook*-tawr
   instructor
internet ⓜ een-ter-net *Internet*
   — **kafić** *ka*-feech *Internet café*
intervju ⓜ een-ter-*vyoo* *interview*
invalidska kolica ① pl een-*va*-leed-ska
   kaw-*lee*-tsa *wheelchair*
inženjer ⓜ een-*zhe*-nyer *engineer*
inženjerstvo ⓝ een-*zhe*-nyer-stvaw
   engineering
Irska ① *eer*-ska *Ireland*
isključen ees-*klyoo*-chen *excluded*
iskustvo ⓝ ees-*koost*-vaw *experience*
isplata ① ees-*pla*-ta *payment*
   (to someone)
ispod ee-spawd *below*
ispovijed ① ee-*spaw*-vee-yed *confession*
   (at church)
ispravan ee-*spra*-van *right (correct)*
isti ⓜ ee-stee *same*
istok ⓜ ee-stawk *east*
Italija ① ee-*ta*-lee-ya *Italy*
iz eez *from*
iza ee-za *after • behind*
izabrati/izabirati ee-*za*-bra-tee/
   ee-za-bee-ra-tee *choose*
izaći/izlaziti ee-za-chee/ee-zla-zee-tee
   go out
izaći/izlaziti sa ee-*za*-chee/
   eez-la-zee-tee sa *go out with*
   (date) a person
izbjeglica ① eez-*byeg*-lee-tsa *refugee*
izbočina ① eez-*baw*-chee-na *ledge*
izbori ⓜ pl eez-baw-ree *election*
izdavanje ⓝ eez-*da*-va-nye *publishing*
izgoren eez-gaw-ren *burnt*
(iz)gubiti (eez-)goo-bee-tee *lose*
izgubljen eez-goob-lyen *lost*
izlaz ⓜ eez-laz *departure gate • exit*
izlazak ⓜ eez-*la*-zak *night out*
izlazak sunca ⓜ eez-*la*-zak soon-tsa
   sunrise
izlet ⓜ eez-let *trip (journey)*
izložba ① eez-*lawzh*-ba *exhibition*
između ee-zme-joo *between*
iznad eez-nad *above*
iznajmiti/iznajmljivati eez-*nai*-mee-tee/
   eez-naim-*lyee*-va-tee *hire • rent*
iznenađen ⓜ eez-*ne*-na-jen *surprise*
Izrael ⓜ ee-zra-el *Israel*

J

ja ya *I*
jabuka ① ya-*boo*-ka *apple*
jabukovača ① ya-*boo*-kaw-va-cha *cider*
Jadranska obala ① ya-dran-ska *aw*-ba-la
   Adriatic Coast
Jadransko more ⓝ ya-dran-skaw *maw*-re
   Adriatic Sea
jagoda ① ya-*gaw*-da *strawberry*
jahanje konja ⓝ ya-*ha*-nye *kaw*-nya
   horse riding
jahati imp ya-*ha*-tee *ride (horse)*
jahta ① *yah*-ta *yacht*
jaje ⓝ *yai*-e *egg*
jajnik ⓜ *yai*-neek *ovary*
jak yak *strong (physically)*
jakna ① *yak*-na *jacket*
janje ⓝ ya-nye *lamb (animal)*
janjetina ① ya-*nye*-tee-na *lamb (meat)*
Japan ⓜ ya-pan *Japan*
jarac ⓜ ya-rats *goat*
jaslice ① pl ya-slee-tse *creche*
jastučnica ① ya-*stooch*-nee-tsa
   pillowcase
jastuk ⓜ ya-stook *pillow*
javni yav-nee *public*
   — **parkovi** ⓜ pl par-kaw-vee *public
     gardens*
   — **telefon** ⓜ te-*le*-fawn *public telephone*
   — **zahod** ⓜ za-hawd *public toilet*
je ⓝ ye *her*
jedan ⓜ ye-dan *one*
jednake mogućnosti ① pl *yed*-na-ke
   maw-*gooch*-naw-stee *equal opportunity*
jednokrevetna soba ①
   yed-naw-*kre*-vet-na *saw*-ba *single room*
jednom *yed*-nawm *once*
jednosmjeran *yed*-naw-*smye*-ran
   one-way (ticket)
jednostavan *yed*-naw-*sta*-van *easy*
jedrenje na dasci ⓝ ye-*dre*-nye na
   das-tsee *windsurfing*
jeftino ⓝ *yef*-tee-naw *cheap*
jelo ⓝ ye-law *dish (food item)*
jelovnik ⓜ ye-*lawv*-neek *menu*
jesen ① ye-sen *autumn • fall*
(po)jesti (paw-)ye-stee *eat*
jetra ① ye-tra *liver*
jezero ⓝ ye-ze-raw *lake*
jezik ⓜ ye-zeek *language*
joga ① yaw-ga *yoga*

jogurt ⓜ *yaw*-goort *yogurt*
(ne) još (ne) yawsh *(not) yet*
jučer yoo-cher *yesterday*
jug ⓜ yoog *south*
Jugoslavija ⓕ yoo-gaw-*sla*-vee-ya
  Yugoslavia
juha ⓕ *yoo*-ha *soup*
jutro ⓝ *yoo*-traw *morning*

K

kabanica ⓕ ka-*ba*-nee-tsa *raincoat*
kabina za presvlačenje ⓕ pl ka-*bee*-na za
  pres-*vla*-che-nye *changing room*
kablovi za punjenje akumulatora ⓜ pl
  ka-blaw-vee za *poo*-nye-nye
  a-koo-moo-*la*-taw-ra *jumper leads*
kaciga ⓕ ka-*tsee*-ga *helmet*
kada ka-da *when*
kafić ⓜ ka-*feech café*
kajsija ⓕ *kai*-see-ya *apricot*
kakao ka-*ka*-aw *cocoa*
kako ka-*kaw how*
kalendar ⓜ ka-*len*-dar *calendar*
kamen ⓜ ka-men *stone*
kamion ⓜ ka-mee-awn *truck*
kamp ⓜ kamp *camping ground*
kampirati imp kam-*pee*-ra-tee *camp*
Kanada ⓕ *kan*-a-da *Canada*
kanta ⓕ *kan*-ta *bucket*
  — za smeće za *sme*-che *garbage can*
kapi za oči ⓕ pl *ka*-pee za *aw*-chee
  eye drops
kaput ⓜ ka-*poot coat*
karantena ⓕ ka-ran-*te*-na *quarantine*
karavana ⓕ ka-ra-*va*-na *caravan*
karta ⓕ *kar*-ta *map (of country)* • *ticket*
karte za igranje ⓕ pl *kar*-te za ee-*gra*-nye
  cards (playing)
kartonska kutija ⓕ *kar*-tawn-ska
  koo-*tee*-ya *carton*
kasan ka-san *late*
kasino ⓜ ka-*see*-naw *casino*
kasnije ka-snee-ye *later*
(za)kašljati (za-)*kash*-lya-tee *cough*
kat ⓜ kat *floor (storey)*
katedrala ⓕ ka-te-*dra*-la *cathedral*
Katoličanstvo ⓝ ka-taw-lee-*chan*-stvaw
  Catholicism
katolik ⓜ ka-*taw*-leek *Catholic*
kava ⓕ *ka*-va *coffee*
kazalište ⓝ ka-za-leesh-te *theatre*

kazati/kazivati ka-za-tee/ka-*zee*-va-tee
  say
kazeta ⓕ ka-*ze*-ta *cassette*
kći ⓕ kchee *daughter*
keks ⓜ keks *biscuit*
kemijska ⓕ ke-meey-ska *pen (ballpoint)*
keramika ⓕ ke-*ra*-mee-ka *ceramics*
kikiriki ⓜ *kee*-kee-*ree*-kee *groundnut* •
  peanut
kila ⓕ *kee*-la *kilo*
kilogram ⓜ kee-*law*-gram *kilogram*
kilometar ⓜ kee-law-*me*-tar *kilometre*
kino ⓝ *kee*-naw *cinema*
kiosk ⓜ *kee*-awsk *kiosk*
  — za prodaju novina za *praw*-dai-oo
  naw-vee-na *newsstand*
kip ⓜ keep *statue*
kiropraktor ⓜ kee-*raw*-prak-tawr
  chiropractor
kiseli krastavci ⓜ pl kee-*se*-lee
  kra-stav-tsee *pickles*
kiselo vrhnje ⓝ kee-se-law *vrh*-nye
  sour cream
kisik ⓜ *kee*-seek *oxygen*
kiša ⓕ *kee*-sha *rain*
kivi ⓜ *kee*-vee *kiwifruit*
klasa ⓕ *kla*-sa *class (category)*
klasičan kla-*see*-chan *classical*
klasni sistem ⓜ *kla*-snee *see*-stem
  class system
klavijatura ⓕ kla-vee-ya-*too*-ra *keyboard
  (instrument)*
klima ⓕ *klee*-ma *air-conditioning*
klimatiziran klee-ma-*tee*-zee-ran
  air-conditioned
ključ ⓜ klyooch *key*
knjiga ⓕ *knyee*-ga *book*
knjižara ⓕ *knyee*-zha-ra *bookshop*
knjižnica ⓕ *knyeezh*-nee-tsa *library*
kockice ⓕ pl *kawts*-kee-tse *dice*
kočnice ⓕ pl *kawch*-nee-tse *brakes*
kod kawd *at* • *with*
kofer ⓜ *kaw*-fer *suitcase*
koji koy-ee *which*
koji/koja/koje ⓜ/ⓕ/ⓝ koy-ee/koy-a/
  koy-e *what*
kokain ⓜ kaw-*ka*-een *cocaine*
kokos ⓜ *kaw*-kaws *coconut*
koktel ⓜ kawk-tel *cocktail*
kola za ručavanje ⓝ *kaw*-la za
  roo-*cha*-va-nye *dining car*
kolač ⓜ *kaw*-lach *cake*
kolačić ⓜ kaw-*la*-cheech *biscuit* • *cookie*

koledž ⓜ *kaw*·lej *college*
kolega/kolegica ⓜ/ⓕ kaw·*le*·ga/ kaw·*le*·gee·tsa *colleague*
koliba ⓕ *kaw*·lee·ba *lodge*
kolica za prtljagu ⓕ kaw·*lee*·tsa za prt·*lya*·goo *trolley*
količina ⓕ kaw·lee·*chee*·na *number (quantity)*
koliko kaw·*lee*·kaw *how much*
koljeno ⓜ *kaw*·lye·naw *knee*
kolo ⓜ *kaw*·law *circle dance*
kolovoz ⓜ *kaw*·law·vawz *August*
komad ⓜ *kaw*·mad *piece*
komarac ⓜ *kaw*·ma·rats *mosquito*
kombi ⓜ *kawm*·bee *van*
komedija ⓕ kaw·*me*·dee·ya *comedy*
komisija ⓕ kaw·*mee*·see·ya *commission*
kompas ⓜ *kawm*·pas *compass*
kompjuterska igra ⓕ kawm·*pyoo*·ter·ska ee·gra *computer game*
komunikacije ⓕ pl kaw·moo·nee·*ka*·tsee·ye *communications (profession)*
komunista ⓜ kaw·moo·*nee*·sta *communist*
komunizam ⓜ kaw·moo·*nee*·zam *communism*
konac ⓜ *kaw*·nats *thread*
  — za čišćenje zubi ⓜ za *cheesh*·che·nye zoo·bee *dental floss*
koncert ⓜ *kawn*·tsert *concert*
konferencija ⓕ kon·fe·*ren*·tsee·ya *conference (big)*
konj ⓜ kawn' *horse*
konjunktivitis ⓜ kaw·*nyoonk*·tee·vee·tees *conjunctivitis*
konobar ⓜ *kaw*·naw·bar *waiter*
konop za sušenje rublja ⓜ *kaw*·nawp za soo·she·nye *roob*·lya *clothesline*
kontakt leće ⓕ pl *kawn*·takt *le*·che *contact lenses*
konverter ⓜ kawn·*ver*·ter *adaptor*
konzervativan *kawn*·zer·va·tee·van *conservative*
konzulat ⓜ kawn·*zoo*·lat *consulate*
koralj ⓜ *kaw*·ral' *coral*
korisnik droga ⓜ *kaw*·ree·sneek *draw*·ga *drug user*
koristan *kaw*·ree·stan *useful*
kosa ⓕ *kaw*·sa *hair (head)*
kost ⓕ kawst *bone*
koš ⓜ kawsh *basket*
košarka ⓕ *kaw*·shar·ka *basketball*

košer ⓜ *kaw*·sher *kosher*
košulja ⓕ *kaw*·shoo·lya *shirt*
kotač ⓜ *kaw*·tach *wheel*
kozmetički salon ⓜ kawz·*me*·teech·kee sa·lawn *beauty salon*
koža ⓕ *kaw*·zha *leather · skin*
kraj ⓜ krai *end*
kraj krai *beside*
kralj ⓜ kral' *king*
kraljica ⓕ *kra*·lyee·tsa *queen*
krasno *kra*·snaw *great (fantastic)*
(u)krasti (oo·)*kra*·stee *steal*
kratak *kra*·tak *short*
  — životopis ⓜ zhee·*vaw*·taw·pees *CV*
kratke hlače ⓕ pl *krat*·ke hla·che *shorts*
krava ⓕ *kra*·va *cow*
krčenje šuma ⓜ *kr*·che·nye shoo·ma *deforestation*
kredit ⓜ *kre*·deet *credit*
kreditna kartica ⓕ *kre*·deet·na *kar*·tee·tsa *credit card*
kreker ⓜ *kre*·ker *cracker*
krema ⓕ *kre*·ma *cream (cosmetic)*
krevet ⓜ *kre*·vet *bed*
krevetnina ⓕ kre·vet·*nee*·na *bedding*
kriket ⓜ *kree*·ket *cricket (sport)*
krila ⓜ pl *kree*·la *wings*
kriška ⓕ *kreesh*·ka *slice*
kriv kreev *guilty · wrong*
krivnja ⓕ *kreev*·nya *fault (someone's)*
križ ⓜ kreezh *cross*
krojač ⓜ *kroy*·ach *tailor*
kroz krawz *across · in*
krsno ime ⓜ *kr*·snaw ee·me *given name*
krš ⓜ krsh *karst*
kršćanin/kršćanka ⓜ/ⓕ krsh·cha·neen/ krsh·chan·ka *Christian*
krštenje ⓜ krsh·*te*·nye *baptism*
kruh ⓜ krooh *bread*
krumpir ⓜ *kroom*·peer *potato*
krupan *kroo*·pan *large*
kruška ⓕ *kroosh*·ka *pear*
kružni tok ⓜ *kroozh*·nee tawk *roundabout*
krv ⓕ krv *blood*
krvna grupa ⓕ *krv*·na groo·pa *blood group*
krvne pretrage ⓕ pl *krv*·ne pre·tra·ge *blood test*
kuća ⓕ *koo*·cha *house*
kući koo·chee *(at) home*
kućni poslovi ⓜ pl *kooch*·nee paw·slaw·vee *housework*

kuglice vate ⓕ pl koo·glee·tse va·te
cotton balls
kuhanje ⓝ koo·ha·nye cooking
kuhar/kuharica ⓜ/ⓕ koo·har/
koo·ha·ree·tsa cook
(s)kuhati (s)koo·ha·tee cook
kuhinja ⓕ koo·hee·nya kitchen
kukuruz ⓜ koo·koo·rooz corn
kukuruzne pahuljice ⓕ pl
koo·koo·rooz·ne pa·hoo·lyee·tse
cornflakes
kupaći kostim ⓜ koo·pa·chee kaw·steem
bathing suit • swimsuit
kupaonica ⓕ koo·pa·aw·nee·tsa bathroom
kupiti/kupovati koo·pee·tee/
koo·paw·va·tee buy
kupka ⓕ koop·ka bath
kupon ⓜ koo·pawn coupon
kupovati imp koo·paw·va·tee shop
kupovina ⓕ koo·paw·vee·na shopping
kupus ⓜ koo·poos cabbage
kusur ⓜ koo·soor change (coins)
kutija ⓕ koo·tee·ya box • packet
kvačilo ⓝ kva·chee·law clutch (car)
kvalifikacije ⓕ pl kva·lee·fee·ka·tsee·ye
qualifications
kvaliteta ⓕ kva·lee·te·ta quality
(po)kvariti se (paw·)kva·ree·tee se break
down

L

labav ⓐ la·bav loose
lagan la·gan light (not heavy)
laki obrok ⓜ la·kee aw·brawk snack
laksativ ⓜ lak·sa·teev laxative
lanac ⓜ la·nats chain
laneno platno ⓝ la·ne·naw plat·naw
linen (material)
lažljivac/lažljivica ⓜ/ⓕ lazh·lyee·vats/
lazh·lyee·vee·tsa liar
leća ⓕ le·cha lens • lentil
leći/ležati le·chee/le·zha·tee lie (not stand)
led ⓜ led ice
leđa ⓝ le·ja back (body)
leptir ⓜ le·pteer butterfly
let ⓜ let flight
(po)letjeti (paw·)let·ye·tee fly
lezbijka ⓕ lez·beey·ka lesbian
ležaljka ⓕ le·zhal'·ka deck chairs
lice ⓝ lee·tse face
liječnik ⓜ lee·yech·neek doctor (medical)

lijekovi ⓜ pl lee·ye·kaw·vee medicine
(medication)
lijen lee·yen lazy
lijep lee·yep beautiful • nice
lijevi lee·ye·vee left (direction)
limenka ⓕ lee·men·ka can (tin)
limun ⓜ lee·moon lemon
limunada ⓕ lee·moo·na·da lemonade
linija ⓕ lee·nee·ya stereo
lipanj ⓜ lee·pan' June
list ⓜ leest leaf
listopad ⓜ lee·staw·pad October
litica ⓕ lee·tee·tsa cliff
lokal ⓜ law·kal venue
lokot ⓜ law·kawt padlock
(s)lomiti (s)law·mee·tee break
lomljiv lawm·lyeev fragile
lonac ⓜ law·nats saucepan
lopov ⓜ law·pawv thief
lopta ⓕ lawp·ta ball
loptica za golf ⓕ lawp·tee·tsa za gawlf
golf ball
losion law·see·awn lotion
— **za dobijanje tena** za
daw·bee·ya·nye te·na tanning lotion
— **za upotrebu poslije brijanja** za
oo·paw·tre·boo paw·slee·ye bree·ya·nya
aftershave
— **za zaštitu od sunca** za zash·tee·too
awd soon·tsa sunblock
losos ⓜ law·saws salmon
loš lawsh bad
lov na životinje ⓜ lawv na
zhee·vaw·tee·nye hunting
lubanja ⓕ loo·ba·nya skull
lubenica ⓕ loo·be·nee·tsa watermelon
lubrikant ⓜ loo·bree·kant lubricant
lud lood crazy
luk ⓜ look onion
luka ⓕ loo·ka harbour • port (sea)
lutka ⓕ loot·ka doll

Lj

(po)ljubiti (paw·)lyoo·bee·tee kiss
ljubomoran lyoo·baw·maw·ran jealous
ljudi ⓜ pl lyoo·dee people
ljudska prava ⓝ pl lyood·ska pra·va
human rights
ljudski resursi ⓜ pl lyood·skee
re·soor·see human resources
ljutit lyoo·teet angry

M

mačevanje ⓝ ma·*che*·va·nye
fencing (sport)
mačka ① *mach*·ka *cat*
madrac ⓜ *mad*·rats *mattress*
Mađarska ① *ma*·jar·ska *Hungary*
magazin ⓜ ma·*ga*·zeen *magazine*
maglovit ma·*glaw*·veet *foggy*
majica ① *mai*·ee·tsa *T-shirt*
majka ① *mai*·ka *mother*
Makedonija ① ma·*ke*·daw·nee·ya
Macedonia
mali *ma*·lee *small*
malo *ma*·law *little (not much)* • *some*
mama ① *ma*·ma *mum*
mandarina ① man·da·*ree*·na *mandarin*
mandolina ① man·*daw*·lee·na *mandolin*
mango ⓜ *man*·gaw *mango*
manje *ma*·nye *less*
manji *ma*·nyee *smaller*
marakuja ① ma·ra·*koo*·ya *passionfruit*
margarin ⓜ mar·*ga*·reen *margarine*
marihuana ① ma·ree·*hoo*·a·na
marijuana
marina ① ma·*ree*·na *marina*
marmelada ① mar·me·*la*·da *marmalade*
masaža ① ma·*sa*·zha *massage*
maser/maserka ⓜ/① ma·*ser*/ma·*ser*·ka
masseur/masseuse
maslac ⓜ *ma*·slats *butter*
maslina ① *ma*·slee·na *olive*
maslinovo ulje ⓝ *ma*·slee·naw·vaw
oo·lye *olive oil*
me(ne) *me*(·ne) *me*
med ⓜ med *honey*
medeni mjesec ⓜ *me*·dee·nee *mye*·sets
honeymoon
medicina ① me·dee·*tsee*·na *medicine*
(profession)
medicinska sestra ① me·dee·*tseen*·ska
se·stra *nurse*
mediji ⓜ pl *me*·dee·yee *media*
meditacija ① me·dee·*ta*·tsee·ya
meditation
melodija ① *me*·law·dee·ya *tune*
menadžer ⓜ *me*·na·jer *manager*

menstrualni bolovi ⓜ pl
men·stroo·al·nee *baw*·law·vee
period pain
mesar ⓜ *me*·sar *butcher*
mesnica ① *me*·snee·tsa *butcher's shop*
meso ⓝ *me*·saw *meat*
metal ⓜ *me*·tal *metal*
metar ⓜ *me*·tar *metre*
metro ⓜ *me*·traw *metro (train)*
   — stanica ① *sta*·nee·tsa *metro station*
mi mee *we*
migrena ① mee·*gre*·na *migraine*
(po)miješati (paw·)mee·*ye*·sha·tee *mix*
mikrovalna pećnica ① mee·kraw·*val*·na
pech·nee·tsa *microwave (oven)*
milijun ⓜ mee·*lee*·yoon *million*
milimetar ⓜ mee·lee·me·*tar* *millimetre*
mineralna voda ① mee·ne·*ral*·na *vaw*·da
mineral water
ministar predsjednik ⓜ mee·nee·star
pred·*syed*·neek *prime minister*
minuta ① mee·*noo*·ta *minute*
mir ⓜ meer *peace*
miris ⓜ mee·*rees* *smell (pleasant)*
misa ① *mee*·sa *mass (Catholic)*
(po)misliti (paw·)mee·*slee*·tee *think*
miš ⓜ meesh *mouse*
mišić ⓜ mee·*sheech* *muscle*
mišljenje ⓝ *meesh*·lye·nye *opinion*
mito ⓜ mee·*taw* *bribe*
mjehur ⓜ mye·*hoor* *bladder*
mjesec ⓜ mye·*sets* *month* • *moon*
mjesečnica ① mye·*sech*·nee·tsa
menstruation
mjesni mye·*snee* *local*
mjesto ⓝ mye·*staw* *place*
   — kontrole kawn·*traw*·le *checkpoint*
   — rođenja raw·*je*·nya *place of birth*
   — za kampiranje za kam·*pee*·ra·nye
camp site
mlad mlad *young*
mlijeko ⓝ mlee·*ye*·kaw *milk*
mljeveno meso ⓝ mlye·ve·naw *me*·saw
mince
mnogi *mnaw*·gee *many*
mobilni telefon ⓜ *maw*·beel·nee
te·*le*·fawn *mobile phone*
moći imp *maw*·chee *can (be able)*
moćnica ① *mawch*·nee·tsa *shrine*
moda ① *maw*·da *fashion*
modem ⓜ *maw*·dem *modem*
modrica ① *maw*·dree·tsa *bruise*
moguć *maw*·gooch *possible*

moj ⓜ moy *my*

moja ⓕ *moy*-a *my*

moje ⓝ *moy*-e *my*

mokar ⓜ *maw*-kar *wet*

(po)moliti se (paw-)*maw*-lee-tee (se) *worship*

molitva ⓕ *maw*-leet-va *prayer*

molitvenik ⓜ *maw*-leet-ve-neek *prayer book*

momčad ⓕ *mawm*-chad *team*

mononukleoza ⓕ *maw*-naw-nook-le-*aw*-za *glandular fever*

more ⓝ *maw*-re *sea*

most ⓜ mawst *bridge*

motel ⓜ maw-*tel motel*

motocikl ⓜ maw-taw-*tsee*-kl *motorbike*

motor ⓜ *maw*-tawr *engine*

motorni čamac ⓜ *maw*-tawr-nee cha-mats *motorboat*

možda *mawzh*-da *maybe*

moždani udar ⓜ *mawzh*-da-nee oo-dar *stroke (health)*

mračan *mra*-chan *dark*

mrav ⓜ mrav *ant*

mraz ⓜ mraz *frost*

mreža ⓕ *mre*-zha *net*
  — **za komarce** za kaw-*mar*-tse *mosquito net*

mrkva ⓕ *mrk*-va *carrot*

mrtav *mr*-tav *dead*

mučnina ⓕ mooch-*nee*-na *nausea*
  — **od vožnje** awd *vawzh*-nye *travel sickness*

muesli ⓜ pl *moo*-zlee *muesli*

musliman/muslimanka ⓜ/ⓕ moo-*slee*-man/moo-*slee*-man-ka *Muslim*

muškarac ⓜ moosh-*ka*-rats *man (male person)*

muzej ⓜ *moo*-zey *museum*

muzičar ⓜ *moo*-zee-char *musician*

muž ⓜ moozh *husband*

N

na na *at • in • on • per (day)*
  — **vrijeme** vree-*ye*-me *on time*

nabrojan ⓜ *na*-broy-an *itemised*

nacionalni park ⓜ *na*-tsee-aw-*nal*-nee park *national park*

nacionalnost ⓕ *na*-tsee-aw-*nal*-nawst *nationality*

način ⓜ *na*-cheen *way (manner)*

naći/nalaziti *na*-chee/*na*-la-zee-tee *find*

nad nad *to*

nadimak ⓜ *na*-dee-mak *nickname*

nafta ⓕ *naf*-ta *oil (petrol)*

najam automobila ⓜ *nai*-am a-oo-taw-maw-*bee*-la *car hire*

najbliži *nai*-blee-zhee *nearest*

najbolji *nai*-baw-lyee *best*

najmanji *nai*-ma-nyee *smallest*

najveći *nai*-ve-chee *biggest*

nakit ⓜ *na*-keet *jewellery*

namirnice ⓕ pl *na*-meer-nee-tse *groceries*

namještaj ⓜ *na*-mye-shtai *furniture*

naočale ⓕ pl *na*-aw-cha-le *glasses (spectacles)*
  — **za skijanje** za skee-*ya*-nye *goggles (skiing)*
  — **za sunce** (za *soon*-tse) *sunglasses*

naplata za usluge ⓕ *na*-pla-ta za oo-sloo-ge *service charge*

(na)praviti (*na*-)*pra*-vee-tee *make (bring about)*

naprijed *na*-pree-yed *ahead*

naranča ⓕ *na*-ran-cha *orange (fruit)*

narančast *na*-ran-chast *orange (colour)*

narediti/naređivati na-*re*-dee-tee/ na-re-*jee*-va-tee *order (demand)*

naručiti/naručivati na-*roo*-chee-tee/ na-roo-*chee*-va-tee *order (request)*

nastavnik ⓜ *na*-stav-neek *lecturer*

nastup ⓜ *na*-stoop *gig*

nasuprot *na*-soo-prawt *opposite*

naš nash *our*

naša ⓕ*nash*-a *our*

naše ⓝ *nash*-e *our*

naturoterapije ⓕ pl *na*-too-raw-te-*ra*-pee-ye *naturopathy*

naušnice ⓕ pl *na*-oosh-nee-tse *earrings*

navigacija ⓕ na-vee-*ga*-tsee-ya *navigation*

navijač ⓜ na-*vee*-yach *supporter (sport, etc)*

nazvati/nazivati *naz*-va-tee/na-zee-va-tee *ring (of phone)*

ne ne *no • not*

nebo ⓝ *ne*-baw *sky*

nedavno *ne*-dav-naw *recently*

nedjelja ⓕ *ne*-dye-lya *Sunday*

nedostajati imp ne-*daw*-stai-a-tee *miss (feel absence of)*

nedostatak ⓜ ne-daw-*sta*-tak *shortage*

negativan *ne*-ga-tee-van *negative*

nekoliko *ne*-kaw-leek-aw *few • several*
nektarinka ① *nek*-ta-*reen*-ka *nectarine*
nemoguć *ne*-maw-gooch *impossible*
neobičan *ne*-aw-bee-chan *strange • unusual*
neoženjen *ne*-*aw*-zhen-yen *single (man)*
nepotpuno pečen *ne*-pawt-poo-naw *pe*-chen *rare (meat)*
nepravedan *ne*-pra-ve-dan *unfair*
nepromočiv *ne*-*praw*-maw-cheev *waterproof*
nepušački ⓜ *ne*-poo-shach-kee *nonsmoking*
nesiguran *ne*-see-goo-ran *unsafe*
nešto *nesh*-taw *something*
netko *net*-kaw *someone*
neudata *ne*-oo-da-ta *single (woman)*
neudoban *ne*-oo-daw-ban *uncomfortable*
nevezan *ne*-vez-an *free (not bound)*
nevin ⓜ *ne*-veen *innocent*
nezaposlen *ne*-za-paw-slen *unemployed*
nezavisnost ① *ne*-za-*vee*-snawst *independence*
nezgoda ① *nez*-gaw-da *accident*
nijem *nee*-yem *mute*
nikada *nee*-ka-da *never*
nikakav *nee*-ka-kav *none*
ništa *neesh*-ta *no • nothing*
niti *nee*-tee *neither*
nizak *nee*-zak *low •short (height)*
nizbrdo *neez*-br-daw *downhill*
Nizozemska ① *nee*-zaw-zem-ska *Netherlands*
noć ① nawch *night*
noćni klub ⓜ *nawch*-nee kloob *nightclub*
noga ① *naw*-ga *leg*
nogomet ⓜ *naw*-gaw-met *football (soccer)*
Norveška ① *nawr*-vesh-ka *Norway*
nos ⓜ naws *nose*
nositi imp *naw*-see-tee *carry • wear*
nov nawv *new*
novac ⓜ *naw*-vats *money*
novčana globa ① *nawv*-cha-na *glaw*-ba *fine (penalty)*
novčanica ① *nawv*-*cha*-nee-tsa *banknote*
novčarka ① *nawv*-char-ka *purse*
novčići ⓜ pl *nawv*-chee-chee *coins*
Novi Zeland ⓜ *naw*-vee *ze*-land *New Zealand*
novinar(ka) ⓜ/① *naw*-vee-nar(-ka) *journalist*
novine ① pl *naw*-vee-ne *newspaper*

novogodišnji dan ⓜ *naw*-vaw-*gaw*-deesh-nyee dan *New Year's Day*
nož ⓜ nawzh *knife*
nožni prst ⓜ *nawzh*-nee prst *toe*
nuklearna energija ① *noo*-kle-ar-na *e*-*ner*-gee-ya *nuclear energy*
nuklearna testiranja ⓜ pl *noo*-kle-ar-na te-*stee*-ra-nya *nuclear testing*
nuklearni otpad ⓜ *noo*-kle-ar-nee *awt*-pad *nuclear waste*

Nj

njegov ⓜ *nye*-gawv *his*
njegova ① *nye*-gaw-va *his*
njegovo ⓝ *nye*-gaw-vaw *his*
njen ⓜ nyen *his*
njena ① *nye*-na *his*
njeno ⓝ *nye*-naw *his*
Njemačka ① *nye*-mach-ka *Germany*
njihov ⓜ *nee*-hawv *their*
njihova ① *nyee*-haw-va *their*
njihovo ⓝ *nyee*-haw-vaw *their*

O

o oo *about • on*
oba ⓜ&ⓝ *aw*-ba *both*
obala ① *aw*-ba-la *coast*
obaren aw-*ba*-ren *boiled*
obečati/obečavati aw-*be*-cha-tee/ aw-be-*cha*-va-tee *promise*
običaj ⓜ *aw*-bee-chai *custom*
običan ⓜ *aw*-bee-chan *ordinary*
obična pošta ① *aw*-beech-na *pawsh*-ta *surface mail (land)*
obična voda ① *aw*-beech-na *vaw*-da *still water • tap water*
obitelj ① *aw*-bee-tel' *family*
oboje ⓜ *aw*-bye *both*
oblačan aw-*bla*-chan *cloudy*
oblak ⓜ *aw*-blak *cloud*
oblik ⓜ *aw*-bleek *shape*
obližnji aw-bleezh-nyee *nearby*
obrano mlijeko ⓝ *aw*-ba-naw mlee-*ye*-kaw *skim milk*
obrazovanje ⓝ *aw*-bra-zaw-*va*-nye *education*
obrtnik ⓜ *aw*-brt-neek *tradesperson*
ocat ⓜ *aw*-tsat *vinegar*
ocean ⓜ *aw*-tse-an *ocean*

oči ① pl *aw*-chee *eyes*

od awd *from* · *since (May etc)* · *with*

odbiti/odbijati awd-bee-tee/ awd-*bee*-ya-tee *refuse*

odbojka ① awd-*boy*-ka *volleyball (sport)* — **na pjesku** na *pye*-skoo *beach volleyball*

odgovor awd-*gaw*-vawr *answer*

odjeća ① awd-*ye*-cha *clothing*

odlazak awd-*la*-zak *departure*

odličan awd-*lee*-chan *excellent*

odložena prtljaga ① awd-*law*-zhe-na prt-*lya*-ga *left luggage*

odlučiti/odlučivati awd-*loo*-chee-tee/ awd-loo-*chee*-va-tee *decide*

odmoriti/odmarati se awd-*maw*-ree-tee/ awd-*ma*-ra-tee se *rest*

odnos ① awd-*naws* *relationship (not family)*

odnosi s javnošću pl awd-*naw*-see s *yav*-nawsh-choo *public relations*

odrasla osoba ① aw-*dra*-sla aw-*saw*-ba *adult*

odredište ① aw-*dre*-deesh-te *destination*

odrezak aw-*dre*-zak *fillet* · *steak*

odsjesti/odsjedati awd-*sye*-stee/ awd-*sye*-da-tee *stay (at a hotel)*

odvojen awd-*voy*-en *separate*

oglas aw-*glas* *advertisement*

ogledalo ① aw-*gle*-da-law *mirror*

ograda ① aw-*gra*-da *fence*

ogrlica ① aw-*gr*-lee-tsa *necklace*

ogroman aw-*graw*-man *huge*

ogrtač aw-*gr*-tach *cape (cloak)*

oklada ① aw-*kla*-da *bet*

oko ① aw-*kaw* *eye*

oko aw-*kaw* *about*

okrenuti/okretati aw-*kre*-noo-tee/ aw-*kre*-ta-tee *turn*

okrug ① aw-*kroog* *county*

okrugao aw-*kroo*-ga-aw *round*

Olimpijske igre ① pl aw-*leem*-peey-ske *ee*-gre *Olympic Games*

olovka ① aw-*lawv*-ka *pencil*

oltar awl-*tar* *altar*

oluja ① aw-*loo*-ya *storm*

omekšivač (za kosu) aw-*mek*-*shee*-vach (za *kaw*-soo) *conditioner (for hair)*

omlet aw-*mlet* *omelette*

omotnica ① aw-*mawt*-nee-tsa *envelope*

on awn *he*

ona ①&② aw-*na* *she* · *they* ①

one ① aw-*nee* *they* ①

onesposobljen aw-ne-*spaw*-sawb-lyen *disabled*

oni aw-*nee* *they*

ono aw-*naw* *it* · *that (one)*

opasan aw-pa-*san* *dangerous*

opatica ① aw-*pa*-tee-tsa *nun*

opeklina ① aw-pe-*klee*-na *burn*

opekline od sunca ① pl aw-pe-*klee*-ne awd *soon*-tsa *sunburn*

opera ① aw-*pe*-ra *opera*

operacija ① aw-pe-*ra*-tsee-ya *operation*

operator aw-pe-*ra*-tawr *operator*

operna dvorana ① aw-*per*-na dvaw-*ra*-na *opera house*

opet aw-*pet* *again*

(o)prati (aw-)*pra*-tee *wash (something)*

(o)prati se (aw-)*pra*-tee se *wash (oneself)*

oprema ① aw-*pre*-ma *equipment*

Oprez! aw-*prez* *Careful!*

oprostiti/opraštati aw-*praw*-stee-tee/ aw-*prash*-ta-tee *forgive*

opruga ① aw-*proo*-ga *spring (coil)*

optičar awp-*tee*-char *optometrist*

opustiti/opuštati se aw-*poo*-stee-tee/ aw-*poosh*-ta-tee se *relax*

orah aw-*rah* *nut*

orgazam awr-*ga*-zam *orgasm*

originalan aw-ree-gee-*na*-lan *original*

orkestar awr-*ke*-star *orchestra*

ormar awr-*mar* *cupboard* — **za odjeću** za aw-*dye*-choo *wardrobe*

osiguranje ① aw-see-goo-*ra*-nye *insurance*

osim aw-*seem* *but*

osip aw-*seep* *rash* — **od pelena** awd *pe*-le-na *nappy rash* — **u struku** aw-*seep* oo *stroo*-koo *shingles (illness)*

osjećaj aw-*sye*-chai *feeling*

osjećaji ① pl aw-*sye*-chai-ee *feelings*

osoba ① aw-*saw*-ba *person*

osobna iskaznica ① aw-*sawb*-na *ee*-skaz-nee-tsa *identification card (ID)*

ospice ① pl aw-*spee*-tse *measles*

ostati/ostajati aw-*sta*-tee/aw-*sta*-ya-tee *stay (in one place)*

ostaviti/ostavljati aw-sta-*vee*-tee/ aw-*stav*-lya-tee *quit*

suh sooh *dry*

ošamućen aw-*sha*-moo-chen *dizzy*

oštrige ① pl awsh-*tree*-ge *oyster*

otac aw-*tats* *father*

oteklina ⓕ aw·te·klee·na *swelling*
otići/odlaziti aw·tee·chee/aw·dla·zee·tee *depart (leave)*
otirač ⓜ aw·tee·rach *mat*
otkako awt·ka·kaw *from • since (May etc)*
otok ⓜ aw·tawk *island*
otrovan aw·traw·van *poisonous*
otvarač awt·va·rach *opener*
— za boce za baw·tse *bottle opener*
— za limenke za lee·men·ke *can opener*
otvoren awt·vaw·ren *open*
otvoriti/otvarati awt·vaw·ree·tee/awt·va·ra·tee *open*
ova ⓕ aw·va *this*
ovaj ⓜ aw·vai *this*
ovca ⓕ awv·tsa *sheep*
ovdje awv·dye *here*
ovisnost ⓕ aw·vee·snawst *addiction*
— o drogama aw draw·ga·ma *drug addiction*
ovo ⓝ aw·vaw *it • this (one)*
ozbiljan aw·zbee·lyan *serious*
ozonski omotač ⓜ aw·zawn·skee aw·maw·tach *ozone layer*
ožujak ⓜ aw·zhoo·yak *March*

P

pad ⓜ pad *fall*
padavica ⓕ pa·da·vee·tsa *epilepsy*
paket ⓜ pa·ket *package • parcel*
Pakistan ⓜ pa·kee·stan *Pakistan*
palača ⓕ pa·la·cha *palace*
pamuk ⓜ pa·mook *cotton*
pansion ⓜ pan·see·awn *boarding house*
PAPA test ⓜ pa·pa test *pap smear*
papar ⓜ pa·par *pepper*
papir ⓜ pa·peer *paper*
papirnati rupčići ⓜ pl pa·peer·na·tee roop·chee·chee *tissues*
paprika ⓕ pa·pree·ka *bell pepper • capsicum*
par ⓜ par *pair (couple)*
paraplegičar ⓜ pa·ra·ple·gee·char *paraplegic*
parfem ⓜ par·fem *perfume*
park ⓜ park *park*
parkiralište ⓕ par·kee·ra·leesh·te *car park*
parkirati imp par·kee·ra·tee *park (a car)*
pas ⓜ pas *dog*
— vodič vaw·deech *guide dog*

pasta za zube ⓕ pa·sta za zoo·be *toothpaste*
patka ⓕ pa·tka *duck*
patlidžan ⓜ pa·tlee·jan *aubergine • eggplant*
pauk ⓜ pa·ook *spider*
pčela ⓕ pche·la *bee*
pećnica ⓕ pech·nee·tsa *oven • stove*
pedala ⓕ pe·da·la *pedal*
pegla ⓕ pe·gla *iron (for clothes)*
pekara ⓕ pe·ka·ra *bakery*
pelene ⓕ pl pe·le·ne *diaper • nappy*
pelud ⓜ pe·lood *pollen*
peludna groznica ⓕ pe·lood·na grawz·nee·tsa *hay fever*
penis ⓜ pe·nees *penis*
peniša ⓕ pe·nee·sha *lighter*
pepeljara ⓕ pe·pe·lya·ra *ashtray*
peron ⓜ pe·rawn *platform*
petak ⓜ pe·tak *Friday*
peticija ⓕ pe·tee·tsee·ya *petition*
piće ⓝ pee·che *drink*
pijan pee·yan *drunk*
pijesak ⓜ pee·ye·sak *sand*
piknik ⓜ peek·neek *picnic*
piletina ⓕ pee·le·tee·na *chicken (as food)*
pinceta ⓕ peen·tse·ta *tweezers*
pisac ⓜ pee·sats *writer*
pisač ⓜ pee·sach *printer (computer)*
(na)pisati (na)pee·sa·tee *write*
pismo ⓝ pee·smaw *letter (mail)*
pita ⓕ pee·ta *pie*
pitanje ⓝ pee·ta·nye *question*
(u)pitati (oo)pee·ta·tee *ask (a question)*
(po)piti (paw·)pee·tee *drink*
pivnica ⓕ peev·nee·tsa *beer hall*
pivo ⓝ pee·vaw *beer*
pjena za brijanje ⓕ pye·na za bree·ya·nye *shaving cream*
pjenušavo vino ⓝ pye·noo·sha·vaw vee·naw *sparkling wine*
pjesma ⓕ pye·sma *song*
(pro)pješačiti (praw·)pye·sha·chee·tee *hike*
pješačenje ⓝ pye·sha·che·nye *hiking*
pješački put ⓜ pye·shach·kee poot *hiking route*
pješak ⓜ pye·shak *pedestrian*
pjevač/pjevačica ⓜ/ⓕ pye·vach/pye·va·chee·tsa *singer*
(za)pjevati (za·)pye·va·tee *sing*
plaća ⓕ pla·cha *salary • wage*
plahta ⓕ pla·hta *sheet (bed)*

plan grada ⓜ plan *gra*·da *map (of town)*
plan puta ⓜ plan *poo*·ta *itinerary*
planeta ⓕ pla·*ne*·ta *planet*
planina ⓕ pla·*nee*·na *mountain*
plastičan pla·stee·chan *plastic*
(u)platiti (oo·)*pla*·tee·tee *pay*
plato ⓜ pla·*taw* *plateau*
plav plav *blue*
plaža ⓕ *pla*·zha *beach*
plesanje ⓝ *ple*·sa·nye *dancing*
(za)plesati (za·)*ple*·sa·tee *dance*
pletenasti ukras ⓜ *ple*·te·na·stee oo·kras *plaited ornamentation*
plima i oseka ⓕ *plee*·ma ee aw·se·ka *tide*
plin ⓜ pleen *gas (for cooking)*
plinski uložak ⓜ *pleen*·skee oo·law·zhak *gas cartridge*
plivanje ⓝ *plee*·va·nye *swimming (sport)*
(za)plivati (za·)*plee*·va·tee *swim*
(o)pljačkati (aw·)*plyach*·ka·tee *rob*
pločnik ⓜ *plawch*·neek *footpath*
plosnat *plaw*·snat *flat*
pluća ⓝ pl *ploo*·cha *lung*
po paw *after • per*
pobačaj ⓜ *paw*·ba·chai *abortion • miscarriage*
pobijediti/pobjeđivati paw·bee·ye·dee·tee/paw·bye·je·va·tee *win*
pobjednik ⓜ *paw*·byed·neek *winner*
pobožan paw·baw·zhan *religious (person)*
početak ⓜ paw·che·tak *start*
 — **radnog vremena** rad·nawg vre·me·na *opening hours*
pod pawd *floor (ground)*
podatci ⓜ pl paw·*dat*·tsee *details*
podijeliti perf paw·dye·*lee*·tee *share (with)*
podne ⓝ *pawd*·ne *midday*
područni paw·drooch·nee *regional*
podzemna željeznica ⓕ pawd·zem·na zhe·lye·znee·tsa *subway • underground railway*
poezija ⓕ paw·e·zee·ya *poetry*
pogoditi/pogađati paw·*gaw*·dee·tee/paw·*ga*·ja·tee *guess*
pogreb ⓜ *paw*·greb *funeral*
pogreška ⓕ *paw*·gresh·ka *mistake*
pokazati/pokazivati paw·*ka*·za·tee/paw·ka·zee·va·tee *point • show*
poklon ⓜ *paw*·klawn *present (gift)*
pokretne stepenice ⓕ pl *paw*·kret·ne ste·*pe*·ne·tse *escalator*

pokušati/pokušavati paw·koo·sha·tee/paw·koo·sha·va·tee *(attempt)*
pokvaren paw·*kva*·ren *broken down • corrupt • faulty • spoiled*
polica ⓕ *paw*·lee·tsa *shelf*
policajac ⓜ paw·lee·*tsai*·ats *police officer*
policija ⓕ paw·*lee*·tsee·ya *police*
policijska stanica ⓕ paw·*lee*·tseey·ska *sta*·nee·tsa *police station*
političar ⓜ paw·*lee*·tee·char *politician*
politika ⓕ paw·*lee*·tee·ka *politics*
poljodjelac ⓜ paw·lyaw·dye·lats *farmer*
poljodjelstvo ⓝ paw·lyaw·djel·stvaw *agriculture*
poljubac ⓜ paw·*lyoo*·bats *kiss*
polovina ⓕ paw·law·*vee*·na *half*
polovni paw·lawv·nee *second-hand*
pomoć ⓕ *paw*·mawch *help*
pomoći/pomagati paw·*maw*·chee/paw·*ma*·ga·tee *help*
ponedjeljak ⓜ paw·ne·*dye*·lyak *Monday*
ponekad paw·ne·kad *sometimes*
poništiti/poništavati paw·*nee*·shtee·tee/paw·nee·*shta*·va·tee *cancel*
ponoć ⓕ *paw*·nawch *midnight*
popeti/penjati se paw·pe·tee/*pe*·nya·tee se *climb*
poplava ⓕ paw·pla·va *flood*
popraviti/popravljati paw·pra·vee·tee/paw·prav·lya·tee *repair*
popularan paw·poo·la·ran *popular*
popunjen paw·poo·nyen *booked out*
popust ⓜ *paw*·poost *discount*
pored paw·red *beside • next to*
poredak ⓜ paw·re·dak *order*
poremećaj srca ⓜ paw·re·me·chai *sr*·tsa *heart condition*
porez ⓜ *paw*·rez *tax*
 — **na dohodak** na *daw*·haw·dak *income tax*
 — **na promet** na *praw*·met *sales tax*
 — **na zračni prijevoz** na *zrach*·nee pree·ye·vawz *airport tax*
poriluk ⓜ *paw*·ree·look *leek*
poruka ⓕ *paw*·roo·ka *message*
posao ⓜ *paw*·sa·aw *job*
poseban paw·se·ban *special*
poširan paw·shee·ran *poached*
posjetiti/posjećivati paw·sye·tee·tee/paw·sye·chee·va·tee *visit*
poslano expres poštom paw·sla·naw *eks*·pres *pawsh*·tawm *by express mail*
poslastice ⓕ pl paw·sla·stee·tse *dessert*

poslije paw·slee·ye *after*

(ovo) poslijepodne ⓝ (aw·vaw)
paw·slee·ye·pawd·ne *(this) afternoon*

poslodavac ⓜ paw·slaw·da·vats *employer*

poslovna osoba ⓕ paw·slawv·na
aw·saw·ba *business person*

pospan paw·span *(to be) sleepy*

posramljen paw·sram·lyen *embarrassed*

post ⓜ pawst *Lent*

posteljina ⓕ paw·ste·lyee·na *bed linen*

poster ⓜ paw·ster *poster*

postići/postizati paw·stee·chee/
paw·stee·za·tee *score*

postotak ⓜ paw·staw·tak *per cent*

posuda ⓕ paw·soo·da *dish (plate)* • *pot
(ceramics)*

posuditi/posuđivati paw·soo·dee·tee/
paw·soo·jee·va·tee *borrow*

pošta ⓕ pawsh·ta *mail (letters)* • *postal
system*

poštanska marka ⓕ pawsh·tan·ska
mar·ka *stamp (mail)*

poštanski broj ⓜ pawsh·tan·skee broy
postcode

poštanski sandučić ⓜ pawsh·tan·skee
san·doo·cheech *mailbox*

poštanski ured ⓜ pawsh·tan·skee oo·red
post office

poštarina ⓕ pawsh·ta·ree·na *postage*

potkošulja ⓕ pawt·kaw·shoo·lya *singlet*

potomak ⓜ paw·taw·mak *descendant*

potpis ⓜ pawt·pees *signature*

potpuno paralizirana osoba ⓕ
pawt·poo·naw pa·ra·lee·zee·ra·na
aw·saw·ba *quadriplegic*

potreban paw·tre·ban *necessary*

potres ⓜ paw·tres *earthquake*

— **mozga** maw·zga *concussion*

potvrda vlasništva automobila
ⓕ paw·tvr·da vlas·neesh·tva
a·oo·taw·maw·bee·la *car owner's title*

potvrditi/potvrđivati pawt·vr·dee·tee/
pawt·vr·jee·va·tee
confirm (a booking) • *validate*

povijesni paw·vee·ye·snee *historical*

povijest ⓕ paw·vee·yest *history*

povrat novca ⓜ pawv·rat nawv·tsa
refund

povratan paw·vra·tan *return (ticket)*

povrće ⓝ paw·vr·che *vegetable*

povreda ⓕ paw·vre·da *injury*

povremeni posao ⓜ paw·vre·me·nee
paw·sa·aw *casual work*

povrijeđen ⓜ paw·vree·ye·jen *injured*

pozadina ⓕ paw·za·dee·na *back
(position)*

pozitivan paw·zee·tee·van *positive*

poziv na račun nazvane osobe ⓜ
paw·zeev na ra·choon naz·va·ne
aw·saw·be *collect call* • *reverse
charge call*

pozvati/pozivati pawz·va·tee/
paw·zee·va·tee *invite*

požar ⓜ paw·zhar *fire*

prah ⓜ prah *powder*

pranje rublja ⓝ pra·nye roob·lya *laundry
(clothes)*

praonica ⓕ pra·aw·nee·tsa *laundry
(place)*

pratiti imp pra·tee·tee *follow*

pravilo ⓝ pra·vee·law *rule*

pravnik ⓜ prav·neek *lawyer*

pravo ⓝ pra·vaw *law (study, professsion)*

prazan pra·zan *empty* • *vacant*

praznici ⓜ pl praz·nee·tsee *holidays* •
vacation

praznovjerje ⓝ praz·naw·vyer·ye
superstition

pred pred *in front of*

predgrađe ⓝ pred·gra·je *suburb*

predmenstrualna napetost ⓕ
pred·men·stroo·al·na na·pe·tawst
premenstrual tension

prednje svjetlo ⓝ pred·nye svyet·law
headlights

predsjednik ⓜ pred·syed·neek *president*

predstava ⓕ pred·sta·va *play (theatre)* •
show

pregled ⓜ pre·gled *review (article)*

prehlada ⓕ pre·hla·da *cold*

prekid ⓜ pre·keed *intermission*

prekjučer ⓜ prek·yoo·cher *day before
yesterday*

preko pre·kaw *across*

— **noći** naw·chee *overnight*

prekomjerna cijena ⓕ pre·kawm·yer·na
tsee·ye·na *rip-off*

prekomorska pošta ⓕ pre·kaw·mawr·ska
pawsh·ta *surface mail (sea)*

prekosutra ⓕ pre·kaw·soo·tra *day after
tomorrow*

prekršaj ⓜ pre·kr·shai *foul*

prema pre·ma *to* • *towards (direction)*

prenoćište za mladež ⓝ
pre·naw·cheesh·te za mla·dezh
youth hostel

prenosivi računar ⓜ pre-*naw*-see-vee ra-choo-nar *laptop*

preporučenom poštom pre-*paw*-roo-che-nawm pawsh-tawm *registered mail (by)*

preporučiti/preporučivati pre-paw-roo-*chee*-tee/ pre-paw-roo-*chee*-va-tee *recommend*

preporuka ⓕ pre-*paw*-rooka *reference*

prepun pre-*poon crowded*

prethodni pred-*hawd*-nee *last (previous)*

pretinac za odlaganje prtljage ⓜ pre-*tee*-nats za awd-*la*-ga-nye prt-*lya*-ge *luggage lockers*

pretpostaviti/pretpostavljati pret-*paw*-sta-vee-tee/ pret-*paw*-stav-lya-tee *prefer*

prevelika doza ⓕ pre-ve-leeka *daw*-za *overdose*

prevesti/prevoditi pre-ve-stee/ pre-*vaw*-dee-tee *translate*

prezervativ ⓜ pre-zer-va-*teev condom*

prezime ⓕ pre-*zee*-me *surname*

pri pree *at • on*

pribor za jelo ⓜ *pree*-bawr za ye-law *cutlery*

pribor za prvu pomoć ⓜ *pree*-bawr za pr-*voo* paw-mawch *first-aid kit*

priča ⓕ *pree*-cha *story*

pričest ⓕ *pree*-chest *communion*

prigovor ⓜ *pree*-gaw-vawr *complaint*

prijatelj/prijateljica ⓜ/ⓕ *pree*-ya-tel'/ pree-ya-*te*-lyee-tsa *friend*

prijazan *pree*-ya-zan *kind (nice)*

prije *pree*-ye *ago • before*

prijemni šalter ⓜ *pree*-yem-nee *shal*-ter *check-in (airport)*

prijevoz ⓜ pree-ye-vawz *transport*

primjer ⓜ *pree*-myer *example*

primorje ⓜ *pree*-mawr-ye *seaside*

pripremiti/pripremati pree-pre-mee-tee/ pree-*pre*-ma-tee *prepare*

priredba ⓕ *pree*-red-ba *performance*

priroda ⓕ pree-*raw*-da *nature*

prirodna okolina ⓕ *pree*-rawd-na aw-kaw-lee-na *environment*

pristaša ⓜ *pree*-sta-sha *supporter (politics)*

pritisak ⓕ *pree*-tee-sak *pressure*

privatan *pree*-va-tan *private*

privatni smještaj za najam *pree*-vat-nee smyesh-tai za *nai*-am *guesthouse*

privlačan *pree*-vla-chan *sexy*

priznanje ⓝ *pree*-zna-nye *confession (admission)*

priznati/priznavati *pree*-zna-tee/ pree-zna-va-tee *admit (confess)*

prizor ⓜ *pree*-zawr *view*

prljav pr-lyav *dirty*

probati/probavati praw-ba-tee/ praw-*ba*-va-tee *try*

probavne smetnje ⓕ pl *praw*-bav-ne smet-nye *indigestion*

prodati/prodavati *praw*-da-tee/ praw-*da*-va-tee *sell*

prodavač droga ⓜ praw-*da*-vach draw-ga *drug dealer*

prodavač duhana ⓜ praw-*da*-vach doo-ha-na *tobacconist*

prodavaonica ⓕ praw-da-va-*aw*-nee-tsa *shop*

　— **alkohola** al-kaw-haw-la *bottle shop • liquor store*

　— **bicikala** bee-*tsee*-ka-la *bike shop*

　— **cipela** *tsee*-pela *shoe shop*

　— **električne robe** e-*lek*-treech-ne *raw*-be *electrical store*

　— **foto-aparata** *faw*-taw-a-pa-ra-ta *camera shop*

　— **igračaka** ee-gra-cha-ka *toy shop*

　— **metalne i tehničke robe** me-tal-ne ee *teh*-neech-ke *raw*-be *hardware store*

　— **muzike** moo-zee-ke *music shop*

　— **novina i časopisa** naw-vee-na ee cha-saw-pee-sa *newsagency*

　— **odjeće** aw-dye-che *clothing store*

　— **opreme za kampiranje** *aw*-pre-me za kam-*pee*-ra-nye *camping store*

　— **polovne robe** paw-lawv-ne *raw*-be *second-hand shop*

　— **ribe** ree-be *fish shop*

　— **sa produženim radnim vremenom** sa praw-doo-zhe-neem *rad*-neem vre-me-nawm *convenience store*

　— **sira** see-ra *cheese shop*

　— **sportske robe** spawrt-ske *raw*-be *sports store*

　— **suvenira** soo-ve-*nee*-ra *souvenir shop*

　— **uredskog materijala** oo-reds-kawg ma-te-ree-*ya*-la *stationer's (shop)*

produženje ⓝ *praw*-doo-zhe-nye *extension (visa)*

program ⓜ *praw*-gram *program*

proizvesti/proizvoditi praw-eez-ve-stee/ praw-eez-*vaw*-dee-tee *produce*

projektor ⓜ proy·*ek*·tawr *projector*
prokulica ⓕ praw·koo·lee·tsa *Brussels sprout*
prolaz između sjedišta ⓜ praw·laz eez·me·joo sye·*deesh*·ta *aisle (plane etc)*
proljeće ⓝ praw·*lye*·che *spring (season)*
proljev ⓜ praw·lyev *diarrhoea*
promet ⓜ praw·met *traffic*
promjena ⓕ praw·*mye*·na *change*
prosinac ⓜ praw·see·nats *December*
prosjak ⓜ praw·syak *beggar*
proslava ⓕ praw·sla·va *celebration*
prostitutka ⓕ praw·stee·*toot*·ka *prostitute*
prostor praw·stawr *space*
prosvjed ⓜ praws·vyed *protest*
prosvjedovati imp praw·svye·daw·va·tee *protest*
prošli prawsh·lee *last (week)*
prošlost ⓕ prawsh·lawst *past*
provesti/provoditi se praw·ve·stee/ praw·*vaw*·dee·tee se *enjoy (oneself)*
provjeriti/provjeravati praw·vye·ree·tee/ praw·vye·*ra*·va·tee *check*
provod ⓜ praw·vawd *party (night out)*
prozor ⓜ praw·zawr *window*
prsa ⓕ pr·sa *breast (body)* · *chest (body)*
prsluk za spasavanje ⓜ pr·slook za spa·*sa*·va·nye *life jacket*
prst ⓜ prst *finger*
prsten ⓜ pr·sten *ring (on finger)*
prtljaga ⓕ prt·*lya*·ga *luggage*
prvenstvo ⓝ pr·*vens*·tvaw *championships*
prvi pr·vee *first*
— **razred** ⓜ ra·zred *business class* · *first class*
prženi pr·zhe·nee *fried*
(is)pržiti (ees·)pr·zhee·tee *fry*
ptica ⓕ ptee·tsa *bird*
puder za bebe ⓜ poo·der za *be*·be *baby powder*
pumpa ⓕ poom·pa *pump*
pun poon *full*
punac ⓜ poo·nats *father-in-law (of husband)*
punica ⓕ poo·nee·tsa *mother-in-law (of husband)*
punim radnim vremenom poo·neem rad·neem *vre*·me·nawm *full-time*
(na)puniti (na·)poo·nee·tee *fill*
puno ⓝ poo·naw *(a) lot*
puran ⓜ poo·ran *turkey*

pustinja ⓕ poo·*stee*·nya *desert*
(is)pušiti (ees·)poo·shee·tee *smoke*
puška ⓕ poosh·ka *gun*
put ⓜ poot *route* · *track* · *trail*
(u)pucati (oo·)poo·tsa·tee *shoot*
putna agencija ⓕ poot·na a·gen·tsee·ya *travel agency*
putna karta ⓕ poot·na *kar*·ta *road map*
putnički čekovi pl poot·neech·kee che·kaw·vee *travellers cheque*
putnik ⓜ poot·neek *passenger*
putovanje ⓝ poo·taw·*va*·nye *journey*
(pro)putovati (praw·)poo·*taw*·va·tee *travel*
putovnica ⓕ poo·*tawv*·nee·tsa *passport*
puž ⓜ poozh *snail*

R

račun ⓜ ra·choon *account (bank)* · *bill (account)* · *check* · *receipt*
računalo ⓝ ra·choo·na·law *computer*
rad ⓜ rad *work*
— **za barom** za ba·rawm *bar work*
radijator ⓜ ra·dee·*ya*·tawr *radiator*
radio ⓜ ra·dee·aw *radio*
radionica ⓕ ra·dee·aw·nee·tsa *workshop*
raditi imp ra·dee·tee *work*
radna dozvola ⓕ rad·na dawz·vaw·la *work permit*
radnik ⓜ rad·neek *labourer*
— **u tvornici** oo *tvawr*·nee·tsee *factory worker*
radno iskustvo ⓝ rad·naw ee·skoos·tvaw *work experience*
ragbi ⓜ rag·bee *rugby*
rajčica ⓕ rai·chee·tsa *tomato*
rak ⓜ rak *cancer*
rakija ⓕ ra·kee·ya *brandy*
rame ⓝ ra·me *shoulder*
rani ra·nee *early*
raniti/ranjavati ra·nee·tee/ra·*nya*·va·tee *hurt (physically)*
raskošan ra·skaw·shan *luxury*
rasna netrpeljivost ⓕ ra·sna ne·tr·pe·lyee·vawst *racism*
rasprodaja ⓕ ra·spraw·dai·a *sale*
(po)rasti (paw·)ra·stee *grow*
rat ⓜ rat *war*
ravan ra·van *straight (not crooked)*
ravnopravnost ⓕ rav·naw·prav·nawst *equality*

razbijen ra-*zbee*-yen *broken*
razlika u vremenu ① *raz*-lee-ka oo vre-me-noo *time difference*
razlog ⓜ *raz*-lawg *reason*
razmažen raz-*ma*-zhen *spoiled*
razmijeniti/razmijenjivati raz-mee-ye-nee-tee/raz-mye-*nyee*-va-tee *exchange*
razmjena ① *raz*-mye-na *exchange*
razuman ra-*zoo*-man *sensible*
razumjeti/razumijevati ra-zoo-mye-tee/ra-zoo-mee-ye-va-tee *understand*
razveden raz-ve-den *divorced (of man)*
razvedena raz-*ve*-de-na *divorced (of woman)*
realan re-a-lan *realistic*
rebro ⓝ *re*-braw *rib*
recept za lijekove ① *re*-tsept za lee-*ye*-kaw-ve *prescription*
reciklirati perf re-tsee-*klee*-ra-tee *recycle*
reći perf *re*-chee *tell*
red ⓜ red *queue*
redovnik ⓜ re-*dawv*-neek *monk*
refleksologija ① *re*-flek-saw-*law*-gee-ya *reflexology*
registarska tablica ① *re*-gee-star-ska *ta*-blee-tsa *numberplate*
registracija re-gee-*stra*-tsee-ya *car registration*
rejv parti ⓜ reyv *par*-tee *rave*
reket ⓜ *re*-ket *racquet*
relikvija ① re-*leek*-vee-ya *relic*
rep ⓜ rep *tail*
republika ① re-*poo*-blee-ka *republic*
restoran ⓜ re-*staw*-ran *restaurant*
rezanci ⓜ pl re-*zan*-tsee *noodles*
(na)rezati (*na*-)*re*-za-tee *cut*
rezervacija ① re-zer-*va*-tsee-ya *reservation (booking)*
rezervirati perf re-zer-*vee*-ra-tee *(make a booking)*
rezime ⓜ re-*zee*-me *résumé*
riba ① *ree*-ba *fish*
ribar ⓜ *ree*-bar *fisherman*
ribarsko selo ⓝ *ree*-bar-skaw *se*-law *fishing village*
ribolov ⓜ *ree*-baw-lawv *fishing*
riječ ① *ree*-yech *word*
rijedak *ree*-ye-dak *rare (uncommon)*
rijeka ① *ree*-ye-ka *river*
ritam ⓜ *ree*-tam *rhythm*
riva ① *ree*-va *waterfront*
rizik ⓜ *ree*-zeek *risk*

riža ① *ree*-zha *rice*
rječnik ⓜ ryech-neek *dictionary*
robna kuća ① *rawb*-na koo-*cha* *department store*
rock grupa ① rawk *groo*-pa *rock group*
rock ⓜ rawk *rock (music)*
roditelji ⓜ pl raw-de-*te*-lyee *parents*
rođendan ① *raw*-jen-dan *birthday*
romantičan raw-*man*-tee-chan *romantic*
ronilačka oprema ① raw-*nee*-lach-ka aw-*pre*-ma *diving equipment*
ronjenje ⓝ *raw*-nye-nye *diving (underwater)*
  — s disalicom s *dee*-sa-lee-tsawm *snorkelling*
  — sa bocama sa *baw*-tsa-ma *scuba diving*
rošulanje ⓝ raw-*shoo*-la-nye *rollerblading*
rošulati se imp raw-*shoo*-la-tee se *skate*
rotkva ① *rawt*-kva *radish*
rt ⓜ rt *cape • promontory*
rubeola ① roo-be-*aw*-la *rubella*
ručak ⓜ roo-chak *lunch • meal*
ručna svjetiljka ① *rooch*-na svye-*teel*-ka *flashlight • torch*
ručna torbica ① *rooch*-na tawr-bee-tsa *handbag*
ručni radovi ⓜ pl *rooch*-nee ra-*daw*-vee *handicrafts*
ručni zglob ⓜ *rooch*-nee zglawb *wrist*
ručnik ⓜ *rooch*-neek *towel • wash cloth*
  — za lice za *lee*-tse *face cloth*
ručno izrađen *rooch*-naw eez-ra-jen *handmade*
rujan ⓜ *roo*-yan *September*
ruka ① *roo*-ka *arm • hand*
rukavica/e ① sg/① pl roo-*ka*-vee-tsa/e *glove(s)*
rukomet ⓜ *roo*-kaw-met *handball*
ruksak ⓜ *rook*-sak *backpack*
rum ⓜ room *rum*
rupčić ⓜ *roop*-cheech *handkerchief*
ruševine ① pl *roo*-she-vee-ne *ruins*
ruž za usne ⓜ roozh za *oo*-sne *lipstick*
ružičast roo-zhee-chast *pink*

S

sa sa *with*
sabor ⓜ *sa*-bawr *parliament*
SAD ① pl es a de *USA*
sada *sa*-da *now*

sadašnjost ① sa-dash-nyawst *present (time)*
salama ① sa-la-ma *salami*
salata ① sa-la-ta *salad*
saldo ⑪ sal-daw *balance (account)*
salveta ① sal-ve-ta *serviette*
sam sam *alone*
samo sa-maw *only*
samoposluga ① sa-maw-paw-sloo-ga *self-service*
samostalno zaposlen sa-maw-stal-naw za-paw-slen *self-employed*
samostan ⑪ sa-maw-stan *convent • monastery*
san ⑪ san *dream*
sandala ① san-da-la *sandal*
sanjkanje ⑪ san'-ka-nye *tobogganing*
sapun ⑪ sa-poon *soap*
sardina ① sar-dee-na *sardine*
sastanak ⑪ sa-sta-nak *appointment*
sastojak ⑪ sa-stoy-ak *ingredient*
sašiti/šivati sa-shee-tee/shee-va-tee *sew*
sat ⑪ sat *clock • hour • watch*
sauna ① sa-oo-na *sauna*
savjet ⑪ sa-vyet *advice*
savršen sa-vr-shen *perfect*
sebičan se-bee-chan *selfish*
sedlo ⑪ sed-law *saddle*
seks ⑪ seks *sex*
sekunda ① se-koon-da *second (clock)*
selo ⑪ se-law *village*
semafor ⑪ se-ma-fawr *scoreboard • traffic light*
senf ⑪ senf *mustard*
seosko područje ⑪ se-aw-skaw paw-drooch-ye *countryside*
sestra ① se-stra *sister*
sezona ① se-zaw-na *season (for activities)*
shiatsu ⑪ shee-a-tsoo *shiatsu*
sići/silaziti sa see-chee/see-la-zee-tee sa *get off (a train, etc)*
sićušan ⑪ see-choo-shan *tiny*
SIDA ① see-da *AIDS*
sigornosni pojas ⑪ see-goor-naw-snee poy-as *seatbelt*
sef ⑪ sef *safe*
siguran see-goo-ran *safe*
— seks seks *safe sex*
siječanj ⑪ see-ye-chan' *January*
silovanje ⑪ see-law-va-nye *rape*
silovati perf see-law-va-tee *rape*
sin ⑪ seen *son*
sinagoga ① see-na-gaw-ga *synagogue*

Singapur ⑪ seen-ga-poor *Singapore*
sintetičan ⑪ seen-te-tee-chan *synthetic*
sir ⑪ seer *cheese*
siromašan see-raw-ma-shan *poor*
siromaštvo ⑪ see-raw-mash-tvaw *poverty*
sirov ⑪ see-rawv *raw*
sirup za kašalj ⑪ see-roop za ka-shal' *cough medicine*
sitan see-tan *fine (delicate)*
siv ⑪ seev *gray • grey*
sjedalo za dijete ⑪ sye-da-law za dee-ye-te *child seat*
sjedište ⑪ sye-deesh-te *seat (place)*
sjekira za razbijanje leda ① sye-kee-ra za raz-bee-ya-nye le-da *ice axe*
sjena ① sye-na *shadow*
sjesti/sjedati sye-stee/sye-da-tee *sit*
sjever ⑪ sye-ver *north*
skalp ⑪ skalp *scalp*
skijanje ⑪ skee-ya-nye *skiing*
— na vodi na vaw-dee *water-skiing*
skijati imp skee-ya-tee *ski*
skočiti/skakati skaw-chee-tee/ska-ka-tee *jump*
skoro skaw-raw *almost*
skulptura ① skoolp-too-ra *sculpture*
skup ⑪ skoop *rally*
skup skoop *expensive*
slab slab *weak*
sladak sla-dak *sweet*
sladoled ⑪ sla-daw-led *ice cream*
sladoledarna ① sla-daw-le-dar-na *ice-cream parlour*
slanina ① sla-nee-na *bacon*
slanutak ⑪ sla-noo-tak *chickpea*
slastičarnica ① sla-stee-char-nee-tsa *cake shop*
(po)slati (paw-)sla-tee *send*
slavan sla-van *famous*
slavina ① sla-vee-na *faucet • tap*
sleđ ⑪ slej *herring*
sličan slee-chan *similar*
slijedeći slee-ye-de-chee *next (month)*
slijep slee-yep *blind*
slijepo crijevo ⑪ slee-ye-paw tsree-ye-vaw *appendix (body)*
slika ① slee-ka *painting (a work)*
slikar ⑪ slee-kar *painter*
slikarstvo ⑪ slee-kars-tvaw *painting (the art)*
slikati perf slee-ka-tee *photograph*
slobodan slaw-baw-dan *free (available)*

slobodno mjesto ⓝ *slaw*·bawd·naw *mye*·staw *vacancy*

Slovačka ⓕ *slaw*·vach·ka *Slovakia*

Slovenija ⓕ *slaw*·ve·nee·ya *Slovenia*

složiti/slagati se *slaw*·zhe·tee·tee/*sla*·ga·tee se *agree*

(po)slušati (*paw*·)*sloo*·sha·tee *listen (to)*

slušni aparat ⓜ *sloosh*·nee a·*pa*·rat *hearing aid*

službenik/službenica ⓜ/ⓕ *sloozh*·be·neek/*sloozh*·be·nee·tsa *office worker*

službeno putovanje ⓝ *sloozh*·be·naw poo·taw·*va*·nye *business trip*

smeće ⓝ *sme*·che *garbage*

smeđ ⓜ smej *brown*

(na)smijati se (na·)*smee*·ya·tee se *laugh*

(na)smiješiti se (na·)*smee*·ye·shee·tee se *smile*

smjer ⓜ smyer *direction*

smješan *smye*·shan *funny*

smještaj ⓜ *smye*·shtai *accommodation*

smjeti imp *smye*·tee *can (have permission)*

smokva ⓕ *smaw*·kva *fig*

smrad ⓜ smrad *smell (unpleasant)*

snaga ⓕ *sna*·ga *power*

snijeg ⓜ snee·*yeg* *snow*

snimak ⓜ *snee*·mak *recording*

snimiti/snimati *snee*·mee·tee/ *snee*·ma·tee *record (music etc)*

soba ⓕ *saw*·ba *room*

soba za pranje rublja ⓕ *saw*·ba za *pra*·nye roob·lya *laundry (room)*

socijalistički saw·tsee·ya·*lee*·steech·kee *socialist*

socijalna skrb ⓕ saw·tsee·yal·na skrb *social welfare*

soja ⓕ *soy*·a *soy sauce*

sojino mlijeko ⓝ *soy*·ee·naw mlee·*ye*·kaw *soy milk*

sok ⓜ sawk *juice*
— **od naranče** awd *na*·ran·che *orange juice*

sol ⓕ sawl *salt*

soli za rehidrataciju ⓕ *saw*·lee za re·hee·dra·*ta*·tsee·yoo *rehydration salts*

spavaća kola ⓕ *spa*·va·cha *kaw*·la *sleeping berth*

spavaća soba ⓕ *spa*·va·cha *saw*·ba *bedroom*

spavaći kupe ⓜ *spa*·va·chee koo·*pe* *sleeping car*

(od)spavati (awd·)*spa*·va·tee *sleep*

spilja ⓕ *spee*·lya *cave*

spirala ⓕ spee·*ra*·la *IUD*

spoj ⓜ spoy *date (appointment)*

spolna bolesta ⓕ *spawl*·na *baw*·les·ta *venereal disease*

spolna diskriminacija ⓕ *spawl*·na dee·skree·mee·*na*·tsee·ya *sexism*

spomenik ⓜ *spaw*·me·neek *monument*

spor spawr *slow*

sporo *spaw*·raw *slowly*

sport ⓜ spawrt *sport*

sportaš/sportašica ⓜ/ⓕ *spawr*·tash/ spawr·*ta*·shee·tsa *sportsperson*

spreman *spre*·man *ready*

spriječiti/sprječavati spree·*ye*·chee·tee/ spree·ye·*cha*·va·tee *stop (prevent)*

Srbija ⓕ *sr*·bee·ya *Serbia*

srčani udar ⓜ *sr*·cha·nee oo·dar *heart attack*

srce ⓝ *sr*·tse *heart*

srebro ⓝ *sre*·braw *silver*

sreća ⓕ *sre*·cha *luck*

srednja škola ⓕ *sred*·nya shkaw·la *high school*

sredstva za sprječavanje neželjene trudnoće ⓜ pl *sreds*·tva za sprye·cha·*va*·nye ne·zhe·lye·ne trood·*naw*·che *contraceptives*

sresti/sretati sre·*stee*/*sre*·ta·tee *meet (run into)*

sretan *sre*·tan *happy • lucky*

srijeda ⓕ sree·*ye*·da *Wednesday*

srodstvo ⓝ *srawd*·stvaw *relationship (family)*

srpanj ⓜ *sr*·pan' *July*

stablo ⓝ *sta*·blaw *tree*

stadion ⓜ *sta*·dee·awn *stadium*

stajati imp *stai*·a·tee *cost*

staklenka ⓕ *sta*·klen·ka *jar*

staklo ⓝ *sta*·klo *glass (material)*

stan ⓜ stan *apartment*

stanica ⓕ *sta*·nee·tsa *station • stop (bus etc)*

Stanite/Stani! pol/inf *sta*·nee·te/*sta*·nee *Stop!*

stanovati imp sta·*naw*·va·tee *live (somewhere)*

star star *old*

staviti/stavljati *sta*·vee·tee/*stav*·lya·tee *put*

staza ⓕ *sta*·za *path • track (sport)*

stepenica ⓕ ste·*pe*·nee·tsa *step*

stepenište ⑩ *ste·pe·neesh·te* stairway
stići/stizati *stee·chee/stee·za·tee* arrive
stidljiv *steed·lyeev* shy
stijena ① *stee·ye·na* rock
stil ⑩ steel style
stjenica ① *stye·nee·tsa* bug (insect)
sto staw hundred
stol ⑩ stawl table
stolica za sklapanje ① *staw·lee·tsa za skla·pa·nye* chair
stolni tenis ⑩ *stawl·nee te·nees* table tennis
stolnjak ⑩ *stawl·nyak* tablecloth
stopalo ⑩ *staw·pa·law* foot
stopirati imp *staw·pee·ra·tee* hitchhike
strana ① *stra·na* side
stranac ⑩ *stra·nats* stranger
strani *stra·nee* foreign
stranica ① *stra·nee·tsa* page
stranka ① *stran·ka* client • party (politics)
strašan *stra·shan* terrible
stražnji *strazh·nyee* rear (seat etc)
stražnjica ① *strazh·nyee·tsa* bottom (body)
strm strm steep
stroj ⑩ stroy machine
— **za pranje rublja** za *pra·nye roob·lya* washing machine
stručnjak ⑩ *strooch·nyak* specialist
struja ① *stroo·ya* current (electricity) • stream
struna ① *stroo·na* string
studeni ⑩ *stoo·de·nee* November
student ⑩ *stoo·dent* student
stupnjevi ⑩ pl *stoop·nye·vee* degrees (temperature)
subota ① *soo·baw·ta* Saturday
sud ⑩ sood court (legal)
sudac ⑩ *soo·dats* judge • referee
sudar ⑩ *soo·dar* crash
suknja ① *sook·nya* skirt
sunčan *soon·chan* sunny
sunčanica ① *soon·cha·nee·tsa* sunstroke
sunce ⑩ *soon·tse* sun
suncobran ⑩ *soon·tsaw·bran* umbrella
supermarket ⑩ *soo·per·mar·ket* supermarket
sušeni *soo·she·nee* dried
(o)sušiti (aw·)*soo·shee·tee* dry
sutra *soo·tra* tomorrow
— **popodne** paw·*pawd·ne* tomorrow afternoon
— **ujutro** oo·*yoo·traw* tomorrow morning
— **uvečer** oo·*ve·cher* tomorrow evening

suvenir ⑩ *soo·ve·neer* souvenir
suviše *soo·vee·she* too (expensive etc)
suvremen *soo·vre·men* modern
svadbena torta ① *svad·be·na tawr·ta* wedding cake
svadbeni dar ⑩ *svad·be·nee dar* wedding present
(po)svađati se (paw·)*sva·ja·tee* se argue
svaki *sva·kee* each • every
svatko *svat·kaw* everyone
sve sve all • everything
svećenik ⑩ *sve·che·neek* priest
svekar *sve·kar* father-in-law (of wife)
svekrva ① *sve·kr·va* mother-in-law (of wife)
svemir ⑩ *sve·meer* universe
svetac/svetica ⑩/① *sve·tats/sve·tee·tsa* saint
sveučilište ⑩ *sve·oo·chee·leesh·te* university
svi svee all • everything
svibanj ⑩ *svee·ban'* May
svijeća ① *svee·ye·cha* candle
svijet ⑩ *svee·yet* world
svila ① *svee·la* silk
svinja ① *svee·nya* pig
svinjetina ① *svee·nye·tee·na* pork
svinjska kobasica ① *sveen'·ska kaw·ba·see·tsa* pork sausage
(od)svirati (awd·)*svee·ra·tee* play (instrument)
svjedodžba ① svye·*dawj·ba* certificate
svjetao svye·ta·aw light (of colour)
svjetiljka ① svye·*teel'·ka* light (lamp) • flashlight • torch
svjetlomjer ⑩ svyet·*law·myer* light meter
svjetlost ① svyet·*lawst* light (illumination)
svjetski kup ⑩ svyet·*skee* koop World Cup
svjež svyezh fresh
svrbež ⑩ svr·bezh itch
svrha ① svr·ha point (logic)

Š

šah ⑩ shah chess
šahovska ploča ① sha·*hawv·ska plaw·cha* chess board
šal ⑩ shal scarf
šala ① sha·la joke
šalica ① sha·lee·tsa cup

šalter ⓜ *shal*-ter ticket office
— **za podizanje prtljage**
za *paw*-dee-za-nye prt-*lya*-ge
baggage claim
šampanjac ⓜ sham-*pa*-nyats champagne
šampon ⓜ sham-*pawn* shampoo
šank ⓜ shank counter (at bar)
šansa ① *shan*-sa chance
šator ⓜ *sha*-tawr tent
šatorski kolčić ⓜ *sha*-tawr-skee
kawl-cheech tent peg
šarmantan shar-*man*-tan charming
šećer ⓜ *she*-cher sugar
šef kuhinje shef koo-hee-nye chef
šešir ⓜ *she*-sheer hat
šibice ① pl shee-bee-tse matches
(for lighting)
širok shee-rawk wide
šišanje ① *shee*-sha-nye haircut
škamp ⓜ shkamp prawn
škare ① pl *shka*-re scissors
škarice za nokte ① pl shka-ree-tse za
nawk-te nail clippers
škola ① *shkaw*-la school
Škotska ① *shkawt*-ska Scotland
šlic ⓜ shleets zip • zipper
šljiva ① *shlyee*-va plum
šminka ① *shmeen*-ka make-up
šmrkav nos ⓜ shmr-kav naws runny nose
Španjolska ① *shpa*-nyawl-ska Spain
šparoga ① shpa-raw-ga asparagus
špinat ⓜ *shpee*-nat spinach
štakor ⓜ *shta*-kawr rat
štapići za jelo ⓜ pl shta-pee-chee za
ye-law chopsticks
štrajk ⓜ shtraik strike
štrcaljka ① shtr-*tsal*'-ka syringe
šuma ① *shoo*-ma forest
šunka ① *shoon*-ka ham
šutnuti/šutirati shoot-noo-tee/
shoo-*tee*-ra-tee kick
Švedska ① *shved*-ska Sweden
Švicarska ① shvee-*tsar*-ska Switzerland

T

tableta ① ta-*ble*-ta pill
— **protiv bolova** *praw*-teev *baw*-law-va
painkiller
— **za spavanje** za *spa*-va-nye sleeping pills
tajnik/tajnica ⓜ/① *tai*-neek/*tai*-nee-tsa
secretary

također ta-*kaw*-jer also
taksi ⓜ *tak*-see taxi
— **na vodi** na *vaw*-dee water taxi
— **stanica** ① *sta*-nee-tsa taxi stand
taman ta-man dark (of colour)
tamo ta-maw there
tampon ⓜ *tam*-pawn tampon
tanak *ta*-nak thin
tanjur ⓜ *ta*-nyoor plate
tastatura ① ta-sta-*too*-ra keyboard
(computer)
tata ① *ta*-ta dad
tava ① *ta*-va frying pan • pan
tečaj razmjene ⓜ *te*-chai raz-mye-ne
exchange rate
tečaj stranih valuta ⓜ *te*-chai *stra*-neeh
va-*loo*-ta currency exchange
tegovi ⓜ pl *te*-gaw-vee weights
tehnika ① *teh*-nee-ka technique
tekućina za kontakt leće ①
te-*koo*-chee-na za *kawn*-takt *le*-che
contact-lens solution
telefaks ⓜ *te*-le-faks fax machine
telefon ⓜ *te*-*le*-fawn telephone
telefonirati imp te-le-faw-*nee*-ra-tee
telephone
telefonska centrala ① te-*le*-fawn-ska
tsen-*tra*-la telephone centre
telefonska govornica ① te-*le*-fawn-ska
gaw-vawr-nee-tsa phone box
telefonska kartica ① te-*le*-fawn-ska
kar-tee-tsa phonecard
telefonski imenik ⓜ te-*le*-fawn-skee
ee-me-neek phone book
telegram ⓜ *te*-le-gram telegram
teleskop ⓜ *te*-le-skawp telescope
teletina ① *te*-le-tee-na veal
televizija ① te-le-*vee*-zee-ya television
(general)
televizor ⓜ te-le-*vee*-zawr television set
temperatura ① tem-pe-ra-*too*-ra
temperature (weather)
tenis ⓜ *te*-nees tennis
tenisko igralište ⓜ *te*-nee-skaw
ee-gra-leesh-te tennis court
tepih ⓜ *te*-peeh rug
teren za golf ⓜ *te*-ren za gawlf golf course
teretana ① *te*-re-ta-na gym (place)
termofor ⓜ *ter*-maw-fawr water bottle (hot)
tesar ⓜ *te*-sar carpenter
test ⓜ test test
— **na trudnoću** na trood-*naw*-choo
pregnancy test kit

tetka ① *tet*·ka *aunt*
težak *te*·zhak *difficult* • *heavy*
težina ① *te*·zhee·na *weight*
ti tee *you* inf
tih teeh *quiet*
tijelo ⑩ tee·ye·law *body*
tijesan tee·ye·san *tight*
tipičan tee·pee·chan *typical*
titlovi ⑩ pl *teet*·law·vee *subtitles*
(ovaj) tjedan ⑩ (aw·vai) tye·dan
(this) week
tjelovježba ① tye·law·*vyezh*·ba *workout*
tjestenina ① tye·ste·*nee*·na *pasta*
tkanina ① *tka*·nee·na *fabric*
tko tkaw *who*
tlak krvi ⑩ tlak *kr*·vee *blood pressure*
to ⑩ taw *it*
toaletni papir ⑩ taw·a·*let*·nee pa·*peer*
toilet paper
točno *tawch*·naw *exactly*
toksični otpad ⑩ *tawk*·seech·nee
awt·pad *toxic waste*
ton ⑩ tawn *volume*
topao ⑩ *taw*·pa·aw *warm*
topla voda ① *taw*·pla vaw·da *hot water*
toplice ① pl *taw*·plee·tse *spa*
toranj ⑩ *taw*·ran' *tower*
torba ① *tawr*·ba *bag*
tost ⑩ tawst *toast*
toster ⑩ *taw*·ster *toaster*
trajekt ⑩ *trai*·ekt *ferry*
tramvaj ⑩ *tram*·vai *tram*
tranzitna čekaonica ① *tran*·zeet·na
che·ka·*aw*·nee·tsa *transit lounge*
traperice ① pl tra·pe·ree·tse *jeans*
trava ① *tra*·va *grass (lawn)* • *pot (dope)*
travanj ⑩ *tra*·van' *April*
(po)tražiti (paw·)*tra*·zhee·tee *look for*
(za)tražiti (za·)*tra*·zhee·tee *ask (for
something)*
trčanje ⑩ *tr*·cha·nye *running*
(po)trčati (paw·)*tr*·cha·tee *run*
(za)trebati (za·)*tre*·ba·tee *need*
treći *tre*·chee *third*
trener ⑩ *tre*·ner *coach (sports)*
trešnja ① *tresh*·nya *cherry*
trg ⑩ trg *square (town)*
trgovac ⑩ *tr*·gaw·vats *trader*
— **drogama** *draw*·ga·ma *drug dealer*
— **povrćem** *paw*·vr·chem *greengrocer*
— **ribom** *ree*·bawm *fishmonger*
trgovački centar ⑩ *tr*·gaw·vach·kee
tsen·tar *shopping centre*

trgovina ① *tr*·gaw·vee·na *trade*
— **drogama** ① *draw*·ga·ma *drug
trafficking*
trišlja ① *treesh*·lya *pistachio*
trkači bicikl ⑩ *tr*·ka·chee bee·*tsee*·kl
racing bike
trkalište ⑩ *tr*·ka·leesh·te *racetrack*
trudna ① *trood*·na *pregnant*
trudnička jutarnja mučnina ①
trood·neech·ka yoo·tar·nya
mooch·*nee*·na *morning sickness*
tržnica ① *trzh*·nee·tsa *market*
tucet ⑩ *too*·tset *dozen*
tuča ① *too*·cha *fight (fisticuffs)*
tumač ⑩ *too*·mach *interpreter*
tumor ⑩ *too*·mawr *tumour*
tuna ① *too*·na *tuna (fish)*
tunjevina ① *too*·nye·vee·na *tuna
(as food)*
turist ⑩ *too*·reest *tourist*
turistička agencija ① *too*·ree·steech·ka
a·*gen*·tsee·ya *tourist office*
tuš ⑩ toosh *shower (bathroom)*
tužan *too*·zhan *sad*
tvoj ⑩ tvoy *your*
tvoja ① *tvoy*·a *your*
tvoje ⑩ *tvoy*·e *your*
tvornica ① *tvawr*·nee·tsa *factory*
tvrd tvrd *hard (not soft)*
tvrdo kuhan *tvr*·daw koo·han *hard-boiled*
tvrdoglav tvr·*daw*·glav *stubborn*

U

u oo *aboard (train, bus)* • *at* • *in* • *on* • *to*
— **inozemstvu** ee·naw·*zemst*·voo
abroad
— **vezi** *ve*·zee *about* • *to do with*
ubiti/ubijati oo·bee·tee/oo·*bee*·ya·tee
murder
ubod ⑩ oo·bawd *bite (insect)*
ubojstvo ⑩ oo·*boys*·tvaw *murder*
ubrizgati/ubrizgavati oo·breez·ga·tee/
oo·breez·*ga*·va·tee *inject*
učitelj ⑩ oo·chee·*tel'* *teacher*
(na)učiti (na·)oo·chee·tee *learn*
uči/ulaziti oo·chee/oo·la·zee·tee *enter*
udaljen oo·*da*·lyen *remote*
udati/udavati se oo·da·tee/oo·*da*·va·tee se
marry
udvarati se imp oo·*dva*·ra·tee se *chat up*
uganuće ⑩ oo·ga·*noo*·che *sprain*

ugao ⓜ oo·ga·aw *corner*
ugodan oo·gaw·dan *comfortable*
ugovor ⓜ oo·gaw·vawr *contract*
ugriz ⓜ oo·greez *bite (dog)*
ugrožene vrste ⓕ pl oo·graw·zhe·ne vr·ste *endangered species*
uhititi perf oo·hee·tee·tee *arrest*
uho ⓝ oo·haw *ear*
uključen ook·lyoo·chen *included*
ukraden ⓜ oo·kra·den *stolen*
ukrcan na oo·kr·tsan na *aboard (boat, plane)*
ukrcati/ukrcavati se oo·kr·tsa·tee / oo·kr·tsa·va·tee se *board (a plane, ship etc)*
ukusan oo·koo·san *tasty*
ulaz ⓜ oo·laz *entry*
ulaznica (cijena) ⓕ oo·laz·nee·tsa (tsee·ye·na) *admission (price)*
ulica ⓕ oo·lee·tsa *street*
ulična tržnica ⓕ oo·leech·na trzh·nee·tsa *street market*
ulični zabavljač ⓜ oo·leech·nee za·bav·lyach *busker*
ulje ⓝ oo·lye *oil*
ultrazvuk ⓜ ool·tra·zvook *ultrasound*
umak ⓜ oo·mak *sauce*
umirovljen oo·mee·rawv·lyen *retired*
umirovljenik ⓜ oo·mee·rawv·lye·neek *pensioner*
umjetnički obrti ⓜ pl oo·myet·neech·kee aw·br·tee *crafts (handicrafts)*
umjetnik/umjetnica ⓜ/ⓕ oo·myet·neek/oo·myet·nee·tsa *artist*
umjetnost ⓕ oo·myet·nawst *art*
umoran oo·maw·ran *tired*
umrijeti/umirati oo·mree·ye·tee/ oo·mee·ra·tee *die*
uniforma ⓕ oo·nee·fawr·ma *uniform*
unovčiti/unovčavati oo·nawv·chee·tee/ oo·nawv·cha·va·tee *cash (a cheque)*
unuk/unuka ⓜ/ⓕ oo·nook/oo·noo·ka *grandchild*
unutra oo·noo·tra *inside*
unutrašnji oo·noo·trash·nyee *indoor*
upala ⓕ oo·pa·la *inflammation*
upaljač ⓜ oo·pa·lyach *cigarette lighter*
uplata ⓕ oo·pla·ta *payment (by someone)*
Upomoć! oo·paw·mawch *Help!*
upoznati/upoznavati oo·pawz·na·tee/ oo·pawz·na·va·tee *meet (for first time)*
upozoriti/upozoravati oo·paw·zaw·ree·tee/ oo·paw·zaw·ra·va·tee *warn*

uprava ⓕ oo·pra·va *administration*
ured ⓜ oo·red *office*
　— za izgubljene stvari za eez·goob·lye·ne stva·ree *lost property office*
　— za odlaganje prtljage za awd·la·ga·nye prt·lya·ge *left luggage (office)*
urednik ⓜ oo·red·neek *editor*
urod ⓜ oo·rawd *crop*
uska ulica ⓕ oo·ska oo·lee·tsa *alley*
uskoro oo·skaw·raw *soon*
uskrs oos·krs *Easter*
usluga ⓕ oo·sloo·ga *service*
usne ⓕ pl oo·sne *lips*
uspinjača ⓕ oo·spee·nya·cha *cable car*
usta ⓝ oo·sta *mouth*
ustajao oo·stai·a·aw *stale*
uši ⓝ pl oo·shee *lice*
utakmica ⓕ oo·tak·mee·tsa *match (sports)*
utikač ⓜ oo·tee·kach *plug (electricity)*
utorak ⓜ oo·taw·rak *Tuesday*
utrka ⓕ oo·tr·ka *race (sport)*
uvala ⓕ oo·va·la *bay*
uvijek oo·vee·yek *always*
uvjetna karta ⓕ oo·vyet·noo kar·ta *stand-by ticket*
uz ooz *beside*
uzbrdo ooz·br·daw *uphill (to go)*
uzeti/uzimati oo·ze·tee/oo·zee·ma·tee *take*
uznemiravanje ⓝ ooz·ne·mee·ra·va·nye *harassment*
uzrast ⓜ ooz·rast *age (person)*
užasan oo·zha·san *awful*
uže ⓝ oo·zhe *rope*
uživati imp oo·zhee·va·tee *(have) fun*
užurban oo·zhoor·ban *in a hurry*

V

vadičep ⓜ va·dee·chep *corkscrew*
(iz)vagati (eez·)va·ga·tee *weigh*
vagina ⓕ va·gee·na *vagina*
val ⓜ val *wave*
vani va·nee *outside*
važan va·zhan *important*
večer ⓕ ve·cher *evening*
večera ⓕ ve·che·ra *dinner*
večeras ve·che·ras *tonight*
već vech *already*

veći ve-chee *bigger*

vedar ve-dar *fine (weather)*

vegetarijanac ⓜ ve-ge-ta-ree-ya-nats *vegetarian*

veleposlanik ⓜ ve-le-paw-sla-neek *ambassador*

veličina ① ve-lee-chee-na *size (general)*

velik ve-leek *big*

veliki tjedan ⓜ ve-lee-kee tye-dan *Holy Week*

veljača ① ve-lya-cha *February*

vena ① ve-na *vein*

Venecija ① ve-ne-tsee-ya *Venice*

venecijanski ve-ne-tsee-yan-skee *Venetian*

ventilator ⓜ ven-tee-la-tawr *fan (machine)*

veslanje ⓝ ve-sla-nye *rowing*

veza ① ve-za *connection*

vi vee *you* pol sg & pl

video kazeta ① vee-de-aw ka-ze-ta *video tape*

video rekorder ⓜ vee-de-aw re-kawr-der *video recorder*

vidik ⓜ vee-deek *lookout*

vidjeti/vidjati vee-dye-tee/vee-ja-tee *see*

vijesti ① pl vee-ye-stee *news*

vikend ⓜ veek-end *weekend*

viknuti/vikati veek-noo-tee/vee-ka-tee *shout*

viljuška ① vee-lyoosh-ka *fork*

vino ⓝ vee-naw *wine*

vinograd ⓜ vee-naw-grad *vineyard*

vinova loza ① vee-naw-va law-za *vine*

virus ⓜ vee-roos *virus*

visina ① vee-see-na *altitude*

viski ⓜ vee-skee *whisky*

visok vee-sawk *high • tall*

visoka stolica za bebe ① vee-saw-ka staw-lee-tsa za be-be *highchair*

višak prtljage ⓜ vee-shak prt-lya-ge *excess (baggage)*

više vee-she *more*

vitamini ⓜ pl vee-ta-mee-nee *vitamins*

viza ① vee-za *visa*

vjećanje ⓝ vye-cha-nye *conference (small)*

vjenčan vyen-chan *married (of man)*

vjenčana vyen-cha-na *married (of woman)*

vjenčanje ⓝ vyen-cha-nye *wedding*

vjera ① vye-ra *religion*

vjeren vye-ren *engaged (marriage)*

vjerenica ① vye-re-nee-tsa *fiancée*

vjerenik ⓜ vye-re-neek *fiancé*

vjerenje ⓝ vye-re-nye *engagement*

(po)vjerovati (paw-)vye-raw-va-tee *trust*

vjerski vyer-skee *religious (concerning religion)*

vjetar ⓜ vye-tar *wind*

vjetrobran ⓜ vye-traw-bran *windscreen*

vlada ① vla-da *government*

vlak ⓜ vlak *train*

vlasnik ⓜ vla-sneek *owner*

voće ⓝ vaw-che *fruit*

voda ① vaw-da *water*

vodene kozice ① pl vaw-de-ne kaw-zee-tse *chickenpox*

vodič ⓜ vaw-deech *guide (person) • guidebook*

vodka ① vawd-ka *vodka*

vodopad ⓜ vaw-daw-pad *waterfall*

vojna obveza ① voy-na awb-ve-za *military service*

vojnik ⓜ voy-neek *soldier*

vojska ① voy-ska *military*

volan bicikla ⓜ vaw-lan bee-tsee-kla *handlebars*

voljeti imp vaw-lye-tee *like (a person) • love*

vozačka dozvola ① vaw-zach-ka dawz-vaw-la *driving licence*

voziti imp vaw-zee-tee *drive*

— bicikl imp bee-tsee-kl *cycle*

vozni red ⓜ vawz-nee red *timetable*

vožnja ① vawzh-nya *ride (trip)*

— biciklom bee-tsee-klawm *cycling*

— na skateboardu na skeyt-bawr-doo *skateboarding*

vrač vrach *fortune-teller*

vrata ① vra-ta *door*

vratar ⓜ vra-tar *goalkeeper*

vratiti/vraćati se vra-tee-tee/vra-cha-tee se *return (come back)*

vreća za spavanje ① vre-cha za spa-va-nye *sleeping bag*

vremenski uvjeti ⓜ pl vre-men-skee oo-vye-tee *weather*

vrh ⓜ vrh *summit*

vrhnje ⓝ vrh-nye *cream (food)*

vrijednost ① vree-yed-nawst *value (price)*

vrijeme ⓝ vree-ye-me *time*

vrlo vr-law *very*

vrsta ① vr-sta *type*

vrt ⓜ vrt *garden*

vrtić za djecu ⓜ vr·teech za dye·tsoo *kindergarten*
vrtlar ⓜ vrt·lar *gardener*
vrtlarstvo ⓝ vrt·lars·tvaw *gardening*
vruć vrooch *hot*
vrućina ① vroo·chee·na *heat*
(po)vući (paw)·voo·chee *pull*
vuna ① voo·na *wool*

Z

za za *to • with*
zabavan za·ba·van *fun*
zaboraviti/zaboravljati za·baw·ra·vee·tee/za·baw·rav·lya·tee *forget*
zabrinut ⓜ za·bree·noot *worried*
zagađenje ⓝ za·ga·je·nye *pollution*
zaglavljen za·glav·lyen *blocked*
zagrijan za·gree·yan *heated*
zahod ⓜ za·hawd *toilet*
zahvalan za·hva·lan *grateful*
zahvaliti/zahvaljivati za·hva·lee·tee/za·hva·lyee·va·tee *thank*
zajedno zai·ed·naw *together*
zakašnjenje ⓝ za·kash·nye·nye *delay*
zaključan za·klyoo·chan *locked*
zaključati/zaključavati zak·lyoo·cha·tee/zak·lyoo·cha·va·tee *lock*
zakon ⓜ za·kawn *law*
zakonit za·kaw·neet *legal*
zakonodavstvo ⓝ za·kaw·naw·davs·tvaw *legislation*
zalazak sunca ⓜ za·la·zak soon·tsa *sunset*
zaleđen za·le·jen *frozen*
zalihe hrane ① pl za·lee·he hra·ne *food supplies*
zamijeniti/zamijenjivati za·mee·ye·nee·tee/za·mee·ye·nyee·va·tee *change (money)*
zamrznuti/zamrzavati za·mr·znoo·tee/za·mr·za·va·tee *freeze*
zanimljiv za·neem·lyeev *interesting*
zapad ⓜ za·pad *west*
započeti/započinjati za·paw·che·tee/za·paw·chee·nya·tee *start*
zaposlenik/zaposlenica ⓜ/① za·paw·sle·neek/za·paw·sle·nee·tsa *employee*
zaraditi/zarađivati za·ra·dee·tee/za·ra·jee·va·tee *earn*
zaraza ① za·ra·za *infection*

zastava ① za·sta·va *flag*
zaštićen zash·tee·chen *protected (species)*
(za)štititi (za·)shtee·tee·tee *protect*
zašto zash·taw *why*
zato za·taw *because*
zatvor ⓜ zat·vawr *gaol • jail*
zatvoren zat·vaw·ren *closed*
zatvorenik ⓜ zat·vaw·re·neek *prisoner*
zatvorenje ⓝ zat·vaw·re·nye *constipation*
zatvoriti/zatvarati zat·vaw·ree·tee/zat·va·ra·tee *close (shut)*
zaušnjaci ⓜ pl za·oosh·nya·tsee *mumps*
zaustaviti/zaustavljati za·oo·sta·vee·tee/za·oo·stav·lya·tee *stop (cease)*
zauvijek za·oo·vee·yek *forever*
zauzet za·oo·zet *busy • engaged (phone)*
zavoj ⓜ za·voy *bandage*
završiti/završavati za·vr·shee·tee/za·vr·sha·va·tee *finish*
zbirka fraza ① zbeer·ka fra·za *phrasebook*
zbog zbawg *about*
Zbogom. zbaw·gawm *Goodbye.*
zdjela ① zdye·la *bowl*
zdravlje ⓝ zdrav·lye *health*
Zdravo. zdra·vaw *Hello. (not answering telephone)*
zec ⓜ zets *rabbit*
zelen ze·len *green*
zelena salata ① ze·le·na sa·la·ta *lettuce*
zemlja zem·lya *country • Earth • land • soil*
zgodan zgaw·dan *handsome*
zgrada ① zgra·da *building*
zid ⓜ zeed *wall (outer)*
zima ① zee·ma *winter*
zimski kaput ⓜ zeem·skee ka·poot *overcoat*
zlato ⓝ zla·taw *gold*
zmija ① zmee·ya *snake*
znak ⓜ znak *sign*
znanost ① zna·nawst *science*
znanstvenik ⓜ znanst·ve·neek *scientist*
(sa)znati (sa·)zna·tee *know*
zob ⓜ zawb *oats*
zodijak ⓜ zaw·dee·yak *zodiac*
zoološki vrt ⓜ zaw·lawsh·kee vrt *zoo*
zora ① zaw·ra *dawn*
zračna luka ① zrach·na loo·ka *airport*
zračna pošta ① zrach·na pawsh·ta *airmail*
zračnica ① zrach·nee·tsa *tube (tyre)*
zrak ⓜ zrak *air*
zrakoplov ⓜ zra·kaw·plawv *airplane*
zrakoplovna tvrtka ① zra·kaw·plawv·na tvr·tka *airline*

Ž

zrakoplovna ulaznica ①
  zra·kaw·plawv·na *oo*·laz·nee·tsa
  boarding pass
zub ⓜ zoob *tooth*
zubar ⓜ *zoo*·bar *dentist*
zubi ⓜ pl *zoo*·bee *teeth*
zubobolja ① zoo·*baw*·baw·lya
  toothache
(po)zvati (paw·)*zva*·tee *call*
zvjezda ① *zvyez*·da *star*
(sa četiri) zvjezdice ① pl (sa *che*·tee·ree)
  zvye·zdee·tse (*four-)star*

Ž

žal ⓜ zhal *beach*
(po)žaliti se (paw·)*zha*·lee·tee se
  complain
žarulja ① zha·*roo*·lya *light bulb*
žbica ① *zhbee*·tsa *spoke*
žedan *zhe*·dan *(to be) thirsty*

(po)željeti (paw·)*zhe*·lye·tee *like •
  want • wish*
željeznička stanica ① *zhe*·lyez·nee·chka
  sta·nee·tsa *railway station*
želudac ⓜ zhe·*loo*·dats *stomach*
žemička ① zhe·*meech*·ka *roll (bread)*
žena ① *zhe*·na *wife • woman*
ženski *zhen*·skee *female*
žica ① *zhee*·tsa *wire*
žičara ① zhee·*cha*·ra *chairlift (skiing)*
Židovski zhee·*dawv*·skee *Jewish*
žitarica ① zhee·*ta*·ree·tsa *cereal*
život ⓜ *zhee*·vawt *life*
životinja ① zhee·*vaw*·tee·nya *animal*
žlica ① *zhlee*·tsa *spoon*
žličica ① *zhlee*·chee·tsa *teaspoon*
žmigavac ⓜ zhmee·*ga*·vats *indicator (car)*
žohar ⓜ *zhaw*·har *cockroach*
žulj ⓜ zhool' *blister*
žut ⓜ zhoot *yellow*
žvakača guma ① *zhva*·ka·cha *goo*·ma
  chewing gum

R

S

T

V

W

don't just stand there, say something!

o see the full range of our language products, go to:
lonelyplanet.com

What kind of traveller are you?

A. You're eating chicken for dinner *again* because it's the only word you know.

B. When no one understands what you say, you step closer and shout louder.

C. When the barman doesn't understand your order, you point frantically at the beer.

D. You're surrounded by locals, swapping jokes, email addresses and experiences – other travellers want to borrow your phrasebook or audio guide.

If you answered A, B, or C, you NEED Lonely Planet's language products ...

- **Lonely Planet Phrasebooks** – for every phrase you need in every language you want
- **Lonely Planet Language & Culture** – get behind the scenes of English as it's spoken around the world – learn and laugh
- **Lonely Planet Fast Talk & Fast Talk Audio** – essential phrases for short trips and weekends away – read, listen and talk like a local
- **Lonely Planet Small Talk** – 10 essential languages for city breaks
- **Lonely Planet Real Talk** – downloadable language audio guides from lonelyplanet.com to your MP3 player

... and this is why

- **Talk to everyone everywhere**
  Over 120 languages, more than any other publisher
- **The right words at the right time**
  Quick-reference colour sections, two-way dictionary, easy pronunciation, every possible subject – and audio to support it

Lonely Planet Offices

Australia
90 Maribyrnong St, Footscray,
Victoria 3011
☎ 03 8379 8000
fax 03 8379 8111
✉ talk2us@lonelyplanet.com.au

USA
150 Linden St, Oakland,
CA 94607
☎ 510 250 6400
fax 510 893 8572
✉ info@lonelyplanet.com

UK
2nd fl, 186 City Rd,
London EC1V 2NT
☎ 020 7106 2100
fax 020 7106 2101
✉ go@lonelyplanet.co.uk

lonelyplanet.com